Doris Lessing

was born of British parents in Persia (now Iran) in 1919 and was taken to Southern Rhodesia (now Zimbabwe) when she was five. She spent her childhood on a large farm there and first came to England in 1949. She brought with her the manuscript of her first novel, *The Grass is Singing*, which was published in 1950 with outstanding success in Britain, in America, and in ten European countries. Since then her international reputation not only as a novelist but as a non-fiction and short story writer has flourished. For her collection of short novels, *Five*, she was honoured with the 1954 Somerset Maugham Award. She was awarded the Austrian State Prize for European Literature in 1981, and the German Federal Republic Shakespeare Prize of 1982. Among her other celebrated novels are *The Golden Notebook*, *The Summer Before the Dark* and *Memoirs of a Survivor*. Her short stories have been collected in a number of volumes, including *To Room Nineteen* and *The Temptation of Jack Orkney*; while her African stories appear in *This Was the Old Chief's Country* and *The Sun Between Their Feet*. *Shikasta*, the first in a series of five novels with the overall title of *Canopus in Argos: Archives*, was published in 1979. Her novel *The Good Terrorist* won the W. H. Smith Literary Award for 1985, and the Mondello Prize in Italy that year. *The Fifth Child* won the Grinzane Cavour Prize in Italy, an award voted on by students in their final year at school. *The Making of the Representative for Planet 8* was made into an opera with Philip Glass, libretto by the author, and premièred in Houston. Her most recent works include *London Observed* and the first volume of her autobiography, *Under My Skin*.

By the same author

DORIS LESSING

African Laughter

Four Visits to Zimbabwe

Flamingo
An Imprint of HarperCollinsPublishers

Flamingo
An Imprint of HarperCollins*Publishers*
77–85 Fulham Palace Road,
Hammersmith, London W6 8JB

Published by Flamingo 1993
9 8 7

First published in Great Britain by
HarperCollins*Publishers* 1992

Photograph of Doris Lessing © Ingrid von Kruse

ISBN 0 00 654690 0

Set in Palatino

Maps by TPI

Printed and bound in Great Britain by
Omnia Books Ltd, Glasgow

CONTENTS

AUTHOR'S NOTE

When I was at the Wellington Literary Festival in 1994, people in the audience I was addressing said it was not true that the New Zealanders had tried to 'kill out' the Maoris. When I was signing books afterwards two people (white) in the queue said I should stick to my guns: it was true. Maoris I asked said it was true. This is probably a question of definition. What does 'kill out' mean? There were brutal and dreadful wars. It is agreed that the New Zealand government policy now is to reconciliate, and try to make amends. Some say this involves softening the truth about the past.

With most particular gratitude to Dr Antony Chennells of the University of Zimbabwe for his help, his patience, his generosity, the energy of his commitment to Zimbabwe and his knowledge of the history of Southern Africa. Gratitude, too, for the use of his library of books and material from the earliest days of the country.

And my most grateful thanks to the members of the Book Team of the Community Publishing Programme. This programme was initiated by the Ministry of Community and Co-operative Development. The Women's Book, the third in the series, is being jointly produced with the Ministry of Political Affairs.

And with grateful thanks to Peter Garlake for generously sharing his expert knowledge of Bushmen painting in Southern Africa.

Acknowledgements to:
Anton Chekhov, *The Island – A Journey to Sakhalin*; Loren Eiseley, *The Unexpected Universe*; the *Independent* for material used in articles; F. C. Selous, *Travel and Adventure in South-East Africa*; Lloyd Timberlake, *Africa in Crisis*; *The Times* obituary page; D.C. De Waal, *With Rhodes in Mashonaland*; the *Observer*, Jan Raath.

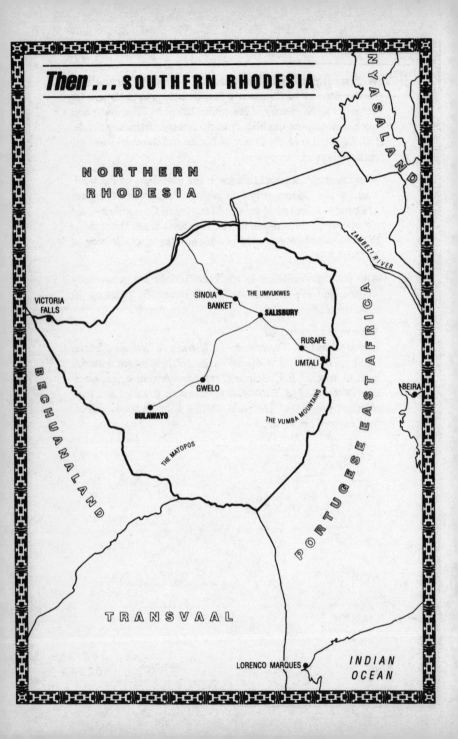

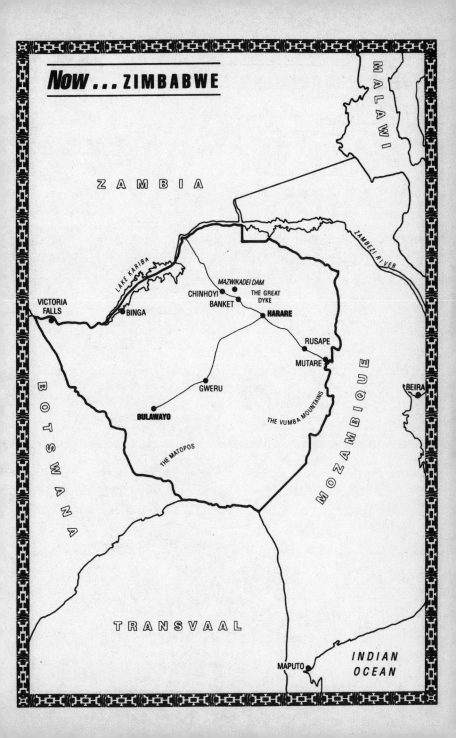

GLOSSARY

Words borrowed from Afrikaans

vlei	a valley
kopje	a hill
skellum	a bad person or animal, a rascal, a crook
lager	a camp, a defended place
mealies	maize
donga	a gully
dorp	a small town or village
spoor	tracks – of animals, of people
biltong	dried meat

Word borrowed from Swahili

boma	a safe place, a headquarters

Words borrowed from the Portuguese

Chef	a boss, a leader
povos	the poor
viva!	hail! hurrah!

Indigenous words

mombies	cattle
sadza	a stiff porridge made of maize meal
nganga	a shaman, male or female, a 'witchdoctor'
mudzimo	a spirit or soul
musasa	the most common tree in Mashonaland
guti	mist
honkey	slang word for a white. Because whites talk through their noses, say Africans. Should there be degrees of honkiness, with the French and the Americans at an extreme end of the scale?

Notes

The Matabele the inhabitants of Matabeleland. But more and more they are called the Ndebele which is the word once used for the language. Once the Matabele lived in Matabeleland and spoke Ndebele, but now the Ndebele live in Matabeleland and speak Ndebele.

The Mashona Similarly, the Mashona lived in Mashonaland and spoke Shona. More and more the Shona live in Mashonaland and speak Shona.

The War It was called the Liberation War, or, popularly, the War in the Bush, and the fighters on the black side were the Freedom Fighters, or the Boys in the Bush, or the Comrades. Or, from another point of view, Terrorists or the 'terrs'.

With our short memory, we accept the present climate as normal. It is as though a man with a huge volume of a thousand pages before him – in reality, the pages of earth time – should read the final sentence on the last page and pronounce it history. The ice has receded, it is true, but world climate has not completely rebounded. We are still on the steep edge of winter or early spring. Temperature has reached mid-point. Like refugees, we have been dozing memoryless for a few scant millennia before the windbreak of a sun-warmed rock. In the European Lapland winter that once obtained as far south as Britain, the temperature lay eighteen degrees Fahrenheit lower than today.

On a world scale this cold did not arrive unheralded. Somewhere in the highlands of Africa and Asia the long Tertiary descent of temperature began. It was, in retrospect, the prelude to the ice. One can trace its presence in the spread of grasslands and the disappearance over many areas of the old forest browsers. The continents were rising. We know that by Pliocene time, in which the trail of man ebbs away into the grass, man's history is more complicated than the simple late descent, as our Victorian forerunners sometimes assumed, of a chimpanzee from a tree. The story is one whose complications we have yet to unravel.

Loren Eiseley, *The Unexpected Universe*

AFRICAN LAUGHTER

Then

▐▓▌

1982

Early next morning we left the river and journeyed through a region the scenery of which was exceedingly pretty – more picturesque I have hardly ever seen. Hills and valleys, spruits and rivers, grass and trees – all combined to present a most charming variety of landscape views.

Major Johnson and I were driving in a cart some distance ahead of the waggon, and, when we arrived at the summit of a small hill, we stopped and waited for Mr Rhodes and Dr Jameson. I was so struck with the beauty of the country there that I decided to choose the site of the farms, which Mr Venter and I were to have in Mashonaland, at the foot of that hill. Mr Rhodes soon guessed my thoughts, for when he came up to our cart he said to me, before I had spoken a word, –

'Don't tell me anything De Waal, and I shall tell you why you've stopped the cart and waited for me!'

'Well, why?' I asked.

'Because you wish to tell me that you have here chosen for Venter and yourself the site of your farms.'

'Precisely,' I replied, 'you have guessed well.'

'Well,' he said, 'I've just been speaking to my friends in the waggon about the grandeur of the place, and I told them that I was sure you would not pass it by without desiring a slice of it.'

Mr Rhodes then requests Mr Duncan, the Surveyor-General of Mashonaland, who was with us just then, to measure out two farms there, one for Mr Venter and one for myself. I am sure the landed property in that part of the country will soon become very valuable, especially when the railway runs – as it soon will – between Beira and Salisbury.

D. C. De Waal, *With Rhodes in Mashonaland*

This excerpt describes the country near Rusape, on the road between Salisbury and Umtali. The journeys were made in 1890 and 1891, during the Occupation but before the military conquest.

A LITTLE HISTORY

Southern Rhodesia was a shield-shaped country in the middle of the map of Southern Africa, and it was bright pink because Cecil Rhodes had said the map of Africa should be painted red from Cape to Cairo, as an outward sign of its happy allegiance to the British Empire. The hearts of innumerable men and women responded with idealistic fervour to his clarion, because it went without saying that it would be good for Africa, or for anywhere else, to be made British. At this point it might be useful to wonder which of the idealisms that make our hearts beat faster will seem wrong-headed to people a hundred years from now.

In 1890, just over a hundred years from when this book is being written, the Pioneer Column arrived in grassy plains five thousand feet up from the distant sea: a dry country with few people in it. The one hundred and eighty men, and some policemen, had a bad time of it, travelling hundreds of miles up from the Cape through a landscape full of wild beasts and natives thought of as savages. They were journeying into the unknown, for while explorers, hunters and missionaries had come this way, homesteaders – people expecting to settle – had not. They were on this adventure for the sake of the Empire, for Cecil Rhodes whom they knew to be a great man, for the Queen, and because they were of the pioneering breed, people who had to see horizons as a challenge. Within a short time there was a town with banks, churches, a hospital, schools and, of course, hotels of the kind whose bars, then as now, were as important as the accommodation. This was Salisbury, a white town, British in feel, flavour and habit.

The progress of the Pioneer Column was watched by the Africans, and it is on record they laughed at the sight of the white men sweating in their thick clothes. A year later came Mother Patrick and her band of Dominican nuns, wearing thick and voluminous black and white habits. They at once began their work of teaching children and nursing the sick. Then, and very soon, came the women, all wrapped about and weighed down in their clothes. Respectable Victorian women did not discard so much as a collar, a petticoat or a corset when travelling. Mary Kingsley, that paragon among explorers, when in hot and humid West Africa was always dressed as if off to a tea party. The Africans did not know they were about to lose their country. They easily signed away their land when asked, for it was not part of their thinking that land, the earth our mother, can belong to one person rather than another. To begin with they did not take much notice of the ridiculous invaders, though their shamans, women and men, were warning of evil times. Soon they found they had indeed lost everything. It was no use retreating into the bush, for they were pursued and forced to work as servants and labourers, and when they refused, something called a Poll Tax was imposed, and when they did not pay up – and they could not, since money was not something they used – then soldiers and policemen came with guns and told them they must earn the money to pay the tax. They also had to listen to lectures on the dignity of labour. This tax, a small sum of money from the white point of view, was the most powerful cause of change in the old tribal societies.

Soon the Africans rebelled and were defeated. The conquerors were brutal and merciless. There is nothing in this bit of British history to be proud of, but the story of the Mashona Rebellion and how it was quelled was taught to white children as a glorious accomplishment.

At all times and everywhere invaders with superior technology have subjugated countries while in pursuit of land and wealth and the Europeans, the whites, are only the most recent of them. Having taken the best land for themselves, and set up an efficient machinery of domination, the British in Southern Rhodesia were able to persuade themselves – as is common among conquerors – that the conquered were inferior, that white tutelage was to their advantage, that they were bound to be the grateful recipients of a superior civilization. The British were so smug about themselves partly because they never went in for general murder, did not attempt to kill out an entire native population, as did the New Zealanders, and is happening now in Brazil where Indian tribes are being murdered while the world looks on and does nothing. They did not deliberately inject anyone with diseases, nor use drugs and alcohol as aids to domination. On the contrary, there were always hospitals for black people, and white man's liquor was made illegal, for it had been observed what harm firewater had done to the native peoples of North America.

If it is asked, How did these people, no more or less intelligent than ourselves, manage to accommodate so many incompatibles in their minds at the same time, then this belongs to a wider query: How and why do we all do it, often not noticing what we do? I remember as a child hearing farmers remark, with the cynical good nature that is the mark of a certain kind of bad conscience: 'One of these days they are all going to rise and drive us into the sea.' This admission clearly belonged in a different part of the brain from that where dwelled the complacencies of Empire.

By 1900 there was Southern Rhodesia, bright pink all over, inside its neat boundaries, with Mozambique, or Portuguese East Africa on one side, Angola (Portuguese West Africa) and the Bechuanaland Protectorate (pink) on the other, and Northern Rhodesia (pink) just above it.

The Transvaal, arena for the Boer War, was to the south.

The same neat shape is now stamped Zimbabwe. The trouble is that these boundaries ignore a good deal of history, mainly to do with the Portuguese influence, for Portuguese traders, adventurers, explorers, travelled and sometimes lived in areas that later were painted pink. There were no frontiers then, and if any European country were to claim the territory by right of precedence, it should have been Portugal. These histories are in Portuguese archives, not so much in the British, and school children were not taught about the Portuguese in Monomotapa or the kingdom of Lo Magondi. Yet that the Portuguese had been before them could hardly have been overlooked by the British adventurers. There is a certain wonderfully fertile valley, still full of citrus groves planted by the Portuguese, who also brought in maize and other crops.

The boundaries also ignore the pre-European politics of the Shona – for instance the Mutapa state which in the sixteenth century included much of central Mozambique.

The picture of Mashonaland presented as history to the heirs of the Pioneer Column went something like this: When we whites came we found the Matabele, an offshoot from the Zulus. They had travelled north to escape from murderous Zulu kings, and taken land from the Mashona, whom they harried and raided. The Mashona were groups of loosely related clans always on the move, for they stayed in one place only long enough to exhaust the soil and scare away the animals. We, the British, brought the Mashona people peace as well as White Civilization.

In fact the Mashona were skilled farmers and miners, whose techniques are only now being investigated by researchers. It was necessary for the British to see them as ignorant savages who owed everything to their conquerors.

The British administered sullen populations, but not for long, for quite soon, in the early 1950s, resistance movements began to form. In the late '40s people like myself, interested in the possibilities of black resistance, found very little, though there was 'a dangerous black agitator' Joshua Nkomo, who inflamed crowds with his oratory in Bulawayo and another called Benjamin Burombo. Ten years later the national movements were powerful. They had been given impetus by a frothy notion called the Central African Federation, which aimed at uniting Northern Rhodesia, and Nyasaland and Southern Rhodesia. The idea of this Federation appealed irresistibly to large numbers of idealistic souls, nearly all white. Yet it was attempting to unite incompatibles. The two northern countries were British Protectorates, and their black populations actually believed in promises made to them by Queen Victoria, that their interests would always be paramount, that their countries were to be administered for their good. It never does to ignore the explosive possibilities of 'naive' emotions like this one. Meanwhile Southern Rhodesia had always modelled itself on South Africa, adapting every repressive law passed there, fitting it into an edifice of oppression as comprehensive as South

Africa's. People who wanted to believe in uniting these three countries ignored the wishes of the blacks, and in fact the nationalist movements of Northern Rhodesia and Nyasaland (which became Zambia and Malawi on Independence) at once put an end to the foolish scheme.

Meanwhile the nationalist movements of Southern Rhodesia, encouraged by the success of their northern allies, fomented 'trouble' most successfully, everywhere. Already in 1956 I met a couple of young men, whose names I was not told, who described an underground life smuggling political literature, of police harassment and arbitrary arrest, beatings, imprisonment. This underground war, still minor, did not find its way into the newspapers, though people spoke of it. Throughout the 1960s the writing on the wall became ever more visible, but the whites, who had learned nothing from Kenya, chose to ignore it. The War of Independence in Southern Rhodesia, like many other wars, need not have happened. The whites numbered 250,000 at their maximum. Of these, many, if differently led, I believe would have compromised and shared power with the blacks. But a minority of the whites, led by Ian Smith, were determined to fight for White Supremacy. There was no date for the start of that war, which slowly simmered into one of the nastiest conflicts of our time. The opposing armies were not neatly separated into black and white. On the white side fought black soldiers and black police. The whites, far from united at the start, became united by the passions of war, and the few who thought the War was a mistake, and should be ended, and could not be won (for look what was happening in Mozambique where the whites were thrown out after a terrible war) were treated with hysterical hatred, were persecuted, victimized, vilified. The blacks, too, were infinitely divided. Not only were there different armies with different leaders and ideas, there was division in the armies themselves. Robert Mugabe's army was only one, but was the most extreme, communist, or marxist, and while the War went on most people thought that the majority of the blacks would choose Joshua Nkomo or Bishop Muzorewa, moderates and democrats.

The War was fought with cruelty on both sides. People living

in the villages had a hard time, for both the government forces
and the black armies punished them for aiding the other side,
but they had to help whichever soldiers arrived and demanded
it. Large numbers of villagers were taken by force from their
homes and put into what amounted to concentration camps –
of course 'for their own protection'. Young men and girls, as
soon as they were old enough, ran away to join guerilla armies,
in Zambia, or Mozambique, or even the forests of Southern
Rhodesia itself, for there at least they would not be subjected
to harassment, torture or death by the government troops. Part
of a whole generation of black youth was educated in guerilla
armies, sometimes to the accompaniment of marxist slogans,
but always unified by their hatred of the whites.

The War over, the atrocities on both sides were gently
allowed to be forgotten, for when the black population voted
– for the first time in their lives – it was Robert Mugabe they
chose, and he at once announced a multi-racial society and
the end of race hatred. It is known that Samora Machel of
Mozambique (and others) said to Robert Mugabe: 'Don't make
our mistake, don't throw out the whites, because you will be
left with a devastated economy.' The devastation was not all
the result of war, but because the departing Portuguese made
a point of burning and destroying everything they could before
they left – behaviour we saw recently when Saddam Hussein
was forced out of Kuwait.

The young nation Zimbabwe came into being in 1980. That
is to say, from the arrival of the Pioneer Column at the foot of
the small hill that would mark the beginnings of Salisbury,
called the Kopje, to Independence, took ninety years. Ninety
years – nothing. Yet in that time the culture of that large area
– roughly the size of Spain – had been destroyed; the people
had been kept subdued by all the power of modern weapons,
policing, propaganda; finally they had rebelled against armies
equipped with the most advanced weaponry, and they had
won. Now they had to take power as equals in a modern world.
Their chief difficulty was the same as in all new black nations.
They did not have enough people trained in administration,
though Southern Rhodesia had done better than most, particu-

larly in agriculture, for Zimbabwe began with a good number of already trained black agricultural workers. That is one reason why Zimbabwe, unlike the black nations that surround it, feeds itself, and has healthy surpluses which it is proud to sell to South Africa and to donate to famine areas in the Horn of Africa. Zimbabwe is a success for all its faults, for all its mistakes, and although it has had to sustain Mozambique, which is a disaster. To help police Mozambique, feed its refugees, keep the oil flowing in the pipeline from Beira, costs Zimbabwe, a poor country, a million pounds a day. Mozambique has been kept alive by Zimbabwe, while South Africa has done everything to destroy it. If South Africa has stopped trying to 'destabilize' its black neighbours, then the damage that has been done will not heal itself overnight, and the rebel bands it armed and financed have not all become good citizens, they still sabotage and destroy. South Africa dominates Southern Africa, for better for worse, and will continue to do so: already in 1991 the ex-communist government of Mozambique invited in South African capital to heal and develop the shattered country.

Zimbabwe, like other new black countries, has a corrupt ruling élite. This is a far from apologetic class of robbers. On the contrary they are proud of themselves, boast and display their wealth. Joshua Nkomo who, like Robert Mugabe, had tried to check the corruption, finally had to capitulate to fact, and to what he was observing all around him. In a speech in 1989 he said, 'I suppose we have to learn how to be rich as well as having to learn everything else.'

The first decade of Zimbabwe's history was a tale of violence and discord; was contradictory, ebullient, and always surprising. The worst chapter was the murders and arson by the 'dissidents' of Matabeleland, seen as representing all the Ndebele, the whole province. Mugabe's armies terrorized the area, decimated villages, were merciless, treated Matabeleland as an enemy province. It turned out that the dissidents, believed to be a guerilla army, were a few desperadoes who, far from representing their people, were refused entrance by their villages when they returned home. It is not – perhaps – without significance for the future, that it is said the Mashona troops, despoiling or killing or raiding through Matabeleland, said, 'This is in return for . . .' some incident of well over a hundred years before, when the Matabele drove off cattle, burned crops and huts, took women.

The best of the Zimbabwe story is the vigour, the optimism, the determination of the people. You may return from a several-weeks' visit to Zimbabwe and realize, finding yourself again in the enervating airs of Europe, that you have been day and night with people, white and black, who talk of nothing else but how to make Zimbabwe work, of new ideas that may be adopted there, and who have an identification with the processes of government and of administration that means nothing can happen which does not at once attract the most passionate reactions, for or against. People coming to Zimbabwe after Mozambique, or Zambia, where nothing is a success, where cynicism poisons everything, say their faith in Africa is restored, and that Zimbabwe, for whatever reason, is unique in Africa because of the creative energies of its people. They are proud of themselves . . . thus you may hear a black person remark of Zambia, or of Mozambique: 'They don't know how to do anything, we shall have to show them.' This self-respecting, or perhaps one might say, bumptious, attitude is a continuation of the Southern Rhodesian white love of themselves and 'their' country, which goes on though the country is no longer theirs. Talking of a success in South Africa, some new enterprise, or farm, you may hear a white remark: 'Of course the Rhodies down South are bound to come out on top: we know how to do things.'

Before Independence the whites were all convinced that Southern Rhodesia was the best place on earth, and their administration better than that of any other white-dominated country. During my trip in 1989 I kept hearing that so and so had said (notably President Chissano to President Mugabe): 'You were lucky to have had the British, at least they leave behind a decent infrastructure.'

1982

When I returned to the country where I had lived for twenty-five years, arriving as a child of five and leaving as a young woman of thirty, it was after an interval of over twenty-five years. This was because I was a Prohibited Immigrant. An unambiguous status, one would think: either a good citizen or a bad one, Prohibited or Unprohibited. But it was not so simple. I was already a Prohibited Immigrant in 1956 but did not know it. It never crossed my mind I could be: the impossibility was a psychological fact, nothing to do with daylight realities. You cannot be forbidden the land you grew up in, so says the web of sensations, memories, experience, that binds you to that landscape. In 1956 I was invited to go to the Prime Minister's office. This was Garfield Todd. Striding about an office he clearly felt confined him, a rugged and handsome man in style rather like Abraham Lincoln, he said, 'I have stretched my hand over you, my child.' He was then ten years older than I was. I attributed his proprietorial style to the fact he had been a missionary, and did not really hear what he was saying: he was welcoming me to Southern Rhodesia because he knew I could give Federation a good write-up. 'I have let you in . . .' I said I could not approve of Federation. We argued energetically and with good feeling for a couple of hours. Later I asked to interview Lord Malvern who, as Doctor Huggins, had been the family doctor, and told him I wanted to visit Northern Rhodesia and Nyasaland, then full of riots, dissidents, social disorder, and other manifestations of imminent Independence. He said, 'Oh you do, do you!' During the course of arguments much less good-natured than those with Garfield Todd, he said, 'I wasn't going to have you upsetting our natives.' I still did not hear what was being said. Finally he said I could go to Northern Rhodesia and Nyasaland for two weeks. 'I don't suppose you can do much harm in that time.' It goes without saying this flattered me: people who see themselves as recorders and observers are always surprised to be seen as doers and movers.

(These long-ago events are of interest now only when I try to come to terms with the irrationality of my reactions.) I came back to London and then began to think there was something here I could be seeing. That I had been Prohibited in Northern Rhodesia and Nyasaland, countries where I had never been, did not affect me, but I could not 'take in' the fact that I could be Prohibited in the country I had been brought up in. At last I asked a lawyer to come with me to Southern Rhodesia House where an official, peevish with what he clearly felt was a false position, said, 'Oh drat it, you have forced my hand.' In this way was I finally informed that I was a Prohibited Immigrant. Prime Minister Huggins had ruled long ago, when I left home to come home, that I must not be allowed to upset his natives.*

As the convention was, I was proud to be Prohibited. Since then it has become clear that countries with the levels of purity of motive high enough to match our idea of ourselves as world citizens are not many.

I did not want to live in Southern Rhodesia, for if its climate was perfection, probably the finest in the world, and its landscape magnificent, it was provincial and tedious. I wanted to live in London. What this Prohibition amounted to was that I would be prevented from visiting relatives and friends. They, however, might visit London. These rational considerations did not reach some mysterious region of myself that was apparently an inexhaustible well of tears, for night after night I wept in my sleep and woke knowing I was unjustly excluded from my own best self. I dreamed the same dream, night after night. I was in the bush, or in Salisbury, but I was there illegally, without papers. 'My' people, that is, the whites, with whom after all I had grown up, were coming to escort me out of the country, while to 'my' people, the blacks, amiable multitudes, I was invisible. This went on for months. To most people at some point it comes home that inside our skins we are not

---

* Doctor Huggins was Prime Minister of Southern Rhodesia for many years. During Federation, as Lord Malvern, he was Prime Minister of the Federation for the year 1956 while Garfield Todd was Prime Minister of Southern Rhodesia.

made of a uniform and evenly distributed substance, like a cake-mix or mashed potato, or even sadza, but rather accommodate several mutually unfriendly entities. It took me much longer to ask myself the real question: what effect on our behaviour, our decisions, may these subterranean enemies have? That lake of tears, did it slop about, or seep, or leak, secretly making moist what I thought I kept dry?

Now I see that refusal, that inability to 'take in' my exclusion, as a symptom of innate babyishness: mine, and, too, the inhabitants of privileged countries, safe countries, for there are more and more people in the world who have had to leave, been driven from, a country, the valley, the city they call home, because of war, plague, earthquake, famine. At last they return, but these places may not be there, they have been destroyed or eroded; for if at first glance, like a child's recognition of its mother's face when she has been absent too long, everything is as it was, then slowly it has to be seen that things are not the same, there are gaps and holes or a thinning of the substance, as if a light that suffused the loved street or valley has drained away. Quite soon the people who have known one valley or town all their lives will be the rare ones, and there are even those who speculate how humanity will have to leave the planet with plans to return after an interval to allow it to regenerate itself, like a sick or poisoned organism, but when they return after long generations they find . . .

AIR ZIMBABWE

In 1982 I booked the seat on Air Zimbabwe, made arrangements, with more than usually mixed feelings.

As I seated myself inappropriate emotions began, all much too strong. For a start, the stewardesses were black, once impossible. Since nearly all the passengers were white, and these black girls had no reason to expect courtesy from them, they were defensive and would not look at anyone. The atmosphere was unpleasant. I had hoped to sit next to a black person, so as to hear what was being thought, but was beside a white race-horse owner, a man of forty or so, who grumbled obsessively for the ten hours of the flight about the new black government. I had heard this note of peevish spite before: at the Independence celebrations in Zambia the white officials of an administration which had done nothing to train blacks for responsibility, recited examples of inefficiency while their faces shone with triumphant malice. Here it was again. This man insisted in one sentence that this was still God's Own Country, and he could raise and train race-horses more cheaply and better here than anywhere in the world; he and his family enjoyed a wonderful life and he wouldn't leave for anything – but the black government . . . I listened with half an ear, thinking that soon, when I had paid my dues to the white world, I could leave it and find out about the new Zimbabwe. Meanwhile I disliked this man with an impatience identical to that I had felt all those years ago, growing up here. Childish, spoiled, self-indulgent, spiteful . . . yes, he was all this, they were all like this, or most of them, but what of it, and why should I remain so involved?

While he grumbled about the deprivations they suffered in the way of food, breakfast was served, slabs of bacon, scrambled eggs, sausages, fried bread, a meal to fuel farm labourers or gravediggers.

The little airport was unchanged: I hardly saw it. The smells, the colours of the earth had undone me, and my emotional balance was gone. Immigration was a shy young man, hesitant, inexperienced, who asked if I planned to come and live here now: too many of 'our friends' had left because of the old government. He enquired about my passport: for I had been born in Persia, and I explained that one could – loosely – equate Persia and Iran with Southern Rhodesia and Zimbabwe. When I changed my money at the airport bank the official asked if I was the author and welcomed me in the name of Zimbabwe. I went out into the dry scented air and wept. And there was the young man who had brought the hired car to the airport. So occupied was I in admonishing my tear-ducts that I hardly saw the streets. I left the young man at the car-hire firm and parked. I was on my own in the streets of the town that was once my big city.

THE BIG CITY

Of course the old one-horse one-storey town had gone . . . though everywhere bits of that town survived among the new tall buildings. What was wrong? Something was – the atmosphere? Yes, it was cold, being winter, and dry, and the skies sparkled with a thin sunshine. There were few people about, and they moved slowly, without animation. A pavement café had customers, not many, and they were all white, and seemed defensive. As I walked about, feeling more dismal every minute, I was accosted by beggars, the wounded from the War. They were aggressive and abusive, thrusting out stumps of arms and legs, and when given a little money, they shook it about in their palms, as if rejecting it, full of hatred. I went into Meikles bar. The hotel, being unique and full of character, had been pulled down and in its place was one exactly the same as many thousands of others, all over the world. That 'they' could have destroyed Meikles made me feel as helplessly angry as we all do when 'they' pull down buildings anywhere. 'Well, it was a mistake,' we know they will soon say airily. The old hotel appears in photographs around the walls of the bar. I felt as if I belonged in those photographs, and could easily have begun surreptitiously to examine them for faces I knew, or even myself, a young woman. I left Meikles, mourning, and went into a bookshop. The young man who came forward was so aggressive I knew at once how white people entered that shop. I asked for novels and stories written by black writers, and he found them for me, never once looking at me, or smiling. I said I was a writer whose books he might even be selling, but he did not ask the name so I told him. He was suspicious, doubtful, then was transformed into a friend. He said he had read one of my short stories. 'Are you coming back to live? All the good white people left in the War.' I said I was visiting.

And who was I visiting? Hard-line whites, who, if they came into this shop at all, being a black enterprise, would behave as they always had. We said goodbye with cautious goodwill, as if bombs lingered somewhere close, and might do us both in at one wrong word.

I decided to leave Harare. I had been in it for less than a morning, and everything about it chilled and dispirited me, and not only because I felt like a sad ghost.

I will say now what the matter was, though it was not that day or the next that I came to the obvious diagnosis. This was a town still recovering from the War. The country had been at war for over ten years, the War had ended two years before. It is not possible to fight this kind of war, a civil war, without the poisons going deep. When I went to Pakistan to visit Afghan refugees and the mujahideen, there was the same atmosphere. Something has been blasted or torn deep inside people, an anger has gone bad, and bitter, there is disbelief that this horror can be happening at all. A numbness, a sullenness, shows itself in a slowness of movement, of reactions.

I went to old Cecil Square, named after the Cecil family and Lord Salisbury, to buy flowers. Really, I wanted to talk to the flower sellers. They were all men, as they had been long ago, but different now, for they crowded around, thrusting the flowers just as the beggars had thrust their wounds, into my face. There were too many flower sellers, and these were hard times, with so few tourists, and they had to sell their flowers. When I said no, two bunches were enough, the sellers who had not been favoured were angry, with the same unconcealed, as it were licensed, anger, as the beggars.

I put the flowers in the back seat of the car and drove east on the old road to Umtali.

THE BUSH

The family went often to Marandellas, whose name is now again Marondera, just as the real right name for Umtali would have been Mutare, if the whites had not overrun these parts. We did not go to Umtali, for it was then a distant place. I did not get to it until I was fifteen or so, and then Marandellas had become only one of the way-stations along a road where I visited farms, sometimes for weeks at a time. But as a child, Marandellas was the other pole to our farm, which was in the District of Banket, Lomagundi (or Lo Magondi) seventy miles to the north-east of Salisbury, and on the road north to the Zambesi valley. Nothing ever happened on our road but the routine excitements of flooded rivers, where we might have to sit waiting for the waters to subside for four or five hours before daring the drift that could have potholes in it from the flood; or getting stuck in thick red mud and having to be pushed out over freshly cut branches laid across the mud; or glimpses of wild animals . . . 'Look, there's a duiker!' Or a koodoo, or a little herd of eland. These being the stuff of ordinary life, and what we took for granted, it was only on the other side of Salisbury that the shock and tug of new impressions began, a shimmer in the air, like mental heat waves, which I knew were proper to the road to Umtali. Marandellas was about fifty miles south-east of Salisbury, but if you ask, What is a hundred and twenty miles? – then that is from the practical, unpoetical perspective. Our car was an Overland, contemporary with the first Fords, now taken out of car museums to star in films of the Great Depression. It was second-hand when we bought it, and thirty miles an hour was a great speed. Add this to the characters of my parents, and the journey became an epic endeavour, to be planned and prepared for weeks in advance. The most often spoken words in our house were, 'But we can't afford it!' – usually, triumphantly, from my father to my mother, to prove something was impossible, in this case to spend a week near Ruzawi at the Marandellas Hotel. My brother was at Ruzawi

School, a prep-school conducted on English lines, and the trip would be so we could take part in a Sports Day, an Open Day, a cricket match, judged as successful according to how they mirrored similar events at prep-schools at Home. Impossible! – thank the Lord! – and he would not have to leave the farm and put on respectable clothes instead of his farm khaki and make small talk with other parents. For his 'We can't afford it,' was not a symptom of meanness, but rather of his need, by now the strongest thing in him, to be left in peace to dream.

But my mother triumphed. Rolls of bedding, boxes of food, suitcases, filled the back of the car where the 'boy' and I fitted ourselves, and we set off. At the speed my father insisted on travelling, the seventy miles to Salisbury took three or four hours. ('A man who has to use a brake doesn't know how to drive a car.') The Packards and the Studebakers shot past us in tumults of dust (these were the old strip roads and you overtook on dirt) for the Fords and the Overlands were already an anachronism. ('Why give up your car when it is still working perfectly well just because *they* want to sell you a new one?') To go from Banket to Marandellas in one day, or an afternoon, even on those roads, was easily done – by everyone else. We stayed at the old Meikles Hotel, but in the annex at the back, because it was cheaper. We ate a picnic supper in our room, because we could not afford the hotel dining-room. Afterwards we drank coffee in Meikles lounge, where a band played among palm trees and gilded columns.

Next morning, the car forced to accommodate even more food, we left early on the road to Marandellas, so there would be plenty of time to set up camp. The drive went on for ever, the miles made longer by the need to concentrate on everything. This is sandveld country, not the heavy red, brown and bright pink soils of Banket, and the landscape has a light dry airiness. Mountains and more mountains accompany the road, but at distances that paint them blue, mauve, purple, while close to the road are clusters of granite boulders unique in the world; at least, I have not seen anything like them elsewhere, or in photographs. The boulders erupt from pale soil to balance on each other so lightly it seems impossible a strong wind will not topple them. The great stones, a light bright grey, with a sparkle to them if you look close, but patched and patterned with lichens, radiate heat waves against the intense blue of the sky. Everyone who passes speculates about how long they have impossibly balanced there and enjoy notions of giants who have played with pebbles. 'That one, there,' I would think, fixing its exact shape and position in my mind, 'it might have fallen off by the time we come back next week.' But that boulder, the size of a hut or a baobab tree, contacting the one beneath it only for a square inch or two, had won the battle against gravity, and was still there in 1982 on that day I sped past on the road, not to Marandellas and Umtali, but to Marondera and Mutare, after so many rain storms, powerful winds, bolts of lightning; after half a century of history and the years of the civil war: the War of Liberation, the Bush War.

The road went up. The road went down. Roads do this everywhere, but never as emphatically as on those journeys at thirty miles an hour, the car labouring to the top of a crest and reaching it in a climax of achievement, then the reward of a descent freewheeling into the valley, then the grind up the next rise, in second gear, because second gear is a solid, responsible state to be in, top gear has something about it of frivolity, even recklessness. Each crest brought another magnificent view, and my mother exclaimed and directed our attention in her way that mingled admiration and regret, as if such beauty must have a penalty to pay in sorrow. Meanwhile I was cramming into my mind, like photographs in an album, these views and vistas that would never stay put, but were changed by memory, as I would find out on the next trip. A 'view' I had believed was fixed for ever, had disappeared. A coil of mountains was lower than I remembered. A peak had come forward and attracted to itself a lesser hill. A river had changed course and acquired a tributary I had simply not noticed. Perhaps there had been a different 'view', and I had been mistaken? No, because *that* hill, there, near the road, had not changed, and I had used it as a marker. Yet how I had laboured over that view, my eyes stretched wide in case a blink shifted a perspective or spoiled my attention, my mind set to receive and record. I was

in a contest with Time, and I knew it. I was obsessed with
Time, always had been, and my very earliest memories are of
how I insisted to myself, Hold this . . . don't forget it – as if I
had been born with a knowledge of its sleights and deceptions.
When I was very young, perhaps not more than two or three
years old, someone must have said to me, 'I'm telling you, it's
like this.' But I knew that 'it' was like that. They said: '*This*
happened, *this* is the truth' – but I knew *that* had happened,
that was the truth. Someone trying to talk me out of what I
knew was true, must have been the important thing that happened to me in my childhood, for I was continually holding fast
to moments, when I said to myself, 'Remember this. Remember
what really happened. Don't let yourself be talked out of what
really happened.' Even now I hold a series of sharp little scenes,
like photographs, or eidetic memory, which I refer to. So when
I fought to retain a 'view', a perspective on a road, the little
effort was only one on a long list. Time, like grown-ups, possessed all these slippery qualities, but if you labour enough
over an event, a moment, you make a solid thing of it, may
revisit it . . . Is it still there? Is it still the same? Meanwhile
Time erodes, Time chips and blurs, Time emits blue and mauve
and purple and white hazes like dry ice in a theatre: 'Here,
wait a minute, I can't see.'

Time passed slowly, so very s-l-o-w-l-y, it crept and crawled,
and I knew I was in child-time, because my parents told me I
was. 'When you are our age, the years simply gallop!' But at
my age, every day went on for ever and I was determined to
grow up as quickly as I could and leave behind the condition
of being a child, being helpless. Now I wonder if those who
dislike being children, who urge time to go quickly, experience
time differently when they get older: does it go faster for us
than for other people who have not spent years teaching it to
hurry by? The journeys to Marandellas, occurring two or three
times a year, were a way of marking accomplished stages:
another four months gone, another rainy season over, and
that's a whole year done with – and the same point last year
seems so far away. The journeys themselves, slow, painstak-
ing, needing so much effort by my mother to get everything

ready, so much effort by my father to rouse himself to face life
and remain this damned car's master ('We would have done
much better to keep horses and the use of our feet!') were each
one like a small life, distant, different from the ones before,
marked by its own flavour, incidents, adventures.

'That was the trip Mrs C. visited us in our camp. I thought
she was a bit sniffy about it. Well, I think we have the best of
it – you don't lie out all night under the stars if you're in the
Marandellas Hotel!' Or, 'That was the time when our boy –
what was his name? Reuben?' – (These damned missionaries!)
– 'went off for two days on a beer drink because he met a
brother in the next village, and he turned up as calm as you
please and said he hadn't seen his brother for five years.
Brother my foot! Every second person they meet is a brother,
as far as I can see.' 'Now, come on, old thing, be fair! Every
second person they meet is a brother – do you remember that
letter in the *Rhodesia Herald*? They have a different system of
relationships. And anyway, we did quite all right without a
servant, didn't we? I don't see what we need a boy for on the
trips anyway.' 'It's the principle of the thing,' said my mother,
fierce. But what she did not say, could not say, and only her
face ever said it for her, like that of an unjustly punished little
girl: 'It's all very well for you! Who gets the food ready and
packs the car and unpacks everything, and finds the camp site
and spreads the bedding and looks after the children? Not
you, not you, ever! Surely I am not expected to do everything,
always, myself?' And yes, she was; and yes, she did, always.

When we reached Marandellas, we turned off the main road
that led to Umtali, drove through the neat little township with
its gardens and its jacarandas and its flame trees, and went for
a few miles along the road to Ruzawi. Here the bush was full
of rocky kopjes and small streams. The sandy earth sparkled.
Well before reaching the school, off the road but within sight
of it, a space was found among the musasa trees. The 'boy' cut
branches to make an enclosure about twenty feet by twenty,
but round, in the spirit of the country. This leafy barrier was
to keep out leopards, who were still holding on, though threatened, in their caves in the hills. We could have lain out under

the trees without the barricade for any leopard worth its salt
could have jumped over it in a moment and carried one of us
off. No, the walls were an expression of something else, not a
keeping out, but a keeping together, strangers in a strange
land. My parents needed those encircling branchy arms. But
my brother, when he was only a little older, went for days
through the bush by himself, or with the son of the black man
who worked in our kitchen, and he slept, as they did, as some
still do, rolled in a blanket near the fire.

Inside this boma were made five low platforms of fresh grass,
long and green and sappy, or long and yellow and dry, according to the season, and on these was spread the bedding. My
brother was given permission to leave school and join us at
these times for at least a night or two. And my parents always
insisted that the black man must sleep inside the lager, safe,
with us.

This involved all kinds of illogicalities and inconsistencies,
but I was used to them, and took them for granted until I was
much older. Reuben (or Isaiah, or Jacob, or Simon, or Abraham,
or Sixpence, or Tickie – for they never stayed long) made up
his own smaller fire outside the boma, and cooked his maize
porridge on it, eating, too, the foods we were eating, bacon,
eggs, steak, cake, bread, jam. While we sat at night around the
big fire, gazing at it, watching the sparks whirl up into the trees
and the stars, he sat with his back to a tree, turned away from
us, looking at his own smaller fire. Later, when we were in our
pyjamas inside the blankets, he was called in, and he wrapped
himself in his blankets, and lay down, his face turned away
from us to the leafy wall. In the early morning when we woke
he was already gone, and his fire was lit, he was sitting by it,
a blanket around his shoulders, and he was wearing everything
he owned – tattered shirt, shorts, a cast-off jersey of my
father's. These mornings could be cold, and sometimes frost
crusted the edges of leaves in cold hollows. In our part of the
country, so much hotter, there was seldom frost.

Later I had to wonder what that man was thinking, taken on
this amazing trip in a car (and few of his fellows then had been
in a car) to a part of the country too far away for him normally

to think of visiting, days and days of walking, with the white family who were choosing – briefly – to live just as his people did, exclaiming all the time how wonderful it was, but preserving their customs as if they were still inside their house. They put on special clothes to sleep in. They washed continually in a white enamel basin set on a soap box under a tree. And they never stopped eating, just like all the white people. 'They eat all the time,' he certainly reported, returning to his own. 'As soon as one meal is finished, they start cooking the next.'

Now I wonder most of all, with the helpless grieving so many of us feel these days, when we remember the destruction of animals and plants, about the reckless cutting down of those boughs, and of young trees. When we left a site the rubbish was well buried, but the wreckage of the encircling boughs remained, and we would see it all there a few months later, on our way to making a new enclosure with fresh boughs. Above where our fires had roared, the scorched leaves hung grey and brittle. In those days the bush, the game, the birds, seemed limitless. Not long before I left Southern Rhodesia to come to London I was a typist for a Parliamentary Committee on sleeping sickness, reporting on the eradication of tsetse fly, recording how, over large areas, the hunters moved, killing out hundreds of thousands of head of game, kudu, sable, bush buck, duiker, particularly duiker, those light-stepping, graceful, dark-liquid-eyed creatures which once filled the bush, so that you could not walk more than a few yards without seeing one.

When I returned to Zimbabwe after that long absence, I expected all kinds of changes, but there was one change I had not thought to expect. The game had mostly gone. The bush was nearly silent. Once, the dawn chorus hurt the ears. Lying in our blankets under the trees on the sandveld of Marandellas, or in the house on the farm in Banket, the shrilling, clamouring, exulting of the birds as the sun appeared was so loud the ears seemed to curl up and complain before – there was nothing else for it – we leaped up into the early morning, to become part of all that tumult and activity. But by the 1980s the dawn chorus had become a feeble thing. Once, everywhere, moving through the bush, you saw duiker, bush buck, wild pig, wild cats, porcupines, anteaters; koodoo stood on the antheaps turning their proud horns to examine you before bounding off; eland went about in groups, like cattle. Being in the bush was to be with animals, one of them.

Lying inside our leafy circle at night, we listened to owls, nightjars, the mysterious cries of monkeys. Sometimes a pair of small eyes gleamed from the trees over our heads, as a monkey or wild cat watched, as we did, how the roaring fire of early evening sent the red sparks rushing up from the flames that reached to the boughs, but then, later, when it died down, the sparks fled up, but fewer, and snapped out one by one, like the meteors that you could watch too, when the fire had died. Or we might wake to hear how some large animal, startled to find this obstruction in its usual path, bounded away into silence. The moon, which had been pushed away by the roar of the fire, had come close, and was standing over the trees in one of its many shapes and sizes, looking straight down at us.

Every night my father, my brother, myself, fought to stay up around the fire, but my mother wanted us to be in bed in good time, to be fresh for her goal, the actual visit to the school. For what was to us the best – the bush, the animals, the birds, the stars, the fire – was to her a means to the moment when she sat with the other parents on the stands watching her son batting or bowling or fielding or running races with the other little boys in their fresh white clothes. The sports field, a large area of pale earth, lay among eucalyptus trees. The school buildings were of a style called Cape Colonial, or Cape Dutch, white and low, with red tiles, green shutters. Everything was clean and tidy and there were green English lawns. I felt alien to the place. This was because I was alien to the English middle class, playing out its rituals here, as if on a stage. I knew even then they were anachronistic, absurd, and, of course, admirable in their tenacity. These were the 'nice people' my mother yearned for, exiled in her red earth district surrounded by people – as she was convinced – of the wrong class. Here we were invited to lunch, tea, supper, with the headmaster, and the other masters and mistresses; the rituals might go on for days, according to strict rules. But often my father was found lying on his back under the gum trees, and would not be budged by my mother, scandalized, hurt, that – as usual! – he so little valued what was her goal, her ambition, her raison d'être. In spite of our poverty, in spite of our struggles as farmers through this terrible Depression, in spite of his lack of interest, we were here, where we ought to be, with our peers, and her son was set on a path proper to him and to us. 'You go, old thing,' said my father, lying flat on his back, staring up through the loose green-fledged white arms of the gum trees and the always blue sky. 'You enjoy it, I don't.' He was letting her down and he knew it, so he might get himself awkwardly up off the ground, manoeuvring that clumsy wooden leg of his, and go with her to tea, and to lunch, and to parents' meetings. Or he might stay exactly where he was. Sometimes he was joined by other fathers, who, seeing him lying there at ease among the scented, brittle, gum-tree leaves, could not resist, so there might be two, three, or ten fathers staring at the blue sky through leaves, until summoned by their wives, while their delighted or shocked children watched them, waiting to hear what their mothers would say. 'But what are you doing there? What will they be thinking of you?'

This place was my brother's place, not mine. Ruzawi was what my mother had to have for him, expressing depths of her nature which we understood and allowed for, even if 'England' and 'Home' were so far off. The Convent was what she had to have for me. Like Ruzawi it was a snobbish choice. To me it was a dark oppressive place full of women loaded with their black and white serge robes who smelled when it was hot. I knew it was a bad place, but not how bad, until I was grown up. I was there for five years and it did me harm: I am still learning how much harm. That unwritten law, that mysterious ukase that forbids children to say to parents more than 'It's all right', when asked 'Well, how was school this time?' made it impossible for my parents to know what went on there. Five years. Five years. Five child-years. What's five years – when you're grown up? Immersed in that time, Convent time, nun-time, with aeons to go before holidays came, which were a different time, equally long, endless, thank God, when I could be free and in the bush, I drowned in helplessness. Above all, I was abandoned by my parents. I was homesick to the point of physical illness: I knew why I was always ill at school, though they didn't. When I asked my brother how he felt about Ruzawi, he said it was all right. But the people who taught him were not nuns, most of them peasants from southern Germany, frustrated and ignorant women. He was taught by brisk, matter-of-fact people who did not hang crucifixes with writhing tortured men on them, or pictures of meaty red hearts dripping with blood, on the walls of rooms where small children slept – children who walked in their sleep, had nightmares and wet their beds. At schools we were in different worlds, he and I, but were in the same world through the holidays. In the bush.

Or in the green circle of the boma. There he might tell stories about the goings-on at his school, but I recognized these as mostly invented to entertain the parents. The convention at his school was that feats and exploits should be described in a way that was both boastful and modest. The feats themselves, climbing dangerous rocks, or forbidden roofs, or trees, or going into pools where crocodiles had been seen – these were boasts, because all were foolhardy. But his descriptions made nothing of the dangers, for that was the modesty prescribed by their school. I recognized the convention from books in the bookcase on the farm: *Stalky and Co.*, Kipling generally, Buchan, Sapper, the memoirs of First World War soldiers. You could cross from one side of a deep gorge on a rope the thickness of an eyelash, or go into fire to rescue a comrade, or wriggle yourself on a six-inch outjut three storeys up a building from one window to another, and you could tell everyone about it, but the voice had to have a certain negligent humour about it, and then it was all right.

I would watch my brother's face, as he told these – permissible – tales out of school. It had the prescribed humorous modesty. Behind that was something else, an obstinate and secret excitement, and for the time he was speaking, he was not there by the fire at all, not with us, he was back in the moment of danger, the thrill of it, the pull of it.

We two had a pact that I don't remember being made, though it must have been: it was that we should help each other not to fall off to sleep, should unite against our mother's determination we should. This meant our two piles of sweet-scented grass must be close together, causing humorous comments from the parents, for usually we were not so affectionate. We lay down on our backs, so as not to miss a moment of moon and stars and up-rushing sparks, but with heads turned towards each other.

'I must stay awake, I must, I must,' I fought with myself, watching my brother's long dark lashes droop on his cheek: I put my hand to his shoulder, and he carefully shook himself awake, while I saw how his body began to shape itself into the curve he would sleep in. I might have time to prod him once, twice – but then he was gone, and in the morning would accuse me of failing as a sentry against sleep. Meanwhile I lay rigid, face absorbing moonlight, starlight, as if I were stretched out to night-bathe. I knew that this lying out with no roof between me and the sky was a gift, not to be wasted. I knew already how Time gave you everything with one hand while taking it back with the other, for this lament sounded whenever my parents talked about their lives. This lying out at night might never happen again. On verandahs – yes, but there always seemed to be mosquito nets and screen wire between you and the night. And it didn't happen again. I never again slept out under the sky in Africa, though I have in Europe. I was right to struggle to stay awake, but soon felt myself failing, and tried hard, and saw my mother bending over the fire in her pyjamas, dropping wood into nests of sparks, her face, for once, not presented to be looked at, but full of emotions I was determined would never be mine. 'I will not, I will not. Remember this moment, remember it,' I admonished myself, seeing the fire-illuminated face of that powerful woman, but she looked like a small girl who had had a door slammed in her face. The moment went to join the others on a list of moments that I kept in my mind, to be checked, often, so they did not fade and go.

And I fell asleep and woke with the sun on my face, not the moon, my brother curled like a cat, my mother already at work folding up the bedding, and perhaps the 'boy' still asleep, his back to us. Or it was in a thick whiteness that sometimes in the very early morning rolled through the trees and over us, a mist that clung to our eyelashes and our skins, and made us all shiver as we sat drinking mugs of hot sweet tea around the revived fire. This mist was the guti of the Eastern districts, and we never saw anything like it in our district, and so it was part of the excitement of these trips, another bonus, to be watched for and welcomed. When it was cold and damp like this, and we sat waiting for the sun to climb higher and dispel the mist, we were kept around the fire and my mother summoned Isaiah – or Joshua, or Aaron, or Matthew, or Luke, or John – away from his little fire and made him sit inside the hot reach of ours, but perhaps a yard further away than we were. 'You'll catch cold,' she fussed at him, as she did at us, pressing on him more mugs of the sweet tea. And then, it seemed always suddenly, the mist thinned and went and left us sitting in the brilliant sunshine.

GIVING LIFTS

It took me two hours to drive that short distance from Harare to Marondera, not because the car went so slowly; on the contrary, it was a powerful car that did not like being slowed. I kept stopping to salute this view, that cluster of toppling boulders, or at a turn-off to a farm I used to visit. No, the landscape had not lost its magnificence, nor grown smaller, the way things do, although I had seen the Arizona deserts, and California and Australia, been immersed in space and emptiness in various parts of the world. The road still rolled high in sparkling air, and, as you reached the crest of one rise, blue distances unfolded into mountains and then chains of mountains. But there was a new dimension to the landscape, because the War

had ended only two years ago, and I was looking at a country
where contesting armies had moved, often secretly, often at
night, for a decade. In these distances you do not see villages,
it is still, apparently, an empty land, but that is only because
huts melt and merge into trees, hills, valleys.

I had been told by white friends, 'On no account give any
lifts to the blacks, it is dangerous.' Public transport is bad and
large crowds of black people waited at every stopping place. If
a car showed signs of slowing, they crowded after it, shouting
and waving. I stopped at a bus-stop and at once the car was
surrounded. Such a scene would have been impossible in old
Southern Rhodesia, where blacks had to know their place. I
said to an old man who bent to peer into the seat near mine,
'Get in,' and he beckoned peremptorily to two women in the
crowd. He opened the door for them to get into the back seat,
and he got in beside me. He made threatening gestures at the
crowd, who were expressing loud dissatisfaction. 'Go on,' he
said to me, in the same peremptory way. I tried to start a
conversation with him but he answered Yes and No, or not at
all. I tried with the women, but he said, 'They don't know what
you are saying.' I could see from their faces this was not true.
I said to him, 'I am back in this country after twenty-five years.
I was brought up in Lomagundi.' He did not reply, and I was
stupidly disappointed. What did I expect? My intelligence
expected one thing, and my emotions another. About ten miles
further on he commanded, 'Stop here.' I stopped. I could not
see a building or road or even a path, only bush. He got out
and went off, leaving his women to follow. They could not
manage the door handle, and wrenched at it, irritated and
angry, meaning these emotions to show. I opened the door for
them. They got out and followed their man. Husband? Father?
He wore long khaki trousers and a good thick jersey. They
wore short colourful dresses and cardigans. Even thirty years
ago, in country districts, this group could easily have been a
man with an animal skin over his shoulders – monkey, leopard,
or buck – and a loincloth, and he would be carrying a bunch
of spears. Behind him women in the traditional blue-patterned
cloth balanced pots on their heads. The man would have to go

first to protect them from enemies or wild animals. These women still walked behind, when all three disappeared into the bush.

There was little traffic. The pipeline bringing oil from Beira to Mutare had just been cut again in Mozambique by Renamo, the South African-backed rebel army, and petrol was hard to get. The newspapers were full of exhortations to save petrol. I did not stop to give a lift again on that stretch of road, because I was soon to see my brother, after so many years, and this needed all my attention.

Going to see my brother was by no means as simple a thing as it might seem to people with normal family relationships. Normal? While the British Empire lasted (a short-lived empire, as empires go) it was common for families to be split, a son or brother somewhere in the army, female relatives working as missionaries (my mother's best friend's sister was in Japan) or (my uncle) being rubber planters in Malaya. When I was growing up in the bush, my parents so woefully in exile, the family was in England: step-grandmother, uncles, aunts, cousins. Since I have lived in London, the family has been in various parts of Southern Africa.

I can say that my brother and I have never got on and, with equal truth, that we always have. We have never agreed about anything, but when we have met (there have been stretches of years when we have not met at all) a mysterious understanding starts to work. It is the genes, so I've read: one shares a ground of genes. Similarly, when one falls in love apparently without rhyme or reason, in fact one yearns for one's own recessive genes incarnate and flourishing in another person. Deep calls to deep. Just as well we cannot hear this conversation, the ultimate in narcissism.

When he came out of the navy and before he married we did see quite a bit of each other, and this was the only time we did, as grown-ups. A year? Not much more. Not long. If I had left the state of being a True Believer behind I was still full of passionate principles, but at least I had learned it was a waste of time arguing about them. He knew that everything I thought was rubbish. In any case discussion, even ordinary talk, was difficult: gunfire in the War had deafened him, and he faced the world with a stubborn, slow, sweet smile, full of a readiness for goodwill. Our father was very ill, and we used to meet in a house where a man was slowly dying. Looking back at then, I see everything slowed, in slow motion, we hung about, we sat for hours on either side of a sickbed, we smiled a lot. When he was conscious my father talked, still talked, talked even now, about 'his' war, and always with grief, with rage. My brother did not talk about his war.

For the thirty years, almost, since we met – briefly – in 1956, we had kept in touch, with letters, at long intervals, giving facts. Sometimes he wrote me a polemic, but in fatherly style, thus: 'If communists like you and McCleod think you can get away with it then I am afraid I have to tell you that our Affs are sensible people, and know which side their bread is buttered.' This was just two months before the end of the War and the election of Robert Mugabe. (Ian McCleod was a Tory Minister.)

From his point of view my very existence was an embarrass-ment, and for him to write at all must have been difficult. After all, the community he belonged to did not have much good to say about me (to put it mildly). It was hard for me to write to him.

Then researchers turned up to interview him, as the brother of the author, and this way he learned that there were people who thought well of me. I understand that, considered as inter-views, the results were unsatisfactory. If I had been asked, I could have said, Don't waste your time. And, too, I was angry because of the lack of courtesy. I preserve the old-fashioned view that a writer's life is her or his property, at least until we die. This view begins to seem quaint, if not eccentric. I was not even middle-aged when a would-be biographer presented himself, with evident confidence that I could scarcely wait to tell him everything about myself. Suppose you decide you don't want a biography written at all? Writers who have left instructions to this effect have been ignored. A British judge decreed that Philip Larkin's wish not to have his life laid open to the curious and the lubricious was 'repulsive'. The only other people treated as if their wishes count for nothing are the mad. This attitude, that writers are fair game, can make life hard for their relatives. My brother had remarked, so someone told me, that the people who came to see him had a very funny way of looking at life, and that he was afraid I was in bad company.

I knew it was unlikely he had ever read a word of what I had written, and at that time he had not. After all, he knew that what I wrote was communist propaganda.

Everything about my life must seem wrong-headed to him. Except for the War years, (his war, the Second World War) and a couple of years after the War ended, his life was spent in the bush. He got up at five or five-thirty, was out of doors all day, and often spent hours walking by himself in the bush. He was always in bed by nine.

Looked at impersonally, and I certainly had been forced to do that, my brother was interesting from a cultural point of view. My parents thought of themselves as modern people, and kept abreast of ideas and new writers. The books on our shelves on the farm, all classics, were only part of it. My mother had progressive ideas about education, admired Ruskin, Montessori. My father might quote Shaw and Wells in an argument. The battering life gave them on the farm shook off that layer of culture. What came to the farm through the 1930s were newspapers from England, and Stephen King Hall's *Newsletter*. It was politics that absorbed them, and that was because of the First World War and its aftermath, which caused both of them anguish and anger, since everything in England was being mismanaged, and what they believed in betrayed. The books on the bookshelves remained unread, except by me. They subscribed to book clubs, but the packages of books that arrived on maildays were nearly all memoirs and histories of the War.

My brother did not read, as a boy, and later spent his life among people who did not read. This was partly because some books have ideas in them, and most of the whites in the Southern Rhodesian lager could not afford to consider ideas that might upset their idea of themselves as the noble and misunderstood defenders of civilization. Later, he took to reading the violent and semi-pornographic books you find in airports.

He told me that when waiting for a flight to leave, he had been surprised to see so many books. He liked Harold Robbins and particularly Wilbur Smith. When he came to visit me in London I asked him, 'Harry, why don't you ever read any good books?' – because of my difficulty in seeing him as a successor to my parents. But he raised a puzzled face – it was genuinely puzzled, and he did not understand the question – and asked, 'Good books? What do you mean?'

It will already have been noticed that my brother was in fact equal with at least two schools of advanced criticism: the one believing that to judge any writer better than another is to be élitist; and the one that says that in any case it is impossible to tell any difference between Goethe, Cervantes, Tolstoy and Barbara Cartland.

I asked him, 'Do you remember all those books we had on the farm?'

'Well, you were always a bookworm.'

'No, *you* – do you remember all those bookcases and the books?'

'I suppose so. But what I liked was being out in the bush, you know that.'

'Do you remember that Mother used to tell us those stories, every night, when we were little?'

'Did she? No, I don't remember.'

'She made up stories about the animals and the birds. Do you remember that long-running serial about the mice in the storeroom and their adventures? What about that story where the mouse knocked a rack of eggs off the shelf and fell into the egg mess and all the other mice came and licked it clean?'

'No, I don't remember, sorry to say.'

'We used to beg her, night after night, more, more, more?'

He looks at me. I look at him.

'Anyway,' he says, 'what could be as interesting in a book as what you see in the bush? An hour in the bush, watching what goes on, has any book in the world beat.'

DO YOU REMEMBER?

All the white farmhouses had, many still have, great security
fences around them, because of the War. I stopped the car
outside a fence that reminded me of pictures of internment
camps, a good twelve feet high, of close mesh. Inside two large
Alsatians bounded and barked, their tails all welcome. I got
out of the car. About a hundred yards away inside the fence
was a stout greying man I did not recognize, coming towards
me. When I had last seen my brother he was young and good-
looking. He stopped to peer at me. We stood at a distance,
gazing, and our faces confessed everything.

'Gosh,' he said.

'*Well*,' was what I said.

And so here I was, back in the life of the verandahs. What
way of life, anywhere in the world, is more agreeable? The
house consisted of rooms set side by side, with kitchen and
storerooms behind them, and at one end a tall trellis to keep
off the wind and carry creepers. The verandah went right along
the front. My brother built his house, working side by side
with a black builder, adding to the place as he could afford it.
A large garden, full of shrubs, sloped to the fence. We relaxed
in deep chairs, looking at the garden, where the gardener was
dragging a hose about. At our feet lay the two dogs. At once
the tea came, brought by the servant: the life of the verandahs
depends on servants. In my time, *then*, this house would have
had three, four, even five servants, all of them underpaid and
underemployed. Now the same work is done by one servant,
usually a man, who cooks, cleans the house, organizes everything. There is a minimum wage.

We sat exposed in strong afternoon light and examined each
other, not concealing it.

'Well,' says Harry at last, 'it does us in, doesn't it, well, I
mean, life does.'

'You could say that,' I say cautiously, thinking that my father
might have said exactly that, in that tone, humorous, philo-

sophic, but with a satisfaction in the inevitable erosion of good which – for some reason or another – justified him.

'In one way and another it does us in. And you look the worse for wear.'

'Fair wear and tear,' I say.

He nodded. 'Fair wear and tear is one thing,' he says, and looked at me in the eyes to make sure I would pay attention. 'I don't think I'm going to get over this one.' His wife had died the year before, and he had taken it hard. 'I have to warn you,' says Harry, 'I'm not the man I was. I feel as if a part of me's been shot clean away.'

'All right,' I say.

Meanwhile I had realized there was something new. Harry became a little deaf when he was not yet twenty. The gunfire in the Mediterranean only made worse what was already bad enough. For a time after the War he was very deaf, in spite of an operation by one of the great ear specialists. You had to shout, and what you said had to be simple. Now he had an efficient hearing-aid. He was talking at his own real pace, in his own style: a cautious man, slow to react, but not cut off by silence from what he saw around him.

'When you're young you think you're going to get over anything that happens to you,' I say.

'Did you think that? I don't believe I ever thought about it. Well, you don't get over some things. There are things that happen . . . and not the obvious things either. Did I tell you I went to the farm?'

This was rhetorical, for how could he have told me?

As he mentioned the farm, a silent *No* gripped me. In 1956, I could have gone to see the farm, the place where our house had been on the hill, but I was driving the car and could not force myself to turn the wheel off the main road north, on to the track that leads to the farm. Every writer has a myth-country. This does not have to be childhood. I attributed the ukase, the silent *No* to a fear of tampering with my myth, the bush I was brought up in, the old house built of earth and grass, the lands around the hill, the animals, the birds. Myth does not mean something untrue, but a concentration of truth.

'You aren't thinking of going back?' asks Harry.

'I was, yes.'

'Then don't. I'm warning you. There are farms all over the place now. And I couldn't even find the hill at first.'

'Couldn't find the hill?'

'I drove past the turn-off because I couldn't see the hill. Then I realized I was expecting to see the old house up there, and so I went back. To cut a long story short, they sliced the top off our hill.'

'Sliced off . . .'

'Yes. There is a plateau up there. It is flat. God knows what it cost them, cutting it off and levelling it.'

I am filled with anguish. Harry gives me a cautious glance and hesitates.

'Go on.'

'Right, but you won't like it.'

'But it was a steep hill. I know things look big when you're a child, but it was a good-sized hill, wasn't it? I used to sit at the door at the back and look down on the hawks circling over the big field.'

'And at the bottom of the hill we had to change into second gear to get up it at all.'

'And the car used to slant so steeply we used to joke it would fall over backwards.'

'And when we rode down the hill on our bicycles we went flying so fast . . .'

'And we looked down over everything, barns, the cattle kraals, the Ayreshire track.'

'You still do that, look down, but wait, they planted fruit trees and you'd never believe it once was just wild, just the bush.'

We look at each other in horror.

'Fruit trees? What happened to the big muwanga tree? The grove of acacias? Do you remember, we called them butterfly trees? The caterpillar tree – it was always full of caterpillars, it looked as if it had felted over and the cocoons were inside the felt . . .'

'I don't remember the caterpillars. But I told you, just don't go back. I don't know how to explain it, but it did me in. When I got back here from that trip, I couldn't sleep, I couldn't get over it. And the animals are all gone. The birds are gone. I kept dreaming about the old house. And then Monica died. I feel everything is gone.'

'Let's go for a walk now,' I say.

And so we go walking, through bush, but now the bush is something that fills spaces between farms and homesteads. It is a suburban bush.

'Do you ever think how bloody lucky we were?' he asks.

'We lived in Eden and didn't know it.'

'It's gone for ever.'

'Gone,' and I hear my own voice, like a Messenger come to announce defeat in battle.

'Gone. But sometimes I see my python in those rocks over there. It's the first I've seen in years. There are so many dogs around here and they give the snakes a bad time. They have all gone. But my python is there. And there are a couple of duiker, too. Sometimes they come around at sundown. And you can see them in the early morning grazing. One night I saw them grazing in the moonlight. Two duikers! Do you remember? We might see a dozen duiker in a mile's walk?'

We stand looking at the pile of rocks where the python lives, but the creature decides to remain out of sight.

Then we walk disconsolately home, while the dogs run around us, coming to put their noses into our hands.

'Time for a drink,' he says, back on the verandah. But it is too cold there, and we go in to a big fire. He pours himself an exact measure of brandy, with an exact allowance of water. His mouth is compressed as he watches his hands at work. His movements are slow, deliberate. Like my father's. Everything in slow motion.

There is a large meal, soup, meat and vegetables, pudding, cheese. Now, as we talk, Do you remember, Do you remember, we both avoid a subject that we are afraid will put an end to this good feeling.

'Do you remember that ridiculous time when you were think-ing of working for a bank?'

'*I* work in a *bank*!'

'Just after the War. And you even had a spell of thinking you would sell insurance.'

'I sell . . . never.'

'Don't you remember you came to see me and said you'd rather die than live your life inside four walls?'

'Are you sure?'

'Quite sure.'

'Funny thing, that I don't remember. I think there's a lot I've forgotten. Someone came to see me the other day and got quite angry with me when I didn't remember . . . it was Jeremy. Do you remember him? He went on a holiday to Madagascar. He came to see me and said he had left the hotel and gone wandering into the bush and then found he was crying. It was because of the bird songs, the butterflies. The insects. He said to me, "It was like old Southern Rhodesia, when we were children. Full of wild life." He hadn't realized how badly everything has changed. And it is getting worse all the time. Suddenly you think, I haven't seen such and such a bird for some time and then you realize, it's gone. Extinct, probably. Butterflies,' says my brother miserably. 'Bees. Insects. Chameleons. Lizards. We do them all in with our spraying. We destroy everything, you see.'

'Do you remember how we used to shoot when we were children? With the old .22? They gave you the .22 and you went out and shot everything you saw.'

'I would never have done a thing like that.'

'When they gave you your first air-gun you went out to the banks of the river – that was on Chappell's farm, and you came back with a pillow case full of birds.'

'I couldn't ever have done that . . . are you sure?'

'If we saw a porcupine, we killed it. If we saw a wild cat, we shot it. Whatever we saw.' He is most dreadfully distressed. 'That is how all us children learned to shoot. We shot everything.'

'But we used to go through the bush pulling out the bird traps the natives put down, and breaking up the game traps.'

'That was later. When we became reformed criminals. That

was when we shot for the pot, just shooting what we needed.'

'Why didn't they stop us – Mother and Father?'

'Because it was that time – it was the end of the Raj. The upper classes used to shoot everything they saw and the middle classes copied them.'

'Well, the Affs killed animals and birds.'

'They killed to eat.'

'Look at all the black kids now, out with their catapults, killing everything.'

'Just as we did.'

His look at me says if he is not challenging me about equating black and white children, that doesn't mean he hasn't noticed.

'What I remember best is going through the bush taking photographs.'

'But how old were you then?'

'Oh . . . well yes . . . I don't remember things the way you do; not the same things. Are you absolutely sure?'

'I don't understand why you don't remember. I remember everything about *then*. I know I've forgotten a lot of things about my life, because people say to me, Do you remember and I don't. They get angry.'

'Yes, they do, don't they.'

'But not about then.'

We are silent, for quite a bit. Harry is drinking steadily and carefully. Brandy. I could never enjoy drinking like that. I have a friend who researches patterns of drinking for a university. Would she be interested to hear about a man who drinks as if taking doses of medicine? My father, before he got diabetes, used to drink a whisky, perhaps two, as if a mentor invisible to us stood by him saying, Thus far and no further.

'If we had really been like brother and sister, grown up together all the way, we would have a sort of – shared landscape. You know, one says, Do you remember and the other does remember, and if not soon thinks he does.'

'I suppose we haven't been brother and sister, not really.'

'No.'

'Well,' he says, carefully and humorously, 'I haven't been all that keen on seeing you the last few years.'

'And the same to you,' I say. Humorously.

'But you aren't so bad, I suppose. Funny thing, if you don't see somebody for a long time, you start imagining all kinds of things about them and it's quite a shock when . . . but I suppose you do still have those funny ideas about – well, about everything.'

'You could say that I have my funny ideas. You could say they've turned out not to be so funny in the end.'

At this he goes red, he is really angry. This is the moment when we could explode into argument. I say hastily, 'Today when I came past Marandellas, I remembered how we used to camp out there, near the school.'

He smiles, and nods, meaning, Yes, you're right, let's not . . . And says, 'Who camped out? When?'

Now I am really astonished, and upset. 'You don't remember how we used to come down, and camp? Sometimes for a week or even ten days? When you had Sports Days and things.'

'Did you?'

'How can you not remember that? The best times of my childhood . . . we couldn't afford the hotel for a night, let alone a week . . .'

'Wait a minute, yes, it's coming back. Yes, you're right.'

'And the school always let you come and camp with us for a night or two.'

He rubs his hands over the back of his head, with a quizzical but frustrated look. I remembered the movement: father, brother.

'We used to cut down branches or young trees and make an enclosure to sleep in.'

'Whatever for?'

'To keep out the leopards.'

He puts his head back and laughs most heartily. It is a young fresh laugh, from quite another layer of his life. Then, soberly, 'Shouldn't have done that. Couldn't have done the bush much good.'

'We used to leave a trampled-down place inside the circle of dead branches, and the burned leaves hanging down where the fire was.'

'But how could we? What did we want to do a thing like that for?'

'That's how we all were in those days.'

'Well, we are all paying for it now.' Many conversations with my brother end like this: I, we, she, he, they, you, are paying for it. Crime and punishment. Invisible walls have always surrounded my brother, signposted, *Forbidden . . . No . . . Keep out. Verboten.* Me, too, of course, but different walls, different forbidden places.

'Do you remember how we hated to go to sleep because it was so marvellous sleeping out?'

'No. But it is marvellous sleeping out. In the Bush War, that was the best thing. Of course I was too old to fight properly, but when we were out on patrol, we often stayed the night in the bush.'

'Do you remember the old prospectors that used to come to the farm? They lived out in the bush all the time.'

'Of course I remember. You don't forget a thing like that. Perhaps that's what I should have done. I often wonder if I've lived my life right. I should have been in the bush.'

'But you have been in the bush.'

'No, I mean really. They had a pan for gold, a rifle and a blanket. They lived off the bush.'

'And most of them died of malaria or blackwater fever.'

'That's all right. Who cares about dying? I don't.'

'Do you remember many of them weren't ordinary prospectors? Some were men who had lost their jobs in the Slump, and they put their wives into some job in the town where they could have the children, usually matrons or housekeepers or something, and they went off to live in the bush till things got better.'

'No. But it makes sense. Good for them.'

'I'm sure Daddy would have been happy living off the bush. If he hadn't been so ill all the time. Do you remember how he used to get fed up with socializing at Sports Days and he lay down under the blue gums and looked up at the sky, and Mother was quite frantic, and said he was letting the side down. And you were embarrassed too.'

'I wasn't. I couldn't have been. I always do that in the bush. I lie on my back looking at the sky. After a few minutes the birds and the animals – well, what birds and animals are still left – they forget all about you. You could be a stone or a bush. Once a yellow cobra went past about five feet away. He didn't care about me.'

'Do you remember . . . ?'

'No. And you don't remember how . . . ?'

'No.'

'And you really don't remember when . . . ?'

'No I don't, I'm afraid.'

At nine o'clock Harry said he was off to bed. He had drunk the exact amount to make him sleep. He didn't sleep easily these days, he said. He wasn't going to lie awake thinking all those thoughts . . . the doctor had given him a prescription, but he wasn't going to take all that chemical rubbish. Brandy was much better for you.

I said I never slept before twelve or one. He said, 'You will here. You can watch the television if you like . . . but the Affs, they can't run anything, let alone television.' He glared at me, standing in the doorway, a glass in his hand, his thumb just above the level of the brandy, like a reminder to himself. He couldn't bear to put off what had been at the back of his mind while we talked, just as it had at mine, and now he delivered a monologue, in a hot, angry, frustrated bitter voice, and it was exactly the same as the one I had listened to only last night, on the plane, from the race-horse breeder.

'Your precious Africans, what is the first thing they do? They take over *our* Government House, and install President Banana, *Banana*, what a name, and he hasn't been in it a week before he has chickens running all over the gardens, *our* gardens, and all his friends and relations are camped in the place, like a kraal. The next thing is, the place is surrounded by a high fence. Young Jack, from the next farm, but he's Taken the Gap now, went and threw in some chicken feed through the wire, and shouted Cluck, cluck, cluck, bloody peasants, peasants in Government House. And Mugabe, *Comrade* Mugabe, he goes around in a motorcade with armed guards, and if someone doesn't get out of the way quick enough, they get shot. *Our* Prime Ministers didn't need to go around in a motorcade with armed escorts, they didn't have anything to be afraid of. And inefficient . . . they can't get anything right . . . let me tell you . . . and let me tell you another thing . . . yes, and that's not all.' It goes on and on, and ends: 'They're inferior to us, and that's all there is to it.'

'It might strike some people as rather touching and even wonderful that the first black President when he moves into Government House, that is, into the symbol of the old regime, makes it clear he is not going to set himself above the people. Peasant people. He lets it be known he is keeping chickens and anyone can drop in, African style . . .'

'No one is going to drop in now. He's surrounded by security fences and guards armed with kalashnikovs.'

'You don't think there might be some connection between putting up security fences and white louts turning up to jeer and shout threats? You don't think Mugabe goes around in a motorcade because you people would cut his throat as soon as look at him?'

'*Louts?*'

'Louts.'

He glares at me.

I glare back.

He went to bed. I went out into the cold dark of the garden and stood there for a long time, hoping that beyond the security fence I would see the dim shape of a duiker moving about in the starlight. But the dogs stood quietly by me, looking straight out, so there was nothing there.

We were up by five-thirty, awakened with that long forgotten amenity, the early morning cup of tea. At seven we sat down to an old-fashioned English breakfast, laid before us by Joseph, a smiling friendly young man who had already asked how he could come to London and work in my house as my servant. I said we didn't have servants: that is, only a few rich people had them. He stared at me, unhappy, because he wanted to live in London where the streets are paved with gold. Then, 'Who does your work for you? Who cleans your house? Who cooks your food?' When I said most people cleaned their own houses and cooked their food, he shook his head, disapproving.

During breakfast Harry was angry, and I listened to The Monologue again. I knew by now I was going to hear it over and over again, during this trip. At any given time, all the people of the same kind will be saying the same things, often using the same phrases. It is this mechanism that journalists rely on: interview two or three people and you know what everyone is saying. (Similarly, if you want to know what the literary world is thinking, in London, you need only to spend half an hour with a representative of it to know what writers are in, what writers are out, and exactly the words used for these pronouncements of the communal mind.)

Harry was angry because of problems with his business, which made pictures from feathers and articles like buttons and key-rings from ox horn. It had been successful before Independence, but now, with so many of the customers gone – they had Taken the Gap – it was struggling. Black girls came from a nearby farm village to work. It seemed there was a troublemaker among the girls, she set all the others off, yet the girls had been given everything they asked for. They brought their babies and small children with them to work, they came and went as they felt inclined . . . no, it was all impossible, he was glad he was Taking the Gap.

Where did the phrase originate? White people who left Southern Rhodesia, and then Zimbabwe, for The Republic,* 'Took the Gap'.

My brother was prepared to leave this pleasant house, built by himself and a black builder whom he said was a good chap – working with him was a pleasure – leave this great garden, laid out by his dead wife, leave this district, where he had lived most of his life, for a lower standard of living in The Republic not only because he had a daughter in The Republic, but because it stuck in his craw to live under a black government.

'And now I've got to put up with their bloody Labour Officer

---

* South Africa is usually referred to as The Republic.

telling me what to do. I have to abide by whatever decision *he* sees fit to come up with. *I* have to do what *he* says.'

After breakfast the Labour Officer arrived. He was on a bicycle. My brother invited him, with cold formality, to sit down. This of course could not have happened in the old days. We three sat on the verandah and Joseph brought out tea. He and the Labour Officer exchanged greetings in the Shona style.

'Good morning.'

'Good morning.'

'Have you slept well?'

'I have slept well if you have slept well.'

'I have slept well.'

'Then I have slept well.'

The Labour Officer was a man of about thirty-five, a strong, healthy, sane, individual with a humorous look imposed on him by this job, which was mostly having to manage difficult, unreasonable, unfair and sometimes abusive whites.

My brother grumbled on and on about the girls who understood nothing about the obligation to give a day's work in return for a day's pay, and about the troublemaker who had all the others dancing to her tune.

The officer sat listening. When my brother had to go in to answer the telephone, I asked him about his work. He had been trained in agriculture under the whites, together with hundreds of others: there had been a policy to train black experts to work in the Native Purchase Areas and the Reserves – no, that is what they were called then, they had different names now – luckily for this government, because he was worked off his feet, all the cultural advisers and Extension workers were worked off their feet, there was not enough of them. It would take two to three years, he said, to train the experts Zimbabwe needed. 'Surely,' I said, 'no one's going to blame you if it takes longer?' Suddenly a direct look, acknowledging me as a friend, and not an enemy. He grimaced, shook his head, and laughed. 'They blame us in any case,' he said, which was his real answer to my question, 'Do you find this work difficult?' To which he formally replied, 'I try to do my best, madam.'

He bicycled off to the village to talk to the girls. Meanwhile my brother grumbled that this Labour Officer 'or whatever he calls himself' of course would be on the side of the girls. After a couple of hours the man came back. The tea tray appeared again. He thought he had sorted everything out, but first of all he would like to see the pay books. Tight-lipped, Harry brought out the pay books. For about half an hour the man worked through them, then snapped them shut, and delivered his verdict. 'The girls told me you hadn't paid them, but I see you have, sir. My recommendation is you should dismiss Mary . . .' (the troublemaker) 'but you should dismiss Sarah too. She's the real trouble. You have got it wrong, sir. Mary does what Sarah tells her. I've told them that when they get work somewhere else, I'll be keeping my eye on them.'

Off he went on his bicycle. He told us he was going to visit a farm where a woman had accused another of putting the evil eye on her. As a result, there had been fighting among the farmer's workers.

'Did you hear that? The evil eye! That's what we have to contend with . . . and those silly girls won't get work anywhere else, because there isn't any work. They'll be jolly sorry they played me up when they find they can't get work. With so many of us Taking the Gap there's less work all the time.'

'Aren't you pleased at the way that was sorted out?' I enquired.

'Let's go and have lunch.'

An enormous meal of meat and vegetables, baked potatoes, salads, pudding, cheese, biscuits.

'I can see I am going to eat far too much here,' I said. 'No one in England eats anything like this amount.' I described the evolving food habits of the British, take-away foods, snack foods, convenience foods, freezers, microwaves. I said we ate Indian food, Chinese food, pizzas, pastas and American hamburgers. 'The old pattern of eating, three solid meals a day and morning and afternoon tea – it's gone.'

'I'm sorry to hear that. I believe standards should be kept up.'

After lunch he slept for exactly half an hour, and then we

sat on the verandah and drank tea. The two Alsatians lay beside us, one at my brother's feet and the bitch Sheba at mine. She has been miserable ever since her mistress died. She wants another woman to love her, and hopes this will be me. Her hunger for a woman's affection makes her trot over to the farmhouse a mile away, where she puts her muzzle into the hand of the mistress of the house, and whines, begging for love. The woman, who understands the dog's unhappiness, sits down on the verandah or on the lawn beside Sheba and hugs her and sweet-talks, until Sheba licks her face, and trots back home. Sheba is overshadowed by the big dog Sparta, a strong intelligent dog who, when we play with them in the garden, always reaches the thrown stick first, and can pick up in his mouth two, three, four sticks, tossing them and catching them for our applause, like a juggler. Sheba can carry only one stick. Sparta knows how to obey orders, Sit, To heel, Lie down, Fetch it, Bark once – twice – three times. My brother trained Sparta, but Sheba was not trained. She is frantic to be like Sparta, is always watching, to find out how it is done, while Sparta shows off.

My brother seemed helpless with Sheba, did not know how to gentle the dog's pain, which is so like his. But later, when Sheba found that no woman came to live in the house, she attached herself to my brother, and bested Sparta in the way of affection, for he could not compete with her need to be one person's dog, with her fierce devotion. She slept on my brother's bed, was always beside him, her head near his hand, or lay with her eyes on his face. When my brother Took the Gap, the dogs went with him. Quite soon Sheba got herself coiled in some wire left loose at the end of a fence. She strangled to death, though there was a man present, with wire-cutters in his pocket, the white stock manager of a local ranch. He said he wasn't going to risk being bitten by an Alsatian.

Later a neighbour telephoned to say he had driven into Marondera for the mail, and could not buy a newspaper: they had all been sold. There had been an 'incident' on the Victoria Falls road from Bulawayo. Terrorists had captured tourists. 'Of course they aren't going to tell us the truth in our papers,' said

the neighbour. 'Ask your sister to ring London.' I did this and
found that the Terrorists, supposed to be Joshua Nkomo's men,
had captured six tourists, but released three women. The men
would be killed if Mugabe did not release some Nkomo men in
prison.

'There you are,' says Harry, 'you have to telephone Home
to get the facts.'

Which were all on the television news.

'There *you* are,' I said.

But he went off into The Monologue. By then I had understood the whites were in a state of shock, just as if there had
been an accident, or a disaster. I was irritated with myself for
not seeing earlier what could have been foreseen before even
leaving London.

After supper we argued: of course I should have known
better. He got a bit tight and talked about the innate inferiority
of the blacks. I was to discover this happens often with whites
when they get drunk. Not all of them, though; and it is interesting to try and guess which old Rhodie will start spouting racial-
ism when they have had a drink or two, for they might just as
well reveal admiration of a wistful Rousseau-like kind: 'They
are much better people than we are, you know.' But some
whites define themselves by insisting on the inferiority of the
blacks. What deep insecurity, what inadequacy, does this
insistence on other people's inferiority conceal? (In 1991 I sat
in a London restaurant with black Zimbabweans who talked to
Indian waiters with the same cold insulting dislike once used
by the worst of the whites to the blacks.) I said he talked as
if the whites of Southern Rhodesia were all remarkable and
valuable, but many were poor material from any point of view.
When they were good they were very very good, skilful, adapt-
able, full of expertise, but the rest were limited, unintelligent,
with that kind of complacency that can only go with stupidity.
They would not easily get jobs anywhere else and the blacks
were only too lucky to have got rid of them. Harry was hurt.
He was bitter, accusing; could not believe I had said these
things or could think them.

Next morning, friends dropped in from Banket, among them

an old woman I had known when we were children. There is a convention among adults that because they are friends, their children must be too. This girl and I were sent off to play together when our parents visited each other. At once we began to play Do You Remember, the game so useful when other conversation is difficult. I remembered that on hot days we were put into a tin bath under a big mulberry tree and cold water poured over us. Snakes love mulberry trees, and we kept looking up into the innocent branches for a stealthy slithering green coil, a flickering tongue. We were both teased 'unmercifully', as was then prescribed, because we were plump. We both played up to what the adults wanted, squealing and splashing water about. She did not remember this. What she knew was that we were sent off into the fields to collect 'witch grass', the witchweed or fireweed the farmers don't like. We were paid pocket money, a few pence for each bundle. 'I don't remember that,' I said, and she was affronted, insulted. 'But whenever I think of you, you are standing in the mealies holding a big bundle of witchgrass.' She turned away from me and went to sit at the table on the verandah. In denying her this memory, part of herself, a 'nice' memory, chosen from others to enable her to think pleasantly about an unsatisfactory childhood friend, I only deepened what she already felt about this deceiving, treacherous and above all unfair time that was taking everything away from her. She and her brother, my brother and a couple of neighbours sat drinking tea and then beer, while they recited versions of The Monologue. I sat a little away from them, and read one of the novels by African writers I had bought only two days ago. There I sat, apart, reading, just as I had as a child . . . they sat together, leaning a little forwards, their shoulders hunched and defensive, sometimes sending me accusing glances from inside their little lager. Their voices were miserable, full of betrayal, sorrow, incomprehension.

When they went off, Harry asked what was I reading, and I told him about the good African writers. Had he ever thought of reading them? He had never heard of them. If he did read them, then perhaps he would understand better how the Africans were thinking? He said he understood quite well what they were thinking, and he couldn't say he liked it much. Encouraged by this note of humour, I handed him a couple of books. During the next few days, I left them lying around, and even read him a paragraph or two. He listened as if to news from a foreign country.

I had no better luck in any of the white households I visited on that trip. In not one was anyone prepared even to open an African novel; I was challenging, threatening, some well-out-of-sight, or even out-of-consciousness, prohibition. *No* said all these faces, when I asked, These are books written by your fellow citizens. Aren't you even interested?

Next day we drove into Marondera to shop. Grumble grumble all the way because there were gaps on the shelves where imported goods used to be. I pointed out there was plenty to eat. Bickering, we drove to the post office, where a group of whites stood talking in a tight circle, faces close, their shoulders repelling invisible bullets. Cheerful blacks milled about, talking, laughing, calling out to each other and took no notice at all of the whites.

On the way home we stopped at a roadside stall to buy mushrooms, and the seller asked if we could lift his wife to the turn-off. With bad grace, my brother said yes. The girl, pregnant and holding a new baby, sat by me on the driving seat. When we had set her down, Harry kept saying, 'But it's no distance,' which statement had layers of meaning. One, that Africans had not lost the use of their legs, as we had, and this was both a matter for admiration, and a symptom of being primitive. Two, he did not see why he should give free lifts to people who had just unfairly beaten his side in the War.

My smug disapproval about the whites not giving lifts was to take a knock, for six years later I found that no one, not 'liberals' or the religious; not 'progressives' or 'reactionaries', no one at all, gave lifts to any person, black or white, whose face was not familiar. It was too dangerous: there had been too many muggings, hold-ups, 'incidents' of all kinds.

We went to take morning tea on another verandah full of wonderful dogs, and luxurious cats, who had to be spilled off the chairs so we might sit down, and I heard The Monologue spoken, first by the wife, and then at lunch, which was served by a black girl wearing a uniform not unlike an Edwardian maid's, black, with white cuffs and lace. This time the husband said The Monologue. Then everyone sneered at President Banana's funny name.

We walked around the garden. Again a garden 'boy' – the old word still used, quite unself-consciously, watered a variety of lawns and shrubs, and when his employers were not listening, asked if he could come and work for me, he needed to better himself. He had an O-level, and was only a gardener because he had not yet found a good job. I live in London, I said. He asked if it was in America, because if so, he would come and work for me. I said in America black people did not necessarily have an easy time. He said he had seen rich black people on television and in films, and he wanted to be like them. This took me back thirty odd years, to when I used to sell communist papers around a certain 'Coloured' (that was the correct word politically then for people of mixed race) suburb in old Salisbury. While I preached informed opposition to white domination, I was being stopped on every street corner by aspiring young men who wanted to go to America where everyone was rich. I used to give them gentle lectures on the need to think of the welfare of All before self-advancement. What a prig. What an idiot. I can see myself, an attractive but above-all self-assured young woman, in a clean and perfectly ironed cotton dress – which in itself was a luxury for people living crammed in shabby rooms; wheeling a nice clean bicycle too expensive for almost everyone I met, and on the carrier piles of newspapers and pamphlets advocating varying degrees of social discontent, with revolution as a cure for everything.

Next day Harry said he would take me to the Club some miles away. I knew he did not want to go, but he said it would do him good. Since his wife died he had got out of the habit of socializing. But I wasn't to expect a good time. Because so many people had Taken the Gap, the Club was nearly empty these days. Once there were two hundred, three hundred people on Saturdays and Sundays, and people had to queue to use the tennis courts or to get drinks at the bar. Yes, yes, he would go, he felt he should: people kept insisting that he must go out to lunch, or to supper, or to the Club. They meant to be kind, he knew that.

When we got there, the Club was a low brick building in the bush, with tennis courts, a squash court, a bowling green. It seemed the weekend before several cars full of youngsters had come down from Harare for a party, and some were still here, lolling on the verandah. A couple slept flat on their backs under a tree, their arms flung out, faces scarlet. On one sun-inflamed forearm sat a contemplative green grasshopper. The cold-thinned musasa trees of winter laid shifting mottled shadow over them. There was a bleak and dusty wind.

'Stupid to drink yourself into this state,' said Harry authoritatively, and shouted: 'Thomas. Thomas!'

A black man in a servant's white uniform appeared on the verandah, said calmly to him, 'Good afternoon, sir,' and walked slowly over.

'They shouldn't be lying here like this, they'll get pneumonia.'

Thomas looked down at the unconscious pair, and then at Harry, saying with his eyes that it was not part of his job to tell the two young whites how to behave.

'Is there a blanket? Anything to put over them?'

The servant strolled off, and came back with his arms full of checked tablecloths, which he and my brother placed in layers over the sleepers.

Among the hungover youngsters, and in a quite different style, were the older people, the Club's real users, mostly farmers. Not many now, and they were putting a good face on things, being brave. They were pitiable.

Harry and I played bowls. He has always been easily good at any physical thing . . . the first time he was put on a bicycle, the first time he took up a cricket ball . . . and he would shin up any tree as soon as look at it. It was not that I was bad, but the comparison with him made me the clumsy one, and so I was styled through my childhood. Later I realized I had been nothing of the kind. Such is family life.

When he had beaten me at bowls, someone challenged him,

and I retired to the verandah, sat by myself and watched. The rooms of the Club were half empty, full of the ghosts of the departed whites. And would it fill soon with blacks?

At the next table sat a group of middle-aged farmers, talking about the Bush War. Among them sat a man who was silent while they went on about the iniquities of the blacks, and recited versions of The Monologue. He was a farmer of about forty. He was apart from them, just as I was. Yet he had been fighting in the Bush War. His silence was felt, and they began teasing him, trying to be pleasant, but sounding peevish, because he was not about to Take the Gap, as they were. He had decided to stay in Zimbabwe, to stick it out. He had made inner psychological adjustments, and was no longer uncritically one of them. He did not look too happy: these were his neighbours, his tribe.

As the sunset began to fire the sky, my brother took on another challenger: he had beaten the first.

The group at the next table broke up. The odd-man-out sat looking at me for a while, then came over. He knew I was my brother's sister, and had funny ideas.

'Well,' he said, 'I've been wondering what you're making of it all.'

His manner was conditionally friendly. I decided not to choose my words. He listened, sitting back in his chair, nodding sometimes, but I could see from his eyes that he was matching what I said with scenes or events he was remembering and the words I used did not fit. 'Everyone's entitled to their opinion,' he summed up. Then I said there were things I would like to ask my brother, but could not: the Bush War, for instance, for he simply clammed up.

'You should remember there's a difference between his generation and our lot.'

'What difference?'

He shrugged.

'Were you brought up in this country?'

'Canada.'

'Ah, I see.'

'All right, what do you want to know?'

'For instance why was it in the Bush War, the black civilian casualties were always so high when "incidents" were reported?'

He sat thinking for a while. Then: 'All right, I'll tell you the story of something that happened. In the *Rhodesia Herald* it said, "One member of the Security Forces killed, five civilians, eleven Terrorists."'

THE BUSH WAR

He was with five others on patrol in the bush. They were travelling fifteen to twenty miles at night, and lying low in the day. He was patrol leader. They each carried food for eight days.

'I had a self-invented muesli, of milk powder, oats, wheatgerm, raisins, and bits of salami. I ate one pound of this a day, with half an onion. We sucked dew off the grass in the morning, if we didn't come on any decent water. The muesli was in a plastic bag and that was good because it didn't make a noise: tins clash, and give you away. Everybody made up their own rations. Biltong came into its own, I can tell you. We saw two men lurking about outside a village. We thought they looked suspicious, probably spies for the 'terrs'. You acquire an instinct, after a bit of practice. We took them prisoner. So there were eight of us. They didn't mind going along with us. We didn't even have to tie their hands. They had no spirit, those chaps, poor buggers, government forces or the 'terrs', they got it in the neck either way. Then we heard the 'terrs' singing their freedom songs in a village we didn't know was there. It was just luck. We knew they didn't know we were there. All the different groups of 'terrs' told each other of their whereabouts, or where we were, through their talking drums. We usually had some Aff with us who could tell us what the drums were saying, but not that trip. But the 'terrs' wouldn't have been singing their heads off if they knew we were half a mile away. We left the two prisoners with two guards. One was shitting in his pants with fear. That is what is meant by the smell of fear.'

The four crawled up to the edge of the village in the dark. It was cold. They lay in the grass just far enough away from the firelight. There was no moon. 'It was the usual thing. A song, and then a speech. Then a song and another speech.'

One of the 'terrs' was sitting on a scotch cart, its wheels within touching distance of the four watchers, who lay as still as they could, trying to breathe quietly.

'Luckily he was drunk. We were watching the leaders going in and out of a hut where we were sure a girl was. They were having a good time with her. We could hear her laugh. The ones who made the longest and most fiery speeches got most time in the hut. I had given orders no one should open fire until I did. I knew they were itching to let go, with all those drunk 'terrs' reeling about. I waited until the girl came out of the hut to have a pee. Then we all threw our bombs into the hut. Girls were screaming, and I realized there were other girls in there. There was general firing for about a minute. The 'terrs' ran away into the bush. They didn't know how many soldiers were out there in the dark. We could have been a whole battalion, not just four. One of us was hit by a ricochetting bullet. He died later.'

The four went on lying in the grass, waiting. They did not know one of them was badly wounded.

'He did feel blood trickling, but he thought it was just a scratch. We were listening to the groans of the wounded. We had no idea how many there were. Several times grenades went off. The usual trick, a grenade put under a corpse, or held under him by a wounded man – kamikaze stuff, the idea was we would get it, when we moved him. But sometimes the grenades went off when they weren't supposed to. When the light came, there were several dead, including civilians, lying on the earth between the huts, and in the huts where I thought there was only one girl, were several dead 'terrs' and three dead girls. The girl who had come out to have a pee had a smashed hip. We gave her morphine and called in the choppers, and they took the girl and our wounded chap, but he was as good as dead by then, to the hospital. I followed the girl's progress. It turned out she was three months' pregnant. We gave her a new hip, and she kept the baby. I visited her in hospital. She was a pretty girl all right. She had already got herself engaged and she's had another baby since. When we got back to where the prisoners were waiting for us, we sent them for interrogation. Then we went on with our patrol. There were no more incidents that trip. Next week I read two lines in the *Herald*: "One member of the Security Forces killed, five civilians, eleven Terrorists. Does that answer your question?' He was brisk, and businesslike, and unemotional, telling his tale.

Then a group of fifteen or so were sitting around a table, joking how, when the election was being prepared, the Security Forces were sent to get evidence that the 'terrs' were contravening Lancaster House rules, with the aid of the Australians 'who distrusted the Brits as much as we did.' The Security Forces were able to wriggle to the edge of clearings where the 'terrs'' meetings went on, and made recordings. 'We got all this evidence they were cheating, but of course the Brits didn't do anything.'

'But we were cheating too,' said the farmer who had told me his story. 'Everyone knew that. Our cheating and theirs cancelled each other out.' He laughed. After a moment the others laughed with him.

As Harry and I went to the car, the two youngsters from Harare were still sprawled under their tree in the dark. It was cold. Another youth bent over them, trying to shake them awake, while they groaned and complained but on a facetious note.

'Never was anything like that in the old days,' said Harry.

'How can you say that!' I demanded.

'We kept up standards, then.'

'Harry, I was part of the old days, have you forgotten? It was only when I got to England I realized how much we all drank. And you must have seen that too, when you got to England.'

But he was not going to admit anything of the kind. Back there, in the old days, *then*, was paradise, a shangri-la, a lost perfection.

At the security fence, he could not find the keys. I said, why not go to the neighbour's house a mile away and get wirecutters. He did not like to think that a pair of wirecutters was all that had been between them and the 'terrs'. No, he was going to climb it. Derring-do. There was I, a small girl again, watching my brother performing impossible physical feats, while I thought, intending the thought to show, Well, what's the point of *that*!

He did not find it easy. The fence was not only high, but at the top there was a three-stranded leaning-out section. It was this that stopped him. Down he slid, a heavy man, out of temper, out of breath, and locked out of his safe place. He banged at the gate and shouted for the servant – who was asleep – while handsome Sparta, elegant Sheba, defenders of the lager, barked and bounded and whined inside. Just as we were off to borrow the wirecutters, he found the key. At once he became humorous and laughed at himself as the big gate swung in, and the dogs overwhelmed us with love. Then the gate was locked, and we looked out through the wire from inside the lager.

That evening, he asked what I had been talking about with Hugh. The fact there had been this long conversation had been reported to him. I told him, we were talking about the Bush War.

'What did you want to do that for?'

'Well, you don't seem to want to talk about it.'

'Nonsense.' And he began on a careful statement, like a formal briefing. 'The men of my age couldn't do the real fighting, worse luck. We did police duties. We visited farms, to make sure everything was all right. Or we investigated villages that were supposed to be sympathetic to the 'terrs'. Sometimes we just drove up and down the roads in army lorries. Showing our teeth, you know. Often we slept out in the bush. Yes of course I enjoyed it, wouldn't you? The bush, you know. Anyway, you people don't understand anything about it. We were fighting for you, against communism. And now look at what's happened.'

Soon, he poured himself another brandy, and another – carefully, as usual – and then he was talking about *his* war, not the Bush War, but the Second World War, how he was in the *Repulse* when it was sunk, and then the fighting in the Mediterranean. His tone changed. I recognized it. What he wanted to tell me was terrible, but he wasn't going to make much of it. How could he? He had been trained not to.

'Did I ever tell you about the *Repulse*?'

'You wouldn't talk about it.'

'Wouldn't I? That's funny. I think about it all a good bit.'

And now that was it, we were off, never mind about the Affs and the 'terrs', the Bush War and the inglorious Brits. This is what he wanted to talk about. *His* war.

'I was down at the bottom of the ship. That's where I was when the Jap bombs hit. We knew there were only a few minutes before the ship went down. The water was pouring in . . . did you know the *Repulse* and the *Prince of Wales* were supposed to be unsinkable?'

'Yes, like the *Titanic*.'

'Yes. Funny, the way we go on believing . . . I was standing at the bottom of the companionway, while the men climbed up past me . . . the stairs were already perpendicular. I just stood there. Someone said to me, "Aren't you going to go up, Tayler? You'd better get a move on." I went up those stairs like a monkey, and I walked down the slanting deck straight into the sea and I swam away as fast as I could. Lucky for me I'm a good swimmer. Some of the chaps couldn't swim fast enough. We were in the water for hours. It was full of oil and rubbish from the ship and dead men floating. I trod water. I used as little energy as I could and I kept my nose and mouth above the oil. Then they came to pick us up out of the water. They said there were sharks but I couldn't see any. They were probably keeping clear of the oil too. Wouldn't want to be a shark in that mess.'

'Well, that wasn't very jolly, was it,' I said, falling from long practice into the mode, or tone.

'No,' he said, looking carefully at me to see what I was saying. 'No. A lot of my friends were drowned, you see.'

'Yes.'

'And it was just luck it wasn't me. If that chap hadn't said, you'd better get a move on, Tayler . . .'

'Yes. And then?'

'Oh, and then they patched me up and rehabilitated me. In Ceylon, that was. They gave us a good time in Ceylon. So I believe. I met someone not long ago, and he said, They gave us a good time in Ceylon. I pretended I could remember, but I couldn't. Ceylon is a blank. I was there for weeks. It's a total blank. It really is a funny thing what we remember . . . you saying things . . . I've been thinking hard the last few days . . . and then after Ceylon was the Med.'

'And you were there quite a time.'

'Yes, the *Aurora*. A good ship, that. A good lot of chaps.'

'And there was that gunfire and you got very deaf.'

'That was nothing, being deaf I mean. They gave me an operation, and then they gave me this hearing-aid. It's a miracle, this hearing-aid. Sometimes I forget I was ever deaf . . .'

A long silence. The fire burned in the wall, and the dogs lay stretched out, firelight moving on their soft fur.

'No,' said Harry. 'That wasn't the point, you see . . .' A pause. 'It wasn't till the Bush War I understood something about myself. I suddenly understood I had been numbed for years and years. Only just the other day I said to myself, you've spent the best part of your life numbed. Frozen . . .' A pause. 'That wasn't a very nice thing, suddenly knowing that.'

'What made you understand, then? Was it something that happened in the Bush War?'

'Something on those lines, yes. It wasn't a picnic, the Bush War.'

'So I've gathered.'

'No. I was watching some of the younger men, the ones who did the bad fighting, you know. I knew when they were switching off – you could see them doing it. I knew, you see, because I'd done it. I wanted to say, No, don't do it, don't do that, you don't want to spend your life as I've done. You know, it's like living inside a sort of glass jar. But they had to switch off. You can't see your best friends being blown to pieces and then just go on as if nothing had happened. So now when I look at someone I can tell – I think, you've switched off: and a lot of the 'terrs' too, I shouldn't wonder.'

'Harry, does it strike you as odd that it's only now you are saying you had a bad time in that war?'

'I never said that,' he protested at once. 'A lot of people had it much worse than I did.'

'I don't think anyone would criticize you for exaggerating if you happened to remark you had a bad war.'

He was silent, looking humorous, rueful, deprecating.

'This bloody stiff-upper-lip business of yours – you pay a pretty heavy price for it.'

He looked genuinely surprised.

'I don't know, I don't think one should make a fuss, that sort of thing.'

'Why not? Do you realize, when I asked you after the War, how was it when the *Repulse* went down, you said, Oh it wasn't too bad.'

He was silent and then he began to talk about his son. My brother's son, whom I have not met since he was seven or so, was in the Selous Scouts. For those who have forgotten, let us put it this way: the whites in new Zimbabwe were not talking about the Selous Scouts as the blacks did, or as they were spoken of in our newspapers in Britain; we do know that one person's thug and murderer is another's hero.

This young man, who had distinguished himself in the Scouts, suffered a sudden conversion to fundamental Christianity, then took himself to Texas where he was trained as a preacher. He now preached to black and white in South Africa.

'Pretty fiery stuff,' says Harry, looking at me in a certain way.

'Ah, you mean you go for it?'

'I've been to some of their services. Quite a bit different from the good old Church of England. It quite sweeps you off your feet.'

'Literally, so I hear. Have you been dancing in the aisles?'

'Well, just about.'

'Funny thing, his having that conversion, after that fighting. Would you agree it wasn't pretty, what he was doing?'

'You could say that, yes.' A pause. 'A conversion, you call it?' he says, casual, pouring himself a drink, offering me one.

'Yes. A sudden thing. Quite common really. People in great danger, scared stiff, they suffer conversion. They get God. The psychologists know about it.'

'Interesting thing, that.'

'Like astronauts.'

'Makes sense.'

'Or people just about to fall off a mountain peak or lost in a small boat in the middle of an ocean.'

'Anyway, I didn't have a conversion. I've always gone to church.'

He drinks, gulp after gulp, but carefully. It was as if he were listening to each mouthful as it went down. Suddenly I understood something: again, I could have seen it before: nothing is more exasperating than this, that you can flounder about in a mist, and then, all at once, everything is clear. What my brother and my father had in common was not genes: at least, genes were not why both were slow, hesitant, cautious, dream-logged men who seemed always to be listening to some fateful voice only they could hear: they were both men hurt by war. This thought was such a shock to me, illuminating all kinds of old puzzles, old questions, that I had to set it aside for the moment: Harry was obviously planning to say something difficult. His lips were moving together over words he was discarding as they came to him: his eyes stared inward. At last he lifted his head and made himself look at me.

'You say we spent a lot of time together in the bush?'

'Yes, every school holidays, sometimes all day. We used to take a bottle of cold tea and sandwiches and stay out from sunrise till after the sun went down.'

'After that Japanese was here – funny chap he was – I read one of your short stories.'

'Well, what did you think?'

'It was about you and me in the bush. And the dogs. But it really got to me, that story. I couldn't finish it. I didn't remember anything, you see.'

'What, nothing?'

'No. I realized then I didn't remember anything very much before I was about eleven or twelve. At least, I remembered quite a bit about school, but nothing about the farm.'

'Nothing?'

'You could say nothing.'

'You don't remember things like lying in the rocks on Koodoo Hill and watching the wild pig – they were only a few feet away? Or hiding in the long grass at the edge of the Twenty Acres to watch the duiker come down at sunset? Or climbing trees to hide so we could watch what went on in the bush?'

'No, I don't, I'm afraid.'

'You don't remember when that wild pig with piglets chased us up the tree and we threw bits of bark and leaves at her to make her go away? But she actually tried to climb the tree after us . . . stood with her feet on the trunk and grunted at us? And we were laughing so hard we nearly fell out of the tree?'

A long silence.

'I blocked all that off too, didn't I?'

'It looks like it.'

'Then there must have been a reason why I blocked everything off.'

'I think there was.'

'But you didn't block off, you remembered it all.'

'But perhaps we had different ways of surviving.'

'That's a strong word,' he said, his eyes hard.

'It's the word I use.'

He sat thinking, drinking judiciously. At last he said, 'I've told you, I know a thing or two about blocking things off . . .' And now he kept his eyes on my face, to make sure I wouldn't overstep some mark or other. 'I'll tell you something. If you've blocked things off, then there's a reason for it. If you've any sense you let sleeping dogs lie. That's where these psychologist chappies are wrong. In the Bush War things from the other war kept coming back, but I couldn't see why I felt so upset.

Why did I block them off? But I could tell there was something pretty bad there, because if there wasn't, why did they get to me? Anyway, I haven't told you everything, and I'm not going to. There are things you should shut up about. And don't think I regret the Bush War . . . I'm not going to mind kicking the bucket when my time comes. I've had that, lying wrapped in a blanket looking up at the stars and listening to the owls and the nightjars – not that there are many of them around these days. No, I'm glad I'm Taking the Gap.' He turned away, because his eyes were full of tears. He poured himself another dose, and then looked at me again. 'I've visited where I am going. It's in the Transvaal. We think it is getting pretty bad here – the bush, but down there it's all enormous ranches with miles and miles of beaten-down dirty over-grazed grass. *There's no bush.*'

'Makes sense, you're going there, since that's what you care about more than anything.'

'At least I won't have to watch it being destroyed here, and that is what is happening.'

'It's a tragedy,' I said, not knowing I was going to. 'Do you realize who would understand you best in this country? About the bush, I mean. The Africans, that's who, and you won't talk to them.'

'What do you mean, I won't talk to them? When I was out in the bush as a boy with the cook's son, what do you think we did? What about the builder at the school? Solomon, his name was. We used to sit and jaw for hours and hours about life and everything. What about the chap who built this house with me?'

He waits for me to challenge him with some point of my dogma, and then says, 'Anyway, it's not true that only the Affs would understand me. Any old Rhodie would.'

'Nonsense. Half the old Rhodies know as much about the bush as some poor black kid in Brixton knows about the English countryside.'

'Of course I mean the right kind of Rhodie.'

'People like you.'

'If you like.

'Nine o'clock,' he says. 'Time for bed.' He gets up, goes to the door, turns and sees me reaching for my notebook. 'Are you taking down things I say to use in evidence against me? I don't care provided you write down the bloody stupid things you say, too.'

In the morning he drove me to a road that ran past a plantation of blue gums. When he was working at his old school, Ruzawi – for he went back as manager of the place, because there he could be out of doors all day – he asked to be allowed to plant trees. We left the car well-locked, though he was unhappy about it. 'You can't leave a car for five minutes without some skellum stealing it. Everything has to be locked up. Everything has to be barred. It's like living inside cages.'

We walked through the enormous sweet-smelling eucalyptus trees.

'I often come here. I come here whenever everything gets me down. At least I planted all these trees. But not long ago I began to think, what a pity I didn't plant musasas. Indigenous trees. In those days who would have believed musasas could be under threat? You know those TV programmes they make, about animals? Every one ends with, This animal's habitat is under threat. I can't bear to watch them any more. If I had planted musasas they would just about be getting mature now. That would have been something, wouldn't it . . . we could be walking here through musasas. A protected plantation.' He laughed. 'We make these wrong decisions,' he said, and stood with his hand on the smooth creamy trunk of a blue gum. It was a diagnostic, affectionate hand, and he even patted the tree. Meanwhile Sparta and Sheba ran about among the leaves, noses down, after smells. Harry stroked the tree. 'All the same, it's a good place.'

He took me to where a notice, stuck on a board among rocks, said, 'Please Remember to Bury your Rubbish.' At the same moment we burst out laughing. 'It's the Scouts' and Cubs' camp site,' he said. 'That's where they put up the tents. That's where they build the fire. That's where they sit in rows to eat. That's the rubbish pit. That's where the vans park when they bring cornflakes and sliced bread and orange squash from the supermarket.'

We laugh, staggering about in the dead leaves and the dust, while the dogs leap up to lick our faces.

GIVING LIFTS

Some miles on from my brother's house, I drove – without so much as a premonitory catch of the breath – over the place where, a few days later, four other people and I were in a car accident so bad the only explanation for our all not being killed is that five guardian angels were on the alert.

The trip to Zimbabwe had been planned like this . . . I would spend two weeks with members of the family and then take off into the new Zimbabwe, allowing to happen to me what would: the only way to travel. Meanwhile I was impatient to talk to Africans, any African, to find out what lay behind the rhetoric of war. The black man in my brother's kitchen was a friendly soul, but he was not likely to talk frankly to his employer's sister. He had supported a lost cause, the Bishop Muzorewa, that was all I knew.

I had stopped the car to admire a particularly beautiful stretch of country. If, as a child, on the slow journeys to Marandellas I took in every turn and twist of the road, every heap of boulders, on the hurtling journeys to Macheke, as a young woman, I was always in a car full of people in emotional juxtapositions with each other, and we did not notice much outside the car. I did not remember this view. A beaten-up lorry came skidding to a stop near me, a black youth got down, and the lorry turned off on to a side road. The youth stood looking after the lorry for a long time. Then he turned, and saw me sitting there. He came slowly towards me, his face a plea. This was very different from the importunate clamour of the crowds at bus-stops. I opened the door and he got in beside me. At once he bent himself away from me, in a disconsolate curve, his hands limp

between his thin knees. He was trembling in little spasms, as
people do who have been cold for some time: it was a sharp,
sparkling, highveld morning. He wore a suit, a white shirt, a
tie, all clean and pressed, but the materials were cheap. I asked
where he was going. He said it would be after Macheke.

I had hoped he would want to be set down before Macheke,
called Mashopi in *The Golden Notebook*, because I had planned
to stop, walk around, sort out memory from what I had made
of it.

I asked, 'Why are you so sad?' and his whole body made a
convulsive struggling movement, as if it were invisibly bound,
and he was trying to get free. Tears welled sparkling from
under his tightly pressed lids. He shook his head: it was too
terrible to talk about. We drove smartly on, while I tried to
recall sights and signs that belonged to the road to Macheke,
but we were going too fast: there is not only a different road
for those who walk, or go by bicycle, but for those who drive
at thirty, and sixty. The cars we used to go to Macheke were
all on their last legs. During the War we drove what we could
get.

He began a dreary and hopeless sobbing. It was clear he had
been doing a lot of crying.

'Please tell me, what is the matter? Perhaps I can help?'

'No one can help. I lost my job this week. They said I am not
good enough. I got my Certificate but they said I'm no good.'

'Who said?'

'My Department. Mr So and So . . .' The name of a black
man. 'Mr Smith liked me and said I was good at my job and
Mr So and So . . .' He wept.

To get a job in the big city is the goal of every young person
in Zimbabwe, like everywhere in the world. The usual pieties
go on about the delights and virtues of village life but people
cannot wait to leave the villages. Here sat a young man condemned to return to his village. His big city had not even been
that metropolis Harare, but Marondera. He had been a citizen
of urbanity, and now he would take his Certificate and his
brave thin suit to his village where they would be wrapped in
plastic bags and put on a high shelf out of the reach of dogs

and chickens, or better still, hung from a nail so ants and insects could not reach them. He would be one of the unemployed, the workless, taking up a hoe sometimes when the women nagged at him enough. The high moments of a life spent dreaming about the delights of that centre Marondera would be when he walked to the main road and got a lift – if he was lucky – so he could spend an afternoon in the little town, looking up former colleagues for whom he was now a country cousin. They had been able to clutch tight to the ladder of success. Perhaps they would allow him to go with them to the beer house or the cinema.

'It is because all the white people are going. They are taking all the jobs with them.'

'But this is only temporary. It's only two years since Independence. There will be all kinds of new jobs.'

'Where are the new jobs? I don't see any new jobs.'

This struck me as unreasonable. As I had been saying to my brother, 'What can you expect in two years?' This, though I did not know it then, so close to the start of the trip, was to be my strongest impression of it, and it remains with me now as a consistently surprising fact. Two years before, in 1980, had ended a very brutal war, involving the whole country. Comrade Mugabe had come to power as the strongest group that had fought in the bush against Smith and Co., which meant there must be large numbers of people disappointed he had won and who were looking for reasons to disapprove of him. The people he had put into government had proved they were good at guerilla warfare, but now they had to govern a modern country in the modern world. Without any tradition of training in administration. Without enough educated people. Without any of the background of experience every child, no matter how poor or deprived, takes for granted in developed countries – which means everyone knows about telephones, letters from government departments, electricity, post boxes, buses, trains, aeroplanes, magistrates' courts, social security, clinics. Without this background of culture of a practical kind, these people had at a moment's notice to take on the task of running a country the size of Spain. In a country devastated and shocked by war.

You would think they would be given a few years to get used
to it. Not at all. Every newspaper, television programme, or
international expert talked about Zimbabwe as if it were an
established country to be judged by the highest standards. If
some authority had pronounced, This is a young administration, taking on almost impossible problems, it must be given
time to find its feet – then I had missed that charitable recommendation. Why should the Mugabe administration be
expected to behave like an established member of the family of
nations? I believe, partly, it was because Comrade Mugabe
claimed to be marxist, and it was unconsciously assumed the
authority of marxism would 'count' for good marks, just as, so
recently, a young man of twenty-two from Devon, a friend of
mine, found himself in old Northern Rhodesia governing a
district the size of Yorkshire and sitting in judgement in the
courts; he was not seen as a young man of twenty-two, but
rather as a representative of the British Empire. And then, too,
there had been all that rhetoric during the years of fighting,
always confident, loud, and full of boasts and promises. But
whatever the reason, Zimbabwe was being judged as if there
had not been a war. This often happens. The reality of war, the
suffering and the brutality and the terror – all that is suppressed
almost at once, because it is intolerable and no one can stand
it, and instead the pain (and the horror at the way everyone
behaved) becomes frozen in war memorials, patriotic speeches,
war rhetoric – sentimentality.

'How old are you?'

'I am twenty-two years old, madam.'

'*Please* don't call me madam.'

If he was twenty-two then he was twelve or thirteen when
the War began.

'Where were you during the War?'

'At school, madam. My father wanted me to get my Certificates.' And he wept even harder. 'I'll never get a job now the
whites are going. Mugabe doesn't know anything. The whites
are cleverer than us. We need them to stay here and give us
jobs.'

Weeks later, just before I left the country, when I described this encounter to a black intellectual, he said in a troubled voice, 'Who said those things? Are you sure?' I said, 'But why are you surprised? I don't understand any of you. Why do you expect so much of yourselves? Why does everyone go on as if Zimbabwe has been in existence for fifty years? *The War ended two years ago.* There were all kinds of different opinions during the War and a lot of blacks fought for the government. Why should all that come to an end overnight?' But what I said was so much against the atmosphere of that time I might as well not have said it. People were numbed. People were turned off . . . had turned themselves off. They needed a formula: united black marxist Zimbabwe.

We drove on, south-east, getting closer to Macheke (or Mashopi) through that landscape, all miles of wintersere grass, where the wind made rivers of light, where clumps of musasa stood in their airy green, edged by blue mountains – that scene which somewhere in it held his village, to which he was condemned for ever. As he must think, being twenty-two, when what happens to you is for ever.

'Look,' I said reasonably. 'The white people are not cleverer than you. You are only believing what the whites have been telling you. Did you know that for centuries the people of Europe – that means white people – were considered backward and primitive by the Arab world? When the Romans invaded Britain, the way you were invaded by the whites, they called us stupid and backward and savage. And we were.'

While I said all this I felt increasingly ridiculous.

'Someone wanted my job,' he said. 'That's what happened to me.'

I could have said, the sociological approach, 'Oh well, you see, there are too many people in the world for the number of jobs available. And this situation is likely to get worse, not better.'

Instead, I asked, 'Was the War bad for you?'

He burst out angrily, 'It was horrible, you don't know, no one knows . . .' He wiped the sleeve of his precious jacket across his wet face. 'In the village, first the Security Forces came, then the Comrades came . . . we had to be nice to them,

you see. We had to pretend . . . we couldn't be safe, it didn't
matter what we did.'

I gave him some tissues and he mopped up his face. 'We only
read about it in the newspapers and saw it on the television,' I
said, wanting him to ask, Where are you from? – and he said,
'Were you in Harare in the War?'

'I was in England. I've just come from London.'

He gave a what-do-you-expect sobbing laugh, and a shrug.
'Yes, that's it, of course, from England. You are a white person
from England. Now I understand.'

'We have unemployment in England.' As I said this I
remembered he would not be getting unemployment benefit,
but living off his family.

A black Zimbabwean said to me, 'The extended family is a
very good welfare system. We don't need old people's homes
and mental hospitals and unemployment benefit. I have a piece
of land twenty miles from Harare, about fifty acres. Twenty
to thirty people are always living off it. Grandparents, aunts,
nephews, cripples, crazy people, the unemployed. You despise
that. Subsistence living, you say, as if it's nothing. But subsistence means that people are feeding themselves. They aren't in
institutions being kept by taxpayers. You only admire big farms
that sell surplus produce.'

'Why did you come here to Zimbabwe? Are you going to live
here? Have you got a job for me? Any job. I want it.'

'No, I've just come to visit.' Here I could have said I was
brought up here, then left – and so forth, but all that happened
before he was born, possibly before his parents were born. Far
away in the mists of history this white woman lived here . . .

'Why don't you stay here?' he cried, seeing this job, too,
disappear. 'Or perhaps one day I will come to England. There
everybody has a lot of money and a house.'

On we drove, up towards the crest of a long ridge, and then
down into a valley; up the next rise and then down, while
sometimes he cried silently and trembled, and then dried his
face, and trembled and burst out crying again, while I was, with
part of my mind, in cars going to Macheke for the weekend
thirty-five years ago. Communists, we called ourselves. The

label we used to describe ourselves was that, and it is a short-
hand as useful as most. But in fact we spent little of our time on
the current communist prescriptions for a better world, partly
because the 'line' laid down by the Communist Party of South
Africa, and, therefore, by Moscow, was that the black proletariat would take power and create justice all over this land.
There were, then, few Africans who fitted into this definition.
We thought in fact about what went on everywhere else:
Britain, Occupied Europe, Japan, the Far East, America. The
War was an education in thinking about the world as a whole.
It was a watershed, precisely in this way. The First World War
began the process. My father said that when he was growing
up on the outskirts of Colchester (a Roman town) it never
occurred to anyone to brood about events in America, or China
or – much – even in London. No, the news was that Bill's (his
school friend) father's mare White Star had won the 3.30, and
that there would be a church picnic. But the War put an end
to that. Even on the farm he read newspapers from London,
and listened to the crackling broadcasts from the BBC. He felt
a famine in China or India as his personal responsibility. The
admonition that we should eat up whatever it was on our plates
we wanted to leave was delivered with an incredulous,
passionate, accusing anguish.

Macheke is so vivid in my memory because of the War. Now
I believe we were all mad, all over the world, whether actually
in the fighting or not. Perhaps the world cannot murder on
such a scale without going mad? Is this a consoling thought?
Is it true? Is mutual murder the natural state of humankind?
For us, then, this so terrible war was *of course* the War that
would end all war, for everyone at last would see how terrible
war was. (Just like my parents and the First World War.) All
of us believed, as an article of faith, in a peaceful future world
. . . I was in my mid-twenties, part of a group. *Then* such
groups had to be political. By definition we were in the right
about everything, destined to change the world and everyone
in it, and our opponents were either misguided, or mostly
wicked. We were all in love or not in love but wished we were,
or wished that he or she was in love with us; or we had been

disastrously in love, leading to regretted marriages (but luckily divorce was nothing these days), and because many of the group were pilots in training they were always being whisked off to dangerous parts where they could get killed, and many were. Partings were frequent and painful, but borne because of the state of elation we all lived in, and because we all drank too much. Alcohol, sex and politics: endemic intoxications possessed us. Exhausted with our lives in the big city, Salisbury, we took ourselves down to Macheke at weekends, not every weekend, but often, whole groups of us, in the cars we owned or borrowed. What happened in Macheke I described, changed for literary reasons, in *The Golden Notebook*. But how much changed? All writers know the state of trying to remember what actually happened, rather than what was invented, or half invented, a meld of truth and fiction. It is possible to remember, but only by sitting quietly, for hours or sometimes for days, and dragging facts out of one's memory. That means thinking yourself back into that scene, that car, that bedroom. Thus you create parallel truths: what *really* happened, what did not happen. But you soon begin to think, why all this effort? Memory in any case is a lying record: we choose to remember this and not that.

'Do you remember, Doris, when we . . . ?'

'No. Not a thing. But do you remember . . . ?'

'No. Are you quite sure we did that?'

Mashopi was painted over with glamour, as I complained in *The Golden Notebook*. When we see remembered scenes from the outside, as an observer, a golden haze seduces us into sentimentality. And what we choose most often to remember is the external aspect of events: sparks flying up into boughs lit by moonlight or starlight, their undersides ruddy with flame-light; a face leaning forward into firelight, not knowing it is observed and will be remembered. But what was I really feeling then?

I do remember a good deal of what I really felt at Macheke. Why are those impressions so strong, from that time? After all, the War went on for a long time, years of it. I lived in different places, with different people. I *was* different people. Between the efficient young housewife of my first marriage, and the rackety 'revolutionary' of 1943, '44, '45 there seems little connection. Even less between those two and the young woman who – still always in crowds of people who changed, came from everywhere in the world, were always on the move – was developing the habit of privacy, writing when she could, increasingly thinking her own thoughts, increasingly self-critical. And yet we all know what the connection was: it is the sense of self, always the same – and that is the consoling, the steadying thing, that whether you are two and a half, or twenty, or sixty-nine, the sense of yourself, who you are, is the same. The same in a small child's body, the sexual girl, or the old woman.

Memories of Macheke came from different layers of the past, and the first was when I was still a young girl. From a car window I saw dusty blue gums by the railway lines, and under them two sad baboons with chains around their waists attached to ropes which were fastened to the tree trunks. And why was that so hurtful a sight? Because it was a reminder of another. I was five years old, and in London after Persia but before Southern Rhodesia, and just as you went into the London Zoo was a cage of black iron bars, like a parrot's cage, and in it was a gorilla or a chimpanzee, I don't remember which, only my horror at this creature in a cage just large enough to accommodate it, hands grasping the bars, small red eyes glaring in a rage of hate and misery. On the packed brown earth under the blue gums the two baboons lived out (I hope) short lives, tormented by louts of all ages who came to jeer at them.

Later, during the War, it was under these eucalyptus trees that we, the group from Salisbury, sat drinking white wine from Portuguese East Africa, and where 'we', the group at Mashopi, drank white wine, with the railway lines a few paces away on one side, and the main road, Salisbury to Umtali, on the other.

As the sad black youth and I approached Macheke, I said I wanted to stop for a little, because I had been here during the War. But understood even as I spoke that he would think that I meant the Bush War, 'his' war. The mists of history had begun to seethe and billow like boiling milk and I did not even attempt to explain.

'How long?' he demanded, at once suspicious. I recognized the tone. He thought I was putting him off with a lie, and wanted to get rid of him. Here was another white cruelty and I was reverting to type.

I had hoped to stop here, perhaps for a cup of tea, at the Macheke Hotel, for old times' sake, but now knew that this must not happen. Because times had changed we – black and white – might drink a cup of tea together, but that was not the point. I wanted the past to envelop me, but the pressure of his misery would make that impossible. I said, 'Just for a few minutes, that's all.'

'I can walk,' he said, bitterly.

'No, no. I'll just slow down for a minute or two.'

But now two landscapes were in my mind and I could not make sense of what I saw. The main road was in a different place. Yes, there was the garage, post office, store, a bar . . . and a hotel. A hotel in *that* place? I asked him, 'Do you know if they have changed the route of the main road?'

He said, 'It has always been the main road.'

In his lifetime, the main road had always run here.

I turned off to the left, where the railway had to be, and there were the dusty, dispirited blue gums and the railway lines beyond. The same. I stopped the car. Where was the hotel? Surely that could not . . . it was derelict, unused. A low brick building, like a long shed, had a couple of small doors into rooms that were evidently small, and another door into the bar. Yes, I had seen the wonders of the great world since I was in Macheke or Mashopi, but surely this could not be the Macheke Hotel where through all those weekends we drank, danced, flirted and played politics? How many couples had actually been able to dance in the smallish room I saw through dirty windowpanes? And was that the dining-room where we ate those lengthy and companionable meals, Mrs Boothby maternally on the watch. (I was working hard to retrieve her real name.) How many tables would it, did it, hold? And the bar? It had been crowded with men in the Air Force uniform and with local farmers. But it was a narrow cubbyhole of a place. Yet I had been a grown-up person here, not a child; I was not an adult visiting scenes from childhood . . . the verandah that ran all along the building did have room for a couple of small tables: it was more of a passage than a verandah. Yet here we had certainly sat drinking . . . yes, of course, people sat all along that low wall, which was by the main road from Salisbury to Umtali, and part of the pleasure was watching the occasional car whirl past in clouds of pale dust (sandveld dust, not the heavy red dust of Lomagundi) or perhaps it stopped, and out stepped . . . a stranger, or someone we knew who had driven down from Salisbury to join us . . . or driven up from Umtali, knowing we would be there. A stranger would at once cease to be one, absorbed at once into the elation, the high spirits, for we were good company, and – I later realized – surprising company, because we were such a mixed group, people who in England could never meet because of that class system of theirs, but here cockneys, Brummies, Scotties, everybody, joked with young men who had interrupted Cambridge and Oxford to learn to fly and – possibly – die over Europe, or Burma, or India. And the local girls, and girls from Britain and South Africa or who were refugees from somewhere or other. And yet all these people had squashed ourselves along that verandah? No, that was why we spent so much time under the blue gums, near the tracks, where there was room to spread out.

And now for the bedrooms . . . the strongest, the most disturbing of all my memories of old Macheke was at the back of the hotel, the bedroom block. There were ten or twelve rooms, in two lines, back to back, opening on to narrow verandahs. With an apology to the young man, who was now bent sideways against the seat, an arm over his face, to shut out the cruel and deceiving world – shut me out, probably, who for no reason at all had stopped by this building fit only for demolition – I quickly got out and went around the old hotel to the back, and saw only rubble, crowding overgrown shrubs, trees. I was looking up to find the bedroom block, for it was higher than the hotel itself. When I came out of my room (shared, I was married then), I looked down over a flight of steps into the kitchens and the dining-room windows. I used to stand at the top of stone steps and stare and stare at a moon so bright, so large, I have never seen another like it. Yet most of the nights of my life on the farm were spent sitting out in front of the house watching the sky. There was something about the air of Macheke that enhanced and enlarged the moon – probably my feverish, self-hypnotized state. Yes, in Macheke the moon was always full or near full, no matter what weekend we went down, or if half-grown, then in the shape of a pistachio nut, silver on hazy blue-black. I was always stopping myself outside the bedroom to say: Look at it, there will never be another moon like this one, there couldn't be – while the voices of my friends and comrades rose from the bar or the dining-room. And there hasn't been . . . for the good reason that pollution has overtaken the skies of Africa, just like everywhere else. You forget how skies used to be. Not long ago, in north-west Argentina I went out into the night and thought, My God, look, there it is, that's the night sky – like a Christmas tree, or a jeweller's window, the stars so brilliant and so close you could reach up and pick them one by one out of the dark.

Floating on moonlight, and on a hundred intoxications, I stepped carefully down, down the stone steps that were edged with the sweet-smelling plants Mrs Boothby (Mrs *Who*?) was so fond of and crammed into every crevice, and then . . . but it was impossible to see anything through this litter of planks, rubbish, broken bricks, neglected shrubs. No, this was impossible, there was perhaps another hotel . . . no, nonsense, this was the hotel, and here was the bar and here . . . if I were to sort out what had been here, and what I had made of it, then it would take . . . how long? Weeks? No, it was silly, useless, what was the point, and I must in any case drive on, because of this man beside me who sat squeezing his hands between thin chilly knees, while the tears fell steadily over his already crumpled suit.

I wished there was something in the car to eat. Perhaps I should look for a store and buy him . . . it occurred to me this renewed weeping was because we were about to leave

Macheke, this metropolis of urban delights, the last before his exile must begin.

I drove back to the new main road, recognizing among smart new buildings paltry survivors from the very first days of the Colony. I tried to make out where we had walked away from the little township on a narrow sandy track into the kopjes and vleis where butterflies and birds and grasshoppers were so plentiful that I have only to remember how we, the group, walked there to hear a shrilling of birds, the somnolence of doves, the clicking of grasshoppers. And the scents, the smells, the warm dry herby odours . . . well, enough.

About five miles from Macheke the poor young man said, 'It is here.' I stopped. We were nowhere. I mean, we were on the road, but around us were miles of grass, a clump or two of trees, and the blue mountains. He did not at once get out, but sat staring miserably ahead.

He said violently: 'I shall never see any of my friends again. I shall never see you again. I shall never . . .' He scrambled out of the car, and went off into the long grass by the road, clutching his little suitcase. I watched his head and shoulders move above the grasses, and then he was not there.

This year, 1991, it is thought that there are a million unemployed in Zimbabwe.

I began watching the sides of the road for someone to lift. Far from the big town Harare, still a good distance from the smaller big town Mutare, there were fewer people waiting at the bus-stops – places by the road where people came to wait, with perhaps a kiosk for soft drinks, or nothing at all, not even a turn-off to somewhere else. When I slowed the crowd surged forward, but I drove on until I saw by the road, by themselves, three men who looked pleasant, so I stopped. They were going to Mutare and would be my companions for the rest of that journey. They were all three middle-aged, or at least, not young. They were shabby. But they were amiable and I knew I had found what I had been wanting, people of the country, black people, I could talk with. Talk, that is, without being overheard by antagonistic whites, by the new breed of ideological blacks.

The two men in the back seat spoke a little English. The man beside me spoke it well. I at once said I was from England, without going into complicated histories, and he said I was welcome, and he hoped I would stay, because all the whites were leaving the country. I asked if he liked Mugabe. Yes, he liked Robert Mugabe very much, but he didn't like the Comrades. If Mugabe knew what the Comrades did, he would punish them, but perhaps no one told him. I have heard this in too many countries, or read it, not to find it discouraging, so I asked about the War. And that was what we mostly talked about for the rest of the journey. He had spent the first part of the War in his village, not very far from here (close to where De Waal and Venter decided to buy their farms), in a district where the government troops and the guerillas came all the time, both sides taking people away for questioning, beating up even children, even girls. The women couldn't get to work in the gardens, they were too afraid, so everyone was always short of food. If there was food in the huts, soldiers of both sides might take it. Cows and goats disappeared, and soldiers of either side might have driven them off. It all got so bad he left his village with his family and went to live with relatives in Mutare. The War was horrible. No one could know, if they hadn't lived through it.

The man in front, whose name was Gore, referred continually to the men at the back, and they said Yes, Yes, and sighed, and shook their heads and clicked their tongues, and as we passed this gully or that kopje, or apparently friendly piece of bush, one, then all, might point and say, There . . . they killed three people there . . . all the huts burned in that village . . . there was a terrible fight on that hill . . . the helicopters came down there and shot bullets into the bush, and afterwards there were dead people lying everywhere.

The helicopters had to be Smith's men, but otherwise there was no way of knowing who 'they' had been, in this incident or that.

In England, I said, we had read about the War in the newspapers and sometimes seen it on television, but Gore shook his head and said, No, newspapers do not tell you what a thing like that is like. Newspapers can only say, This happened, That happened, but they do not tell you what is in the hearts of the people. We lived all the day and every night afraid. We were afraid to sleep. If you slept you might wake to find the thatch over your head on fire. And who had done it? It could be someone living in the next hut. If someone disappeared you'd know that person was a spy for the government or for one of the armies. Someone you had known since you were both children could be paid money to kill you. Children disappeared and then you heard they were in the bush with the fighters. You knew they might appear any minute with guns. Because they knew about the village and could guide the others. The War made soldiers out of ten-year-olds. And what will happen to them now? They never went to school.

'The Comrades had schools for the children,' said one of the men at the back, being fair.

'Yes, but what could they learn?'

'The Comrades taught them to read and write.'

'Some of them can read and write a little. And they learned a lot of other things. Will they forget those things?'

They sighed, they shook their heads, they smiled, while we drove along this road that for me meant memories of many decades ago, but for them meant war. Ambushes, bombs, mines, armoured vehicles, prowling aircraft, and helicopters who might use it to land on, scattering troops like seeds of death into the bush on either side.

Gore asked about Britain, and his two friends leaned forward to hear what I said. I talked, knowing the images my words made had little to do with Britain. Gore had always lived in his village with his wife and children till they moved to Mutare, and now they were in a single-roomed hut in a township outside Mutare. He worked in a garage. One of the men at the back was a watch-mender and had never been far from Mutare. He had not even visited Harare. The third was a watchman in a hotel in Mutare's main street. The big hotel, he said, with pride, but laughing, mocking the hotel's pretensions and his pride in it. There people came who had been in every country in the world! As for him, he had visited relatives in Portuguese

East, before the War. Mozambique, Gore corrected him. He said, laughing and shaking his head, 'It's hard to remember all the new names. I sometimes say Salisbury, and then somebody says, Watch out, or you'll be reported to the Comrades.'

'Soon everyone will forget,' said Gore. 'Only old people like me will remember Mutare was called Umtali.' And he shook with laughter, the marvellous African laughter born some-where in the gut, seizing the whole body with good-humoured philosophy. It is the laughter of poor people. If we were not talking about the War, when they were tense and sombre, they laughed.

They wanted to know what changes I had seen since I had left so long ago for England.

I wanted to talk about the emptying and thinning of the bush, how the animals had gone, and the birds and the insects, how this meant everything had changed; how myriads of small balances, hundreds in every small patch of bush, necessary for water, soil, foliage, climate, had been disturbed. I had already begun to suspect that these changes were more important than, even, the War, and the overthrow of the whites, the coming of the black government. Now, years later, I am sure of it. But I could not talk like this to these people then, at that time. It would have sounded an irrelevance: at best, like one of the eccentricities the whites go in for.

It is, I think, almost a law that what one is afraid to say because it will be rejected by the atmosphere of a time, will turn out to be a few years later the most important thing of all.

So I did not say anything about that; instead, that when I had left in 1949 there had been a quarter of a million whites, and one and a half million blacks. Now, so the experts claim, it is eight million. Eight million of mostly very young people. In a generation there will be twenty-five million.

'Eight million,' said Gore, laughing and shaking his head. Because of the word *million*, as much a block to his imagination as it is to mine. Mutare, his 'big city' had never had more than thousands in it.

'We are poor people,' he said, gravely, when he had stopped laughing.

This was a comment, not only on the eight million, who would have to find food to eat and clothes to wear, but on what I had been saying about Britain.

I knew what he found particularly interesting in what I told them, when he translated it for his friends. He at once translated when I talked about unemployment benefit, which for them was like news from another galaxy; about the Underground system in London; when he heard that every child went to school until the age of sixteen; that there the shops were full, and there were no shortages of anything, ever. He did not translate when I was ready to talk about our system of government, political parties, elections, town councils.

For the two hours it took to reach Mutare I was with men who knew about what other people had from the talk of travellers, from newspapers, from television – but they seldom saw television or films; they saw aeroplanes in the sky and sometimes got lifts in cars, but they would never travel in an aeroplane or own a car. They were excluded from the marvels of modern living but had come close when for ten years they had been in the front line of a war fought with modern weapons, for about these they talked with knowledge and expertise. In short, they were like most of the people in the world.

Their way of telling me what their lives were like was quiet, ironical, in stories where poverty was something like a character in a folk tale.

I put them down in Mutare's main street, and was sorry to see them walk away, turning to wave and call back farewells. Then I parked and went into the new hotel.

FATHERS AND SONS. NOT TO MENTION MOTHERS AND DAUGHTERS

I sat in the Leisure Area. I do not see how it could be called a lounge or even a sitting-room. I was reflecting that recently, in one of the most expensive hotels in the world, the Four Seasons

in Hamburg, I had breakfasted in that dining-room once found
in every hotel, a long tall-ceilinged room with chintz curtains
at long windows. There were white damask tablecloths, heavy
cutlery and – this is what marked it out from your common
hotel – jam in pots, with a spoon. Old-fashioned charm is what
rich people want to pay for. No doubt, quite soon, a hundred
thousand characterless modern hotels will be pulled down and
replaced with loving copies from the past. Meanwhile, new
countries hastening to prove their worth in the company of
nations, are building modern hotels.

At the table next to me sat two middle-aged men, white,
farmers, and I listened to The Monologue – President Banana
and the chickens, Mugabe's motorcade, and, too, angry
exchanges about Squatters and the inadequacies of the Minister
of Agriculture. With my other ear I listened to two Swedes,
man and woman, who were working on a scheme for retraining
and resettling Freedom Fighters. They were talking about the
whites near their Resettlement Scheme, who were doing everything to make their work difficult. They lowered their voices to
say the new bureaucracy was impossible, almost as hampering
as the retrograde whites. They decided to go to Harare and see
a certain Minister (black), first making sure his assistant (white)
would put some sense into his head. 'Of course you can't
expect things to come right so quickly,' said these reasonable
souls. I went on sitting with the two farmers on one side and
the two Swedes on the other, and watched people coming in
and out, white and black, in groups and families, and among
them quite a few of that new breed, the international Aid
workers. The waiters were all black, lively, and with a confidence and ease it was pleasant to watch.

Soon a young couple, white, came to join the Swedes. They
were of that immediately recognizable kind, children of the
1960s who, if too young to have actually partaken of the
delights of that decade, were stamped by it. They are genial,
anxious always to present to everyone a willed innocence, are
open to every idea going, sensible or not, from pacifism to
vegetarianism or aromatherapy and UFOs, and they know that
if it does not seem everything is for the best in all possible

worlds, then in some mysterious way this will come to pass. These were in their late twenties. They had to discuss with the Swedes if they could come to the Resettlement Scheme to work. The young woman was a physiotherapist, the young man wanting desperately to help people, but without special training. Both were Zimbabweans, and from this area.

Now, out of its sequence, I shall describe a later visit to a couple I had known well in the old days. The middle-class everywhere complain about poverty; for some reason or other, no matter how much money they have, it is never as much as they are due. This is not an original observation, but on this trip it was being given startling new life. The couple I was visiting were both getting on, like me. They were in their sixties. They had retired from civil service jobs. Both were full of health, energy and complaints. Their house was a large bungalow, many-roomed, with verandahs all around it, and it sat in two acres of land, full of fruit trees and vegetables and flowers. Everything in the house had the sparkling cherished look which is not often seen in Britain, where women work, or do not have the time for this level of housework. It is the look that goes with servants. This couple employed two servants, men. 'But I am afraid poor Anne has to do some of the cooking these days.' 'Yes, I am afraid it is a bit of a burden.' The servants cleaned the house, grew the vegetables, tended the fruit trees, laid the table, served the food. When we had finished they cleared the table, made coffee and washed up. Meanwhile my friends of thirty years ago complained. The Monologue, of course. But they were also complaining about their poverty, their deprivation, and in the nagging peevish voices of spoiled children.

Towards midnight, having spent some hours saying Dear me and Tut tut, I cracked and asked how many people in the world did they suppose lived on the level they did? This cruel question did not at once reach them. They sat blinking, unable to believe I could be so treacherous. 'In Britain you'd have to be rich to live like this. Even in America, to have two servants, you'd be rich. Your way of life is an unreachable dream to ninety-nine point nine per cent of the world's people.' Silence.

What they could not credit was such a degree of disloyalty to the white cause. Loyalties, particularly those confirmed by war, have never had anything to do with reason, commonsense – nothing of that boring sort.

It was already late when the two young people came in I had seen at the hotel that first morning in Mutare. Their son and their daughter. Two different generations, two kinds of people. How did they manage to talk to each other? With difficulty, is the answer. The young couple had begun work with the Swedes, and had rung up their parents to tell them. This was the first physical encounter. The two elderly people sat there in their neat, correct clothes, she with her newly waved silvery hair, he with his buttoned-in tidiness – and gazed with hurt eyes at their careless, casually dressed offspring who were helping those enemies, the Terrorists. The young ones had come in so late because it meant less time in this atmosphere of accusation. 'We would have dropped in earlier but we don't get much time off,' said the daughter, and her father said at once, 'Of course they're going to exploit you for what they can get out of you.'

'Look,' said his son, his voice already angry, 'this is a Swedish relief organization. They can't afford to pay us much.'

'Of course they aren't going to pay you,' said the mother, brisk and in the right. 'All they are ever interested in is getting everything they can.' *They* here meant the blacks, though the attack might as easily have been against the Swedes, who were supporting the 'terrs' against the whites.

'Look, Mum,' said the young woman. 'I keep trying to explain it to you. We want to do something to help the country. It's our country too now, and we want . . .'

'It's not our country, it's *their* country,' was the bitter reply.

At this, the two young people exchanged glances. The young woman shook her head slightly, but was noticed, and her father said, 'That's right, just treat us like fools. We are too stupid to understand anything.'

The mother said, 'Oh Paul, don't quarrel with them, or we won't ever see them at all.'

'I'm sorry, Mum,' said the daughter. 'But it's hard work, and everyone works till all hours. It's not just an eight-to-four job, but we'll come when we can.'

'Oh yes, we know! We're too old to change, we're no use.'

'I never said that,' said the girl, for this was too unprogressive a thought for her to own. 'Of course you aren't. No one ever is.'

'But,' said her mother, 'your fiancé didn't like it either, did he?' She tittered and went red, because she knew this was below the belt.

The girl also reddened, but from anger, and said, 'It's just as well I found out what he is like in good time.'

'Her fiancé didn't like all this living with the Terrorists,' said the father, triumphant.

'He's gone south,' said the young woman to me. 'He's Taken the Gap. Well, it's the right place for him, isn't it?'

'If we could take our pensions out we would Take the Gap too,' grumbled the father.

'You wouldn't be living like this in The Republic,' said the son. 'I had a letter from Rob, and he's earning half what he did and there's no question of servants.'

This talk went on, the young people getting more exasperated, but patient, while now it was the parents who exchanged looks that said, There's no point, keep quiet.

But as their children left, the parents said, 'Now you've got your Zimbabwe, I hope you'll like it.'

THE VERANDAHS

And now here is the life of the verandahs at its best, because the houses are high in the Vumba mountains and the one where I am to spend a few days looks down on valleys and hills, forests and lakes. Also the border with Mozambique, four miles away. Sometimes there are little puffs of smoke, and the small sound of distant explosions. Renamo are again blowing up the pipeline, the railway, the road. Farmers who spent years fighting against the 'terrs' listened to the sounds, noted the exact size and shape of the smoke-puffs, and diagnosed such and such a mortar . . . type of explosion . . . gun. They spoke with the nostalgia of those who have learned expertise they will never use again. The Selous Scouts appeared in every conversation. I had known that as soon as I was in Zimbabwe, the certainties of 'progressive' Britain would recede, become less black and white (black, good; white, bad) but the hardest thing was to find myself in an atmosphere where it was taken for granted that the Selous Scouts were all heroes. I met as many people proudly claiming to have started the Selous Scouts, or whose uncles, brothers, nephews started the Selous Scouts, as in London I know people who invented the CND logo.

Among its other accomplishments the Selous Scouts ran training courses for people like farmers who could not be full-time soldiers. One course was how to survive in the bush. Initiates were given a piece of string and a knife, told which plants were edible and which might have water in them, and left in the bush for a week or so to get on with it. It seems to me few people, or perhaps I should say few of a certain type, would not respond with all the energy of fantasies made real. No one brought up in, or near the bush, for a start. Because of the heroic and romantic aspects of the Selous Scouts many Rhodesian whites found it easier to overlook the brutality, the ruthlessness.

Within a couple of years, in South Africa, in every bookshop would be shelves full of books on the Selous Scouts (mostly ghosted, since the type of person who excels in commando or SAS styles of fighting are seldom those who take easily to writing books) and the Selous Scouts had become for the white right wing a symbol of excellence and of the heroic War for the survival of white Rhodesia. The expertise of the Scouts contributed to the brutalities and excesses of the South African troops in Angola and Namibia.

And who was this Selous? He was Frederick Courtney Selous, an illustrious and esteemed hunter. How many hundreds of thousands of animals did he kill during his years in the bush? He lived from 1851 to 1917 so he watched old Africa being overrun by the whites. He wrote a book called *Travel and Adventure in South-East Africa*, and here is a bit of it.

That evening we slept on a Kafir footpath not far from Lo Magondi's kraals. About two hours after sunrise on the morrow, when we were quite close to the foot of the hills where the kraals are situated, we met a fine old eland bull face to face, coming from the opposite direction, upon which we at once shot him. As we had a little business to transact with Lo Magondi, in whose charge we had left several trophies of the chase in the previous July, and from whom I expected to be able to buy some ivory, this supply of meat, so near his town, was very opportune. We at once sent two Kafirs on, to apprise the old fellow of our arrival, and then off-saddling the horses (there was a beautiful running stream of water in the valley just below us) set to work to cut up the eland and camp.

In the afternoon our messengers returned, accompanied by Lo Magondi and about twenty of his followers. We at once presented the old fellow with a hind quarter and half the heart fat of the eland, while on his side he gave us a large pot of beer, a basket of ground nuts, and some pogo meal. That night there was great feasting and rejoicing in our camp, our own boys, who had long been living upon meat and longing for a little vegetable diet, buying large supplies of maize, beans, meal, beer and tobacco from the equally meat-hungry Mashonas. Lo Magondi had brought with him all the rhino horns, etc. that we had left in his charge, but no ivory. He however said that he would send for two tusks the following day, upon which I showed him my stock-in-trade consisting of cotton shirts, beads, coloured handkerchiefs, etc.

It seems the district Lomagundi was named after Chief Lo Magondi. There is confusion because close to Lomagundi, stretching from northern Mozambique up into Malawi, is a tribe* called The Makondi, known for their work in wood and

---

* I am told the word 'tribe' is unacceptable. One should say, ethnic group. But everyone knows what 'tribe' means. Most people I think would find 'ethnic group' confusing, certainly at the time this book is being written.

in stone, which is bought by collectors. Wonderful, enigmatic, beautiful statues – but that was long before any whites saw value in African art. They are also storytellers. As well as all that, their women are famed for their skills in lovemaking. If, having heard this, you ask a black man from almost anywhere in Central and East Africa, How about those Makondi women, then? – his face will at once put on the look of one who knows he has to pay tribute. But ask just what these skills are – for after all they might contribute to the joy and well-being of humankind – and nothing more is forthcoming. One man said that the women scar their stomachs. All right: a rough surface, fine – and then? But so far, that's it.

POLITICS

If, as soon as you arrived in Zimbabwe, first London . . . then Britain . . . then Europe . . . then the rest of Africa, receded, dwindled, instead rose up, threatening and powerful and unscrupulous, South Africa, the southern neighbour, the exemplar, the 'last bastion of White Supremacy in Southern Africa'. In 1982 few conversations did not come around to South Africa, either as a threat or a promise. Not only civilians left every day to this bastion: the soldiers of the disbanded white armies, their occupation gone, talked of Taking the Gap and then forming guerilla groups who would return to fight against the black government. In fact Renamo had been born in white Rhodesia as just such a group. The South Africans employed 'Rhodies' not only to train Renamo, but in all kinds of ways subversive to Zimbabwe. They incited 'incidents' that reached the British newspapers as the work of isolated adventurers, but in Zimbabwe they were believed to be the long arm of South Africa. (Nothing is more useful as a diagnosis of Britain than going to a country remote from European sets of mind and finding out what has not been reported in Britain, or reported inadequately.) Everyone, black and white, believed that the anti-Mugabe Terrorists, mostly supporters of Joshua Nkomo, whether he welcomed their support or not, were inspired by South Africa. 'Near Bulawayo there are whole areas of bush the government troops can't go into at all.' Everyone knew South Africa sent agents to the international conferences where investment and development were discussed, to spread rumours of the precariousness of Zimbabwe, every achievement minimized, every setback exaggerated. And, in 1982, newspaper correspondents met bombastic blacks, or whites who confidently talked Treason. I listened to feverish whites, in Harare, in Mutare, mostly ex-army, plotting the downfall of Mugabe. Crazed, they were, but could not see it. Smith was their hero. Smith, Smithie, Good-old-Smithie, in every conversation. Easy to hear, instead, 'Daddy', 'Nanny', even 'Mummy', and the terror of children left alone in the dark, children who had been brought up to know they were due everything, and could not lose what they had, for safety had been promised them by 'Smithie'. But they had lost everything; they had lost their White Supremacy, and still could not believe it. And their plots and intrigues could not have the consequences of Treason because how could it be treason to take back what is rightfully your own? While listening to these infants I used to think of the black man in London (on Liberation he returned home and took his place in the new Zimbabwe) who at the height of the War, when emotions were at their most violent, remarked calmly: 'We can't expect that type of white to change. They never will. They are like children and will have to be treated like children. Or like sick people.'

A week into my stay in a new Zimbabwe I finally understood that these were indeed sick people. As I moved from one verandah to another – morning tea, lunch, afternoon tea, drinks, dinner – on the flanks of those incomparable mountains, I listened to The Monologue, and reminded myself that these were normally cool, self-reliant, resourceful and humorous people. The Monologue up here was bitter, self-pitying, peevish, began with the day at six or so and went on till bedtime. Now it was not only President Banana and the chickens, Mugabe and his motorcade, but the new bureaucracy, inefficient, arbitrary, weighted against the whites. The Swedes and their Aid operations were hated with a cold rage that now I find hard to believe. Did I really sit listening for hours of malicious anecdotes about the Swedes? Indeed I did: I have my notes. The Swedes were the first, or the most generous, or the most visible of the new armies of international benefactors, and particularly attracted resentment, but so did anyone who had supported the 'terrs' or who had assisted the birth of Zimbabwe. Cold Comfort Farm, that exemplary settlement where, for years under the whites, black and white lived and worked together, had always attracted criticism, but now what it stood for had triumphed, every kind of gossip circulated among the whites, some so stupid and so petty I had to keep telling myself: a political enemy is not described as someone who disagrees with you, almost certainly from motives as idealistic as your own, but as vicious, twisted, immoral, and incompetent.

Above all, there were the Squatters . . . one could encapsulate the whole grievance of the blacks thus: They came and stole our land.

Land, the soil, the earth, this is what had been taken from the blacks. Throughout the War of Liberation, the Bush War, Mugabe was making a promise, that when the whites were defeated, every black person would have land. What Comrade Mugabe meant was that they would be part of communal schemes and settlements, but every black wants to own land as the whites do, to have and to hold and to pass on to heirs. Comrade Mugabe was fighting a hard war and his was only one of the armies. He did not know he was going to win. Perhaps even in the midst of such uncertainties it would be wiser for guerilla leaders not to make impetuous promises. It is not possible for every black person to own land or even live on the land. There will never be enough land, particularly with the population doubling, doubling, doubling, at such short intervals. But when the War ended, every black person who had supported Mugabe because of his promises, and many who had not, waited for land, and for Paradise to begin.

This Paradise was in fact more like an anarchist's utopia. No one would need a licence to drive a car. Cars would not need licences. No one would have to pass school exams, yet everyone would have qualifications and certificates, and any job at all would be at once available. No need for tickets on buses or on trains. Electricity and water would flow as free as air through pipes. Of course not every black believed in every article of this creed, but every black believed something on these lines, or, at least, this fantasy was believed in by the more childish part of the blacks. And who knows how much despondency and betrayal is felt by that sensible and adult part of a person whose childish fantasies have to die?

By the time Zimbabwe was born there were three countries to learn from. Mozambique's economy was in ruins, partly because the whites had been thrown out, with all their expertise. In Tanzania Nyerere, inspired by the examples of the Soviet Union and China, where collectivization had led to the deaths of tens of millions of people, introduced forced collectivization and the peasants practised passive resistance, so that in the shops of that fertile country was little food or none: peasants always win in the long run. In Zambia, due to mismanagement, agriculture was such a disaster most of the food was being grown by the few remaining whites. (This remains true in 1992.)

Comrade Mugabe learned from all this, and only two years after Liberation there was a careful, cautious, thoughtful policy of buying up white farms as they became available, settling selected people on them, but only when elementary services had been guaranteed. The rhetoric that accompanied this policy was as senseless and torrential as in any communist country, but luckily there was (and is) little connection between what was happening and the words used to describe it.

Inflamed and justified by the years of rhetoric, black people rushed on to the new farms, not waiting to be properly settled, but were removed again, if unsuitable. Who was suitable and who not? Well, that's it, the promises of the Bush War did not mention suitability.

'The whites stole our land, and now we want it back.'

'Yes but slowly does it. Do you want Zimbabwe to be a mess, like Mozambique, like Zambia, like Tanzania?'

'We don't care about all these big thoughts, long-term perspectives. Just give us the land you promised us.'

'But there isn't enough land to go around.'

'Then throw the whites off their farms and give us their land.'

'There still wouldn't be enough land.'

'That isn't what you were saying when you were the Boys in the Bush.'

'Yes, but the exigencies of that period of time prohibited in-depth analysis, and now we have examined the situation from all angles and taken into consideration the parameters of the parastatial infrastructure and relevant co-ordinates, it is evident that . . .'

'*Give us our land.*'

The new farms are an extension of the already existing settlement areas and Native Purchase Areas set up under the whites, just as the Master Farmer Certificates given to good farmers are a continuation of policies begun under the whites. It was not possible to give credit to the whites for anything in 1982, so the new policies were presented as if born out of the head of the new regime.

On the white verandahs, the most important article of The Monologue was the Squatters. When I was not sitting on verandahs, I sat in cars, being driven through areas crowded with every kind of shack, hut, shanty, each surrounded by straggling mealies and a few pumpkins. The earth was eroding into gullies, the trees were being cut for fuel. Who drove me? Explosive, splenetic whites.

'Just look at that, look at it, there won't be any soil left . . .'

'For God's sake, calm down!'

'It's not as if they are even living there . . . the men have jobs in town, they bring their wives and kids to the land they've squatted, they can't live on what they grow, they can't even grow more than a few meals of sadza.'

'You are going to have a stroke if you aren't careful.'

'And the Minister won't do anything . . . when he addresses meetings of the Faithful he just promises them land . . . he's scared not to. When he speaks to us, the white farmers, he says, "Yes, yes, yes, you're right, no of course we don't want soil erosion." But he doesn't do anything.'

The soil was washing away. The gullies deepened. Bad enough on mealie-growing land, but on the steep hillsides of the Vumba perched and huddled the shanties with a few thin maize stalks about them, and some chickens. But this shallow forest soil could never grow maize, and whole hillsides were sliding into gullies. '*Just look at that!*' shouted the white farmers, who these days are all conservationists to a man, woman and child.

Half an hour's drive from this high valley in the mountains that grows coffee, kiwi fruit, soft fruit, passion fruit, you have dropped a couple of thousand feet and there you are in the tropics: pineapples, bananas, mangoes, any tropical fruit, but what united these different landscapes was the Squatters. On to every farm crept the people from the towns hoping to be farmers, real farmers, with title deeds. And every farm repelled them: it was a new and energetic guerilla war.

Which sometimes took surprising forms. A certain liberal white farmer (but the word liberal is a malediction) on Liberation called his workforce to him and said, 'And now we shall all work together as equals. No more migrant labour on this farm. I shall give every one of you two acres of land to build a permanent home. The land will be yours. What you grow on it will be yours.'

'And what do you suppose happened?' demanded the white woman who was telling this tale, her face lit with hatred. 'Well, what do you think? All the relatives moved in at once, there were hundreds of them. That idiot went to his permanently employed men and said, "Can't you see that there won't be any soil left here in five years' time? It'll be desert. Your friends are cutting all the trees down. You must send them away." But of course they wouldn't go. They could recognize a good thing when they saw it.'

'And what happened?'

'He went to Australia and he's farming near Perth. And all his Squatters got their comeuppance anyway because his farm was purchased by the government.'

Verandah talk was not only of Squatters. When Mugabe was
fighting his desperate war in the bush, he said other things that
were less than intelligent. One was that compulsory dipping of
cattle* was a sinister plot by whites to destroy the cattle – the
mombies – which are warp, woof and weft in traditional African life. Compulsory dipping was in any case hard to keep up
while the War was going on, but at Liberation the blacks at
once stopped dipping, and as a result there were all kinds of
diseases. Hard for the government to begin enforced dipping
again. 'But we thought you told us . . .'

The Comrades in the bush announced that making contour
ridges to stop erosion was another ploy to undo the blacks.
The bad results from this were in 1982 already visible. On African farms they were ploughing right across the contour ridges.
Gullies formed, which became ravines, water rushed down
them carrying precious soil. 'You wait a few years,' said ill-
wishing or conservationist whites, 'they won't have any land
left – but they'll blame us for it, as usual.'

This concern for the land impressed me. When I was growing
up the whites were land pirates in more ways than by grabbing
it. When the government made contour ridging compulsory,
and sent out surveyors to map the land, they grumbled. All
that has been forgotten. If The Monologue in its various forms
was boring, and you wished only to be somewhere else as it
started up again – again, again – when these people talked
about farming techniques, it was a very different thing. These
reformed pirates and landgrabbers know about inventions and
discoveries from every part of the world. They experiment,
they innovate, they wonder if tree planting in Scotland or the
thousands-of-years-old tricks used to wring water from deserts
being used by Israel could be applied to Zimbabwe. They discuss wind power, solar power, water-screws from the Middle
East and Egypt, new ways of building dams, the introduction
of drought-resistant plants from semi-deserts, the control of

---

* Farm animals have at regular intervals to be made to swim through a
bath of chemically treated water to kill the insects which cause disease.

pests by other pests or helpful plants, the farming of eland instead of cattle.

I was taken to visit a farm which was 'a bit of a show place, you won't find many farms like this one'.

The couple had farmed in Northern Rhodesia, were among the hundreds of white farmers who left when it became Zambia. They went to the Transvaal and farmed successfully, but 'They don't know how to get on with the Affs down there. The Affs there aren't friendly and nice like our Affs. They are sullen. I never saw a smiling face all the time I was there. So we decided to try Southern Rhodesia.'

Again history caught up with them, and inflicted on them a black government.

He was a remarkable farmer. The farm was more like a medieval manor, or perhaps a white farm in the old days, than farms now; full of workshops and mills, dairies, a blacksmith's, a leather-worker's shed. The farmer resembled a stereotype Texan, for he was tall, tough, rangy, slow-talking. He had a genius for improvisation. During the War, with machinery and spare parts hard to get, he had attended every farm sale, bought up the machines, and rehabilitated them. His farm was a museum of farm machinery: I recognized ploughs and harrows and planters from the 1920s and '30s. There were a couple of acres full of these machines, and every one was in working order. He had taught a couple of farm workers all he knew, and these men looked after their machines like – well, like mombies. This joke was made by the farmer to the men, and returned to us by the men, laughing. 'Nearly as good as mombies,' they said, showing off wagons, planters, reapers The place was almost self-sufficient, with storerooms full of preserves, jams, honey, cheeses, pickles, and bins full of grain. Supper was a feast, and breakfast another, and nothing on the table had been bought. The farmer's wife was as remarkable as her husband. When her husband went off for months at a time to fight, it was she who ran the farm. She did not find it easy to take a back seat again – like all the wives who managed farms while the men went to war, and who tended to exchange resigned looks when their husbands said things like, 'So and

so came to look after my wife when I was away fighting.' Now,
with peace restored, as well as being a farmer's wife of the old
kind who could turn their hands to anything, she was running
what amounted to a training school for house servants. These
were all female, not male, but the decision to employ women
had not been made by her. 'Oh, I do what I'm told,' she said,
and then, 'Come and see the Princess. Yes, I have a Princess
working in my kitchen.' This was not said unpleasantly, as it
certainly would have been in the old days, for she was trying
to come to terms with the new Zimbabwe. In the kitchen a
pretty black girl was learning to cook elaborate cakes and puddings. 'They come up to me from the village every day, they
beg me to teach them, they cry and if I say no, they just go on
coming back till I give in. Please teach me, please teach me and
so I have five girls working for me, whatever next, my husband
tells me I'm silly, but I say, I'm doing my bit for Zimbabwe,
aren't I? There isn't any work for these poor girls, you see.
They know I give them a good training, and they try to get
work somewhere in the towns in a hotel or one of the embassies. They all want to work in a hotel. I show them everything,
how to cook and serve and make beds and keep the verandah
plants nice. I teach them how to answer the telephone and take
messages.' Before I went to bed they warned me that if I went
for a walk before breakfast then I must be careful. 'There are
all kinds of skellums about you know, because of the War. And
if you hear a lorry, get into the bush. If it's just our soldiers,
then it's all right, but if it's the North Koreans . . .'

Comrade Mugabe accepted an offer by the North Koreans to
supply soldiers to train a regiment especially to guard him and
act as exemplars of military efficiency to the rest of the citizens.
They were thugs, bullies and, more than once, murderers, for
it was they who were blamed for the recent murder of two
tourists not very far from this farm. Everyone feared them. In
1982 only one issue united blacks and whites: loathing of the
Koreans, the infamous Fifth Brigade. 'They'd kill you as soon
as look at you,' said my host. Said too, the five girls who were
off to their villages through the dark bush, together for safety,
with a man from the farm as escort. When I went walking early,

about six, it was through fields full of coffee bushes that were dusty and limp from lack of rain. I was listening for the birds, even hoping to see an animal or two. There were some birds, not very many, but no animals. Suddenly appeared a lorry full of men in uniform, jolting past in clouds of dust. They were a local regiment, not the Koreans. I stood in the dust at the side of the road, ready to run if necessary. They did not look friendly, but then, why should they?

Soon after I returned to London, I heard this couple decided they didn't want to live under a black government: it was the bureaucracy, the incompetence, the Squatters, and, above all, fear for their future. They took their skills and experience and expertise, and returned to the Transvaal, sullen blacks or no, and started again from the beginning, because they could not take money out of the country. What happened to that farm, full of workshops and machinery and animals? That great house, full of rooms? To the young black women so desperate to be cooks, parlour maids, waitresses?

At supper – fifteen people, family friends, visitors, a scene of peace and plenty – all the talk had been of war. Again I heard the note of bitter longing and regret, when they remembered how at nights they lay in the bush under the stars, and tried to stave off sleep because of the splendour of the skies, and listened to the silence of the bush – full of danger, and that was at least half the point. 'The best time of their lives' – what else? And with a thousand times more reason than when my father talked of the best time of his life, meaning the companionship of soldiers. 'I've never known that again . . .' But that was the trenches. Longing, regret, nostalgia – for what? More and more I think that these, our most powerful emotions, longing or regretting, are about something else, some other good or lack. There's a Companionship few of us have known, which we dream of, and in war it comes close, for a time. With Death as its price. Then the War is over, and suddenly everything tells these men they are no longer young. It is not a long slow attrition, which is how most people experience the onset of middle age. During the War years they have been valued and have valued themselves for the attributes of

young men: physical strength, toughness, endurance, bravery.
And for years they have been in an earlier stage of culture,
where men hunted other men, to kill them. No wonder memories of war are such a strong drug. And all over Zimbabwe
black men who had fought for six, seven, eight years, in the
forests and kopjes and vleis, sometimes from the age of ten, or
eleven, had endured that cruel war, so much worse than we
were ever told in the newspapers, had fought inadequately
equipped, and often untrained – these men were remembering
a time of hope. For years they had lived in and off the bush,
their fathers' heritage, if not their own; they had been with
equals and friends, the white man and his cold cutting ways
held in focus as an enemy, and a long way off. They were
permanently drunk on the most satisfying rhetorics, so much
better than alcohol, and on danger. Now they were back in
civilian life, most in poorly paid jobs, or jobless and clinging
on to the often semi-criminal fringes of town life, or jobless
in villages. Or they were crippled and being 'rehabilitated',
sometimes being taught to read and write. Probably the people
who could understand each other best of all in Zimbabwe, in
1982, were the white and black veterans of that war. But they
had to hate and condemn each other.

ANIMALS

The 'gun-boy', a man of fifty or so, is out every night after
baboons and wild pigs. Driving along the side of a mountain
through the bush, in these parts more like rain forest, suddenly
there is a troop of baboons and their young crossing the dangerous exposed road.

'Ahhhhh,' sighs the visitor from Europe.

'Vermin,' snaps the farmer.

A group of wild pigs, the little ones running after mother
. . . 'Oh, look, look at the little pigs.'

'Vermin, rubbish,' says the farmer.

Baboons raid the coffee fields, can lay waste a whole field in a night, and have learned they can get high on coffee beans. They do get high on coffee beans. Pigs root up the vegetable gardens and chase the house dogs and kill them when they can.

The man with the gun is essential to the mountain valley and its farmers. Baboons and pigs and people cannot live together, too bad.

In the forests of Mozambique there is no game left, because of the War. Nothing, all killed.

But every morning, when I got up, about five-thirty, to be in time to see the sun rise, I sat on the verandah and observed, a hundred yards down the hill, a vervet monkey sitting in the top of a tree, lolling there like me on my chair, and he was watching the sunrise too, as he warmed himself after the cold night. He stayed for about half an hour. Friends, or family, more frivolous characters than this philosopher, cavorted about in the lower branches or chased each other across the ground from tree to tree.

HOTELS

On the road up to the Vumba are two hotels, old style, full of space and character, with verandahs, lawns and – birds. You sit out on a sunny lawn, overlooking mountains and forests, and drink tea, beer, and watch the birds flashing about in the trees. The game warden for this area is also linked with the hotel industry. He is full of woe because the kidnapping of the six tourists will put people off coming to visit. We sit about drinking this and that and play the game, 'If I were . . .' In this case, Minister for Tourism. We would advertise package tours for bird-watchers, promising old-fashioned hotels, full of charm.

THE NEW CLASS

In one of these hotels I sat with a friend in a corner of the bar. At the bar four very young, very smart black people. The two girls wore evening dresses, all bare backs and shoulder straps. The men were in dinner-jackets. They flirted and chattered and behaved stylishly. Film behaviour. My friend, an old-time white, and I were experiencing quite different emotions. Those girls, there – thirty-five years ago – that was me. I knew they felt as I did, aged nineteen, twenty, in my ever-so sophisticated dance dresses. They were desperate and unsure. My companion said, 'They are civil servants from Mutare, up here on a night out. Well, good luck to them.' Meaning, If that's what they want, then that proves they are stupid.

ANTHROPOLOGY

Certainly not on the verandah, for it is too cold, but around the great fire, a dozen people, some visitors from Harare, talk about the news: if three of the six tourist hostages taken on the Victoria Falls road have been released, their captors say they will kill the others by a certain time. Several say it is a bluff, no one has been killed or will be killed. Then a man from Bulawayo says, 'If the Matabele say they will do a thing, they do it. It is their culture.' He told us he had lived with the Matabele during the War for months, had eaten and slept with them. When he came out of the bush it was hard to remember English, for a day or two. On cold nights, with one thin blanket each, he slept in a sandwich between two Matabele. He has nothing but admiration for the Matabele. When later it was confirmed the hostages had been killed, he said, 'I told you so.' Quite a few of the company love the Matabele, it turns out, and even more the Zulus, from whom the Matabele descended. There is present an historian and anthropologist, and he teases a South African girl. 'Why do you love the Zulus? It's because they are military people by nature. Soldiers. The Prussians of Africa. I can tell what a person's like according to whether they like the Matabele or the Mashona. The Mashona are easy-going, creative, artistic, and witty, just like the Italians. That's why the Italians who settled here after the Second World War got on so well with them. Both have a great gift for living. But white South Africans adore the Zulus, and certain types of white Zimbabweans adore the Matabele. Like to like.'

They talk, they talk, they talk obsessively about the new black leaders. They cannot stop talking about them. But already the harsh and angry judgements of my first few days are changing. Mugabe has this or that good quality. Nkomo isn't too bad – a pity he's in the dog-house. This is far from the hysterical turnabout that the Kenyan whites showed a surprised world: one week Jomo Kenyatta was a devil and a thug, the next a Grand Old Man.

One leader has no redeeming features at all: Edgar Tekere who when drunk went into a white farmhouse and murdered the farmer. Tekere is a fanatic, he is beyond redemption, and Mugabe should get rid of him. Edgar Tekere comes from this part of the world, he is a local hero. Bad luck for Manicaland, these whites say.

They talk, they talk, they talk . . . about the regiment that is stationed just a couple of miles away. No, they are not the Koreans, nothing like the Fifth Brigade, but they are far from the nice tidy soldiers of modern Europe, kept tucked out of sight when not in use. They behave very badly, not above stealing what they find unguarded. They terrorize women they find alone, join beer drinks when they should not and get very drunk. There is no redress.

Why are they here?

When the boundary between Portuguese East Africa and Southern Rhodesia was drawn, two officials met for drinks and settled the matter, by throwing dice . . . true or false? When an anecdote is told and retold, and it is, and has been, about frontiers all over Southern Africa, then you have to wonder. It is told with relish, by the whites – tamed characters admiring their buccaneering predecessors. ('Drake was really a terrible ruffian, you know.') I have also heard it told, with relish, by blacks, in the spirit of, *Well, what can you expect!*

Lord Salisbury said: 'We distributed mountains, rivers and lakes among us without knowing where they were.'

Presumably he would not have approved of the two raffish young officials, one Southern Rhodesian and one Portuguese, sharing sundowners and dicing for the frontier that runs four miles away.

The trouble is, it cuts a certain African tribe in two. One part is now in Mozambique, the other in Zimbabwe. Because Mozambique is having such a bad time, and there is famine, and because the Africans on that side see no reason to love or respect the frontier, they come over to Zimbabwe to get food from their relatives, who are well off. This is against the law of the new Zimbabwe, which has to be enforced by Comrade Mugabe's soldiers, referred to by the locals as the Comrades. This battalion is the real ruler of the area. The whites hate them because wherever they are, there is anarchy. The blacks hate them because they are always raiding homes to see if they are harbouring 'brothers' from across the frontier.

The whites: 'They behave as if they own the place.'

'Do you think the fact they have just won this war has anything to do with it?'

'I'm not having it, that's all! The women have been up complaining again. I've sent a message to the chap in command. But what can he do? There's no discipline.'

But the battalion had its uses, too.

'Something is under way,' goes the talk on the verandahs. 'We'll tell you when it's over.'

We stand on hillside looking down at the little huts of the Squatters, poor, makeshift, and, instead of being grouped like a traditional village, they are isolated, dotted here and there, in clearings in the forest where the trees have gone and the soil is slipping away down the mountainside.

This is what was under way . . . the battalion had been ordered by the government to clear some Squatters off a farm.

In charge of The Operation was a young Scotsman, who hated what he had to do: he had not slept for two nights, he said. After The Operation he came in for a drink. The army had gone in with lorries, cleared everything out of the huts, set fire to them. The women had stood watching the huts burn. There were over seventy women. It was considered significant that two sewing-machines were found, twenty sacks of mealies, and a suite of store furniture. It was taken for granted that these goods were for the anti-Frelimo Terrorists, or Renamo, who – the people around here believe – are sure to win. I ask, 'But surely these people wouldn't support South Africa? That's what it amounts to?' 'Look, these are peasants, behaving like peasants – like all the people in villages, poor bastards, while the War was on. They kept their heads down and survived. They know how to survive. Those poor bastards want to eat. People need to eat you know. They don't eat under Samora Machel. They think they will eat better under the other crowd. That's all there is to it.'

The lorries took the Squatters down to Mutare, to be resettled, I was told. But it turned out only ten per cent were going to be given a place on the land. 'Most of them have jobs in Mutare, or have husbands or brothers in work there. They have homes already.'

'Did they get their sewing-machines back?'

'Impounded.'

'And the maize?'

No one was comfortable. The Operation was a victory for the whites, giving them reassurance that the black government would at least sometimes enforce the law.

There was anger later when these Squatters were taken before a magistrate and ordered never to return. Not fined. Not remanded. Not put on bail. Told: Don't do it again.

'Of course they'll do it again. They're walking back up the mountain through the bush at this moment. The Minister of Agriculture keeps promising us, Yes, Yes, of course you can't have Squatters on your farms, but the next thing he has one of those rabble-rousing meetings of theirs and he says the white farms are up for grabs, and promises them land. He knows there isn't enough land. He never tells them that. He gets them all worked up roaring and shouting, and next day he comes to us, Oh don't worry about a thing, just go on growing your crops, Zimbabwe couldn't do without you.'

A few days after driving towards the Indian Ocean, Harare to Mutare, I drove back, not stopping, Mutare to Harare. Negotiations had gone on with the petrol station, where no one without a permit was served unless you were part of the local mechanisms of barter – services or favours or farm produce in return for a tank of petrol. The pipeline had just been cut again by Renamo, and the road was empty for miles at a time. Sometimes I find myself thinking, What luck to be living now, and it is often when driving alone in wild country, alone, or, as today, companioned. Not only is it permitted, this driving about where one wills, it is actually approved – though probably not for long. Make the most of it while it lasts, I guiltily admonished myself, dawdling or racing in the poisonous machine. On that day in Eastern Zimbabwe, through that landscape, under the tall cool sky, it was no good reminding myself that this was, in the minds of all the citizens, still a war country, with every tree or hill or turn of the road a reminder of killing.

Is there a more beautiful country in the world than this one? – combining magnificence, variety, freshness of colour with a way of speaking to you intimately about our story as a species (we originated hereabouts, so they say) as if you, this item of a moment in history were truly the heir of everything humankind has done and achieved. Survival is what this dangerous grandeur reminds you of: if we have all survived so much, then surely we can confidently hope . . . but we were nearing Harare and the road was no longer empty, and my companion was pointing out this car, or that lorry or bus, expostulating about the standards of driving. Liberation had released on to the roads thousands of vehicles that were not licenced and could never be licenced because of their decrepitude, but, 'This government doesn't care about a little thing like that, it's shit-scared of its own people. It never prosecutes one of its own. If one of us offends, then that's it, the police have time enough for that.' But if many of the black drivers were bad, then the black men who drove the coaches and buses of the regular services were all good chaps: 'I'd trust my life to them anywhere, any day.' Certainly now my attention was withdrawn from the bush, the mountains, the sky, and all the associated scaly and furry thoughts banished, I had never seen a more interesting collection of jalopies, tin cans tied up with string, rusting mementoes of the days when 'everyone' had cars. They were, in short, just like the cars driven by the poorer white farmers of the old days. Each vehicle pumped out black smoke. Long before you glimpsed one of them toiling up a slope ahead, the greasy black clouds were drifting across the trees, and soiling the cool blue of the winter sky.

THE SHOW

The Harare Show was on. The Salisbury Show in the old days was part agricultural show, part industrial, with horse-racing, song and dance of all kinds, parades, fashion, not to mention the Show Ball. The Show Ground covers many acres, and people came in from everywhere, South Africa and Northern Rhodesia too. This year apprehension darkened anticipation: last year, in 1981, the first Show after Liberation, a group of drunk and armed Freedom Fighters had rampaged, overthrowing stalls, threatening to beat people up, singing snatches of revolutionary songs. The War was only a year away, and everyone knew that all over the country were these men, and not a few women, who had fought for Liberation and who – many, if not all – were bitter that the whites had not all been instantly thrown out of Zimbabwe. 'This is not what we fought for,' was what they yelled, seeing so many white faces behind the stands and stalls. But it was not only white people they insulted and threatened. They were people who needed to fight, to hurt . . . and suppose it all happened again this year? My brother had decided not to take his feather pictures, bone

buttons and key-rings to the Show, but then said he was not
going to be panicked by a bunch of 'terrs'.

I walked past the place where prize cattle were being led in
front of the judges, their foreheads adorned by large rosettes,
Second Prize, First Prize, Champion, like girls with bunches of
flowers in their hair at an old-fashioned dance. At Light Industry groups of men, white, stood together talking in low voices,
their shoulders held defensively. There were quite a lot of
people, but 'in the old days' – but that was only three or four
years ago, on the other side of The Divide – the Show had been
so crowded you could hardly move. Around a large circle of
bare earth were the stalls of Arts and Crafts, and there was my
brother waiting for customers.

'There's no one here,' says Harry, calm but angry. 'I might
just as well not have come.' All the people behind the stalls
selling the kinds of beads, belts, flowers, clothes you would
find anywhere from Camden Lock to the Market Square in
Helsinki or a country fair in the States were white. The thin
crowd was mostly white.

I sat in a deck chair in the sun outside his booth and watched
the people drift past, slow, slow, with the steering loitering
look of fish in a tank, hesitating at this stall, nosing gently at
the next, wandering about over the great circle of brown dust.
The faces . . . many were dream faces, distorted but familiar.
These were people I had gone to school with, danced with at
the Salisbury Sports Club, raced dangerously about with in
cars, before one had to feel that cars were a threatened species.
I knew them and I didn't know them. And since I do dream so
much about old Rhodesia, probably I had encountered them
disguised in my sleep.

An elderly woman, in a tea-party suit, with a flowered hat
and white gloves, stops, stares, and advances cautiously to my
brother.

'Is that you Harry? I thought it was. Long time no see. I've
been in The Republic to have a look. But I'm sticking it out
here. I like our Affs better. They're a nice lot compared with
there. You can always have a good laugh with our Affs.'

He did not say he was Taking the Gap, only remarked that

the Show was not what it used to be. 'I'm only here because I thought we should show the flag a bit.'

A pause. She looks hard at me. She goes close to my brother. She lowers her voice. 'Harry, who is that lady in the deck chair?'

'That's my sister,' he says, lowering his.

'You mean that's . . . ?'

The two faces turn to stare at me.

'But I thought she was . . .'

'Yes, but with this government – she's on their side. So she's not Prohibited now.'

Her face is harassed, with that it's-all-too-much-for-me look, like a housewife whose saucepan is boiling over while her baby has spilled the custard over her clean floor. She laughs nervously, while Harry confides, 'She's still got all those funny ideas of hers, you know.'

As she walks off, she gives me a dignified inclination of the head, while the flowers on her hat nod gently. I raise my hand in that gesture that says, Hi there!

Harry comes to me and says carefully, 'That's Joannie.'

'Ah. Well. It's nice to see everyone again.'

A customer arrives, a black woman with three large daughters. She wants buttons for cardigans she knits for sale through mail order. I wander off to African Agriculture. Here there are real crowds, but while they are animated, and having a good time, they are cautious too, for they are as afraid of an eruption of drunk freedom fighters as the whites are. They are absorbed in the plants and vegetables. Very few of these people are cut off from their villages, the country, the bush. I thought of Finland where they said there is not one person who does not have a toehold in the countryside: parents, a brother, a sister married to a farmer. These people crowding to examine the produce knew what they were looking at. All kinds of maize, millet, rapoka, munga – these grains I knew, but there were many others. Roots and leaves from the bush that are used to make relishes for the porridge: I knew the leaves only as plants I saw when walking through the bush. Legumes – dozens of different kinds. Potatoes and sweet potatoes, and pumpkins

like yellow boulders, and all the varieties of gourds and
squashes. These plants were what the Africans knew and grew,
and have always grown, but Zimbabwe, the paradise country,
can grow anything at all, from the soft fruit, plums and peaches
and apples of the Eastern Districts, to the tropical fruits of the
Burma Valley, to the oranges and lemons and grapefruit of the
Mazoe Valley, to avocado pears, and mangoes and lichees and
kumquats, to . . . is there anything this sun-blessed, star-
blessed country cannot grow?

Crowds drifted from admiring their food, displayed in pots
and baskets and laid out on cloth, to the stands beside the place
where tribal dancing was going on. The drums livened our feet,
and made us move together, and some of the women were
dancing, in groups, while men stood by clapping. The tiers
were so full you would think not one body could possibly find
room to squeeze in, but all the time people, who stood looking
wondering where they might fit, found that a space had
opened somewhere, and the impossible was happening.
Groups of whites stood watching. One group was the new race
of Aid workers, or perhaps people from an embassy, friendly,
casual, as at home here as they would be, next year, in Ethiopia,
Jakarta, Peshawar. Another group was South African soldiers.
There was something about them, just as there used to be about
the Vietnam veterans. The year before I had come to know a
South African who had done two years in Namibia. His face
was ravaged, destroyed. The South African soldiers from
Angola and Namibia have had to forgive themselves too much.
Their faces, many of them, were like wounds. These young
white South Africans, here as tourists, looking at Zimbabwe,
saw something that they, in The Republic, had fought to prevent. No one looked at them, except covertly, as I was doing.
The Africans going past unconsciously (or perhaps knowingly)
gave them plenty of space, and lowered their voices.

Generally, the black crowds here ignored the whites. They
did not want to have to see us, or, perhaps, genuinely did not
see us.

The South African soldiers went on standing where they
were, looking at the dancing which here was not a show put

on for tourists. The soldiers were all high on something, and it was not alcohol.

I went off and was stopped by a young woman dressed in a wonderful combination of smart red suit, black heels half a yard high, and a head cloth in many colours. 'Will you give me an interview for my newspaper?' she wanted to know. We sat opposite each other in the Press Pavilion, and chatted about this and that. Then she asked, 'What do you think about Zimbabwe?' We were getting on pretty well, so I risked, 'At the moment it is breaking my heart.'

She at once sobered out of her smiling professionalism, and says, 'Yes, I agree. But perhaps a positive message?'

'Viva Zimbabwe,' I say. For no reason at all, there are tears in my eyes, and, I see, in hers too. We realize we might easily begin crying.

'It's going to take time,' she says, almost under her breath, glancing around to make sure no one had overheard.

'It's going to take time, but Zimbabwe is on the right path.'

'Very good,' she says. 'I like that.'

AT A BAR

That evening I am standing at a bar in a restaurant in a suburb, with some friends. The bar is full. A black man has been told that it is now against the law to forbid a black person from going into a 'white' bar or club. He is bobbing about among the white drinkers, smiling ecstatically, a bit drunk perhaps, or elated with the emotions of the time. The whites, as they notice him, not at once since they are pretty drunk, make room for him, and one says, 'Whoa there, Jim, mind my glass.' 'Yes, baas, yes, my baas,' says the brave one, smiling, bobbing, turning himself right around to make sure he is here, actually here, by right, in this white place. 'Do you want a drink?' asks another white, and to the barman: 'Give this nice chap a drink.

What do you want to drink?' 'A beer, baas.' 'No, have a whisky, go on, be a devil.' 'Yes, baas, a whisky please, baas.'

Next morning, sober, he will be beside himself with rage. 'I'll kill them, I'll kill them,' he will certainly say, banging his fists against the wall, weeping.

Then our party goes to a table. A Zimbabwean evening. Just like a Southern Rhodesian evening. I sat there, the women sat there, while the men got drunker and drunker. They had long ago passed that alas very short period when drunks are inventively funny, wondrously witty, and had become stupid. How many hundreds of evenings had I, a young woman, sat literally stupefied with boredom, swearing I would leave this country, leave it if it was the last thing I did. 'I've got to get out of here or it'll do me in . . .' Boredom, obliterating boredom . . .

THE RESTAURANT

This is the Jameson Hotel, which was inter-racial years before Liberation, and has always been a good-natured place. In the restaurant a husband is urging his wife to order food she has never tried. 'You can't eat only sadza,' says he, like a school master. She is a fat woman, laughing helplessly as she points to an item on the menu, then covers her mouth with both palms and sits shaking. The waiter stands smiling, other waiters interrupt their work to watch, the restaurant manager comes over. Everyone, black and white, is involved in this moment of social evolution.

She tastes a cheese dish, wrinkles up her face, shakes her head then shudders with her shoulders, so that a collar of tangled necklaces flash and tinkle. But we can see she is committed on principle to liking only sadza, and we do not have to take the rejection seriously. A waiter removes the cheese dish with a great philosophical shrug. Another dish is set before her. She pokes her finger into it, rolling her eyes. 'No, no, you must use a fork,' says her husband, with appropriate severity. She compromises with a spoon, takes up a little edge of whatever it is, lifts it to her lips, makes a big astonished face, purses her mouth, shakes her head, sits back wheezing out laughter and pressing the napkin to her whole face.

By now everybody is laughing.

The waiter sets down a plate of pudding, with a flourish and a last-ditch gesture that involves us all. Her eyes stretched wide, she stands bravely at the precipice edge, she plunges in a spoon, she takes it in slow jerks to her mouth, groaning with apprehension, she encloses the spoon with her lips, she tilts back her head and allows a look of ecstasy to overcome her, she removes the spoon from her mouth, and uses it to eat up her pudding very fast, with little cries of appreciation, while the waiters reel about laughing. 'My dear,' says her husband smiling, 'you are a very foolish woman.'

'Yes, yes, I am a foolish woman, my dear, but I will have some more of whatever it is. I like it.'

IN A POET'S HOUSE

A house in Harare. A black poet is married to a white woman. French. She has a job in the university, works long hours. He has no job. She is cooking a meal for eight people, and more keep arriving. I ask if I can help her. 'No, it is her work, she must do it,' says the husband.

A writer exiled from Kenya has just arrived in Zimbabwe. He has the restless aggressive humour so useful for his situation and is being funny about the anomalies and injustices in Kenya.

Present, too, is a man of about thirty, ex-freedom fighter, who, it is rumoured, will be the Minister for Arts. He is also being funny, joking with the host that if Zimbabwe goes along like Kenya, it will not be long before he as Minister will be ordering his arrest, because a certain new periodical he works for shows signs of seditious thoughts.

'Seditious thoughts,' says he, 'we can't have that, boy. Better watch those seditious thoughts or we'll have to take steps.'

Two white journalists have just been arrested, no explanation given: they work for *The Herald*. This is not the first time journalists have been in trouble. We joke at intervals all evening about the journalists and the degree of their seditious thoughts.

When the meal is served by the hostess, who is tired, and – it is easy to see – pretty angry, she waits on us all.

'It is our African custom,' says the poet, when I comment.

'Then I don't think much of it,' I say.

'Seditious thoughts,' says he, and we all laugh again.

It was not good laughter.

Again I was thinking how much everyone was in shock, the post-war shock which, not long afterwards, I was to experience in Peshawar among the Mujahideen, among the refugees. And where else? Yes, it was long ago, and I was on a railway platform in Berlin, at night, with a friend. Suddenly we realized that all the people waiting for the train were men, and all were cripples from the War. (That is, the Second World War.) All were drunk, black drunk, sick drunk, and they were full of anger, but like a volcano that has grown a crust of cold ash. My friend and I had been laughing, talking – and then heard how uncomfortably our voices echoed here, along the bitter wintry platform. We saw these angry men, and one said, in English, 'All right, laugh. If you've nothing better to do. You'll learn better.'

Quite late arrived two Freedom Fighters – guerillas – Boys from the Bush – 'terrs' – Terrorists – heroes. They were related to one of the guests, and had been put in a rehabilitation camp outside Harare. They wore new civilian clothes, suitable for work in offices, which is what they were being trained for. They were drunk. Soon everyone was unhappily drunk.

THE ACCIDENT

Again we were on the road Harare to Mutare, and the car was crammed with people and with suitcases. After we had stopped at a roadside delicatessen stall, the car was even fuller, with hams, smoked meats, sausages, bacon. To get food of anywhere near this quality in London, you would have to go to specialist food shops. The Coffee Farmer was doing the driving. We went on safely until ahead of us on the almost empty road appeared a bus, or coach, so crowded with young black men it seemed they would start falling out of the windows. They were the police off to a football match. There is a rule, not in any rulebook, known by every driver in Zimbabwe, which is that one does not overtake if there is a turning off to the right, because drivers so often forget to use mirrors, and do not signal – but it is hard always to remember it. We rapidly caught up with this rollicking-along bus, and ahead was a turn to the right, with a culvert beyond that. We accelerated to pass as the bus, which had not signalled, turned to enter the right-hand road. Our driver tried to swerve, but the culvert was in the way. The bus, having seen us, ought to have turned sharp in a U-turn behind us, but it straightened and hit us to the rear, pretty hard. Our car fell on its right side, was pushed along by the bus a few yards, then turned over on its back. Inside the car everything went into slow motion. I was aware of how I slid, carefully, as if my intelligence was directing it, into the well of the car, bumping my head. The doors burst open in showers of glass. I crawled out, wondering how many of our bones had been broken, asking, 'Is everyone all right?' I stood by the wrecked car, listening to one of the little girls in the back calling, 'Mummy, Mummy, are you all right?'

In no time we were all sitting by the car, on the tarmac. Our wrecked car and the police bus that stood askew but upright across the road were the only vehicles in sight. Groups of policemen were wandering about, shocked, as we were. Then we got cautiously to our feet, dazed, behaving according to our natures. The driver, as famed for his stiff-upper-lip as for his many lucky survivals in accidents and dangerous escapades, was standing as if to attention by the car, announcing, when asked, that he was fine. In fact he was the worst damaged of us all, with a broken shoulder. The young woman, mother of the two girls, spends her life running things, cushioning tender human beings from harsh events, being attentive to everyone's needs. She was smartly lifting suitcases to the edge of the road, getting things into order again. The little girls were crying, 'Why me? Why me?' as we all do the first time disaster strikes, when we have not yet learned how often life moves from expressing itself through statistics – that is, other people – to oneself. As for me, I was leaning against the car while my head swam, clutching my handbag, and thinking, 'Well at least I don't have to go through all that nonsense of filling in forms for passport, driving licence, cheque cards; I haven't lost lists of addresses and telephone numbers.' I was fine too.

A car came travelling fast from the Mutare direction. It stopped, and out jumped a woman who turned out to be a doctor. She exclaimed we were all lucky to be alive, a fact we had not yet taken in. 'And you weren't even wearing seat-belts,' she deplored, unable to believe in our stupidity. She shooed us to the opposite side of the road, just in case one of the rare cars did come along. There we obediently went, and she swiftly examined us, while the thirty or so young men who had filled the festive bus came crowding around us. Now they knew none of them was hurt, they were full of concern for us. They were not drunk, as everyone assumed they must have been, when told about the accident. They had been full of high spirits, non-alcoholic. Now they clucked, and shook their heads and demanded sympathetically, were we hurt. 'What a bloody stupid question,' snapped the driver: by now blood streamed from us all. 'Are you all right?' they asked me, laying affection-ate hands on shoulder, arm, back, and patting me here and there, as if trying to push back into place any dislodged bits. By this time I had a bump on my forehead like those volcanic cones you see in comic strips, with lightning flashes radiating from it. A black eye still had to reach perfection, and one foot was painful. As for ribs, bruised, they had not yet made themselves felt. 'Of course I am not all right,' I said irritably, ready to engage in serious discussion. Some of them were crowding around the little girls, who screamed, 'Keep your hands off me, keep off.' This was not because they were from South Africa, for they came from a good liberal household, but because they were bruised. But the young men's feelings were hurt. As for their mother, by now hardly able to stand, she reasoned with them, thus: 'But you must see that it's a silly thing to say.'

The doctor said she would take us to the nearest hospital, and then put in a report to the police station. At this the young men looked put out, since they were the police station. It was agreed by the driver and the doctor that the police would hush it all up and the report would be ignored. As turned out to be the case. The doctor, a missionary doctor, recently had had to certify the death of one of the tourists murdered by the Koreans, or Fifth Brigade. She was wonderfully kind, but irritated, the way people are who spend their lives treating humanity for wounds so often earned by their own folly. Our driver, though in a bad way, insisted on staying at the site of the accident, to establish details for insurance. I do not remember being driven to the hospital, for by then the pain had begun to take us all over.

What happened in the hospital was a little encapsulation of various trends in Zimbabwe that year, that time – then.

THE COUNTRY HOSPITAL

It was a Saturday, and there was only a skeleton staff at the hospital. It is a country hospital, of that homely kind, liked by everyone, which we have so efficiently got rid of in Britain. Our doctor said she would wait with us until the doctor on call had arrived. She could not treat us herself. Protocol. We were admitted by two friendly black nurses, taking temperatures, filling in forms, blotting up the blood that flowed from us all.

We staggered, and limped about, and laughed, because we were such an absurd sight, particularly me. I had not yet seen my face, with its Vesuvius bump and its blue-black eye. The little girls had finished crying and wailing and were every inch worthy of their stiff-upper-lip heritage. Then arrived from the scene of the crash the Coffee Farmer, who by now was evidently in bad pain, but he was not going to admit it. The black doctor arrived, driving rapidly and scattering gravel through the flowering bushes that surrounded the hospital. He skidded, and parked with an elegant swoop, while the missionary doctor sighed and said, 'Oh look at that, hasn't anybody got any sense?'

Then, a problem: an atmosphere of difficulty and suspense. The black nurses were afraid we would not allow a black doctor to examine us. This said everything about the problems this hospital had to deal with every day. They were tactful, charming, and relieved when the little girls were taken by their mother into the examining room. Meanwhile the white doctor was telling the black doctor that in her opinion only the man was seriously hurt, and he was – and she lowered her voice – a difficult patient. The two professionals exchanged looks, and then smiles, brows raised. She went off saying she would telephone a certain number in Mutare for us, so that we could be collected. She left us grateful. As I was taken off for antitetanus and penicillin injections, I saw a black nurse trying to get the 'difficult' patient to sit down and rest. 'But I'm perfectly all right,' he kept announcing, striding about the room.

I was in a side room with an old nurse, a fat black woman, all competence and comfort. We instantly established a woman-to-woman rapport, and as I took my clothes off, she prodded me for breaks, and we talked. Politics . . . at once, politics, just like everybody at that time. A young nurse came into the room, and the old woman asked her to go and attend to the others, and firmly shut the door after her. She waited a moment, opened the door again to check, shut it, lowered her voice. 'It's dangerous to talk in front of the young ones, they report you to the Party,' she said. She then began a fast monologue of complaint, which I at once recognized as the one I would be likely to hear from other people, like herself. While she skilfully bandaged and injected, she said Mugabe was no good, he wanted everyone to be communists, and she was religious. Bishop Muzorewa was good, and so was Nkomo – they would not frighten the whites. She said that 'we' – meaning the two of us – could remember when things were very good, life was sweet, but now everything was bad, the War had been terrible. The whites enjoyed the War, for it was their war. The blacks suffered in the War, but the whites didn't care about that, and the Comrades didn't care either.

I said, as it seemed I was already doing several times a day, that I simply could not understand why people expected things to change so quickly. We – she and I – knew at our age that nothing changed quickly . . . at least I did not mention the Romans. If there was one thing I had been impressed by, coming here, was this: no one seemed to remember the War had ended only two years ago, that is, they talked about how awful it had been, but not about the damage it had done. Damage to people. Here she remained silent for a while, handling yards of white bandage, and going 'Tsk, tsk,' when I winced. She asked, 'So you weren't here in the War?' 'No, I am from England.' Here she simply nodded, dismissing me from the possibility of understanding. We discussed family matters – husbands, children. She was shocked to hear I had been divorced, and shocked again when she heard that the mother and the two children now with the doctor were from South Africa, and the difficult patient was a coffee farmer. Yet, with these dubious associates, I talked like a supporter of Mugabe. She gave me curious looks and soon was calling me madam.

When I was taken into the X-ray room, I apologized to the young technician for spoiling his Saturday afternoon, but he said, 'I am on call and I like to help people.' I found this young man charming; I found the black doctor charming. The Coffee Farmer was being much too polite to be natural; his shoulder had been pronounced not too bad, like my foot, and various other bits of our anatomies.

Meanwhile, the local police had arrived. He was a young

black man who, having written down my name, said he had
read this and that short story of mine, and he wanted to be a
writer himself, for his life had been interesting. Could I tell him
how to do it?

There we sat, all bandaged up, and clutching our X-rays,
waiting to be collected by the friend from Mutare who was
speeding towards us, doubtless cursing us because of the waste
of precious petrol. I explained to the young policeman, who
had a sweet sensitive face and was quite unlike the conventional idea of a policeman, how to write a novel. He set aside
the business of asking questions and filling in forms while he
listened and wrote down particularly useful phrases. Every
writer has to do this far too often, and it is hard to deliver the
lecture as if for the first time. 'You see, the trouble is that young
writers seem to think that talent is enough; but there are plenty
of people with talent. What you need is to do a lot of work.
Probably because one can write stories and indeed whole
novels with no more than an exercise book and a biro, people
subconsciously believe that it is easy. But if you want to be a
writer then you have to write – and tear up: write – and tear
up. Every writer goes through that stage when what you write
is almost good but not quite good enough. What takes you
from this stage to the point of being good enough is the process
of writing and tearing up, writing and tearing up. And, of
course – reading. You cannot tell any aspiring writer how to
write: only that this writing, and writing, and trying again,
does it.' And so on. This admonition was delivered while the
little girls tried hard not to groan, as they lay stretched out on
two wooden benches, and while their mother and their uncle,
pale as their bandages, sat upright, behaving well, and while
blood stained the bandages on my foot. My ribs were beginning
to hurt horribly. The young policeman said he would look on
me as a mother and he would take my advice.

It goes without saying that this scene outraged what the
Coffee Farmer believed was correct for the occasion. He was
saying loudly that what mattered was to get all the details
of the accident down properly, so that the guilty bus-load of
policemen would be brought to justice. He was in the right, a

thousand times over. The three black nurses, who now had nothing to do, sat in a row on a bench, hands folded, listening and thinking their own thoughts. The black doctor roared off, and we could hear his car a good mile away.

NERVES

Then came the friend from Mutare. Something began that surprised us; we were all afraid, and reluctant to get into the car. Our nerves jumped and winced because every bend in the road, every bump, announced a new accident. When we saw the corpse of the car we had travelled in lying, as in a hundred other accident scenes, at the side of the road, it all got worse. We felt better when we confessed this weakness to each other. Not, however, our stiff-lipped hero who, even more because now he was sitting in the front seat with another hero from the War, was not going to admit weakness. Not for one second now, nor in the painful weeks ahead.

The long drive to Mutare in a fog of pain was the start of a psychological process that now seems as interesting as the accident itself. My mind ticked over comfortably as usual, making this or that comment, but 'my nerves' (what nerves? where situated?) jumped and suffered, but on a parallel track to my intelligence. Nothing I told them made any difference. It was not fear I was feeling, but the neurological results of shock. It was dark by now, and we could not see the road to Mutare, and that made it all worse. The well-known timidity of old women is because they know what can, and does, happen, but young people do not know, and therefore bounce about half-drunk in cars going at a hundred miles an hour on bad roads, and fearlessly do things their 'nerves', still unschooled by experience, will not allow them to do later.

My nerve-sickness continued for weeks. I know – and who does not? – how heart and mind can run on parallel tracks, heart craving what mind forbids, mind's ordinances derided by the heart, but until this accident I had taken for granted that my physical self did more or less what I wanted. Now I was afraid of heights, to the point I could not stand on a hillside whose worst threat was that I might roll over cushions of grass into a gentle hollow: I came out in a sweat, I was paralysed, if not with fear, then with a generalized inhibition. In a car I could not drive faster than fifty miles an hour: a governor inside me I knew nothing about would not let me. If there is one thing I adore it is being taken up in a small aeroplane: given a ride in one through the mountains of the Vumba, I felt sick and silly. I could not cross a road without sweating, or descend a staircase without clutching the stair rail. My mind observed all this helplessly, and if it tried mockery, that made no difference. Then, one day, in London, I found myself dodging through traffic from one pavement to another, the way we all do, and knew I was cured. The mysterious ailment had lifted: it was not a wearing-off, but a sudden deliverance.

A WHITE LAGER

A large house in Mutare, spread about with rooms and verandahs in a large garden. A welcoming hostess. Children. Young people . . . a lot of people . . . We were at once absorbed into kindness and efficiency. A 'proper' doctor was summoned. Again we were examined. The X-rays at the country hospital had been misinterpreted, some were inexpert. More X-rays were ordered. The shoulder was very bad . . . there were cracked ribs . . . a damaged tendon . . . a hairline fracture. I might have remarked that it is not unknown for misdiagnoses to be made in the advanced hospitals of Britain. But: 'Well, what do you expect?' was in the air, was being said loudly, with the smugness of the righteous. In this house it was essential to prove the Africans wrong as often as possible. For all the years of the War, the house had been a lager, a central point. People from exposed farms came in to stay a night, or several, if 'terrs' were reported to be around, or during periods of bad fighting. Women whose husbands were doing a spell with the Security Forces came with their children. The fighters came, between spells of duty, for meals, a bath, a good sleep.

Strong in this house was the atmosphere I was brought up with: in the farmhouses of The District were men and women with unambiguous roles: there was women's work, and there was men's work. Coming from London where every house one goes into has a different pattern, a different balance between men and women, this colonial society was a shock. Salutary, I suppose, as a reminder: this is what I and my kind reacted against. Next morning, as we left, one of the men was barking orders at his young woman. He did this because other men were watching: he was proving he knew how to keep a woman in her place.

All the men had fought in the War. People kept whispering, 'That man, over there, he was the best helicopter pilot in the War.' Or, 'He rescued such and such a family from beneath the noses of the 'terrs'.' Or, 'She fought off a 'terr' who got inside the security fence, and he got scared and ran for it.' The women had cooked, bandaged, nursed, and looked after others all through the War. Some had gone armed, day and night, for years. The War filled their minds still, not as a continuing vendetta or crusade, rather as a memory of when they were all stretched to the best and utmost, and when this house reached its fulfilment as a refuge, a fortress.

One young woman was a daughter-in-law, who had gone to The Republic for good, and was here on a visit to her family. Her husband had been Chief of Police. She said the moment they had decided to Take the Gap was when a black man her husband had arrested several times as a suspected sympathizer with the 'terrs', had put his arm around her at an official cocktail party and said, 'And now we shall call each other Comrade and all work together for the good of Zimbabwe.'

'I said to my husband: That's it, now it's time we left.'

This incident was related as if there could be no other reaction than deciding to leave at once. The same young woman described, without any self-consciousness, that traditional colonial scene: 'When I left for The Republic I cried when I said goodbye to the cook and the houseboy and the garden boy and our nanny. They were part of the family. They said: You are our father and mother. They were crying too.' Now it was evident she was wondering whether to come back to Zimbabwe. In The Republic they were worse off, had a small house, poor jobs, and did not have even one servant. Many people who had left, they said, were trying to come back.

In the room that night was a man who had worked for Intelligence during the War. He was asking me the carefully casual questions that are such a give-away. Not for the first time I was reflecting that it must be an enjoyable business, being a spy, for few of them seem able to let it go: power, I suppose: the agreeable illusion that one is able to control events.*

The questions he was asking might have been appropriate if I had been fighting with the Comrades in the bush, not living at ease in liberal London. And that is the other thing: all these security departments seem to create for themselves a devil figure of their opponents, and then believe in it. Look at Angleton in the CIA . . . they become paranoid. If, however, one is on the same side as the spy department, then one has to worry because of their incompetence, years out of date with their information, if it was ever genuine information in the first place.

That night I shared a verandah with the Coffee Farmer. He would rather have died than complain when awake, but, asleep, he groaned and suffered. I lay in one position all night, since it hurt to move, and I groaned freely when I had to. In the early morning he started up out of sleep, and before even conscious shouted into the void, 'Bring tea!' And, lo, tea was brought at once, by the cook, for both of us.

All over the big house people were bathing, showering, shaving, dressing, putting clothes on children, chatting, drinking tea. Some of the men drove off to get in some golf before breakfast. The women helped the servants get breakfast. The

---

* It turns out that many of the Secret Police under the whites went on working under the blacks.

doctor arrived. Only the broken shoulder was serious. By now my black eye was a wonder, and children appeared from houses up and down the street to admire it. Then there was breakfast, everything the English breakfast has at its best, and, too, fresh fruit and fruit salads and bottled fruit and jugs of cream. Thirty or so people took breakfast. Easy to imagine this scene during the War, the atmosphere of lager, the unlimited hospitality.

BACK ON THE VERANDAH

After breakfast we were packed into a station-wagon and driven up the Vumba, over those roads that wound and swerved and swooped through mountains, and while my 'nerves' jumped and shuddered, I grew more irritated with them and with myself. All of us, the wounded, were in a much worse way than yesterday: bruises that were silent then were complaining now. On the verandah of the house in the mountains we counted our sore places, and lay about stiffly, and were waited on by the devoted Milos, the servant, all tender solicitude, and later we moved indoors to the great fire and neighbours came and were helpful and infinitely skilled. No people on earth are more kind, more hospitable, more resourceful than the whites of Southern Africa, when it is a question of one of their own kind . . . and what is the point of saying it again?

And so began the convalescence. The little girls recovered first and were playing ping-pong and tennis at the Club a mile away. Their mother and I were slower. The Coffee Farmer was in a bad way, facing a difficult operation on a shoulder already damaged twice.

People appeared and disappeared on the verandah.

It is evening around the winter fire, and the room is crammed with people and with animals. The shy young assistant from the next farm, the champion parachutist of Zimbabwe, sits with his new puppy and a great white Persian cat he is looking after and does not want to leave alone. The new puppy Vicky, a clever, scheming little bitch, sits by Josh, the half-grown sweet and stupid ridgeback. The fierce guardian of the estate, Annie, the bull terrier, who is a mass of scars and wounds, puts her head on her master's knees and groans with agonized affection. A man whose job is to settle Africans on the new farms, has brought his dog, a setter. A little black cat, who is timid, finds all this astonishing and is frightened, and slips in and out between the legs of dogs, puppies, people, until she finds a safe place on a rafter, from where she watches us all. There are two couples from the farms lower down the hill, with three labrador puppies, brought to please the little girls, by their own little girls, who are teenagers. We, the wounded, sit carefully in corners, fending off friendly animals who are a threat to our sore ribs and our bruises. Who waits on us all? Milos, and beer and tea and coffee and cakes arrive all evening. It is noisy and cordial and we all watch the animals and discuss them and their behaviour as if they are people.

PAY NIGHT

Scene on a farmhouse verandah in old Southern Rhodesia. On every farmhouse verandah, once a month, this scene took place, through the 1920s, the '30s, the '40s, the '50s . . .

The sun has gone down in its glow of sorrowful red. The stars are coming out. On a small table are piles of cotton bags from the bank in town, full of coins. Beside the table sits the farmer and behind the table stands the bossboy. If this is a raised verandah, then the table is at the top of a flight of steps, the polished red cement steps of prosperity, with plants crowded on both ends of every step. A lamp is on the low wall, if there is no electricity. Or, as on our farm, a hurricane lamp is set on the table which is in front of the house. Another hangs from the branch of a tree. A crowd of black people stand waiting. The bossboy calls out a name and out steps a man wearing a pair of old shorts, and a ragged vest. No shoes. In the pay envelopes are a few coins. The bossboy earned a pound a month, ordinary labourers ten shillings, twelve shillings. What could one buy with this money? A pair of shorts cost two shillings. A vest cost less. No one wore shoes. To buy a bicycle cost five pounds, and could take a couple of years to earn. Food was supplied.

The women had come up from the compound, though they did not do farm work. Pay night was an occasion, a spectacle, something to liven things up. They stood to one side, all together. They were handsome, and wore blue and white patterned cloth wound around them, or as skirts, or as full flouncy dresses. They had head scarves and bangles and earrings. These things were likely to be all they owned.

Sometimes there were arguments about the coins in the envelopes. Then the bossboy, speaking for the farmer, would say, 'But you were away from work three days. You went to the beer drink on boss Jones's farm.' The man would stand there patiently, his face puckering with distress, which had to do as much with his life as with this small incident in it, a shilling taken off his pay. 'But I didn't go to the beer drink,' he might argue. 'I went to visit my brother.' 'But you can't go visiting every time a brother arrives in The District!' The man would shake his head, take the money and walk back to the little crowd which received him with sighs, sympathy, shakes of the head and then – marvellously – they might laugh, warm, irrepressible, infectious. Hearing that laughter the farmer might sit staring at the farm workers, his face a history of contradictory emotions. My father, for instance, who, contemplating 'the system', might conclude with his characteristic testy exasperation at the ways of the universe, 'Bloody farce, that's all it is. I mean, it's a *farce*. What else can you call it?'

Now, looking back, things I took for granted come forward: for instance, what the women wore. For decades every black woman in Southern Rhodesia and Northern Rhodesia and Nyasaland wore blue and white, indigo and white, patterned cotton stuff. Whose idea was it? At some point somebody must have said – who? – 'We are going to manufacture this type of blue and white cloth for the women of Southern Africa.' The patterns look Indonesian. The cloth was manufactured in Manchester along with kenti cloth for North Africa and the kangas of Kenya. The great bales from England arrived in ships, were put on to trains, and the rolls of cloth, smelling of dye, found themselves on the shelves of hundreds of 'kaffir truck' shops. It was beautiful material, strong, good quality. The women looked beautiful. This cloth could not be worn by poor women now, for it is associated with the shameful past. Meanwhile, it is made up into luxury items for boutiques in the big cities of The Republic, and bought by fashionable white women and fashionable black women who may have never known its history. In Zimbabwe I saw it covering sofas and chairs in a farmhouse, and as curtains in Harare. Unwritten social history: in this case probably in the records of the great cotton manufacturers of the Midlands.

The farm workers who stood in the dusk waiting to be paid, the sunset fading behind them, were not the same from one year to the next. They moved from farm to farm, if there might be a shilling or even a sixpence more in their pay envelopes at the end of the month, or a kinder farmer, or a better water supply – a good well, a nearby river. Only the bossboy and his assistant, and a man skilled at driving the teams of oxen, and the carpenter and a man who knew about machinery, stayed on from year to year.

Now, in 1982, I again sit on a verandah on a pay night, watching. It is an enclosed verandah, not a large one. On one side is the kitchen, on the other a bathroom, and doors lead off to the main part of the house. The dogs sleep here on three car tyres covered with old sacks. They sit beside us now, one, two, three, watching, interested.

There is a small table with money on it and the farm manager, who is no longer called a bossboy, sits beside the mother of the little girls, as an equal. She has spent the whole day working out the money due to everyone, because the Coffee Farmer is in too much pain. A dog has leaped up and jarred his broken shoulder. 'A little setback, I am afraid,' he says, and will not laugh when we tease him for being so heroic.

Outside the verandah is a crowd of labourers, men and women. It is five in the afternoon, and the sun is slipping behind the tall dark mountain.

The workers are of two kinds, the regulars who are paid the legal minimum wage, thirty pounds a month, or more, and the casual labourers who come for the harvest. They are paid very little, but work is short. Every day men and women arrive to ask the farmers for work, and say they will work for less than the minimum wage, ask how are they going to feed their families? 'I can't pay you less,' say the farmers virtuously. 'It would be against the law. Well, don't blame me, take it up with the government – it's your government now, isn't it?'

This is, in short, one of those well-known 'grey' areas that spoil the maps of theoreticians. Casual labour does not, or should not exist . . . hardly exists at all . . . soon will not exist . . . is almost illegal . . . without it a whole range of economic activities could not go on.

This pay night, just as it was *then*, is a colourful scene. All the women wear bright store dresses, headcloths, flashing bangles and beads, and it is they who contribute the gaiety, for the regular workers are dressed no better nor worse than the farmers, which is to say casually, if not scruffily. The seasonal male workers cannot begin to compete with their women. Everyone has shoes, these days. Nearly everyone wears a good cardigan or jersey.

It is a noisy scene, too. I sit there with my black eye, my bruised forehead, and the women are joking about the eye. No need to know the local language: women all over the world would be joking in just this way.

The paying out of the money goes like this. A name is called, and into the verandah comes a man or a woman. The little girls' mother says a greeting in Shona: she has a good friendly way with her, and a brief conversation ensues, with jokes and laughter. The manager opens the relevant envelope and the money is spread out on the table, to be checked – the pitiful few notes and coins, but no one complains.

Throughout this scene the two little white girls stand watching. One is twelve, one ten. They wear very brief shorts and heavy sweaters. Their sweaters cover the shorts, and they look as if they are naked under them. They are innocent, and unaware of how they must strike the Africans, who are eyeing them, shocked. Since they were born they have lived among Africans and it has always been their right to wear anything they fancied, go about almost naked if they liked. I remembered how, in the 1930s, the girl from the next farm to ours, who had just reached fourteen and the age for self-assertion, appeared on the rocky crown of our hill, getting out of the car in tiny shorts, a halter top and high heels. My mother was shocked. My father was agonized. 'What must they be thinking? Their women never show themselves like that.' 'What about their breasts?' demanded my mother. 'They sometimes go about with bare breasts.' 'Yes, but that's their custom. You'd never see a black woman with a brassière and shorts that wouldn't cover a mango.' 'Well, that's *our* custom,' said my mother, defending what she hated. 'But we should be setting a good example,' he said, and again, as he did so often, *'What can they be thinking of us?'*

The decades roll past and behold there is the new university on the hill near Harare, and a letter in the newspaper. 'After a dance at the University you see the black students lying entwined on the grass in the dark, two by two, kissing and much more than that. When they were asked why they behaved like this, since it is not any part of their traditional behaviour, they replied, with straight faces, "But we learned it all from you."

Similarly, a delegation of black women went from Zimbabwe to Israel to visit kibbutzim. They behaved arrogantly, using high peremptory voices, ordering people about. When asked why they were so rude to their hosts, they answered: 'But that is how our white madams behave, so we thought it was the way we should behave.'

Next afternoon I was walking with Annie along the road on the mountainside above the house when an old man in ragged clothes, with a thick staff like a Biblical patriarch, came towards me. He stopped when he saw Annie, held out his staff horizontally against her, gripped in fists that trembled, and angrily said, 'Call the dog.' Annie was not threatening him but she blocked his way and knew that she did: she was full of wicked enjoyment. 'To heel,' I said, uncertain whether she would obey me. I was remembering this dog was a bull terrier, and part of the house's defences, like the security fence whose gates these days stood open. The old man's fear said everything about her function. She did not come to heel. The man could have killed me and the dog: all the terrors and the hatreds of the Bush War were in his eyes. 'Sit,' I tried. Slowly Annie lowered her scarred haunches, but did not take her eyes off the old man's face. He could not pass her. 'She won't hurt you,' I said. 'You hold the dog,' he said. I gripped her by the loose folds of neck flesh and he slowly edged past, holding out his cudgel level with her head. 'She's just a silly old dog,' I said, and was at once incandescent with embarrassment: but I actually had said those stupid words. The old man did not turn his back on Annie until he had gone a good twenty yards. 'You hold that dog,' he shouted back. I did. I was afraid she might chase him.

Coming towards us came a flock or flight of girls, ten or so of them, returning from an afternoon's tennis at the Club. They dawdled or skipped about or made little runs out of excess energy. They giggled and their high excited voices rang out over the steep slopes of the mountain. They wore their little shorts and their little shirts; they were all long pale frail limbs, but one had new jeans which she had carefully torn to be fashionable, so her plump knees showed. Their shining tresses blew about, and pretty eyes and pink mouths were lightly sketched on plump faces. They were like an Impressionist's little girls caught in a moment of self-absorbed pleasure.

The old man strode straight past them, and now his cudgel was held out in front of him, at the ready.

It is not often one sees oneself as others see one.

That night all the girls were in front of the great fire, occupying chairs, the sofa, or lolling on the floor with Annie. Two of them were wrapping her around with green paper streamers left over from a party at the Club. She sat, with her head slightly

lowered, looking at them as she had at the old man, a measured
patience and control.

'Annie, silly old dog Annie . . .' They collapsed, laughing,
and rolled about the floor, while the servant carefully stepped
past them with the tray loaded with supper. Annie stood up,
burst her bonds, and went to lie nose to the fire, decorated
with frilly green bits like seaweed or lettuce.

RAIN

One night, not on the verandah, but inside, with the fire roaring up, the rain began to bang down on the corrugated iron
roof, and the company applauded. The long drought . . . dry
dams . . . the coffee plants standing with slightly wilted leaves,
the dogs coming all day panting to the water bowls – and
now, unexpectedly, rain. At once everyone's spirits revived.
Happiness. An intoxication.

THE ASSISTANT

One afternoon, when the verandah was full of guests, some of
them girls from down the hill, there was an apparition in the
sky: Zimbabwe's champion parachute jumper was floating
down from a tiny aeroplane, a neighbouring farmer's. He
floated slowly, for the new parachutes allow plenty of adjustment, and it can take five minutes to make a descent. He'd
better not land over in Portuguese East, cried somebody, and
a Swedish girl visiting at a near farm said fiercely, '*Really*, it's
Mozambique!' 'Renamo or Frelimo, they'll have his guts for
garters,' said the offender. The girl has been, is, silent, observant, and shocked, because she thought that after Liberation,
everything, everyone, would at once be different. 'I suppose

you find us very strange?' she has been asked, by a visiting old-style white from a tea plantation. 'I find *you* very strange,' she said fiercely. 'You, the white people.' 'That's because you don't understand us,' came the amused, impervious-to-criticism reply. 'It takes time, you know.' She had burst into tears and then everyone was very kind to her. 'They patronize me,' she said fiercely. 'How dare they!'

Down, down, floated the handsome hero, over the mountains and the bush, while the little girls and the not so little girls sighed . . . he disappeared into the trees, and appeared an hour or so later walking up the mountain carrying his parachute. Frowning, modest, and – as usual – inarticulate, he subsided in a chair, grabbing up a beer, blushing because of his many admirers.

The Farm Assistant . . . The Tutor appears plentifully in literature, but where is The Assistant? He is very young, an object of sympathy because he has no money, and is lonely in this house so full of family and their friends. He works like a demon all day, because his future depends on it. The farmer's wife is bound to be in love with him in an aching, motherly way. The daughters lie awake at night for him. The daughters of neighbouring farmers take to arriving at all hours. The farmer, who was almost certainly once an assistant is laconic, sardonic and watchful.

This particular farm assistant was – well, of course – shy. He was handsome. He knew nothing, and yearned to know everything. 'Tell me a book to read,' he might demand, and, when handed one, turned it over with lanky respectful fingers. 'Yes, I'll give this one a try.'

He dropped in often. Dropping in, dropping over, is the style of the life of the verandahs and not only for people. Animals visited, too. The great Alsatian from the next farm, who got lonely when his people went off down to Mutare, which they often did, came over to us for company. I might wake in the night – I was sleeping on the verandah – and feel the warm muzzle on my face or arm. A soft pleading whine and he climbed on to the bed, 'Tarka! *What* are you doing here, you should be at home.' If Tarka turned up in the day, a telephone call. 'Your dog Tarka is here *again*.' A servant came to fetch him. 'Come on, Tarka, come home.' Tarka went off, disconsolate, with a hundred wistful glances back at the house full of people and the three dogs, his friends.

PARTINGS

The little girls and their mother departed for Cape Town, just as I soon would leave for London. Then thousands of miles would again separate us. This was when I should leave to find out about new Zimbabwe, but I could still hardly move, what with the bruised ribs and leg. I lay in a long chair on the verandah and looked out over that view of mountains and hills and rivers and lakes that no one could ever get tired of. Sometimes small puffs of smoke just over the border meant that Renamo was at it again, blowing up something or other.

My son sat with me, when not in the fields. He was still in pain. Days passed, then weeks. We were both bored. We told each other we were bored. In a small field down the hill were some sheep, put there to pasture by a neighbour. The sheep had brought flies with them. We sat on the verandah with rolled-up newspapers and swatted flies. Nine, twelve, fifteen, twenty-nine . . . 'I've killed thirty flies,' I would boast. 'Jolly good show. But I've killed thirty-five.'

'You're cheating!'

'No, you're cheating. That's my fly, not yours.'

People came and people went. Sometimes the verandah seemed to me like a seashore, with tides rushing in, depositing sea-drift, and out again. A car full of people might turn up from Harare, and they were all fed, and slept on the living-room floor. 'Milos! Bring tea . . . bring beer, make supper for ten. Make breakfast for sixteen.'

I lay on the verandah, and thought how alike in general pace and style are the lives of the blacks and the whites, the easy hospitality, the generosity. (Nor can we now say, But the whites are rich and the blacks poor.) Why then, if they are so alike . . . in fact my thoughts were the same as those before I left Southern Rhodesia in 1949. But in those days I had nothing to make comparisons with. My thoughts tended to be a blur of incredulity: how could people go on like this when it was obviously stupid? But now I had seen the world and knew that people went on like this everywhere.

Once I had wondered why Europeans were so obsessed with their racial superiority, and if it was a compensation for their having been so backward, so uncouth, while the civilizations of the Middle East and the East glittered and despised theirs. The European arrogance was only the boastfulness of the nouveau riche? Pride in white skin was because there was nothing much else to be proud of? But that was before I had watched an Indian girl trying all afternoon to make her dark face lighter: she was about to meet a possible bridegroom. Before I had read the poems of an Arab who was praising the pearl-white skin, the milk-white skin, of his girl, for, he said, Europeans did not know what they were talking about, when they were proud of their 'white' skins. For real poetic whiteness, you needed a girl who had been shut up in a shady room all her life, and never allowed near strong light.

What is this thing about whiteness? Yes, this is a naive question, ridiculous . . . but how was it possible, I marvelled, naively, that the Afrikaans right-wing was ready to risk everything in war for racial supremacy, when they had seen what happened in Kenya, and in Southern Rhodesia?

'The trouble with you people,' I say to the Coffee Farmer, 'is that you have no historical sense whatsoever.'

'I don't know about that,' he says. 'Anyway, we gave them a jolly good scrap.'

'But for God's sake, it was all unnecessary, there need never have been a war, everything could have been settled without that, without all the waste and death and suffering.'

'But things can *always* be settled without wars, if people want. So why aren't they?'

So we argue.

In the mornings I was awakened by a soft, shurring, silken

sound, like wind in leaves. The man whose task this was crouched over the coffee beans that were laid out in long rows to dry, on the slope outside the house. They had got damp in the night dews, and needed to be stirred and turned. Shrrrr, shrrrr, shrrrr . . . he crouched there, his hand turning and turning the beans with a movement not unlike that used for turning curds that will be cheese. Sometimes there were two, or three of them. I listened to the low soft sound of African talk, African laughter. What are they talking about? I ask Milos. 'They are talking about the Comrades,' was the usual reply – meaning the battalion stationed a couple of miles away. 'They just want the Comrades to go away.'

But it was not always the Comrades. I stood with the Coffee Farmer watching a crowd of women and half-grown children, the casual labourers – the Grey Area – loading bags of coffee on to a lorry. 'What are they singing?' I ask. 'You'll like this,' said he. 'They are singing, Here we are, as usual, working away, while white people stand watching us. But never mind, quite soon it will be Saturday and we'll have a party and get drunk.'

In the living-room where the great fire burned it seemed there were parties most evenings. 'Milos! Bring beer. Milos, bring coffee, Milos . . .'

'He's a good old chap. When you've gone I'll send him off for a couple of weeks and he can go to his village and get drunk day and night if he wants. Well out of sight of his wife. She gives him a bad time.'

'Do you realize how hard that man works?'

'Of course he works hard. So do I. Anyway, he keeps an army of friends and relations in that house of his back there.'

'House, you call it.'

'It would be perfectly adequate for him and his wife and children. Anyway, if I paid them any more I'd go bankrupt. Well, that's what this government wants I suppose.'

'That hasn't changed, at least – farmers saying they are going bankrupt. Of course this government doesn't want that. You're here to earn foreign currency.'

'Then why doesn't it pay us what it owes us? They'll put off paying us for months. You've got to go down on your knees and beg for the money. They keep it to the last possible second because it's earning interest. Anyway, they're incompetent.'

'Of course they are. You didn't give them training for real responsibility and now you are paying for it.'

And now, a silence, because we do not want to begin, again, the real argument. Instead I make a detour. 'Your trouble is that you people are unkind. Heartless. I wonder what it must have been like living under this cold angry disapproval. What it must still be like, for that matter. Bossy. Cold. *Unkind.*'

'I only disapprove of them when they deserve it. I respect them when they deserve it.'

'You mean, you respect them for qualities you think of as white qualities.'

'If you like.'

So we argue.

Some years ago a book came out called *Operation Rhino*. It described how threatened rhinoceroses were transported by lorry and by air to new habitats. The author wrote about these beasts with the tenderest solicitude, with imaginative sympathy. Helping him in his task were dozens of Africans. They were – had to be in the course of things – poor, needing everything. I read the book through once, enjoying the expertise of the author in the ways of the rhino. Then I went through it again to see how these helpers of his in an after all dangerous operation, were described. They weren't. They were taken for granted. But each rhino was described so that you felt you would recognize it if you met it in a zoo.

It is said that on Liberation certain villagers went out into the bush and slaughtered large numbers of animals, because concern for them had become associated with white values: care for animals, but indifference to themselves.

THE WOMAN WALKING
UP THE MOUNTAIN

On a drive through some particularly dramatic mountains, this happened: in the car were the Coffee Farmer, The Assistant, and I. We were going up a steep hill. In front walked a young black woman. She was very pregnant, had a baby on her back, held a small child by the hand. She was walking slowly. Understandably. I knew that the two men had literally not seen this woman. Her need was invisible to them.

'How about giving her a lift?' My voice was stiff with fury, a build-up from weeks of anger, from years of past anger as a young woman, and the anger due to the moment. I knew we would not be giving her a lift.

'You know she wouldn't expect it.'

'You could establish a precedent, couldn't you?'

The Assistant can't believe his ears. He has been told about my funny ideas, like the ideas of those bad people the Swedes, but brought up as he has been, he has never heard any.

Wrangling, we drive slowly up the steep hill past the pregnant woman.

It is The Assistant who is disarming me. I know quite well that if he had to sit beside this black woman and her children he would probably suffer some kind of nervous attack. Yet he couldn't possibly be a 'nicer' person, as we say. I would remember him, I knew, for his quality of puppyish, unformed, decency.

One evening, when a horde of guests had descended, our host had remarked it was a pity all the hams, sausages, and so forth had vanished in the accident.

'What do you mean, vanished?' asked The Assistant.

'They were stolen,' said the Coffee Farmer.

The Assistant thought. 'You mean the Affs stole *your* food? That's not right. People shouldn't steal.'

'Of course they should have stolen it,' I said. 'Probably none

of them had ever seen such a cornucopia. We were like a travelling delicatessen.'

He thought, he puzzled. For one thing, he did not know the
words cornucopia, delicatessen.

'Just imagine it,' I said, 'what all that food must have seemed
like, hams and bacon and sausages scattered all over the road,
like a miracle.'

'But it's not right to steal,' he said.

The conversation in the car ended: 'And anyway, she's
bound to be a Squatter. I'm not giving lifts to Squatters.'

'I should say not, it wouldn't be right,' said The Assistant.

Since then an obvious thought has added itself to those
already in my mind which I might have had before: no one was
likely to give this woman a lift. Who? Certainly not the new
rulers of the country, flashing about in their great cars, their
motorcades. Perhaps some local missionary, or a doctor . . .
everywhere in the world this peasant woman, with one (or
two) babies inside her, one on her back, one or two clutched
by the hand, is slowly walking up a mountain, and we can be
sure that few people see her.

INNOCENCE

The innocence of the farm assistant made me think of a certain
television programme, towards the end of the Bush War, when
it had become evident the 'Affs' were going to win. Half a
dozen young whites were talking. They were the new type of
young white, to be seen in Australia, South Africa, New Zealand, Canada, different from their elders and from their con-
temporaries who have elected not to change. They are
immediately recognizable by their open and smiling readiness.
Charm. They are like friendly children. These were chatting
away about the War, in a confiding way, offering to the viewers
as an experience we were being privileged to share with them,
their coming to a mature understanding. 'And now we are

going to need your help,' they cried engagingly. 'You must help us!' They meant themselves, the whites, who were about to change their ways and become good citizens of a mixed society. It was *they* who deserved help, and they were appealing to the world with confidence they were going to get it. *It was their due.* All their lives they had been due everything, and they expected everything still. I watched this programme not really surprised, since I know my compatriots. The telephone rang. It was my friend the black man who might ring up to share certain moments. 'Did you see that?' he asked. 'I certainly did.' 'Can you believe it?' 'Well, yes, I am afraid I can.' 'God,' he breathed, 'how is it possible? *We* have been exploited, *we* have been ground down, *we* have had our country stolen from us. But it is *they* who have to be given tender loving care.'

MISSIONARIES

Two young white missionaries, a married couple, have dropped in. They have been six months in Zimbabwe. For the whole of an afternoon they exchange with their hosts critical anecdotes about the Africans and the black government, watching to measure how well they are fitting in with what is expected of them. They radiate the self-satisfied cheerfulness I associate with a certain type of Christian. I find this scene more than usually depressing: I used to watch it as a girl. People who in England would be 'liberal' here can adjust themselves, are even more anti-black than their hosts. Their voices: condemning, sniffy, superior, cold. Again I listened to The Monologue.

LEAVING

It is time to fly home. I have not been back to the old farm, though for the six weeks of the trip I have talked about it. Yes, yes, of course I must go, it is childish not to. But really I don't want to. The same reluctance that in 1956 made it impossible to turn the car's steering wheel into the track to the farm, gripped me still. The person I should have gone with was my brother, already packing to Take the Gap. He had shut a door on the past and I understood him perfectly. 'That's it. Cut your losses! Goodbye!' Besides, petrol was so short. And besides, it was the worst time of the year, the rains had not come to the farms in the north-east, the bush would be dry and the air full of dust.

I said goodbye to the humans, to the little black cat, to wicked clever little Vicky, to the sweet stupid ridgeback, and to the fierce bull terrier. Saying goodbye to humans is one thing: almost certainly you will see them again, but to animals, now that has to be a real goodbye.

THE SQUATTERS

As I turned off the farm on to the main road, which was not more than a track itself, soldiers from the battalion were marching up from the camp, through the gum trees. They were full of the raw confident energy of a recently victorious army.

Two miles from the farm I stopped for two women and they got in the back seat, with their baskets and their bundles. Yes, they were going down to Mutare, and the bus was late. They had already waited two hours. They looked about fifty, were probably younger. They were like poor women everywhere in the world, women you don't notice because there are so many of them, shabby, overweight from poor food, old too early, tough, wary, cunning, surviving. They did not want to talk, though one had a good bit of English. They were Squatters, and I had come off the farm of an enemy. Five miles on I slowed to pick up an old man who was toiling up a hill, and using a stick as if he needed it to keep upright. They did not want me to, made annoyed *sotto voce* exclamations as they moved their things to make room. But when he got in, they all exchanged courteous greetings, and talked like neighbours until, five miles on, the old man tapped my shoulder to make me stop. He carefully got out. He lifted his hand in farewell to the women, and then, the hand allotting more formality, to me. He carefully made his way into trees, leaning on his staff. I drove on, down to Mutare, while the women chatted softly. I knew that if I understood what they were saying, I would be learning more than I had in my weeks in Zimbabwe. But I not only did not know the local language, I did not know Shona. When I was growing up no white child learned Shona.

In Mutare there were complicated negotiations at the garage, over petrol. The women asked if I was going to Harare, and I said yes. They said they would come with me. There was more than a hint of command in their voices. They directed me to go to a certain hotel where they would tell a relation this and that, who would tell another that and this, and then they must buy some presents for Harare relatives. I sat in the car under a flame tree, and looked at the people walking up and down the slow lazy streets of this always slow-moving town, and wondered if this visit would stop the miles-long Main Street appearing regularly in my dreams as a symbol for difficult journeys.

The women returned, with suitcases, and got into the back seat. Off we went. It was going to be a long drive, because my inner monitor or governor still would not let me drive faster than about fifty miles an hour. I began to sweat and tremble if I did. The women were commenting on my slowness, but I did not want to alarm them by explaining I had been in a car accident. I was understanding a good bit of what they were saying, by intonation. They had decided I was one of the 'good' whites, because I was giving them a lift. They asked if I lived on one of the coffee farms and I said, No, I was from England, and this explained everything. We began a real conversation. Their lives were full of difficulties, mostly because between them they had seventeen children. They were sisters. One husband was dead, killed in the War because he was asleep in a hut set on fire by Smith's men. The other husband had a job in Mutare in the supermarket. Some of the children were in school in Mutare. The smaller children lived with them, the mothers – in other words, up in the mountains, in the Squatters' huts. There was one son in good work, in a hotel, but the oldest son of one sister had never worked, and he was drinking. The women were worried because two children would end school this year, and where would they get work?

We talked on and off on the long slow drive from Mutare to Harare, and there was an incident interesting enough to remember. I saw a tall very thin young man flailing his arms about to make me stop and give him a lift. I was slowing when both women leaned forward and energetically shook my shoulders, two strong hands commanding me to drive on. First I thought, But it's like the old man on the mountainside, they want the back seat to themselves, but then they said, 'He's a bad man. He's a skellum from the War. You must not give lifts to bad people.' I said, 'But you have to trust people.' I heard the feebleness of it as it came out of my mouth. Why did I say it? I don't believe it, but something in their picture of me had brought the foolish words out of me. I have more than once been surprised at myself when other people's expectations of me make me say things, do things, I like to think are not in character.

The two women were looking full in each other's faces with wonderful expressions of derision, of amusement. The older leaned forward to give me a lesson. 'You must look carefully at a person's face, then you can see if he is good. That one is very bad. The War made many bad people. He would steal your money and our suitcases.'

They had written me off as a fool, and their manner towards me changed. Soon they tapped my shoulder: a roadside stall had come into view. I stopped. They went to the stall, stood talking for a time with the old woman who was selling. To hurry over a transaction like this is not the way of the country. They brought back cans of soft drinks and opened one for me. Then, without asking me, they peeled an orange for me, and as I drove they handed segments over my shoulder, nodding with approval as I put them into my mouth, as if I were one of their children.

In Harare they asked if they could come with me when I went back to Mutare. I said I was going to England tomorrow. I could hear my voice, forlorn, regretful. They heard it too. 'Then we will be meeting next time.' And to their cries of 'Next time! Next time!', I went into the hotel.

Next Time

1988

When life arises and flows along artificial channels rather than normal ones, and when its growth depends not so much on natural and economic conditions as on the theory and arbitrary behaviour of individuals, then it is forced to accept these circumstances as essential and inevitable, and these circumstances acting on an artificial life assume the aspects of laws.

Anton Chekhov, The Island.
A Journey to Sakhalin

MEANWHILE

It was six years before I returned to Zimbabwe in 1988, and meanwhile all of Southern Africa was on a full rolling boil. This was mainly because of South Africa's determination that all of the southern part of the continent should remain dominated by the whites. During those years The Republic's subversion of her neighbours reached a height of unscrupulousness, of nastiness. South African armies kept Namibia and Angola at war, and it is not possible to exaggerate the cruelty of these armies. In Mozambique Renamo did its worst work. South African agents were busy in peaceful Botswana, and it was not unknown for them to murder South African citizens who had taken refuge there. Zimbabwe stood four-square, confronting South Africa, resisting 'destabilization'.

Internally The Republic reached heights of repression. The world was told about it, but inconsequentially, intermittently: a spotlight touches a place and moves on. There was a law that prevented any journalist, from inside or from outside the country, seeing anything the government did not want to be seen. I think, when we know it all, the story will be much worse than we ever thought.

The horrors of the place were masked, as always has been the case, because what is seen by most visitors is the pleasantness of life for the whites, and because social apartheid improved – no longer were there different queues for whites and blacks in shops and banks, and the races mixed easily in restaurants and hotels. But all my life I have been hearing, 'Never mind about the towns! It's the countryside, it's the farms, it's the little dorps where no journalist has ever gone. If people knew what went on there . . .'

Zimbabwe was surrounded by countries where South Africa played puppet-master – surrounded by civil wars and by failure, as in Zambia to the north. Zimbabwe was suffering from a siege mentality, and its leaders were at least in some things paranoid. In Matabeleland, so they believed, and so all the world was told, guerilla armies lurked in the bush that seems made for guerilla war. There were murders in isolated white farmhouses, and some were burned down. How easy to believe that South Africa pulled the strings here too. Mugabe's response to this threat was to send in troops that were mostly Mashona, and they terrorized villages up and down Matabeleland in a consistent and deliberate and merciless policy of intimidation. They pillaged, they murdered, they raped, they burned. In some villages half the inhabitants were killed. When they talk about this time some people start weeping or cursing or both, for these savage events wounded Zimbabwe's idea of itself.

And then Comrade Mugabe behaved like a statesman and offered an amnesty. This was the famous Unity Accord of December 1987 when Joshua Nkomo came in out of the cold. He was minister first in the President's office, and then became one of two senior ministers. Instead of the expected armies of guerillas, a couple of dozen men gave themselves up. They were former Freedom Fighters who had taken to the bush to express their disapproval of Mashona domination of Matabeleland, and because Joshua Nkomo was not in government, and because – probably the real reason – it is hard for men who have a talent for war to become unregarded civilians.

And something else bad happened in those decisive six years. Corruption has overtaken every newly independent country in Africa, and Zimbabwe too, though Comrade Mugabe exhorted, pleaded, threatened and passed well-intentioned laws. A new class known jocularly by the populace as the Chefs had arrived.

A United Nations official remarked, not in an official report, but during one of those unofficial conversations that are probably more influential: 'It is not exactly unknown for the victorious side in a civil war to line their pockets, but Zimbabwe is unique in creating a boss class in less than ten years and to the accompaniment of marxist rhetoric.'

But reading newspapers from Zimbabwe, letters from Zimbabwe, listening to travellers' tales, what came across was not the flat dreary hopelessness of Zambia, the misery of Mozambique, but vitality, exuberance, optimism, enjoyment.

AIR ZIMBABWE

That night on Air Zimbabwe, November 1988, announcements were made like this: 'Comrade Minister, ladies and gentlemen, please fasten your seat belts . . .' 'Comrade Minister, ladies and gentlemen, the non-smoking sign has been switched off and . . .' The *Comrade Minister* was said as if the minister were a box of sweets to be shared out among us passengers. On board were many large and solidly-suited black men on their way home from international conferences, making us whites seem a casual and unserious lot. There was one person who united us all in respectability, compared to his magnificent otherness: a pop star, a young black man glittering and swaggering, like a bullfighter or a Pearly King. Six years earlier the air hostesses had been as nervous as foster-parents on trial, but now they were maternal and firm, and when the lights were turned down and the troubadour sang gently to his guitar, they would have none of it, and ordered him to sleep, preferring their lullaby, 'Comrade Minister, ladies and gentlemen, the captain and the cabin staff wish you good night.'

Immigration was a confident young man, Customs another, and there at last were the skies of Harare, a deep and sunny blue, and the foliage was rich green, the rains having come last week. I was driven through a suburb that this time I was actually seeing, inappropriate emotions having taken themselves off. What I saw was streets that kept going out of focus and blurring with remembered street patterns and vanished buildings. We are all of us used to towns that collapse here and there in geysers of dust, quickly transforming themselves into towers, gardens, new streets, but I had not gone through this day-by-day process with Salisbury, which is like living with a person: you hardly notice the slow erosion of a face, or how features re-create themselves. When I left in 1949, when I visited in 1956, the town was still a cross-hatching of avenues and streets sketchily laid over the veld, ratified by trees and gardens as a town. Now you drive through the central part, business and administrative, to get to Harare's expanding suburbs, glossy, rich, with gardens that in Britain you would have to pay an entrance fee to see. I said, 'Do you realize what a paradise you people live in?' – and remembered I had said that before, though it was not what I thought when I lived there.

This house is deep under trees that hold the heat off, and there we were in a room with gardens on two sides, and soon we stood in the garden itself, two acres of it, containing, as a quick census established, several hundred different kinds of plants. Birds swooped about, notably the purple-crested lourie, with its creaking fateful cry.

In the old days, visiting a farm, you were 'taken around the place'. It is the settlers' instinct, showing to fellow civilizers of the wilderness what has been achieved, and on behalf of all of them. 'See what I've carved out of the trees, out of the grass-lands, see my house, my animals, my plants, my good strong roof which may very well have to shelter you too some-time . . .' so a dog eases itself into a new sleeping corner, fitting his back into a curve, stretching out his legs. He drops his muzzle gently on his paws . . . 'Yes, that's the size of it, that's what it is like, this place of mine.'

When Ayrton R., my host, showed me his house, his place, he was doing what he had seen done as a child, for he had been born and brought up in the country, just as I had.

We stand in the middle of this garden and breathe in garden air, facing up to the house that lies in a long curving shape, made longer by a discreet wall screening the servants' quarters.

'Well, are they any better than they used to be?' I ask, mean-ing the accommodation for servants, once a small brick room, or two, that held the lives of one, two, three, servants, and often many of their friends as well.

'The rooms are much better, yes, but it depends on what they hold.'

'And what do these hold?'

'The gardener has eleven children, and sometimes he and his wife have them all here. And the cook has three, and they are sometimes all here. And she has her man living here too.'

'Illegally?'

'Not illegally these days. But that isn't what I wanted you to notice. What I've learned living here, is about space.'

'You have plenty of it.'

'Yes, but just take a look down there.'

At the end of the garden were two substantial patches of mealies, standing glossy and thick, and a patch of rape.

'That patch there is my mealies, for sweetcorn, and that other patch is theirs. When an African buys a house anywhere the first thing he does is plant a patch of maize, even if it isn't big enough to give them more than an occasional cob or two. Maize it has to be. It is a symbol. And that patch of maize appeared as soon as I set up house here. It was not a question of asking me: it is their right.'

'And then?'

'The rape is the relish. It makes sense, because that patch will keep them in green stuff, they pull a few leaves at a time. Full of vitamins. And when I dug up a guava tree I thought was in the wrong place – suddenly I was confronted by the cook and the gardener, both in tears, accusing me of an unkind heart. It was really their guava, do you see? So I planted another at once. Parts of this garden are their space. *Their right.*'

'That's something new, then.'

'Yes, it is. And now look up there.'

Up there is a ridge where, among well-established trees, are large houses.

'And up there the new Chefs live. Their houses are three or four times the size of this one. They wouldn't be seen dead even visiting a house like this. They wouldn't be seen talking to a mere university intellectual like me.' He sounds amused, more, full of relish: I was to learn that this relish, this enjoyment in the unexpected, was very much the note of new Zimbabwe.

Inside the house breakfast was on the table, presented by Dorothy, the cook, a plump smiling lady. Then we sat all

morning and talked, about Zimbabwe, with the same relish
and pleasure. I had seen by now that the miserable greyness,
the sullenness, of last time had gone – I had dreaded it, and
there had been no need.

We also talked about the servants as the whites have always
done, not only the minority who were able to see themselves
as a part of a pretty remarkable history. All around them that
sea of black people, whose lives were so different, who thought
so differently; hard ever to know about those lives, those
thoughts, but here, in this house, close as your family, are
these people, and so you talked about them, speculated, as if
from them you could learn everything about the rest.

And in any case Ayrton R. was afflicted by the unappeasable
conscience of the liberal, and suffered for the whole institution
of servants past and present. For the real wrong is that everyone, in the whole world, ought to be living in just such a house
as this one, with its large rooms and its comfort. And without
servants?

Dorothy had a baby at fourteen and was thrown out of
school, her parents seeing no reason why they should make
things easy for her. 'The terrible wastage, the destruction, of
African women,' mourns Ayrton R. seeing in Dorothy the
world's millions of women who get pregnant so young and
have to pay all their lives for their mistake. Dorothy had four
children, by different men. To keep the children, and often the
men, she ran a shebeen – an illegal drinking place. When
Ayrton R. was ill in hospital she came to him and said, 'I want
to come and look after you.' She had heard he was a kind
employer and besides, they were compatriots, both from Matabeleland. That was the luckiest day of his life, says Ayrton R.
Her life, however, is far from easy. Her room houses not only
her and her children but also the man who takes a good part
of her money, although he earns more than she does.
'Wouldn't she be better off without him?' I demand, full of
ridiculous indignation. 'Of course she would, but you must
have a man to walk behind when you go to the races or visiting,
to impress the other women. You should see Dorothy when
she's dolled up for the races! She's a real queen.'

The other servant, the gardener George, is a handsome smiling man who has created this garden under Ayrton R.'s guidance. The big problem in his life is his oldest daughter, who has a Spirit, which in her case shows itself by making her go rigid when she is criticized, and then she has to attack people. She is lazy and stupid, and when working for one of the new security firms – they supply guards for shops and houses, who are nearly all ex-Freedom Fighters – she had sex with all eight of the guards. The family makes visits to one nganga (shaman) after another, to get her accepted as an accredited medium, but they say she is an hysteric. If the ngangas would approve of the girl, the family's fortunes would be made. As it is they are very poor, though he is paid many times the minimum wage.

'Eleven children!'

'That's only the way we look at it,' says Ayrton R. 'He says you can never have too many. The main thing is to keep them fed and you can always do that. His wife has been trying to conceive her twelfth and failing and so she is depressed, because she feels she is no longer a true woman.'

'And what about educating them? How about health?'

'You've got to face it, there are a lot of people like him left. Perhaps more like him than like Dorothy, who is a modern woman. She's clever enough to be in the Cabinet – she'd be better than most of them. She goes to the family planning clinic and saves all the money that man of hers doesn't take off her to get her oldest son an education. *But* – although she is worth more than the gardener many times over, I couldn't pay her as much as he gets because his male pride would suffer. And she approves of that. She has a very strong sense of what is proper. I tried to get the building society to pay for more rooms for the servants, but they said no, it wouldn't add to the value of the house, and so, when there was a crowd back there when all her children arrived, I suggested she and her man should sleep in my spare room. She was terribly shocked. It wouldn't be right. I'm afraid she is a very authoritarian lady. When this AIDS business began, I told her about it, to make her take it seriously – because the government wasn't, then, and her reply was that all the sick people should be killed. I told her what she said shocked me, and she said, Then they should all be put in internment camps with armed guards.'

TALK ON THE VERANDAHS

And so for all of the first day we sit around talking, talking, while people come to visit, and I ease myself into Zimbabwe, this time cool as you like, dry-eyed as a judge, while facts and statistics (passionately offered) pile up in my mind, and pamphlets and reports appear from everywhere. No one talks about new Zimbabwe without partisanship, and during the next day, and then the next, people explain and complain and exhort while I think how pleasant to be in an atmosphere where not only everyone cares so much but assumes they can immediately and effectively influence events. How unlike life in Britain, or anywhere in Europe, where long ago decisions have been removed from the levels where citizens have their being, to summits of power high above their reach. And all this time I listen for the equivalent of The Monologue, but that has gone, as they say, into the mists of history. Instead certain phrases recur in every conversation and the most often heard is 'Why does he . . . Why doesn't he . . .' – that is, Mugabe – do this or that. At this time in Britain we ask why *she* does this or that, but there is this difference: there has never been a governing class or clique more visible than this new one of Zimbabwe, and we are not talking about inaccessible heights shrouded by committees and quangos.

Every conversation at once turns to the Unity Accord, between Zapu and Zanu, Matabeleland and Mashonaland, Mugabe and Nkomo, the Accord which has transformed the atmosphere, everyone optimistic, everyone saying, 'At last Zimbabwe is one country.' Then they ask, Why didn't he do it before? If it worked immediately in 1987, then it would have worked earlier. How was it that Mugabe didn't know the dissidents were so few? Why did the whole country believe that armies of the Ndebele were involved? If Mugabe didn't know the enemy consisted of a handful of men now described by everyone as Terrorists, then why not? Did he not have spies and informers?

Why does President Mugabe not stop his ministers and officials from being so greedy? The reply to this is that the corrupt ones are those who keep him in power. But no one wants to believe this: at this time all talk of Mugabe is fuelled by idealism, of a kind frightening to some people who remember similar talk about despotic leaders. But Mugabe is not a despot . . . but Mugabe could easily become one . . . but now Nkomo is up there with him he won't allow Mugabe to be a despot . . .

Where is President Banana? He is no longer President, he is a Professor in the university, and a popular one.

The university is talked about all the time, because the students have just been on strike over corruption, for every day there is a new scandal about ministers and high-ups, involved in every kind of fraud, embezzlement, theft. The students rioted in the name of the Revolution and its ideals, appealing to Mugabe, expecting Mugabe would stand by them. But he did not. The police went into the university and behaved stupidly. They fired tear-gas grenades into rooms where the students were hiding. Many were hurt. But worst of all was the cynicism and disillusion. It is interesting how people talk about Mugabe when they think he has made a mistake; it is in a sorrowful perplexed tone, repeating the same words through an evening, Why did he let them down? How could he have done it? He was himself a revolutionary and he knows how dangerous it is when young people get cynical . . . he ought to be treating the students as his natural supporters . . . I can't help feeling he is badly advised . . . who is advising him? – why does he let himself be so shut off from everyone, so remote? . . . he shouldn't have let them down. Why? What do you think was in his mind?

Parallel to the Why does he? Why doesn't he? is 'Mugabe says . . .' Nothing is more interesting than what leaders and satraps are supposed to have said, for here speaks the voice of popular myth-making, voices of hope or of cynicism. It doesn't matter whether the Leader has actually used the words attributed to him, for the force and effect are the same.

How very attractive is this talk, is the intense personal involvement in Zimbabwe. The spasms of cynicism, and not only about the current corruption scandals, are only the opposite side of the coin. The people in this room include those who, in the Bush War, supported Mugabe, supported Nkomo, supported Bishop Muzorewa, but now they are all speaking in the same way. What way? I swear this isn't far off being in love. One may be in love with a country or the phase of development of a country as one is with a person. Incredulous, tremulous hope . . . uncertainty . . . amazement at the beloved's perfections and achievements. Exaggerated disappointment at moments of failure. I was listening to people who spoke of corruption scandals with the raging grief appropriate to betrayed love.

For instance, the car scandal. Because Mugabe will not allow cars to be imported into Zimbabwe (or anything else, not spare parts for cars, not farm machinery – nothing, forbidding the necessary with the frivolous) there is a local factory permitted to make Toyotas. They are vastly expensive, three times what they would cost in Europe. Only the rich can afford one, but even the rich can't get hold of one, because they are supposed to be for the Chefs. A minister or similar privileged person is informed by the factory his car is ready. He, or she (there are a few women in high positions) rings up a friend who is not on the list for a car. Before the car is delivered it has already been sold for several times the cost. It is said that 'everyone' is involved in this scandal, 'people you'd never expect would dirty their fingers with it'. Why does Mugabe not . . .

A BETRAYED LOVER

'I expected a period of incompetence. I expected every kind of mess and muddle. I knew nothing would work for a time. How could it when they didn't have the trained people? But what I didn't expect was that these bastards would get into power and then not care about anything but feathering their own nests. There are dozens of them, noses in the trough, getting rich quick. Do you imagine they care about those poor bastards out in the Reserves – yes, they are still the reserves, you can give them a new name if you like – but they don't give a shit. And if you imagine the students were rioting last term because of corruption, don't you believe it. Oh yes they sound pure and noble but that isn't it. They know the layer of jobs in the civil service and the government they ought to get themselves – but they'll never get in there, because all these jobs were filled by the Comrades coming in from the bush, still in their twenties, who have got decades of working life in front of them, and the students will have nowhere to go and they know it. They want to get their noses in the trough too . . .' So he raged.

THE AESTHETIC APPROACH
TO REVOLUTION

'They have all this money, they build themselves houses that would be seen as shocking taste even by Thatcher's *nouveau riche*. You simply wouldn't believe what they are building, nothing to do with the country or the climate, stupid little windows, a mincing suburban refinement, but boastful and ostentatious at the same time. They fill these houses with furniture that no one would be seen dead with in Britain. There isn't one thing in their houses that isn't hideous. You stand there looking at these houses and you want to weep at the awfulness of it all.'

'But surely that is how it always is? First there is the generation that makes the money, all vulgarians full of crude vitality, without scruples. Then their children, who don't make money, they spend it, and who laugh at their parents for bad taste. Then the third generation who go in for art and liberalism and

fine feelings – history often describes them as effete. So why
are you so upset this inevitable process is taking place in
Zimbabwe?'

Because this is Zimbabwe – is the real reply. This man, a white
born and brought up here is in love with the dream of Zimbabwe and he was supporting it when to do so meant ostracism
from his own kind. He cannot endure any blemish on his love.

To be in love with a country or a political regime is a tricky
business. You get your heart broken even more surely than by
being in love with a person. You may even lose your life. I
knew a woman political activist in the old days – in this case,
the 1950s. She spent her days and her nights working to undo
the white regime in South Africa. Needing a rest, she went to
visit Nigeria, to see her dream made flesh, found it was run by
human beings, and committed suicide. Everyone who has been
involved with idealistic, rhetorical, politics knows a thousand
versions of this story, from all over the world.

It has to be recorded that Dorothy admires the new house
being put up half a mile away, a horror of a house you would
think had been designed to illustrate how many mistakes could
be made in a single building – she loves it to the point her eyes
go all misty at the sight or even the thought of it.

'And Zimbabwe has all these fine architects. Did you know
that? Our architects are some of the best in the world. They
win prizes – in other countries. So they are leaving to take jobs
in countries where they are appreciated. These clever boots
employ architects from Eastern Europe whose idea of building
is Stalinesque grandiosity. I tell you, it is enough to break your
heart.'

After 'Why does Comrade Mugabe . . . ?' the most often
heard set of words is, 'The women do everything in this
country. They do all the work. The men sit about, and the
women keep things going. If you want anything done, then
you have to reach the women.'

A VISIT TO SIMUKAI

I was taken by Judy Todd to visit Simukai, established and run by ex-Freedom Fighters, men and women. As the War ended, while they waited at the assembly points to be demobilized, they imagined this farm, decided to make it.

Some miles from Harare a sign said, 'Simukai Collective Farm Welcomes You' near a small store, a shed-like building whose shelves have on them more soft drinks than the nutritionists would be pleased to see. It was after midday, very hot, and people lazed on the store verandah, mostly women knitting and crocheting. The men were asleep. It turned out that the chairman Andrew was away. He is famous, a man of principle, whose socialism refused to envisage differences between men and women. 'Here we have only comrades,' first he – and then they all – decided. This meant that when a certain feminist arrived to discuss the oppression of women, she was told there were no men and women, only people working on equal terms, but probably the person she would like to talk to was the comrade, a woman, who drove the tractor.

This tale has the quality of myth, standing for so much more than its bare facts, symbolizing new Zimbabwe – like other tales about this farm where many visitors are taken.

This was a white farm, and the old pattern of spread-about farmhouse, farm buildings, animal sheds, is here, and it is easy for me to see the old life, the single white family, and its animals – and now the same place is filled with several black families.

The level of poverty, that is the point, and what is so hard to convey: impossible for a person from Europe to imagine, let alone someone from rich America.

A small brick building is the new school and it represents so much hope, effort, work, sacrifice on everyone's part.

And here I meet, and within a few days of my arrival, that note, or theme, which soon I see as the main one, I think, of Zimbabwe at this time. It is this: how much a small thing, a single building, or animal, or little garden, or a dedicated person can mean, transforming a whole district.

This meagre little school where remarkable people teach, will be remembered by – how many children?

There is a new dam, where they plan to grow fish.

Trees are being planted.

Everything here, which to an eye used to the riches of European farming seems so small and bare is like a step taken with feet that have iron weights on them.

We are taken to see a workshop, once part of a tobacco barn, where a young woman is making overalls. Then to a little house where small children and babies are being looked after. A tiny child, not used to white faces, bawls in terror and is hushed by an older child who sends us embarrassed smiles. In another former tobacco barn meals are cooked and eaten communally.

The farm grows maize, cattle, sheep, pigs, tobacco, wheat, sugar beans.

I asked what, if they were given a wish, they would choose.

This is a question which often gets surprising answers.

We had been driving through rich farms where miles of fields showed the brilliant whirling sprays of irrigation machines. These are now called Commercial Farms, meaning individually-owned high-tec farms, either black or white. I expected the reply would be, irrigation, silos, a new landrover, a refrigerated truck.

Two young men, polite but sleepy, for after lunch on a hot day is not the best time to go visiting, replied in the tones of practised speechmakers, 'To raise the standard of living.' 'To improve the lives of our people.' This kind of conversation often disappears into mists of misunderstanding and the need for definitions – and then smiles, full of good feeling, but embarrassed.

'No, no,' I said. 'What technique or machine or piece of equipment would this farm find most useful now, at this time?'

There was a long silence.

'The farmer who had this farm was very rich,' said one young man, offering this to me, I could see, as a starting-off point.

Given this level of poverty, what standard of living did I have in mind? That of the white family who lived here? To give so many families the same would take more money than this farm had even begun to think of. Was I suggesting that every child would have a room full of toys and a bicycle, young people a car each or the use of one, trips to Europe every year or so?

Such questions could be asked, I could see, but I had not been thinking of past white affluence.

Then one young man brought definition to our talk, when he enquired if I had connections with Aid money. Did I work for an Aid organization? Both of them became animated. Some of the amenities on Simukai had been paid for with Aid money. How much money could I give them?

I said I was not connected to an Aid organization.

I saw they were thinking, Here is another visitor, who likes the way we work so hard.

I was thinking that this was rather like being in Pakistan, meeting refugees all day, who had come out from Afghanistan with nothing but what they had on their backs. Our group despaired several times a day: if we had a million pounds to spend, it would all disappear in half a morning, and still do nothing very much.

THE FIGHTERS

Judy Todd has been involved with settling Freedom Fighters in jobs and on farms. Not all the difficulties were foreseen. For instance, a certain young man complained that when he applied for jobs, he was granted an interview but as soon as he gave his particulars a job mysteriously became unavailable. And what name was he giving? 'Comrade Spillblood'. Other names that proved unappealing to employers were Comrade Instant Death, Comrade Advance Zimbabwe, Comrade Lightning, Comrade Ceasefire, and Comrade Drink Blood.

THE DISSIDENTS

A Swedish journalist was present at that anticlimactic event
when the Matabele dissidents gave themselves up under the
amnesty.

The scene was a shabby room in a police station. In the
middle stood a dozen or so desperadoes slung all over with
weapons, including one Gayiguso, famous because he had
recently killed sixteen people with an axe. The police accepting
their submission were unarmed. The world's journalists were
sitting around the walls. They had been told not to ask provocative questions, because 'of the spirit of reconciliation under the
Unity Accord'. Unable to think of anything more interesting,
one cautiously enquired, 'And how do you feel now?'
Expecting – perhaps? – reflections on the key fact that it is
possible indeed, increasingly common, for a few people, even
half a dozen, to bring whole countries into civil unrest, or civil
war – to destroy the very frail stuff of civilization. The reply
from the intrepid Gayiguso was the confidence that they
wanted to sleep in a nice bed and have some food. After all,
they had been living in the bush for ten or so years, in caves
or where they could, raiding food from villages or fields, or
forcing villagers to feed them. An uncomfortable life, even
when not murdering people and burning homes. Their hard-
ships, they seemed to feel, deserved sympathy. 'I've never
seen a rougher crowd of men,' said the journalist.

When these 'dissidents' returned to their villages, their
families rejected them, saying they weren't wanted.

All kinds of people who had supported these men – believed
to be an army – now disowned them, including the students
who had demonstrated for them.

And now, what to do with them? They were put on to a
farm under sympathetic supervision, and soon became good
citizens, with a tendency to lecture the Youth on the need to
keep the law and respect government.

Reformed Terrorists are often taken like this. Many of the

Red Brigades in Italy, who suffered reverse conversions in prison, and demonstrated their capacity for citizenship by turning their prison cells into universities – writing memoirs, learning languages, taking degrees – when let out went about telling already perfectly good ratepayers and householders that it is important to abjure violence and illegality. I was told by a certain Italian that it had not been the least bizarre experience of her life, seeing a female ex-Terrorist who had murdered several harmless people lecture, 'with a sort of modest self-respect' a girl of fifteen (her own daughter) on the need for law and order.

NOVELS

Someone who had the idea of researching the over one hundred novels written by blacks which will never be translated into English, found something unexpected. Whites figure in these novels hardly at all, or when they do, often as helpful and Olympian figures, taking a child to hospital, or giving a lift. But you can read a couple of dozen such books one after another and not meet one white character. 'They are not interested in us,' said the man who told me this, amused, ironic. 'We assume they are fascinated by us, the way we are by them. But we are simply noises off, that is, down there in the villages.'

'Down there . . .' – the phrase is sometimes used ironically, meaning the rapidly enlarging gap between the poverty of the countryside and the riches of the towns, not because the countryside gets poorer but because the towns get richer.

Ayrton R. and I, both brought up in the country, he in Matabeleland, I in Mashonaland, and both remembering how the whites sat around discussing the ways of the blacks, talked about these hundred or so novels as a revelation.

'Then that means that if the whites left this country entirely most of the blacks wouldn't even notice? Perhaps it would become like those countries up north which are rapidly going back to old Africa, as if the whites had never been there,

everything is collapsing, nothing working, transport, telephones, roads, railways, the civil service, hotels – nothing
works.'

'Oh, no,' says Ayrton R. at once. 'The infrastructure here is
too sound.' He speaks protectively, and with pride.

Infrastructure is not a word that usually spends much time
in my mouth, but I seem to be hearing it and using it, several
times a day.

PASSIONATE PROTAGONISTS

A white person said . . . a black person said . . . I was taken
to task by one of the people who loves the new Zimbabwe,
and cannot endure the slightest blemish. Because blemishes
undoubtedly exist, she insists even more on political definitions: a not unusual reaction. 'We are all Zimbabweans now,'
she cries. 'We aren't black or white, we are people.' I say her
attitude is sentimental, unreal. She says mine is unhelpful, and
anyway, what does it mean, black, or white?

I say nothing could be easier. White means all the shades
from the ivory of skins that have never seen the sun to the
café-au-lait of the mixed-race people – usually called Coloured,
but it is a risky word, because the political 'line' changes so
often. Black means the gradations from this same coffee to the
velvety black of tropical Africa.

True that certain politicoes, particularly in the United States,
have decided that 'black' is reactionary, but the people these
sentimentalists claim to defend, namely, the blacks, use it all
the time.

JESUIT ACRES

It was Cecil John Rhodes himself who gave the Roman Catholics so many fat acres. They have always run schools, convents, training centres, missions. Some of the best schools in the country are Jesuit, Dominican. It seems no one grudges them these acres.

If one were to say their record does not deserve unmixed praise, then what does?

For instance, a friend of mine, whose grandmother was the storyteller for her clan, a famous lady, replied when I asked him, Do you remember your granny's tales, for if you do then you should record them before they vanish – 'I knew them when I was small, because that was how we Africans were taught about life then, through stories, but when I was put in Dombashawa School all that was beaten out of me. They said our culture was backward, and now I couldn't remember even one of those tales. They beat us and beat us. They beat us for anything and everything. You have a saying, I think, Spare the rod and spoil the child?' He laughed.

I am being taken on a trip to a Jesuit school, Silveira House, by Sister Dominica. She is a nun, but refuses to wear the uniform or accept discipline which she thinks arbitrary and foolish. She lives in a holy house but makes her own life. She is responsible for the recruitment and welfare of large numbers of young whites who teach mostly in remote parts of Zimbabwe and in very poor schools. She wears dresses, skirts, blouses, but with a large silver cross. A colleague, an equally independent soul, wears culottes and a halter top. They are feminists, critical of the male authority of the Church and the Pope.

I wonder what Mother Patrick would make of them? Kindred spirits, I think.

Sister Dominica was a nun at the convent where I did five years hard, from the ages of seven to twelve. We compared notes, from such different points of view about the administrative and teaching nuns, educated women from Ireland and from Germany, and about the ignorant peasant women, all German, who looked after us. If that is the word for it. For all these years I have remembered Mother Bertranda with gratitude. Once a child literally ill with homesickness crept towards the august office that was surrounded by a sea of grey granite chips crunching under feet trying to be silent, and, daring an upright pillar of black and white, the Dominican habit, climbed on to a lap that sloped away under the many slippery robes, and wept in arms that turned out, after a first stiffness of surprise, to be kind, warm, close, hospitable. Over the child's head Mother Bertranda exclaimed and consoled in German, swinging back and forth as strenuously as a rocking horse.

Sister Dominica said, 'Perhaps, but if you were a very young and frightened novice thousands of miles from home, you would have experienced her differently. She terrified us.'

Silveira House is an old school, privileged, funded, well-known. Comrade Mugabe taught a course on trade unionism here, I was told, with pride. The school consists of many single-storeyed brick buildings scattered among trees, and shrubs and flowers. Cats lie about in shady places expecting to be admired. The place is empty, because the pupils have gone for their holidays. We are taken over it by the principal, whose life links with mine, just as Sister Dominica's does. His family was German. He spent four years of his childhood in an internment camp near Salisbury. During the Second World War. My second husband, Gottfried Lessing, a German, was six weeks in the internment camp, then let out to pursue an ordinary life, instructed only to report once a week to a certain office, so lax a requirement he often did not bother and no one seemed to notice. He was anti-Nazi, but then so was the interned family. I listened to the principal describe his years in the camp, thinking about what makes the so different fates of people: often chance, luck, some small happening. About Zimbabwe he was talking in that voice characteristic for this time: anxious pride, a passionate need to explain and excuse – the pride for what is being achieved, the anxiety for what is needed, so much and for so many.

Under a group of trees was a spread of benches and tables, and on them all kinds of carvings in stone and in wood,

watched over by their creators, young men who are unemployed and hope to better their fortunes in this way.
Some of their creations are on sale in galleries in Harare.

There is also a good crafts shop, run by one of the forceful
women to be seen everywhere. From Sister Dominica I again
hear the words: It is the women that keep this country going.
They do all the work. Everywhere you look women are working
and men lazing about.

THE DIGESTER

Based at Silveira House is an internationally known expert on
alternative technology, Brian McGarry, at once recognizable as
one of that breed, people passionately concerned with saving
the world from our stupidities. He is, among other things,
trying to invent, adapt, devices to save energy, so that Zimbabwe's rapidly vanishing or thinning bush may be saved. In
some areas there are no trees left, and people dig up roots, or
burn thin handfuls of straw, competing with animals who need
to eat it, or even burning the light flat cakes of cow dung – and
this has not been common practice in this country – when dung
is needed for fertilizer.

There exists a solar stove, a natty little device, but it is not
popular, has no emotional appeal. You can't sit around a solar
stove the way you can around a fire, gossiping. If everyone used
the solar stove, then the forests of Zimbabwe would be saved.
Similarly, there is a useful contraption called a digester, easy to
make and cheap to install. A pit is dug near the living hut, and
fed with a slurry of animal dung or plants. Another pit takes the
spent slurry, to be spread on fields. From a small vent near the
main pit a pipe leads methane gas into the hut, to the cooking
area. In the middle of the hut we were shown was a large smok-
ing log with a pot standing beside it, and the gas pipe was not
working. That log has been burning in the middle of a cave, a
hut, a hall for – how long? Thousands of years? Millions? The
centre of communal life, family life, in every part of the world.

A COMMUNAL AREA

We were taken around by an instructor in agricultural and communal expertise, a middle-aged man called Peter Simbisai, an energetic character who was proud of what he and his kind are accomplishing. First to a family place of a traditional sort, a group of huts inside a fence. 'Here,' said he, 'lives an old man with his sons and their families, all here, with him.' Not looking at me, but past me, because of the criticism: 'We aren't like you people. You don't mind if your children leave home at eighteen, perhaps going as far away as South America. We like to keep our families together.' He spoke with reproach.

This kind of hut is not impressive from outside. Inside they are tall, airy, cool. A bench goes part of the way around the inside. About a quarter of the wall space is filled with cooking pots. Shelves hold clothes and crockery.

There is talk of a new tourist venture. Groups of people will be led on walking tours through the bush, spending their nights in villages – that is, in huts like this group of huts. Villages asked if they want to be on this tourist route have said yes.

We were driving through still fresh and uncut bush, the light and airy trees of Mashonaland, which are infinitely various, for unlike the forests of Europe, they have never been subjected to an Ice Age. That is why the trees and plants of Europe are so limited in kind: the Ice Age destroyed the old forests and the trees we know are what have taken hold since the ice retreated.

Peter wanted us to see something he said was important. Soon he was driving us through a Communal Area, an old one, which meant it had been a Reserve. I had known the Native Reserves in the old days. As the Colony of Southern Rhodesia was settled the blacks were moved off good land and put in the Reserves which were poor bleak places, often without roads, schools, clinics, even enough water. When Mugabe came to power he decided that the first necessity was to direct money to improve the rural areas. Someone who did not know what

the Reserves used to be like might not be impressed now, taken
to a Communal Area. They are still poor. What you at once see
is that the bush is impoverished, full of stumps, and most trees
have lost a limb, or two limbs, to the need for firewood. They
have been carefully pruned by people who know very well that
these trees of theirs are precious. The grass is thin. There are
gullies of erosion, or the slope of a field shows a scattering of
grit and pebbles where the rains have washed away the soil.
Groups of huts may be at distances of as much as half a mile.
The general effect is of emptiness, but in fact the soil is carrying
as many people and animals as it can – more than it should in
some areas. But what this imagined observer will not know, as
he speeds comfortably enough along the new good road, is
that the road was so recently a dusty or muddy track, that the
groups of brick buildings that occur here and there are new,
though the idea and the name Growth Points, originated under
the whites; that these Growth Points, consisting of clinic,
administrative buildings, schools, are expected to develop into
little towns, feeding services into the area; that the little fields of
maize and cotton and sunflower which seem so unimpressive
compared to the great rich red fields of the Commercial Farming areas are growing every year more and more of the
country's food – that, in fact, here is a transformation that can
be valued and understood only by people who know what it
was all once like.

THE SHED

Peter Simbisai wants me to see a certain shed. It is a large plain
lock-up shed with a cement floor. It is communally owned. At
its start, a great many families wanted to be in on this scheme.
In the impetuous early days of Liberation everything seemed
effortlessly possible, all kinds of people wanted to join all kinds
of communal schemes, which sounded easy, because in any
case working in groups was part of their tradition. But each

family not only had to put money into the materials to build the shed, but then help build it, and afterwards look after it. Someone always had to be there: this afternoon it was a young woman whose turn had come on the roster. She said that most families had left the scheme, leaving a nucleus who had built it up, and now people wanted to join it again, because it was changing the life of the area.

In the shed is a weighing machine for the sacks of produce, and to weigh people when doctors and nurses come. There is a heap of maize, seed maize, tinted blue and green as a warning not to eat it or feed animals with it. This seed maize is numbered R-201 and SR-52, developed in old Southern Rhodesia and valued now. We are expected to share ironical appreciation of the fact that this precious maize is expertise from the bad old days. In the shed, too, political meetings are held, educational classes of all kinds, and parties. The owners of the shed are proud its facilities are available to everyone, members or not, that it is a centre for the whole area, and such a success that other people in neighbouring areas are talking about building a similar centre. 'In good time this shed will become a Growth Point,' says the young woman, but she and the others are advising caution, having experienced the difficulties. Only people who seem likely to stick with it should be invited into the scheme.

Most of all, the problems of transport have to be solved. Having grown the crops and bagged them and weighed them and stored them here on the good cement floor where the animals cannot get in and eat them, and the white ants cannot tunnel, after all that – transport.

LORRY SERVICES

Everyone, anywhere in Zimbabwe who gets together a bit of money buys a lorry and sets up a transport firm. It is one of the quickest and easiest ways to get rich. The farmers living far from the markets, often far from Growth Points, are easy prey. They are forced to pay more than they should to get their produce transported. They are helpless until they can afford to buy their own lorry, and meanwhile they feel they are being bled by these conscienceless transport firms – which might very well be run by members of their own families. There is no legislation regulating what is charged for transport. 'Why doesn't Mugabe do something to protect us? He says we are the hope of Zimbabwe, we, the black farmers.' 'We are slowly building the infrastructure the whole country can build on . . .' 'The government should match their words with their deeds.' 'Comrade Mugabe should . . .'

THE STORE

This unimpressive shed was changing lives in a large area. Now we were to see something equally important. Again we drove through thinned and impoverished bush, full, however, of fat and contented cattle, because of the rains, to a village where there was a communal store, owned by the usual nucleus of families who had risked every bit of money they had to set it up. There was a regular store, doing well, and this new communal store was in competition with all that capital, wrung from them, the former customers. Their problem was of course the shortage of capital, and so their new clean scrubbed shelves had fewer goods on them than the commercial store. Peter had helped set this store up, and was proprietary and proud, and we were introduced to the owners, all proud and anxious, and there we stood about drinking Coca-Cola, or was it Pepsi-Cola, while I contemplated the cola revolution, for everyone drinks the stuff. These people who may not have enough money to feed their children enough protein will pay money for soft drinks, and on the shelves of the remotest stores are ranks of bottled tooth-rot and gut-rot and there too are the piled loaves of white bread. While I stood there gossiping, up came a young

man all smiles and good nature with that immediate childlike
lovableness that says, This person is not one of Nature's successes. He wanted to know if I would drive him to a place
many miles distant. The people I was standing with watched
me to see if I had understood, and when I replied in the formula
of the country that I would take him 'just now' – which is like
the Spaniard's *mañana* – they nodded approvingly. The young
man went off, satisfied, and one of the men said to me, not
'He is one of the afflicted of God', or 'He is simple', but 'He
has a short wire'. The use of this phrase seemed to me to sum
up pretty adequately what has happened to this society in one
hundred years.

MEAT, SADZA

We had lunch in Greendale Shopping Centre. These centres
are the equivalent of the Growth Points of the Communal
Areas. We ate meat. This was always a meat-eating culture.
You may begin a visit saying you'll stick to your near-vegetarian
habits, which suit you, but in no time give it up: it gets too
difficult. We ate beef. The beef grown in Zimbabwe is marvellous and, when exported, one of the country's successes. So
strong is the bias of the whole culture towards meat-eating it
is hard to believe they could ever agree it is wasteful to feed
grain to cattle instead of eating it direct, as grain. That really
would be a revolution. The whites have eaten meat ever since
they maintained themselves, or at least part fed themselves, on
shot game. The blacks were hunters when the whites came, as
well as farmers. Their main food now may be sadza, but they
always eat meat with it when they can.

During lunch we talk politics, but politics mostly as gossip.
This Minister had done this, that Minister is doing that. Never
has there been a ruling caste so visible to its people, never have
followers been so intensely and personally involved with its
leaders. Mugabe is owed one tone of voice, but the new caste

of fat cats are talked of with a sardonic appreciation of their comic possibilities. Is this, perhaps, politics as theatre? Yes, when politics are followed in places like Zimbabwe, in this close and personal way, it is the dramatic sense that is being fed. Characters really only life-size, are on an enormous stage where they are bound to seem ludicrous, pompous, laughable. But there is charity too: Let's see how they turn out – that's the feeling.

For several days I am driven around and about by people able to take time off work. We always come to rest outside the house or farm of a Chef, for a bout of the scandalous, relishing gossip.

'This house has been bought by . . .' 'That farm belongs to . . .' A Minister, or a businessman.

'The first thing they do, when they move in,' say the whites, 'is a mealie patch. That's how you can tell a Chef's house.'

'And why are you surprised?' demands the black man who is driving me one day. 'Of course we plant mealies.'

'But damn it, they aren't even African. The Portuguese introduced them.'

'And I believe roses were introduced into Europe from the Middle East?' he says, laughing with pleasure at going one better.

'Touché.'

'So why shouldn't we love our mealies?'

'No reason at all.'

'That's what I think.'

We are stationary outside the house of a Chef who was famous long before Liberation. I met him once, long long ago, a gentle, humorous, patient soul, who exemplified every virtue you can think of in the line of passive resistance. The whites loathed him and slandered him; the blacks looked up to him.

The Africans in the car today tell me that he is now famous for quite different qualities. He is bad to his servants. He has too many girlfriends. He drinks. He likes going abroad too much, wangles himself on to the commissions and committees so he can have trips to America and Europe. And it is well known he is one of the Ministers involved in the current car scandals.

After half an hour or so of discussion the driver calls everyone to order. 'Now, wait a minute, just – wait – one – little minute! What is this I hear? I think we have proved it is better to be poor, not rich? This poor Chef here, his character destroyed, ruined by success – a pity he wasn't left just where he was. Better to live like a dog, kicked by Life. Can it be this is what we have decided?'

'If that is what we have decided,' says his wife, 'then we must undecide it. Better to be a good dog than a bad Chef? No. Not me.'

'It's all right,' says her husband, driving on. 'You're safe. My salary won't allow you to be corrupt.'

'A pity, my dear.'

COMMERCIAL FARMERS

Are the Commercial Farmers good when they are black? The reply is that many have gone bankrupt. 'They seem to think' (the speaker is a white farmer who certainly works hard) 'that all you have to do is buy a farm and then it runs itself. They buy a store, a hotel, a transport business and a farm, and try to run them all. The farms are the first to suffer, but they don't always realize that: it's easy to put a few mombies on a farm and call it farming.' (Mombies, the word for cattle, sounds like the lowing of cattle, when soft, contented, conversational. It is a word pleasant to use and to hear.)

'And so they aren't good farmers?'

'They are good farmers when they are good farmers. But the really good black farmers are the small farmers. They do it properly.'

THE SMALL FARMERS

They do it properly on old-fashioned technology. Sometimes a small tractor is labouring across a small field, but the level of technology used by most blacks is the same as that used when my father was farming, by the whites. Oxen, not tractors, pulled ploughs, harrows, cultivators of the sort now to be found in farm museums, in Britain. Oxen dragged the wagon piled with sacks of grain or loads of manure.

The need for working oxen is what keeps the perennial debate between whites and blacks, conservationists and the farmers, alive and often acrimonious.

'Your trouble is that you have too many mombies on your land. It is overstocked.'

'My trouble is that I haven't enough land. I need more mombies to do the work.'

All the Communal Areas I have visited are in wildly beautiful country. The people living here are poor. Their lives when the rains fail are hungry. But surely it is better to be poor here, in this sunlight, this beauty, than, let's say, Bradford or Leeds. There ought to be different words for poverty that grimes and chills and darkens, and this poverty where people live in splendour, lifted up on to the Altitude into ringing windy sunscoured skies.

THE ALTITUDE

I had forgotten about the Altitude. Today, afflicted by a disinclination to do more than sit on the patio and watch the birds, I heard: 'But you are still getting used to the Altitude.' Where I was brought up the Altitude was held responsible for most ills. Being run down, another not easily defined condition, meant you should get off the Altitude, and getting on to it again needed a period of readjustment. The Altitude has a lot in common with contemporary dangers like radioactivity and ultra-violet rays which cannot be seen or felt, but strike you down nevertheless.

THE GREAT DYKE

The map of Zimbabwe shows that all of it stands high, except where certain rivers go, but along a ridge running slantwise on the eastern side, the Altitude is 5,000 to 7,000 feet. Banket is on this ridge, and the road running from Sinoia (Chinhoyi) to Harare, and the road from Harare to Mutare. The Umvukwe mountains are part of the ridge, but the name was heard wrong, the real sound is Mvurwi, and anyway, these days they are called the Dyke. I have been hearing the Dyke, the Dyke, in so many conversations, not realizing it meant only those mountains I spent so many years of my young life staring at, for it turns out this chain of mountains are considered to be the end bit (or one of them) of the Rift Valley, which as we all know, threatens to split Africa in a billion years or so. Perhaps where the Darwendale chrome mine now makes the flanks of the Dyke glitter with its spilled ores, will lap the waters of the Indian Ocean, and then this landlocked country, this plateau so high and dry-windswept, will be damp with sea winds. The Dyke is loaded with the minerals of half a continent, pushed southwards in a tongue through other geological formations, and the whole chain is carved with small workings, both new and abandoned, some from long before the white men came. The hills of the Dyke are bald and bare, so highly mineralized trees won't grow on them. It is hard to imagine an idea more attractive to the myth-making mind than this one, so casually proprietary with units of a million years, as is the way of those arch myth-makers, the geologists. You hear, 'He's farming on the other side of the Dyke'. 'It's on the Dyke, you know,' and you are meant to gather that much more is expected of the situation than if the Dyke never entered it at all.

THE ITCZ

Similarly, there is the ITCZ, which means the Inter-Tropical Convergence Zone, and it seems to crop up in every other conversation. This is mostly because of the tricky rains, which did come on schedule this year, after some unsatisfactory seasons. For years the drought in Matabeleland was serious enough to figure regularly in overseas news and it killed off over a million animals, in a population of eight million already reduced by the Bush War and dissidents. In a run of bad years there can be a good one, or a half-good one, and then the rains fail again. This year began well: but that doesn't mean it will go on well. All Zimbabwe, including Matabeleland, is green and watered, but now it is time the rains came again. The hot dry blue days that succeed each other, delighting me and other fugitives from November in Europe are making all the locals nervous. 'Why doesn't it rain? Those aren't rain clouds.' And we go indoors to watch the ITCZ prowling about on the satellite pictures of the television weather programme.

I remember how, then, we used to watch the skies to the north, from where the rains have to come, we felt the heat building, with a practised sense for the different densities and weights of heat, while the clouds piled higher every day and turned from silver to black. We said, 'The storks have arrived from Russia and from Turkey and East Europe and the chimneys of Germany and Denmark, so now the rains should start.' This year the storks have arrived well, and the fields around Harare are black with their multitudes, but the rains are holding off. It seems that the rains are generally starting later than they used. *Then* October was the rainmaker, some time in October the rains had to come, but now, it seems, November is when they start. The trouble is, the weather is at odds all over the world and temporary anomalies are instantly seized on as evidence for the worst. 'Oh no, the rains never start in October these days, the seasons have changed.'

TELEVISION

Most evenings we watch television, sitting there in front of the screen as if it were a child we expect to do better if it tried. In fact television is going well. In 1982 it was, quite simply, embarrassing. Everything was awful, the presenters gauche, newsreaders unpractised, and the rhetorics of the Revolution, crude. Now the programmes may not be up to much, most of them, but these are professionals who have learned from the best. Dazzlingly pretty girls, young men fit to be film stars, offer us the news – nearly all of it parochial. They inform us of the progress of the ITCZ, and act in advertisements as entertaining, if not as sophisticated, as the ones in Britain. Programmes from Britain are shown, basics, like Dickens, but nobody likes the British programmes, except for 'Yes, Minister'. 'The Povos enjoy watching Chefs having difficulties.' What everybody likes are the American programmes, 'Dallas', 'The Colbys', 'Dynasty' – the good life.

'In Britain I suppose we didn't have a choice – we are an American cultural colony . . .'

'Why Britain? All of Europe!'

'All right. But there is no reason why this country should have made that choice. There isn't money for textbooks in the schools and universities, the libraries are running down because there is no foreign exchange to buy books, you can't send for books from overseas, because Customs makes sure you have to pay on them –' (thirty per cent of the value of the books, as valued, arbitrarily, by ignorant officials). 'But there is plenty of foreign exchange for "Dallas". Not to mention rubbishy magazines from down South full of pornography. How do their minds work, this government, do you think? Why does Mugabe . . . ?'

As in Britain, where people sit around, dazed by incredulity: 'Why does *she* do this or that? What on earth does she think she's doing, running down universities, science, research, libraries, the arts . . . ?'

As always there are the two main kinds of thought, the Muddle Theory, 'It's just a damned cock-up', and the Conspiracy Theory, 'They want to fill the peasants' heads with rubbish, it keeps them quiet.'

Here the Muddle, or Cock-up, Theory inevitably holds sway. Several times a day the talk turns to the general inefficiency, the new bureaucracy.

'Tell me, if you are talking about inefficiency, have you been in Britain recently?'

'Yes, but there are levels of incompetence. And you are surely not suggesting that *he* is allowing all this rubbish into Zimbabwe? He's an educated man. Books were important to him – he has said so. What can be the reason for his penalizing books, culture, serious magazines, libraries? It must be a mistake.'

He of course is Mugabe. The assumption always is that *he* is on the side of the angels, that is, of whatever policy the speaker is favouring.

AN AID WORKER SPEAKS

'If you ever want to understand what we really stand for, in these people's minds, if you feel like having your nose rubbed in it, then go to a remote village in a Communal Area. There you are, sitting in a dusty space between trees – every tree has a branch lopped off for firewood, of course – and you are with five hundred or so people who have come in from miles around for the great occasion. It is not that they don't know what television is. They know. It is "Dallas". It is "Dynasty". There is a moon shining away overhead. A late cicada is still at it. The crickets are clicking. There is one TV set in a hundred miles and there is America presenting itself for the admiration of the world on the small screen. Now, *we* have defences against it: it is only when you watch people who don't have defences that you understand how well-armoured we are. We watch cynically, we think, Well, it's a lot of rubbish but why not? But those village people sitting out there under the stars, they believe it's for real. As murder follows murder, theft, double-cross, swindle, lie and racket, not to mention the fifty-seven varieties of sex, their eyes shine ever brighter with honest admiration: this is what the modern world is all about. 'I wish I could go to America,' you hear, as the programme ends. Off they go back to their huts through the bush, these poor people, but they know that if they are crooked enough, and unscrupulous enough, and cruel enough, they too can enjoy the riches of the world.

'And it is the same in India, in South America – everywhere I've been part of the scene, poor people watching the American dream, in a dozen countries.

'But why does America choose to show itself like this to the world? That's the question.'

GRANITE

Yesterday, being taken around by a man who adores Zimbabwe, chiefly – he says – because of its granite, I heard that granite is radioactive. But Zimbabwe is full of granite, whole mountain ranges of it, or great upthrusting single smooth mountains, or tall clumps of balancing boulders. If granite is radioactive then half the citizens should be shining in the dark or about to evolve in interesting ways – to look at the stuff only from the positive aspect. The point is not how radioactive granite is, dangerously, or mildly, an amount to be expressed in figures, but that the idea of radioactivity is appropriate to granite. Photographs of granite never give any real idea of it. It has a sparkle to it, a liveliness. If you put your hand on it on a hot day it seems to pulse.

This man says that when he is away from Zimbabwe he feels exiled from granite. It is the oldest rock in the world, says he: it came bubbling up from the world's secret interior, slowly rising through layers of other rock to surface here. He can't live without granite . . . I once knew a poet, a Yorkshireman, who spoke about rock in this way, but it did not have to be particular. The feel and the weight of rock, stone – any stone – in one's hands, that was the thing. It gave substance to his life.

Should I ring up some appropriate office and enquire, my voice made stern with the ring of one in search of scientific exactitudes: 'Just exactly how much is granite radioactive?' Of course not: this country is a myth-breeder, it always was. Revolution, that maker of myths, has only made it easier for a voice to slip into that tone, careless, dreamy, proud, where one says, 'Look at that granite mountain over there – I don't know why they make such a fuss over Ayers Rock – imagine some great lizard crawling over it, the size of a railway train. A winged lizard . . . just the place for a dinosaur to lie out and soak in some sun . . .'

A PICNIC

Today I was taken to see the Bushmen paintings some miles from Harare. Again the drive through rich suburbs, then the rich red lands, then a Communal Area. This one is comparatively well-off. Most families have at least one member working in Harare, and the money comes back here. Or cash crops are grown on these small well-worked fields and taken in for sale. There are all types and kinds of dwellings, from the old pattern of groups of huts, to new brick bungalows standing by themselves in little gardens, with cars outside them.

To get to the paintings we had to turn on to a dirt road,

where granite tumbled everywhere about us, in the shape of cliffs, hills and heaps of piled boulders. Heat sizzled out of the granite and down from a sky where there was not one cloud. The road goes through villages, where, if there is a car, then it is likely to be visitors for the paintings. Now there are plans to take small, carefully selected groups of tourists who can afford to pay well. As usual here is a collision between the need to look after these easily damaged paintings and the imperative to earn foreign exchange.

The road became wheel-marks through rough grass. We passed some people sitting out under trees, who greeted us. We greeted them, feeling awkward at being there. Half a mile further the road ended, we parked, and climbed cracked slopes, littered with rock, through granite boulders that always seem about to topple, but never do, to a baby cliff where you pull yourself up and then go crabwise to a ledge where once the Bushmen stood to make their pictures on a low overhang. And here you see why there are so few left of these rock records of the past. Once you could see rock paintings almost anywhere you searched among hills or boulders. There were some on our farm, sprightly half-effaced figures on the underside of a boulder. They were vandalized, deliberately destroyed. I remember watching white schoolboys throwing stones at a rockface covered with paintings, on and on, until they were chipped, cracked. Why? Because they were there? What is this need to destroy?

There is graffiti here, clumsy scrawls, a stick figure like a small child's first efforts: this time, it is the local people who have tried to deface this gallery of lively sketches. They are done in coloured soils or plant juices and have survived here for hundreds of years. Elephants, different kinds of buck, hunting parties with their spears, all with the immediate living truthfulness you see in a sketch done by a Japanese master: half a dozen lines that create a flower, a face.

The experts argue about the meaning of some of these scenes, these figures. The trouble is, we are looking at them through our eyes, and there is no way of knowing, I say, how those people then saw the world. I am with an expert who probably knows as much about Bushmen paintings as anyone in the world. He disagrees with me: we can find out how they thought and understand their cosmology from these pictures.

Sometimes, when you are with an expert you casually say something and then know you have touched an area where people have been arguing, speculating, for years.

He said, 'Perhaps you enjoy the idea that we don't understand them, and can't understand them?'

It is true: there is something restful in the thought that thriving and successful peoples have lived and we have no idea at all how they experienced what we call reality.

If you turn your back on the overhang of pictures you stand high, looking out over a landscape that goes miles, to hills, to mountains, the rim of hot blue sky. Below are patterns of fields: those lines that separate fields, are they contour ridges or fences? If fences, or hedges, then that is not an African concept, but then contour ridges weren't either. The people who made these pictures, little people, short stubby made-for-hardship people, stood here long before the Africans of these times were here, looked out over this landscape and saw – what? How do we know they saw what we see? Perhaps when they looked at hills, valleys, trees, they owned what they saw in ways we don't understand, as the Aborigines in Australia can be part of a landscape through song. Perhaps, looking out, their backs to the pictures they had made, they *were* the landscape, were what they saw. Sometimes people now have flashes or moments when it is as if they are 'part of everything', merge into 'everything'; they flow into trees, plants, soil, rocks and become one with them. How do we know that this condition, temporary and only occasionally achieved, and with rare people, was not their permanent state?

Arguing enjoyably about these possibilities we climbed back down through the rocks to the car, to have lunch. Two black youths have come from the huts to gather yellow fruit lying all over the ground, fallen from the mahobahoba trees that grow here in a grove. That is what they are pretending to do, for politeness' sake, but really they want to watch us. We set out china plates, knives and forks, glasses. We spread out cold

chicken and salad and orange juice. Should we ask them to
join us? But they are keeping just far enough away to make
that awkward. Besides, there is not enough for four. We eat,
while they hang about, watching, watching, leaning to pick up
one of the yellow fruits, putting it in their mouths, leaning
down again, standing up to stretch, and yawn and turn away,
pretending indifference – and then again they pick up fruit and
stare at us.

We forget that it is still rare for poor people far from a town
to observe the lives of rich whites or, these days, the rich blacks.

'They are looking at something unattainable,' says my companion, indicating the big American car, built for a life on rough
roads, and the basket, the plates, the glasses, the cutlery. 'They
are already twenty-five years old, and they aren't young
enough to have taken part in Mugabe's educational revolution
that says every child, girl or boy, must get a secondary education. They have probably done four or five years in school.
They are unemployed. They dream of the good life in town.
They will never have a car and a bungalow made of brick, with
glass windows and curtains and a three-piece suite.'

When we had finished eating, we packed everything into the
basket, buried our rubbish in a hole under a rock, but left the
chicken out on a piece of paper on a rock. To leave it seemed
insulting. Not to leave it seemed cruel. Only the night before I
had been told a story of how in a poor village suffering from
drought, they killed a chicken and made sure that every one
of the forty-odd villagers got at least a shred of chicken and
some broth with their sadza.

As we got into the car baboons were barking from the ledge
where the paintings were. They had been watching us from
some safe place, and now had come to inspect the ledge to find
out what we had been doing, and if we had left anything.
Soon, when the black youths had gone back to their huts, the
baboons would come here to pick up the yellow fruits, perfectly
ripe today, for these fruits have a moment of ripeness, just a
few hours, and before that they are sour and rough on the
tongue, and afterwards slimy, repulsive.

A COMMERCIAL FARM

We drove on the Golden Stairs road, past the Mazoe dam. This area is famous for its oranges, for its various agriculture. The farm is near the Umvukwes, that is to say, Mvurwi – or the Dyke. How did it happen that Mvurwi, a soft rumbling word, was heard with a clacking k? A mystery. That Chinhoyi should be heard as Sinoia, Gweru as Gwelo, Mutare as Umtali – not hard to understand. Soon we were near the Dyke, with its load of billions of years. I have on my mantelpiece a small slice of rock, once clay, and in it a fossil fish that was blithely swimming along when some cataclysm sunk it in choking ooze. The label says this little fish, *Dapalis Macrurus*, is thirty million years old, a matter for awe, but the clay that surrounds it must be thirty millions old too, but no one slices up and sells ancient clay to sit on people's mantelpieces with labels that say, This rock is thirty, or three hundred million years old. Clearly, for awe, we need a form, the outline of a fish as delicate as a skeleton leaf; or the Dyke, which we can see dividing the landscape, a visible announcement of extreme age; we need upthrusts of granite which we gaze at and think, Here we touch the archaic, here is real antiquity, as if the soil they are embedded in, a million or so years younger, is worth less of our human respect.

The farm is an old one, that is to say, was 'opened up' not long after the Colony began. The farmhouse is old and comfortable, with the deep verandahs of those days, like big shady rooms. But first we sit out under trees. Under layers of leafy branches, we sit and listen to ring doves, cinnamon doves, the emerald spotted dove, and the different kinds of louries. The heat is heavy, and the bird sounds, by long association, seem the voice of the heat. The temperature is well up into the nineties, but it is the dry snapping highveld heat that does not sap and undermine like the wet heat of sea coasts. We drink tea. We drink varieties of fruit juice. We discuss, what else, politics. I am on the alert for the babyish querulous grumbling of the whites only six years ago, but no, all that has gone. This is what I listened to all through my childhood on the verandahs: farmers grumbling about the government which always and in every country is hostile to farmers. The government and the weather, between these two anarchic tyrants farmers are for ever ground down, no matter what powerful lobbies they operate, no matter how well they are doing.

The Commercial Farmers have an energetic organization and meet continually with government, to the point that other groups complain the Commercial Farmers are unfairly represented. The Commercial Farmers are always being told how much they are valued, are proud they produce difficult crops that bring in the needed foreign currency.

My room in Harare is now full of reports, analyses and abstracts and those dealing with the Commercial Farmers – still mostly white – are interesting for the number of times they will repeat that Commercial Farmers have nothing to fear. This is because the masses of the black landless look with impatience at these big farms of rich good soil and complain that large areas are not being used. But a recent UN Report has said that on the whole the Commercial Farms are properly used. Here is hidden something else, seldom spoken of openly. It is a Grey Area. Everyone knows the bush of Zimbabwe is disappearing, erosion threatens, soil is overused. But it is in the overcrowded communal areas that the bush is going. You can tell when you pass from a Commercial Farm to a Communal Area not only because the soil often changes from red or chocolate to pale colour but because at once the bush is only a ghost of itself. The comparatively undamaged bush on the Commercial Farms is an asset for the whole country. Yet a thousand polemical articles demand that the Commercial Farms should be expropriated. The government says improperly used farms will be compulsorily bought. But improperly used farms are often owned by rich blacks – Mugabe's supporters.

Recently very large areas of the country have been freed from tsetse fly, and this means that beasts can now live there and the land distributed to the landless. The conservationists are saying: That means a lot more of Zimbabwe will become semi-desert.

On the walls of the farm office are two aerial photographs, one taken when the farm was bought, in the 1950s, and one last year. The early map shows large areas of uncultivated land, now very little is left unused. Any committee, commission, or government inspector coming to assess the situation on this farm will at once be shown these maps.

When this farmer said, 'I'll show you around,' it was with the anxious pride that is the note of *now*. First, to the tobacco barns, whose design does away with the old technology that kept young farm assistants or struggling farmers awake half the night to check barn temperatures. The leaves are strung on movable racks, the furnace uses a minimum of fuel, the whole operation needs little supervision. What has also changed is the number of workers needed to run these barns: just like everywhere else in the world technology has thrown people desperate for work out of a job. The farmer is proud of his barns. 'We developed this technology,' says he, and the *we* means, here, 'we, the white farmers of Southern Rhodesia' and not, as it usually does these days, 'we, Zimbabwe'. The design of these barns has been copied in other countries, and so have devices invented by this same farmer. 'I invented this . . .' 'I invented that . . .'

We are driven around the fields. It is midday, hot, hot. The farm is still growing maize, which more and more is being grown by the small black farmers, it grows tobacco, and, a new venture, granadillas, or passion fruit. There are fields of these, the vines strung along wires. The plants are being attacked by some new disease but the farmer is not worried, for he has confidence that whatever Nature comes up with will get short shrift from science. In the middle of a field are grazing some duiker and a couple of bush buck. Surely these animals lie up in hidden shady places in the daytime and graze at night? To see them here in the blaze of midday upsets my idea of the proper order of things, like the rains coming in November instead of October. 'My chaps are forbidden to kill game on this farm,' says the farmer. 'Of course they do, when I'm not looking. Not that there's much left. Do you remember when . . .'

He talks all the way around the farm, and, as we sit in the shady living-room, waiting for lunch, he cannot stop talking about his accomplishments, the new techniques, new crops, new ideas – full of a restless energy that keeps him on the move: when he sits down he is up almost at once to reach for a pamphlet, an article, a book.

Lunch is served by the black servant, and is the meal that will survive in these British outposts long after it is forgotten in Britain. We eat roast beef. Roast potatoes. Badly cooked vegetables. A heavy pudding. That this should all go on with the temperature at nearly a hundred is certainly an invitation to remember commonplaces about national characteristics.

Through lunch we talk about the unemployed youngsters in the farm village. Of course: everyone talks about the unemployed. On this farm live many times more people than should be here. We discuss the word 'should' in this context. The regular workers – that is, the workers who get the proper wage – are a minority. The seasonal workers come and go. Every hut or small house is crammed with people, mostly relatives, and relatives of relatives, here because of the rights of the extended family.

'They break my heart,' says the farmer's wife. 'What's going to happen to them?'

She says that the young people come up to this house to ask if they can borrow her books. She gives them detective stories, crime stories. She can't keep up with the demand for her books. Ayrton R. protests that they are ready for much better. For instance, a young boy he knows of, from a rural school, reads Thomas Hardy. He has suggested Hardy to teachers in the remotest rural schools: with success. The farmer's wife sounds unconvinced, but says she will offer more difficult books. The conversation slides into a familiar track with, 'One of these Aid agencies could set up mobile libraries. They should offer everything from Enid Blyton to Garcia Marquez.' 'I simply don't understand these Aid people. I wish I had the handling of some of that money.' We amuse ourselves mentally setting up projects that would cost a fraction of the vast sums often wasted by the Aid agencies.

Then, the talk returns to the government: I am listening to what I now know is this time's Monologue – or one of them.

Mugabe's economic policy is ruining Zimbabwe because it is creating stagnation. Zimbabwe is desperate for investment, but why should people invest when they are allowed to take out of the country only five per cent: of course they invest in the Pacific Rim, where everything is booming. Socialist dogma is a killer, as they have found in every country in the world. You aren't allowed to sack an incompetent worker: that means that you don't employ them, for you have to carry them. This is only one of the policies you'd think were designed to prevent economic growth. Another is not being allowed to import farm machinery or even spare parts. You can only buy new machines through complicated deals that go like this. Someone outside the country sends a letter, backed by a bank, to the effect that he, she, is prepared to pay for – whatever it is, a tractor, a lorry. These documents are sent by a Zimbabwe bank to the foreign firm who will then supply the machine. But what of those people who don't have relatives or friends outside Zimbabwe prepared to pay for the machines? As for spare parts . . . the government will not allot the currency, so machines stand idle, or you have to make trips down south to The Republic to get them, or you smuggle them in, or, using the famous ingenuity Southern Rhodesia was, and Zimbabwe is, so proud of, you invent spare parts or run machines on "faith, bits of string, rubber bands. But you can't do that for ever". The only people getting anything out of all this are the crooks in government who set up all kinds of rackets importing spare parts: that is one reason we don't expect the policy to change. Too many people do well out of it. Or when Mugabe does permit a factory to make some machine, he says there can only be one factory, so, no competition and the prices are several times what they should be: all the disadvantages of monopoly capitalism, but in the name of Socialism.'

That is one Monologue.

Another overlaps the first. 'Eight years this lot have been in power! Heroes of the Revolution! Look at them! What a bunch of crooks! One of them came visiting our school last month . . .'

(A school teacher is speaking, an idealistic young black man)
'Where do they get all that fat from, the Chefs? If you pricked
him great spurts of pure white pig's fat would come out. He
didn't care about our pupils. He didn't know about our problems. All he cared was to get through his inspection – but he
didn't know how to inspect, he didn't even go into a classroom.
He wanted to get back to Harare and feed his fat buttocks and
his fat pig's belly.'

As we drove back to Harare there was a road block, to check
for licences and the conditions of tyres. The death-traps, the
rattle-traps, of six years ago are being cleared off the roads.

In 1982 the road blocks were feared. They were often oper-
ated by soldiers, and the raw mood of that time made it a
nervous business, stopping so that the inside of a car, the boot,
even the engine, could be checked for weapons. Now a smiling
young man asked some routine questions and glanced at the
tyres.

'Have you work for me?' he asked Ayrton R.

'What sort of work?'

'Any sort of work. Gardener, housework – I can learn to
cook.'

'I am sorry, but I don't have any work.'

'I am sorry you don't have work for me.'

'Goodbye. Go well.'

'Go well. Goodbye.'

We drive on. It seems that whenever you are stopped by the
police on a country road, they ask for work. They want to be
in town. That is the great basic fact about this country. Everyone, but everyone, wants to be in the towns. Any town. Why
should Zimbabwe be any different from the rest of the world?
Other countries haven't solved the problem, why should we be
expected to? Is Mugabe going to pass a law forbidding people to
come into the towns? If he did, there'd be another revolution
and he knows it.'

A TEA PARTY

The room is full of elderly people, white, middle class. They are retired civil servants, widows of public servants. The atmosphere is pale, relaxed, and I see I have been meeting only passionate partisans of Zimbabwe, whether for idealism or self-interest. It is often said of these people that they might never have left Tunbridge Wells or Cheltenham. This is only partly true. For one thing their side was badly defeated in a war and that means they have had to accommodate failure.

The new Zimbabwe, chaotic, ebullient, violent, full of energy, full of optimism, is not a match for their natural temper, which tends toward the ironic, the philosophical. They cannot leave here, because pensions are not paid outside Zimbabwe. But would they if they could? Probably not. People who precipitously left for South Africa have come back. 'Once we lived in a wonderful country called Southern Rhodesia. Now we live in a wonderful country called Zimbabwe.' Outside a gate in one of the suburbs the house's name is announced as 'The Gap Took Us' – from a family who Took the Gap and returned. Where in the world would these ageing people be able to live as they do here, soaked in sunlight and able to afford a servant? But many do not have servants, pride themselves on their self-sufficiency. The worst is that they cannot now make trips to Britain. The money allotted for travelling is very little. If you do not have well-heeled relatives able to pay for you, then you stay here. 'There are worse places to be stuck in,' I observe and am told: 'It's all very well for you, you fly in, you fly out, but you have no idea of the cultural isolation. The newspapers only carry local news or if it's foreign news it's communist propaganda. Thank God for the BBC. We can't afford to subscribe to overseas newspapers on our pension.'

These people do not talk about politics, or say, 'Why doesn't Mugabe . . .' They cultivate their gardens, and go in for charitable works, just as they would at Home.

But they are not the only refugees from the past. Today,

being driven through the most prestigious suburb of them all, I was told it is full of well-heeled whites who are born-again Christians. 'Yes, that's how losing the War took them! They can't face life just as themselves, without holding on to God's hand. No, this whole suburb is jumping with God, comrade, jumping with God.'

GARFIELD TODD

Garfield Todd, ex-Prime Minister, now a hero of the Revolution, magnificent, white haired, eighty years old and alive with energy and optimism, sits on the verandah of his daughter's house. But it is not really a verandah. Hearing she meant to build herself a house, he said, 'You aren't going to have another of these houses, a string of rooms with a verandah along them? No, I shall design you a house.' So it is more like a Spanish house, Mediterranean, with a central atrium full of plants, and rooms off it. Where we sit is a room that does not have a fourth wall.

He dismisses what everyone else is talking about, the corruption scandals, with 'These little incidents . . .'

He says, 'Eight years, all this in eight years. It's a miracle. They've achieved so much. I know we said they could but who would have believed it, in such a short time? You go into an office or a bank, you look at them, so full of confidence and ability, and remember the old days, when they had all their confidence knocked out of them. You meet young people now who don't remember the bad old days.'

He had a sad time in the War, an enemy of the white regime, confined to his farm, forbidden to speak his mind. He helped the fighters when he could, and now sometimes people come up to him and give him presents. 'Do you remember? You helped my little boy?' 'You gave me medicine when I was sick.' 'You hid my brother when the soldiers were chasing him.'

This Zimbabwe is his Zimbabwe and he loves it with a fierce

innocence. The Unity Accord has made him and his country whole and perfect.

ZIMBABWE

A scene guaranteed to appeal to connoisseurs of political irony . . . some months later Garfield Todd got badly burned when working on one of his ancient cars: restoring old cars is his hobby. When he was in hospital Robert Mugabe and Joshua Nkomo, former enemies, went together to visit him. Garfield Todd, still pretty ill, was being gentled out of a bath. The security guards tried to hurry a nurse into getting her patient quickly out of the bath and into bed. 'Can't you see who is here?' 'You do your job and I'll do mine,' she replied.

'When those two men, Mugabe and Nkomo, stood on either side of Todd's bed that day, man, that was the best of Zimbabwe, I tell you, that *is* Zimbabwe.'

SCHOOL

When Mugabe and his army were still hopeful contenders for power he promised that if he won every child would be given a secondary education. On Liberation he said, 'When an African country gets Independence Aid money flows in, and then dries up. We, Zimbabwe, must decide now what is most important. First of all Communal Areas, the old Reserves, always starved of money. That's the priority. After that, the secondary schools. Yes, it is true we do not have the infrastructure to do it well at once, but there is going to be unemployment for a time in any case, and it is better a young person should be unemployed with some kind of education than with none.'

Did he really say this? Who cares!

Comrade Mugabe
Keep your finger in the dyke,
Pull your finger out,
The water flood about,
Comrade Mugabe, Comrade Mugabe,
We rely on *you*.

(Popular song)

And secondary education was established at once. In 1982 I
met teachers radiant with exhaustion and idealism, who said
they worked in schools converted from barns, shacks, shops –
anything, and there might be two or three shifts of pupils in a
day. 'The benches never had time to cool.' Parents helped to
build schools, giving time, skills, and money, often going without necessities. Secondary education was the key to their children's future, and there was no sacrifice too great.

Eight years since Liberation. Nothing in the life of a country.
Everything in the life of a child. Zimbabwe is now covered
with secondary schools. But there are not enough teachers,
textbooks, let alone – often – electricity, or even clean water,
let alone the facilities taken for granted in Europe. A school
may have one teacher actually qualified to teach: the rest may
have a couple of O-levels. Many teachers, while they are teaching, are trying to get more O-levels or a precious A-level. And
their goal? Certainly not to remain in rural schools, far from
the centres, but to get to a big town, preferably Harare. The
teaching staff in these schools never stay long, they are always
on their way to somewhere better, and many headmasters have
turned out dishonest.

The children at these schools believe they are being given a
future, but only five per cent (1988) actually pass O-levels.
They have nothing in their experience to enable them to make
comparisons, do not know what a properly equipped school
is, often fail and have to return to their villages where they
dream that this half-education of theirs will some day, somehow, earn them the good life. There are hundreds of thousands, perhaps millions by now, of young people who believe
they are getting a real education.

This situation is dangerous, a classic for revolution: numbers of young people who have been promised everything, have made sacrifices and are then disappointed. As the rulers of this country know. It is reported that Mugabe is saying, 'We made a mistake. From now on secondary education will concentrate on quality.' And what does he plan to do with these half-educated populations, not fit for employment in the modern world, but educated out of satisfaction with village life? It is said that fear of these young people is why Mugabe is so hard on discontented students. His repressions are signalling: I will not stand for any nonsense from the youth.

It is also reported, with emotion, that when in Parliament it was announced the budget for education for the first time was larger than for defence, everyone stood up and cheered and wept.

We drive out of Harare, going west. The roads are still, to eyes used to any road in Europe, empty. You drive along, sole user of the road and then ahead of you is a bus, enveloped in black fumes. All the public vehicles emit black clouds. Why? Well, there is this question of not being able to get spare parts, and then, they don't service them often enough. When a large new car overtakes it is a Toyota and belongs to a Chef. These cars do not belch out greasy black smoke that trails across the bush, poisoning plants and beasts. Only public transport vehicles do that, and they often break down, and sit on the roadside surrounded by disconsolate people. There are accidents. This is not because the drivers are bad: the vehicles are. Last week I met a woman whose brother, a driver, was killed because brakes failed and the bus fell over into a ravine. It is astonishing how often you meet people who have been in accidents, or whose relatives and friends have. 'Travelling on public transport . . . you need plenty of courage. Of course, the Africans have no choice.'

The weather is bad. This November is cold and grey. I swear that never, ever, was it cold in November, in the old days. The ITCZ is still in the wrong place, too high, and not engaging with the air masses from the Indian Ocean. I would never have believed I could long for a thick sweater in November.

Under a low, cold, grey sky we go on west, through small towns that appear at long intervals, and then stop for lunch at a hotel which is the social centre for a large district: the dining room and bars are too many and too large for the number of people who stay in the hotel. The menu is still the old British menu, roast and grilled this and that, meat wonderful, vegetables less than wonderful, salads and fruits perfection. Everything as it was, except that now on every menu is sadza, and a common meal is steak and sadza, fried fish and sadza. Teachers from schools miles around come here for a meal, and to enjoy electric light, and to use the telephone. Hotels in remote towns like this are places of wonder to most people in the villages. They have never been in one.

In 1956 I drove here on my way to the still being built Kariba dam, through bush that has stayed in my mind as what forest ought to be. Tall and stately trees were full and graceful and above all infinitely various. For hours I drove through this bush, on the look-out for elephants, I saw game of all kinds, and stopped more than once to listen to the birds. On this trip I waited for what I remembered to begin, but it did not. If trees still stood, then every third or fourth tree had been cut down, and the stumps were raw or weathering. Or there were large stumped areas. Or each tree had lost a branch or two branches.

'People have to eat,' says Ayrton R. 'People have to keep warm.' He is as upset as I am.

We drive through this denuded bush on a large road, then a smaller one, and turn off, and off again, each time on to rougher tracks, past notices that say, 'The Happiness Secondary School Welcomes You!' 'The New Dawn School Welcomes You!' Now we are on a rutted track in a Communal Area. There are few trees left. On we go, several miles, past a store, over a little bridge where women are washing clothes in a pool full of detergent suds, and there, ahead, is the school. Two schools in fact, the primary school, the secondary school. All the schools in the country are the same, built to a pattern, long, low, shed-like buildings, sometimes with narrow verandahs. This assembly of buildings occupies a large area, several acres. There are trees, most whole, and not mutilated, there are shrubs and even attempts at gardens. What you might think you were seeing, if you had not already learned these patterns of building say 'school', could be something on the lines of an army camp or depot or an internment camp, places that have to be quickly and cheaply erected.

We have been invited by a friend, a young man from England, who contracted to teach for a year, but volunteered for another year, with the possibility of a third. There is Jack, waving from outside a minute shed, or so it looks. The big Volvo makes the house look even smaller. The house has two small rooms. In one is a bed, a corner with hooks to hang a jacket or a shirt, a shelf for books. In the other is a table, gas stove, and a higgledy-piggledy of pots, pans, jugs, cans of water, kerosene for the hurricane lamp, vegetables, bags of mealie meal, tomatoes, a couple of onions. We have arrived in the middle of a school day. Jack goes off to his pupils, putting on a tie, rolling down his sleeves, according to regulation: teachers must set an example. Ayrton R. and I sit crammed among the paraphernalia while people drop in on pretexts, to look at us, for it is known that Jack is expecting 'important visitors from Harare, from the University.' They want to borrow a match, get a glass of water, or simply to say they are friends of Jack's. They are a succession of lively, very young people, mostly boys. Some are teachers, but it is not easy to tell teachers from pupils.

Then Jack reappears and engages them in conversation in Shona. Ayrton R. who was born and brought up in the country does not know as much Shona as this young man does after a few months.

The Shona patterns of greeting at once melt you in admiration, and in apology for our gracelessness. Nothing like, How are you? or, Hello!

'Good afternoon.'

'Good afternoon.'

'Have you spent the day well?'

'I have spent the day well if you have spent the day well.'

'I have spent the day well.'

'Then I have spent the day well.'

Jack can now converse in Shona, not, he deprecates, about

philosophy or politics, but on the, How is your sister? How is
your health? Have you done your homework? level.

At sundown we walk off to the store about a mile away,
over the little bridge where women are still washing clothes,
through trees. We sit on a stone under a tree drinking Coca-
Cola, watching the comings and goings at the store, and above
is the sunset, backlighting heavy black clouds with scarlet and
gold rays. The bird calls, the voices of the passing groups of
people acquire the softened, distant note appropriate to night-
fall, and we walk carefully in the dark over the rough track to
the tiny house. On the way we are offered green mealies, sold
much harder and older than we would choose to eat them. But
Jack says, buying some for our supper, 'If you are short of food
you aren't going to eat mealies before they have acquired their
maximum size.' We light the paraffin lamp, and in the dim
light we eat the hard mealies and talk about the school. This
headmaster, like the headmasters of three other schools in the
area is 'suspended' for embezzling funds. He has also been
having sex with the pupils. 'He is a man without a character,'
says Jack. This diagnosis interests us and we discuss at length
whether Jack is saying he is a man without the principles
expected of a functionary in a European country with a tradition of public service. 'But this is a school set up on European
principles. That is what they have chosen. It can't run at all
without those principles,' says Jack.

'But it *is* running without those principles,' I say. 'What about
all those young people we were talking to?'

'No, it is not running, it is not running at all. The whole place
is neglected, demoralized and dirty.' And Jack is in despair.

We then embark on that discussion that I have already been
part of several times, but not in a tiny brick room full of insects
buzzing around the lamp, the frogs going hard at it outside.
These ideas sound different in a house in Harare, not exactly
abstract, since Corruption – the scale and the shamelessness of
it – is frightening everyone, but certainly not as urgent.

What is extraordinary about all these embezzlements and
thievings is that the perpetrators do not seem able to believe
they will be caught. You will see in a newspaper – usually the

Chronicle in Bulawayo, not the *Herald*, which is a conformist paper – a headline like, 'Minister So and So – 99 Counts of Fraud'. This headmaster here was stealing money and sleeping with schoolgirls for months, with everyone watching.

'It is as if they have some area in their minds that blanks out the normal expectations of results of wrong-doing,' says Jack. 'If you don't want to say, They're barmy – which they obviously aren't.'

Is this another Grey Area, where old customs, or ways of thinking, blur in contact with new ideas, new laws? Except that in the old society theft was theft, and severely punished. How is it that sane and intelligent people go in for large-scale theft apparently believing they are invisible, or that The Law has no eyes? 'Or,' says Jack, 'that everybody isn't talking about them.'

As for the schoolgirls, that is easy to understand. A girl of fourteen or fifteen is considered nubile, and, indeed, marriageable. The young teachers often sleep with the older girls, and then marry them.

'But surely a headmaster should set a good example?' demands Jack. And repeats that the headmaster is a man without character. This formula is allowed to sum up the conversation.

By now it is half-past seven, nearly time for bed. Jack says he is so tired by the end of the day he is asleep by eight.

Time to make a last trip to the toilet.

Zimbabwe has just held celebrations for the 100,000th Blair toilet. This toilet was evolved as part of the War against fly-borne diseases, and, too, against bilharzia, hookworm, dysentery.

The life-cycle of bilharzia goes like this. It doesn't matter at what point you enter it. Let us take the moment when the snail that harbours the bilharzia fluke ejects it in the water of the river. This entity then enters the skin of some human bathing or washing clothes in the river. It makes its way to the liver, or bladder, or kidney, or some other suitable organ. There it does great damage. This disease afflicts millions of people in Africa, and in other countries too. But Africa is the worst. People die of it, and suffer all kinds of symptoms, one being

lethargy, which is one of the reasons for the accusation that
'Africans are born lazy'. (This is a white formula from the past.)
A friend of my parents, a farmer, an energetic wiry man of the
type described as 'living on his nerves' dropped dead one day,
while apparently in the best of health. He was discovered to
be 'full of bilharzia'. When the fluke leaves the afflicted organ,
it is excreted. The excreta is deposited in the bush – or was
until recently. The rains wash the excreta into the river, and
the bilharzia fluke enters the snail.

It is possible to fill rivers with poison to kill the bilharzia, but
the poison kills a lot else as well. Besides, the next rains will
dilute the poison and make it ineffective. It costs money to
poison a river. It costs much less to treat a person for bilharzia.
Once there were long, and painful, and complicated treatments
for bilharzia, but now it is easier. Much better not to get the
disease at all. Much better if everyone in a village gets into the
habit of using a toilet and not the bush. The Blair toilet was
evolved by one of the real, not sufficiently-sung, benefactors
of humankind, and is being installed in the villages of Zimbabwe to the accompaniment of propaganda campaigns about
the habits of bilharzia and all the other filthy diseases that afflict
Africa. Thus one may find oneself engaged with a schoolchild
in some remote place in discussion that would do credit to a
junior doctor in England. 'You see,' one said to me, 'just
because you can't see something, that doesn't mean it isn't
there. You must always wash your hands.' And she went off
into a chant of, 'Wash your hands and use the soap. Wash your
hands before you eat.'

The Blair toilet is based on the known preferences of the flies
that carry so many diseases. The flies prefer light to dark. The
toilet consists of a very small hole in a cement floor, over what
is known as 'a long drop'. The hole is perhaps seven inches by
about three or four. There is another hole, a large one, full of
light, built outside the toilet. The flies go down into the dark
after the smell, but then try to get out through the well-lit exit,
which has a wire screen over it. They die there. They die in
myriads. Because of this simple idea fly-borne diseases are getting rarer in the villages where they have built the Blair toilet.

To use the thing is not so easy. It consists of two round cement cells, one for men, one for women. With a hurricane lamp in one hand, and a roll of paper in the other I make my way over rough ground to the toilet. Standing on the steps are some goats, who have to be shooed off. It is a question of being as quick as possible, because the lamp attracts moths, insects, bats. The hole, being so small, needs careful aiming. Men, I am told, find it difficult. Going to the loo here is not something to be undertaken without good reason.

Outside, I stand on the path looking at the tiny house that spills dim light from a window. The hurricane lamp is at my feet. I look up at the stars, for it is hard to do this in Harare where the town lights are strong, and the air is polluted. The stars appear and disappear as cloud hurries past. It is very cold. It is very damp. Suddenly a noise around the hurricane lamp. Some frogs have been attracted by the light, and are hustling and pushing at the glass, and more frogs are hopping frantically along the path to join them. They seem crazed. With curiosity? I take up the lamp, and, stepping carefully through the hysterical frogs, go inside. Ayrton R. has a bed in another house. I sleep in Jack's bed. Jack sleeps on the floor among his household goods. A mosquito is trying its chances. It is noisy. The dangerous ones are female and silent. My bloodstream is awash with anti-malarial poisons, so I don't care. I don't care because I have not yet been told that malaria is cunning and evolving itself to outwit our poisons: later I met several people who, in spite of regularly taking two different kinds of pill, have had malaria. Twice Jack and I get up to chase out an invading bat which has decided that this shape of walls and roof is like a cave, and will do it nicely for a home. We block up the hole it came in by. I try to read a paperback I have brought, about the adulterous goings-on in a country house in Wiltshire, but they seem remote. Besides I know that my candleflame will shortly attract other visitors. Rain begins to hammer on the metal roof. The frogs exult. I sleep. It is not yet nine o'clock.

We are awake by five. Outside it is grey and cold. While tea is being brewed I take a can of cold water to the place where one has to wash. There is a curving wall at the back of the little house, enclosing a small concrete-floored space. You strip, hanging your clothes on the top of the wall. You soap yourself, standing naked and shivering, thinking how pleasant it must be on a hot day. You pour cold water over yourself. The water runs out through a hole at the bottom of the wall. Already again at home in a culture where water is precious, I find myself worrying about that water running away into the earth. Shouldn't it be caught and used for watering something? Back inside I drink tea and am relieved to hear the water is not from the pool under the bridge, bound to be full of bilharzia, but from the well a mile away, presumed to be pure. Jack's grin admits he is not sure about the purity of that water either. The well, the little river, are the two sources of water for the school, with its hundreds of people, and for the village. Prominent on a little eminence, sheltered by trees, is a water tank which is supposed to pump water from the well, but there is something wrong, probably the valve, at any rate it doesn't work and there hasn't been water in the tank for months.

Ayrton R. appears from his lodging half a mile away, and remarks that if the Aid organizations had any sense of priorities, they would set up teams of engineers to go around schools, Growth Points, clinics, to mend simple things like valves, which no one bothers to mend. They could take with them youngsters who would learn how to put right a valve, a tap, or a broken pipe.

'The trouble is that all these poor bloody kids, in all the schools of Zimbabwe, have decided that only a literary education is worth having. Where do you find the ultimate bastion of respect for the Humanities? Not in Thatcher's Britain! No, in the bush, where generations of black kids have decided they are too good to be engineers and electricians, and are taking O-levels in English which they mostly fail.'

'Quite so. This is where the English aristocratic contempt for people who work with their hands – engineers or technicians – stops. In schools like this. Do you suppose those effete types who said in England, "I can't ask him to dinner, he's in trade!" or "I can't let Angela marry that man, he's only an engineer" would have believed that, roll on half a century, you'd find black kids stuck in the bush hundreds of miles from Harare unwilling to soil their hands with manual work? Would they recognize their heirs?'

'I was in an office in Harare. An American Aid worker was arguing that the education being given to the children was inappropriate, what was the point of teaching them the British syllabus, with books suitable for Europe? What was needed was a good basic technical education. A black woman who was waiting her turn turned furiously on her. She said, "I see you whites are still just the same. You don't want our children to have a real education. Oh no, that's for your children. We want a good education for our children, just the same as yours."'

'There you are, an aristocrat! Do you suppose she would recognize her predecessors?'

Conversation on these lines entertained us through a break-fast of semolina and tea.

Jack went off to class, to be there by seven-thirty. He pointed out that most of his pupils would have got up by half-past four, or five at the latest. The girls would have fetched water, cut wood and cooked porridge, waiting on the boys as well as on their elders. Some of them would then have walked up to four or five miles to school through the bush. Most do not bring food to school. It is common for pupils to faint from lack of food. This is true too of the small children in the primary school, who might go through until four in the afternoon with-out a bite to eat or even a drink. To get water means walking a mile to the well, and, oddly enough, they lack energy.

When Jack has gone, instructing us to turn up at such and such a time to lecture his pupils, Ayrton R. describes the room he has spent the night in. It belongs to another ex-pat teacher, who has departed to Britain for the holidays. The room is like a time-capsule, for the walls are covered with CND posters, Greenpeace posters, and pictures of heroes like Che Guevara and Castro – the 'progressive' stereotype of five years before. Large numbers of young teachers, inspired by the rhetoric of marxist Zimbabwe, have arrived in bush schools to find them-selves disillusioned. In order to do their job they have to forget the ideals that brought them here. The joke is that the poorest street in the poorest town in Britain would seem full of riches and opportunities to anyone in Zimbabwe.

'Do you realize,' demands Ayrton R., 'the lunacy of it? There isn't a school in Britain that doesn't have television, a computer, telephone, Fax, copy machines, and some sort of library. There isn't a child who doesn't watch television, go to the cinema or on trips to museums and probably to France or Italy. In schools like this one there are classrooms with untrained teachers and too few textbooks, and that's it.'

Some of the ex-pat teachers go home the moment their contracts expire, or, pleading illness, before. The various organizations, religious and otherwise, break in their young teachers by keeping them in Harare for a couple of months. But nothing in Harare can prepare you, says Jack, for the realities of a school like this one. Jack himself became mysteriously ill four months after arrival and had to stay in bed. It was with an effort he dragged himself up and back to work. He comes from a gentle family in the Home Counties, and has taught in London schools which struck him then as rough.

Jack told us to lock the door: *we* might think there was nothing worth stealing. We went through the bush towards the schools, passing the disabled water tank, then through the junior school, whose long low buildings were so crammed with small children it seemed they would spill out of the windows. Goats came to inspect us. There were puddles everywhere and a grey sky pressed down. We left the junior school behind and walked through a sparse scrubby bush, pointing out to each other an orchid and a butterfly: these days they do not go unremarked. Then a small stream, and a path up a rise to a new strong fence. Outside the fence fusses an indignant cow. She has been accustomed to taking this path, but now, for no reason she can understand, there is this fence, designed to keep her and her kind out. She waits there sometimes for hours, hoping for someone to leave the gate unfastened. We find Jack in a classroom in one of the long barrack-like buildings. He is instructing a group of young men and women who have just sat O-levels. Some are as old as twenty. They give an impression of bouncing energy and vigour and confidence. Any group of young Zimbabweans is like this: they are large, strong, glossy with health.

Ayrton R. and I sit at one of the desks, watching Jack finish a lesson. The classroom: two of the windowpanes are cracked. The windows are dirty. There is a cracked rafter. The floor is half an inch deep in dust and rubbish. The room would look derelict, if it were not for the lively people in it.

I notice beginning in me that process known unkindly as 'Africanization'. Well, I think, in this climate they don't really need to shut the windows. As for the rafter, easy to put a bit of wire around it. The floor? You don't need a clean floor to learn lessons. Dirty windows? What of it!

Ayrton R. is miserable. 'There is no headmaster, you see. You can tell a school with a bad headmaster at a glance. I've seen enough of them.'

Jack instructs a couple of the pupils to take us next door and show us the library. His pride and joy. He created it. There was no library at all. No money for books because the headmaster stole the money.

The library is a narrow room, like a wide corridor, and it has perhaps three hundred books in it. Obsolete textbooks. Novels donated by well-wishers or by those who have Taken the Gap, most of the kind read by people nostalgic for dear dead England:

'Edith stood at the window gazing past the buddleia to the road where Geoffrey would come. She had set out her bottle of sherry, but perhaps he would prefer whisky? Where was her whisky bottle? She had had no occasion to offer whisky since last Christmas, when her brother dropped in during his trip home on leave from India. At last she found the whisky bottle pushed to the back of the shelf where she kept her gardening things – insecticides too, she was afraid. She really ought to be more careful! Back in her place at the window she began worrying about supper. It was rather warm this afternoon, at least sixty-five, she was sure. Would steak and kidney pie be too heavy, in this weather? Just as she decided to open a tin of salmon, Geoffrey

came into sight along the road. He was riding his bicycle. Oh
poor thing! He would be so hot and tired . . .'

There were some formidable tomes donated by an American
Foundation, so heavy you could hardly lift them, compen-
diums of literature, history, and so on, designed, you would
think, to put people off for good. The books here that are
actually read are by African writers, and a few American ones.
A survey of what books the teachers read revealed that the only
one who read for pleasure liked Chinua Achebe and Frederick
Forsyth. The distinction between 'good' and 'bad' literature is
not one that means much when it is a question of getting people
to read at all. This pathetic, almost bare room, taught me that
what is needed are simply written stories about different parts
of the world, explaining ways of living, religions, other
people's ideas. These children (only many of them are grown
up) labour through set books too difficult for them. Too difficult
for most of them: there is always that rare spirit who, stuck
in a village miles from anywhere, will read Tolstoy, Hardy,
Steinbeck. Tolstoy, when he was running that wonderful village school of his, talked of the need for simply-told informative
stories. Astonishing how often Russian experience is relevant
to Africa.

Enid Blyton is liked by all the pupils.

Jack had taught the children how a library is run by means
of these few books and an exercise book where borrowed
books are listed: the pupils take it in turns to be librarian.
The books may not be taken home. What would be the
point? Homework is done here, in the school, before the
walk home, which can be a long one. By the time the children
get to their homes, it is dark, or soon will be. They are
expected to help with the work – particularly the girls –
cutting wood, fetching water, cooking. The huts are at best
lit by a candle or an oil lamp but usually the whole family
will sit in the hut in the light of the fire that burns in its
centre. Not easy to do homework or even read a book. The
adults are mostly illiterate or have done four or five years in
a bush school. They passionately want their children to be

educated, but do not know from their own experience how to help them.

The parents in such villages are still close to subsistence farming, and must find thirty pounds a year for a child to attend secondary school, to pay for uniforms and exercise books. If they have several children in school, the burden keeps them, often, short of food and clothing for themselves.

We ask Jack how many of these enthusiastic young people will pass their O-levels.

'I don't think many of this lot will pass them.' He is embarrassed, and makes excuses for them. 'I don't think you understand . . . for instance, there was an exam paper set in Britain, one of the questions had the word "shutter". These people don't have shutters. One of the meanings of the word was a camera shutter. Most of them have never seen a camera, let alone used one.'

Ayrton and I are asked to address this year's O-level class. Few visitors come to this school. Our visit is an event, and not because of the presence of this author, far from it. The star is Ayrton R. who is from the University of Zimbabwe, that abode of the fortunate. The teachers here, with their one or two O-levels each, the one teacher who has an A-level, dream of it . . . the further off, the more unattainable a place is, the more it seems subject, in the imagination, to fortunate chance. It is not easy to imagine oneself suddenly transported to the teachers' training college one hundred and fifty miles away: one would need the requisite number of Certificates, but the University of Zimbabwe – *who knows*? – it might happen, somehow, some time, somewhere.

As for the children here, they have not yet had their results, and the University of Zimbabwe is still part of the landscape of their dreams.

Ayrton R. speaks first. Listening, I understand this is going to be as hard as anything I have done. He is emotional, persuasive, and has behind him the experience of having talked to so many groups of pupils, on so many levels. He makes a statement . . . a suggestion . . . offers a thought – there is the intense and baffled silence which means an idea has not been taken in. He rephrases, tries again. The trouble is, the language he uses, the words, do not find a mirror in the minds of the listeners. In other words, here is the culture gap, illustrated. At the end, trying to give them hope, he says that there is no need to despair, to give up, if they do not pass O-levels, for there are technical schools and this country needs technicians. Their silence is sorrowful, disappointed, if polite.

It is my turn. I have spoken to many different kinds of audiences in many countries, some of them, as we put it, disadvantaged. This is not the first time I say to young people who will never reach university that there are ways of learning open to them, and no one can stop them learning if they want to learn. With a library and perhaps some sympathetic adult to advise them, there is nothing in the world they cannot study. A good library – I am well used to saying, reminding people of our remarkable inheritance – is a treasure house, and we take it for granted. It is possible to pick up a book, perhaps by chance, when you are a child, and find in it a world existing parallel to the one you live in, full of amazements and surprises and delights; you can pursue any interest through different countries and cultures, diving back into history and forward into the future; you can exhaust one interest and then find another; or, turning over books, chance on a subject you had never suspected existed – and follow that, with no idea when you begin where it will lead. With a library you are free, not confined by certainly temporary political climates. It is the most democratic of institutions because no one – but no one at all – can tell you what to read and when and how.

The only trouble with this exhortation, which I have to say has set young people off on explorations of all kinds, was that there was no proper library within three hundred miles. And so I was unable to produce more than a few sentences, while they were thinking, Well, we have a library, don't we?

Then I began to talk about how one becomes a writer, since I've learned that in any audience anywhere there are always people who write novels, or intend to. This went better because there was in fact a man there who was writing, a teacher from another school some miles away.

Jack said afterwards, 'It doesn't matter. What mattered was that someone thought it worth it to come and talk to them. No one takes any notice of them, you see.' And he went on to tell us how 'one of those fat cats from Harare came, an inspector'.

Jack was delighted, hoping he would point out deficiencies to the negligent headmaster. The pupils waited for days in expectation of the event, a visitor from Harare. 'But he went around the school as fast as he could, didn't stop in any class longer than a minute, in some of them he didn't even sit down. He didn't notice the lack of textbooks, he didn't ask questions. Then before he left he said the washing-line should be moved from where it was to somewhere else. The teachers obediently moved it, and moved it back when he left. Off he drove, sweating into his three-piece suit.'

'There are three stages in the flight from the Reserve,' said Ayrton R., 'All right, a Communal Area. The first, a tie. The second, a jacket. The third, a three-piece suit. Then you've made it. You're free for ever from the bush.'

We walk back. The cow, thwarted at the fence, is standing outside the window of a store shed. In the glass she can see another cow who is tossing her horns, and snorting at her. The cow is in two minds about putting her horns right through the glass. Some small children stand watching. They are amused by the deluded cow. Jack calls them, and together they all shoo away the cow from her threatening rival, and persuade her to return to the water tank where there is some new grass. The cow goes, but looks back at the window where she saw the other cow who, she obviously thinks, might decide to pursue her.

In the playground of the junior school the children are squatting on the ground, playing that game that looks like draughts, with smooth stones laid out in holes in the earth. They crowd up to the wire of the playground to watch us, laughing and waving and delighted by the cow.

It is midday. Four or five hours before they get anything to eat.

In Jack's shack we ate bread and tinned herring, feeling like sybarites. Teachers and pupils kept dropping in. What they needed was to see Ayrton R., breathe the same air as he did, be near that elusive paradise, the University of Zimbabwe.

In the afternoon we walked a long way into the bush, which was in the process of ceasing to be bush. Fields were in every stage of preparation. Some had the stumps standing in the bared earth, some stumps were smouldering. There were fields cleared, but untilled. Many trees were ringed for felling. In the bush that was still bush every tree had branches lopped off.

The population of Zimbabwe will triple by 2010. That is, in twenty years. There seems something impossible about this figure.

'Plant trees, we must all plant trees,' urges Comrade Mugabe, shoring what must often seem vain hopes against these ruins of bush. And plant trees they do, miles of the fast-growing blue gums, disliked by everybody as much as we hate the conifer plantations that disfigure Britain. The trouble is, the beautiful indigenous trees grow so slowly.

Mushrooms grew in thousands all along the road. The local people say that mushrooms are poisonous, and came to warn Jack not to eat them. He said that in other parts of the country mushrooms are eaten. But they were unconvinced and await – Jack said – his certain death.

When the sun went down we ate our supper of bread and mushrooms, and tried to listen to the radio. It was not working. Is there no radio in the school? Yes, the other teacher has one, but he is not here. The trouble is, it is hard to get batteries; for most Africans impossibly expensive.

In this school and the other one like it twenty miles away there is no electricity, no telephone, unreliable radio. There is nothing in the way of civilization nearer than that hotel where we had lunch, fifty miles away. When Jack wants to ring up his family in England he takes the bus to the hotel and stays the night there, enjoying electricity, clean water and a decent meal. But often the lines are down, or the connection bad and he can't get through to England on that trip.

His mail comes to the little town where the hotel is. He asks friends to send him books for the school library and we do. The Zimbabwe post office does not encourage an interest in

literature. Any parcel of books over about £10, you have to pay
to receive. If the friends in England are foolish enough to send
two parcels, both under the £10 limit, at the same time, the
enterprising Customs officials tape the two together and you
pay as if they are one parcel. Jack, ever charitable, says he
supposes the officials have trouble feeding themselves and
their families – like the teachers here. Jack does not have any
money because he 'lends' it to the teachers. He has even lent
a good bit to the headmaster – the man without a character.

Next day is the last day of term and there are no classes.
Some of the senior pupils are planting maize: this school has
Agriculture as part of the curriculum. The pupils become bare-
legged gangs, dozens of them invading a field all at once, dropping the maize seeds into holes along lines determined by
strings stretched between pegs. They enjoy this work, and sing
and even dance at the edges of the fields. Jack works with
them. The other teachers, he says, are too good to work in the
fields, but he is white and entitled to eccentricity. The teacher
called the Agricultural Instructor did not know when to plant
the maize, and asked Jack, who did not know, but found out.
The maize from last year's crop was improperly stored, because
of the no-good headmaster, and it all went bad. It is still sitting,
full of weevils, in a shed.

Two end-of-term parties were in preparation. Form One's
meal was to be stewed goat and sadza. The goat had been killed
and its parts were divided into bloody heaps on the ground.
The good bits were already stewing. Form Four were having
superior food – white bread, a treat. Jack had ordered twenty
loaves from the store. They would be eaten without butter or
jam. When he was invited to supper with the parents of a
pupil, he was offered white bread and tea, and they said, 'We
are poor people, we can't afford margarine.'

Before we left we tried to visit the clinic but it was closed.
One of the teachers said bitterly that there was nothing in it
but anti-malaria pills and aspirin. Another said, smiling apolo-
getically, we should take no notice of the first – he was exaggerating, we must understand they were all feeling sad because it
was the end of term. A doctor visited the school once a month.

When there was an accident or someone got really ill, they were taken to hospital. Please remember that not long ago there was no clinic here at all.

It was hard to say goodbye to Jack. By then we had understood that it was he who was running – or at least tried to – this school. His was the real authority. An impossible position, for no one could acknowledge that he was: not he, not the other teachers.

We drove away under the cold sky, and to the hotel and found the space of the dining-room wantonly, wastefully large after the tiny rooms in Jack's house. We ate cold meat and salad, apple pie and ice-cream, surrounded by black people, mostly local businessmen, shopkeepers and Chefs, all lucky enough not to be in a bush school with little hope of escape. We thought – of course – of how electric light and clean lavatories, a telephone and running water were not to be taken for granted; reminded ourselves that both of us had been brought up in the bush in houses that had no electric light or running water or indoor lavatories. We were afflicted by that sense of division, foreboding, and anxious incredulity that comes from moving too quickly from utter poverty to the amenities of the hotel in the little provincial town which owes its importance to being on the road north to Zambia.

Then we visited a woman who is involved with the recruiting and supervision of teachers from America and countries in Europe. She said, 'You would be surprised how many of the headmasters go bad.' We told her a version of the current joke: What is the most dangerous occupation in Zimbabwe these days? Answer: Headmaster. You'll be lucky to get away with five years. (Told us by a teacher in Harare, when he heard we were off to visit a secondary school.) She said that when a headmaster 'goes bad' often his school is run by youngsters from Britain, Sweden, Germany, but she tells them, 'Don't do it. Do what you are supposed to do, no more: you are doing these people no favour by taking over the responsibility. All right – the place goes to pieces. Then one of them will have to face up to it.' She said it was very hard for young people full of idealism to stand by and watch things go to pieces when they have skills to deal with them. She tells them, 'You must remember that from the moment you were born you've been absorbing the skills of the modern world – you've acquired them without even knowing it. But they haven't. How do you think they are going to learn if you just do it all for them?'

One of the Chefs has just made a speech saying that the ex-pat teachers should all be sent home, there was no need for them. How did she feel about that, we asked?

'If you're going to get upset by that kind of thing, you shouldn't be in Zimbabwe,' said this strong-minded lady. 'Anyway, half the speeches they make are for popular consumption.'

We have come away with copies of the school magazine, which Jack started: there wasn't one until he came. He has taught the senior pupils elementary journalism and lay-out, and has taken them for trips into Harare – at his expense – to visit printing works and the offices of newspapers.

Because of Jack fifty or so of these young people can claim they know at least the basics of how to make a newspaper.

Here is a poem written by one of the brightest girls, who has succeeded in spite of difficulties at home in finding a place and light enough to study, or even read. Her father has three wives, her mother being the senior wife. There are twenty children. She is the seventh of eight children. Her family has great expectations for her. She has a thirty-year-old brother who is a primary school teacher.

Where next dear Brothers and Sisters?
  I can't forget the day I came to Kapfunde.
  I was full of love and joy for the beautiful school.
  Happy students cheered for our arrival.
  We were received in a hospitable manner.
  I couldn't believe I was at last at Kapfunde.
  When I think of leaving Kapfunde
  Where students and teachers live in harmony
  I just feel strength going out of me.
  I can't bear the thought of leaving Kapfunde,
  But there is nothing to do.

Time to part, from friends and teachers of Kapfunde
is drawing near.
But the problem is where next, Form Fours?
We have enjoyed every activity,
And every scrap of food at Kapfunde.
We have stayed here four years.
But sooner or later the problem is to come.
The problem is where to go next, what to do,
Whether you will be behind the headmaster's desk,
Or somewhere in the streets, Form Four, think of it,
One day you will find yourself prowling and haunting streets,
Wandering in search of jobs.
Goodbye teachers and students of Kapfunde,
I am grateful for the good times we had together,
Students, please keep the Kapfunde alive in you
Be proud of your beautiful school.
But Form Four, where next from Kapfunde?

                                        by Comrade Ruth Chakamanga

This girl took six O-levels. She passed two, was 'the second-best girl'. She got an A in Shona. She passed maths, the hardest exam. She failed English. Later she retook exams, and now is in teacher training college.

Out of the more than eighty who sat English, six passed. But last year no one passed English.

In Zimbabwe today you need five passes to get a job. With three you can train to be a nurse.

Here is a letter from the school magazine:

Dear Editors. I have a problem concerning our textbooks. I think every student at school has paid $120 but I have found out that when we are in our lessons we always share textbooks. So where is our money going? Does it mean that the money we are paying is not sufficient to buy books? I have noticed that it is a big disadvantage for the Form Fours to share one book between seven people. As we are the people who pay school fees we ought to have one textbook per each person in order for him to get good advantage when reading.

And

A DISASTROUS MEAL

The vagaries of the weather create extremes, periods when food will be abundant and periods of less or no food. This is particularly true with relish problems. There is abundant relish in summer weeds, muboora and okra known as derere. It was in summer, the rains were still going on and people were beginning to fear that the rains would never come to an end. Finally, the rain was over. Muboora and derere were inedible. It was dirty and wet. We had to choose either to go without sadza or to think of something else. Our option was obvious, to think of something else. We had to go and fetch mushrooms. I did this with my two colleagues who were brothers. My mother was happy about our decision.

We arrived at the popular mountain, Chembira, the highest point of Gutu. We found many varieties and many of these were strange to me. I told my other colleagues to adhere to one variety but they just ignored what I was saying. We went back home and we had a delicious meal.

All of us were very much surprised the following day, no one was moving about at our neighbour's yard. Cattle were complaining that they were still in the kraal while some chickens were giving warning that they would break out of their house. A villager then gathered courage and opened the door. He was flabbergasted and petrified by what he saw. They were dead.

The bodies went for an examination at the hospital which was very near. The very first and the obvious targets were the witches. It was an issue debated for a long period. The majority agreed to consult a nganga. Some asked what will be done to the person. One man stood up and said, 'Let's not reason like cowards. When a child comes and defecates on my floor, will I just glare at him? No, I will take a stick and break his head.'

The man encouraged the people to take stern measures against witches.

The person suspected was a doddering old woman, probably of ninety. Her speed was fifty metres an hour. She asked them to look at what they had eaten the previous day: it was mushrooms. The truth was starting to reveal itself. Suspicion of witchcraft was still great. Probably they were not cruel but wanted to find a reason for the deaths.

The post-mortem examination revealed that they had eaten some poison.

WITCHCRAFT

This subject arrives in every conversation, sooner rather than later.

The Passionate Apologists at once insist that in Europe 'everyone' reads horoscopes, that fortune-tellers flourish, that the United States thinks nothing of voting in a President whose schedule is ruled by an astrologer. How about the revival of witchcraft everywhere in Europe? How about Satanism? What do we have to say about those men of priestly magic who so confidently undertake to exorcize evil spirits? Is it not possible that we may yet see (we: Europe) the burning of witches, and mob violence against Satanism?

(If we have not seen mob violence, we have observed the forces of Reason, that is to say, social workers, using methods of interrogation identical to those once used to convict witches on young people and children suspected of complicity with Satanism.)

In other words, who the hell are you (critics from outside Africa) to talk? Put your own house in order first.

FORTRESS HOUSES

We drove in a few hours right across Zimbabwe, west to east. In Harare we had to drop in at several houses before going home. The verandahs of these houses built for air and sun are barred, making them like cages: all windows are barred now. Around the houses and gardens of the new rich (black) the walls are going up, so that you can't see inside. Every evening in a certain place you may watch young men being drilled. The unemployed former Freedom Fighters have created an organization that supplies guards for houses. They drill in the late afternoon, using their expertise from the War, and report for duty at the houses as the light goes. They patrol while the owners sleep. As we drive up to the suburb where Ayrton R.'s house is we pass the President's house. The high walls are heaped with coils of razor wire, and inside patrol guards. When the President drives out through these streets, it is in a limousine with tinted windows, so people cannot see in, and he is in the centre of a motorcade, with armed motorcycle riders. If you are driving through these streets and you hear the sirens of the President's motorcade, you must drive off into a side street. Otherwise you will be shot at. This is no threat to cow the citizens: people have been known to be shot at if they didn't get out of the way. I personally know a rather absent-minded young man who was on a motorbike, and did not understand that the sirens meant the approach of the President. People on the pavement yelled at him to stop or he would be killed. He stopped just in time. A doctor was driving along listening to a pop singer called The Wailer on the car radio: he did not hear those other, more urgent, wailers; did not stop or get off the road. His car was sprayed with bullets, though he was unhurt.

When we got home, the house was opened from inside by Dorothy. The locks for the front door are efficient. At night one part of the house, the bedroom part, is locked against the part that can be entered through the glass of the patio. When I am in my room at the end of the house, I have the door open, but the moment I leave that room, which is on the garden, I lock it and remove the key, inserting a little barrel-like device that makes it impossible to open the door from the outside. The windows of the rooms are barred. At night the car is locked with a chain around the steering wheel. Ayrton R. has had one car stolen already. Everyone you meet has had a car stolen.

Harare is turning itself into a copy of Johannesburg, where for a long time houses have had night watchmen and guard dogs and barred windows, and where in the townships it is taken for granted that whatever can be stolen, will be.

A COMMERCIAL FARM (BLACK)

I meet an Agricultural Extension Worker.

What is an Agricultural Extension Worker? you may ask, if still capable of being amazed at the jargon of bureaucrats.

An Agricultural Extension Worker is an expert in Agriculture. But why Extension Worker?

Don't ask, just don't bother to ask, but from one end of the world to the other, people who know about crops and soil and beasts are called Extension Workers.

Don't you *see*? It is an extension of knowledge.

Never mind.

This man had been visiting a large farm once owned by whites, which grew tobacco as the main crop.

'Tell me,' I said.

The farmhouse and all the outbuildings were crammed with relatives and friends. The manager, a brother of the owner, who is a Chef and a Minister, was in Harare. Another relative took him around. Everybody living there, getting on for a hundred of them, had planted his or her own personal patch of mealies. Many had a cow or two. These beasts were contentedly running together. There were goats. One of the mysteries of Zimbabwe is that you see goats everywhere but these beasts, called 'firemouths' in some countries, don't seem to be doing damage.

'No tobacco?' I asked.

'No tobacco.'

'Just mealies and mombies?'

'And some nice vegetable gardens.'

'Would you say,' I cautiously ask, 'that this is some kind of subsistence farming?'

He looks defensive, but humorous. 'Yes, that is what I would say.'

He does not say: 'Well, what is the matter with that?' since it would contradict government policy.

'I don't see what is the matter with that.'

'I don't either.'

TALK ON THE VERANDAHS

A lot of the whites put on their barrier creams as they get up in the mornings: there is an increase in skin cancer.

More people get killed by lightning in Zimbabwe than anywhere else in the world.

Lightning often strikes through the doors of huts, and kills people sleeping around the hearth.

Why should lightning bother to do anything of the sort?

Perhaps lightning likes the metal in hoes, or axes, or plates or the bangles on the women?

I contribute: When I was a girl we used to drive through a bit of bush not far from the farm where every tree had been struck by lightning.

Then there must be something in the soil, some rock or mineral, that attracts the lightning there.

A certain academic (white) concerned that so many black girls who get pregnant and want to keep their babies have nowhere

to go, because their families throw them out, started a modern
refuge, stretching his own and friends' resources to pay for it.
This roused frenzies of anger and disapproval in some people
(black) who showed all the self-righteous disapproval we call
'Victorian': 'It's their fault if they get into trouble isn't it?' 'Why
should they expect other people to help them if they are
foolish?'

But why 'Victorian'? I was told recently, by someone who
saw it in one of the smart areas of London, that a young couple,
charming products of Mrs Thatcher's Britain, were driving
proudly around in a Porsche with a car-sticker that said, To
Hell With the Poor!

Another person told me she had seen, outside a smart pub
in London's West End, a group of yuppies sitting and drinking.
A beggar came up to them: a young woman took out a five
pound note and burned it, laughing, in front of him. It is
extremely hard not to wish that these unlikeable people are
now out of a job, and downwardly mobile.

A story about the death of Samora Machel supposed to be
murdered by the South Africans. Told by a young white
woman.

'That was the only time I have been scared in Zimbabwe.
The young blacks were rampaging about the streets looking for
whites to beat up. They did beat up some old white women.
My husband saw it. He was looking down from a high window
and thought, What a pretty demonstration, with all those green
branches, and then he saw the beatings. I was at a meeting for
the death of Samora Machel, and it was being addressed by a
famous rabble-rouser, you know, all big mouth and hot air. He
was going on about the CIA, they are the scapegoat for anything and everything. He said, "The CIA are well-known for a
thought technique of inhibiting you from speaking. I was
speaking at a meeting and then suddenly my voice left me. I
knew it was them." The man was crazy, but the audience loved
it. He went from bad to worse, and I was so bored I kept falling
asleep. I thought, this is dangerous, if they see I am asleep
they might start beating me up. One word from this maniac

and they'd do anything. I really understood the word rabble-rouser that day.'

AT A SLIGHT ANGLE

This Commercial Farm is only five miles from our old farm where I still cannot bring myself to go. Ayrton R. thinks – and so do I – that my neurotic behaviour cannot be permitted to go on, and meanwhile this visit will be a bridge – a stepping-stone – a gentle breaking-in.

The hills I grew up with, not to mention the Dyke, are all present, but at an angle.

Where this farm is now was land not 'opened up for development', for it was still bush when as a girl I used to visit a farm just over a ridge from here, for a week or so at a time. The attraction of that farm was stronger than any other because it was full of books, different from those in our bookcases, mostly modern novels of the kind my mother was sure were corrupting. I used to walk by myself in bush different from ours, although so close, for everywhere were kopjes crammed with granite boulders. The house itself was on a hill of boulders, inserted among them, accommodating itself to them, and most of its fabric was granite. What effect on us all did this granite have? I wonder. All the time I was there I was forced to check on 'the view', the hills I knew so well, but this askew perspective created valleys and crags invisible from our verandah. To be whisked from one landscape immovably the same for years through every change of sun and cloud to another, only slightly different, is an assault on some inner balance you have learned to rely on. To return after years to your childhood landscape pulled slightly out of whack tests the landscape you remember, filling you with doubt as dreams do.

We arrived on this new farm in the late afternoon, the shadows black on sunny grass, just as the farmer's wife was leading half a dozen horses towards their field. She didn't feed them, she said, they fed themselves off the bush. Didn't we think they looked well? They never got sick, she never had to dose them, the vet was never needed. They were splendid horses, glowing in the sun, pleased with themselves after their day free in the bush.

And there was the deep verandah, full of furniture designed for lolling about in. This farmer is middle-aged, lean, brown, taut with energy and ideas and before we have sat down he is off – the government, the wrong-headedness of Mugabe, the impossibility of farming without spare parts and machinery, but this complaint is not where his heart lies, for what we then listened to was a cataract of ideas about farming, a philosophy.

At once I am taken right back to *then* because there was always at least one farmer in The District who was obsessed, possessed, with news emanating from some research institute or university – the States, Argentina, Scotland, South America – which would condemn all present farming ideas to the rubbish heap. No need to weed the fields, one should plant among weeds; no need to use fertilizer, if one didn't fertilize the soil itself would adjust and find sustenance in the air; a waste of time to stump out trees and make fields: much better plant among the trees. These ideas and a hundred others appeared on the verandahs, usually because of one farmer. My father for a time was that farmer. More accurate, I think, to see this character, wild, inventive, iconoclastic, less as a person than as an abiding layer or subsidiary personality in every farmer, for one never knew when some chance remark would bring it to the surface. 'Oh, by the way, did you read in the *Farmer's Weekly* that letter saying the way to stop flocks of guineafowl following the planters and eating up the seed as it falls is to perfume the seed-hoppers with garlic, or, better still, plant a clove of garlic with each maize seed?' Expensive? Well, yes, but why be petty? What matters is the *idea*, the perfection of it, abolishing a problem with one majestic flash of the imagination.

Five of us set off on a walk around the farm, or to use the old manorial style, around the lands. I am going down on the lands, he is on the lands, she is on the lands but I'll tell her when she gets back from the lands that . . .

Late afternoon. The sun is preparing to become a sunset. The birds' conversation is still full of daytime concerns, but will soon change key into the minor mode, and what sounds like regret that the day is over. We leave behind in the house various growing children, a fiancée, her brothers, and an assortment of visitors and friends, as in a Russian novel.

We listen to the farmer, whose discourse is a lament for the way we use the world.

'No, you don't understand, if you want to understand agriculture you must look at everything differently. All farming is unnatural, it is an assault on Nature. The moment the first farmer put a spade into the earth it was the beginning of our war on Nature. And now we have reached the point where it is a race between Man and Nature. Who is going to win? I tell you who, it is Nature.' We stand on a muddy track between fields of tobacco, smelling strong because of the rain that is lying in deep puddles along the ruts. 'We fill fields full of just one plant, that isn't Nature's way, it is our way. Nature attacks with a disease or a bug. So we attack Nature with a chemical. Nature evolves the plant so it can deal with the chemical, or the bug mutates. We make another chemical. All these fields are soaked with chemicals. Last year we were spraying this field when the rain came down hard suddenly. We ran for it. The rain washed the poison down into the earth, there wasn't time for it to get weak in the sun and the air. And now look.' At the edge of the field was a twenty-yard area where the tobacco plants were stunted. 'Poisoned. Sometimes you can see what we are doing with our poisons. That one was for eelworm. Do you want to see eelworm?'

We stumble about among plants that send up rank sweet fumes into our brains, tobacco, as seductive green as it is when dry and ready to smoke, and the farmer pulls up a deformed plant and stands holding it in both hands, looking down at it with respect, an enemy contained, not defeated. 'Nature comes up with eelworm. We poison it. But a newly stumped-out field has no pests. You have a couple of years' grace before the pests build up. We laugh at the African's old way, stumping out a bit of land, using it, then moving on – they didn't have the build-up of pests. Of course there isn't land enough in the world now to farm like that. If we farmed like that in Zimbabwe everyone would starve.'

We walk on, listening, avoiding puddles. 'It's all a balance, and you have to understand that. We stake our claim – unnatural practices, plants we grow in fields of hundreds of acres, but Nature likes a mix. She takes a step forward – so do we, it's a race. We have to be a step ahead all the time, but where is it going to end? I'll tell you, we're too damned clever by half and Nature is going to have the last word.'

Now on one side of the road is bush, real bush, and the farmer's wife directs our attention to some orchids. We all step into the bush and admire the plants: there are several in that small patch of bush. 'There you are,' says the farmer, coming to stand by us. 'We don't know why that plant has decided to grow just there, why it likes just this bit of soil. But look . . .' And he stands feet apart, and lifts up a double handful of the earth, which is a mix of soil crumbs, leaf mould, birds' droppings, and minerals washed from the stones. He gazes down at the earth in his hands. 'There, that's real soil,' he says. 'Not the rubbish we have in our fields, full of chemicals, that's not soil. If you saw them without plants . . . the soil is like brick rubble, it's dead. No, that's not earth. This is it.' His hands hold the bush soil delicately, with respect. We stand for a while in silence. The sun is down behind the trees, outlining them in yellow, and the birds' voices make the transition to evening sadness. 'There, look at it,' says he, 'just look.' And he lets it trickle through his fingers, back on to the floor of grasses and flowers and weeds. 'There, you see? I've disturbed the balance just doing that. We stand here and we don't know what damage we are doing with our feet, what organisms we are killing, what pests we have brought in from the road. We are going to step back on to the road and Nature will have to work hard to put right the damage we've done. Before the whites came the blacks moved about in the bush but they didn't harm it, not until they started turning the soil over and planting crops. What crops? Most of them are imports. Look at maize. How do we know what bugs the Portuguese brought in with maize? We don't know! We don't care! Well, don't care was made to care . . . you ought to be able to stick a finger easily into real soil.' He bends and does so. 'See that? Better have a good look, because with what we are doing to the world we won't see that anywhere, soon.'

The farmer's wife silently indicates some Christmas lilies on an antheap. They are also called spider lilies. Each bloom is like a delicate red and yellow claw and once we used to pick them in armfuls to decorate our houses at Christmas. No one would pick them recklessly now. She shows us another plant. 'The horses like this one. We don't know why. When they come in from the bush you can always smell the plant on their noses.'

The men stride off into a field. The farmer's wife and I stand looking at the reddish gold light of sunset touching the white flowers on a bauhinia tree. These flowers are delicate, like the spider lilies or the orchids: the high veld's flowers are never heavy and damp and solid-fleshed like those of the tropics. They are fragile, and light, and their smell is dry, teasing, spicy.

The sunset leaps up the sky in a wash of reddish gold. The trees are black and silent and the birds, if they are awake, have nothing to say. We walk in silence along the farm track. A long way behind us the farmer's lament can just be heard, but now it is hard to distinguish it from the voices coming from the farm township over the ridge – where, of course, side by side with the farm workers, live so many other people who officially are not there at all.

We walk companionably back to the house in the dark. An owl . . . another. The smell of horses. A soft whinny greets the farmer's wife and she calls softly to them. There is a rush of hooves in the dark, and for a while she stands by the fence, a small dark figure reaching up to the horses' heads, brought into sight by white-fringed ears, or the blaze on a forehead.

We join the men as the farmer is saying, 'The blacks are not interested in our ideas about efficiency. Look . . .' A man on a bicycle emerges from the dark. The farmer commands, 'Stop.' The man's dark shape becomes defined as he halts, one foot on the ground. He is smiling. 'Have you got brakes on your bicycle?' asks the farmer. 'No.' 'I can see you haven't got a light.' No reply. 'All right,' says the farmer, 'that's all, off you go.' 'Good night,' says the man, and pedals off.

'There must be dozens of bicycles on the farm and not one of them has lights, not one has brakes that work. They ride the bikes everywhere, through the bush, up hills, along dongas. Slowly everything falls off, brakes, mudguards, handlebar grips, pedal rubbers, everything. Or if they don't fall off they are stolen, and no one bothers to replace them.'

We stand in the dark looking at the black shape of the low wide house, which is spilling out yellow light, and we are thinking, or Africa thinks through us, 'What do you need lights for, when you know the tracks so well? You don't really need brakes, you can always use a foot. Why grips on handlebars? All you need for a pedal is a bar for your foot. Why make life so complicated? The bike goes doesn't it? It carries you from place to place? Well, then, what's the fuss about?'

'Ye-e-e-yes,' says the farmer 'that's how it is.'

And we go in to supper. All the food came off the farm. There was no servant, he had gone home. The family laid the table, served, cleared it and washed up.

At supper I ask about the people who used to live on the farms near here. Some names are instantly remembered. 'Of course! So and so! He had the farm across the river. Yes, and *they* were there until the War. Of course we remember.' But other names get no response at all, yet they were people who lived on farms next to the people who are remembered. 'Who? I've never heard that name. Commander Knight, you say?'

'Yes, he was a character, everyone knew him. He was one of the eccentrics – you know, the larger-than-life characters of those days.' Here various members of the family give the farmer significant looks and smiles which he acknowledges, good-humouredly. 'He was on the farm just four miles away. He tamed leopards. Or tried to.'

'Never heard of him.'

After supper we lolled about over sofas and enormous chairs, arms around dogs and cats. There is an old-fashioned wind-up gramophone, restored as an antique by someone in Harare, and cases of records stand waiting for someone to wind up the gramophone and play them. Ancient tunes like 'Paloma', and 'Red Sails in the Sunset' resound tinnily and I explain to disbelieving youngsters that once on these verandahs were dances that went on until dawn, with no more music than these same wind-up gramophones, that had to be attended to hour after hour by relays of people, wallflowers or people prepared to sacrifice themselves. They murmur that they wish they had been taught to dance, in the same tones one might use to say, What a pity we don't dance the minuet. I say that in Britain this kind of dancing is fashionable again, but their faces have that look: it is interesting to hear of the customs of far-off places.

The farmer is describing his dream: he would like this farm to become a kind of commune, though he does not use the word. The newly engaged couple are already established in the house built for them a hundred yards away. Another little house accommodates parents. A son would like to buy the farm along the road: he has all the qualifications for this kind of high-tec farming. 'Families should stay together,' says the farmer, using the same words used by the black agricultural expert or Extension Worker on the Jesuit farm near Harare. The two men have everything in common, not only their knowledge of farming, for one is a patriarch by tradition, the white man by chance of character. And what do the children of the patriarch think of these plans? They smile, but do not say. And what of a daughter, married to a South African who only understands streets and offices, and could not farm? 'That will be easy,' says the farmer, but frowning a little. He has planned it all out. The daughter can come here for she is a Zimbabwean, and bring her husband. The couple can run canoe trips and manage tourist chalets on the edge of the lake that will soon be here, only three or four miles away. The farmer has agreed to lose forty acres of his farm to the new lake, but he intends to reap the benefits.

'Chalets and canoe trips,' I protest, for he is talking about a particularly magnificent bit of wilderness under the hills.

Ayrton R. protests, 'It will be just like Kariba.'

'Not at all. These things can be done with taste.'

My room, at the back of the house, is vast. There are toys pushed to the backs of cupboards. As well as screening for mosquitos there are heavy bars on the windows: the Bush War was bad in these parts. This kind of country, all kopjes and heaped boulders and ravines and thick trees, was made for guerilla war. In the bathroom spiders and flying ants and moths make for the light or fall into the bath. In London one spider demands appropriate measures: a towel draped over the bath so the creature can climb out, or a tin lid for water, somewhere low, since they die of thirst: they go in search of water under our taps. Here you take no notice, it is Africa, there are too many of them. Once I was visiting a farm near Nairobi, which I remember most for its posse of Arab horses that were brought up to the house to be petted and fed sugar lumps. But I also remember the caterpillars. Occasionally caterpillars invaded the house in thousands, and one had simply to wait for them to go away, brushing them off chairs, beds, the dining table. After a bit you hardly notice them – I was told.

I wake in the night to listen – what for? The tom-toms that used once to beat all night from every farm compound. But it is as if a pulse has ceased to beat. The night is dark and almost silent. Through the bars come the small sounds that say the bush is awake, birds and small animals and once a dog barking from the farm village.

In the morning we wake at different times and sit on the verandah drinking coffee. The farmer's wife is out riding. The farmer has already been out on the lands, and now he is entertaining us. This morning it is medicine. 'We need a cure for a disease, but the doctors don't know about it. We get it often, whites and blacks. Your limbs are like lead, you have a sore neck and shoulders, and you can't move them, everything aches, you wish you were dead. Then it goes. I think it is an insect bite, perhaps it is like tsetse or malaria. You have a certain kind of stomach upset. You go to the doctor, he says it is flu. It isn't flu. The Africans know it isn't flu. We know it isn't flu.'

The farmer's wife comes back, and we set off for a walk, all of us.

The farm's pigs are – it goes without saying – allowed to forage for themselves, no battery pigs on this farm. They are a small energetic company, who present themselves for recognition and greetings.

The farmer says everyone underestimates the intelligence of animals. If we knew what they thought of us, we wouldn't like it. Also, their sense of humour. Pigs play practical jokes on each other. So do calves. Young animals play games, like children. Sometimes he takes himself into a field where the calves are and he sits down quietly under a bush until they forget he is there, and he watches them play king-of-the-castle, pushing each other off an anthill until one of them wins. Then the winner comes down and they start the game again. It is nearly always the same calf that wins: the aristocracy of Nature, you have to understand it, Nature knows nothing about democracy. There is always a buffoon in a crowd of young animals, a prankster who makes the others laugh. You think animals don't laugh? Don't you believe it! See that little pig over there? He's the runt of the litter, he's full of tricks and they laugh at him.

We are shown the vegetable garden. 'If we were allowed to be subsistence farmers we could live like kings on ten acres. Everything grows here. We already grow more vegetables on half an acre than we can possibly use – the Africans get most of them, and we grow things for them they like to eat and we don't. We have cows and pigs. We are self-sufficient already, but we are committed to this business of over-production. What am I growing tobacco for? To earn foreign currency for Mugabe but I'm not allowed any to buy spare parts and new machines. Rich farmers they call us, Commercial Farmers, all they see is the amount of land, not the risk of it. We can be wiped out in a hailstorm in ten minutes. We watch the skies all through the rainy season, the clouds pile up, my God, will it be this time? Hundreds of thousands of pounds' worth of damage while you watch – it's all a gamble. And then, the locusts are back. We've got hoppers on the farm, I'm spraying them but there can be a potential army of locusts in a few square feet of bush hidden away somewhere, you miss them – and that's it. And if you poison them don't imagine it doesn't do harm, all these poisons do harm. We have to pay the penalty for battery chickens and torturing pigs in pens they can't turn around in. Who is going to punish us? God, that's who. Don't think He isn't watching us.'

He is talking about his workforce, paternally, protectively. He and his wife like the Africans. There is never that cold dislike you learn to listen for. And they like him, so he says. 'They call me the Crazy One, but that's all right. If I'm an eccentric all it means I get things done in new ways. They come to me, they ask this and that – loans, or to help them with bureaucrats. I pull out their teeth when they ask, I doctor them, we discuss their problems. They listen to me, and I listen to them. But what you must remember is, they are going along with our ways because it's the modern world and they're stuck with it, but our ways aren't their ways, they don't like them, they like their own ways, it goes against their natures, the way we do things. In the end, it won't be our ways they choose. Well, all right, it's their continent, but I hope they'll let me use a few acres of it. I think they will. You know the important thing about them? All that noise over the War made everyone see things wrong. These aren't vengeful people. They don't go in for hating. When you get talking, you know what you find? They're very philosophical people, they take the long view. So – they're like me and that's why we get along.'

The breakfast table is loaded. The maize meal we knew has gone. It was a grainy mass, full of taste, but now the grain is refined and sadza is white, jelly-like, tasteless. The men, who are going to be working hard all day, are eating plates of it. The scrambled eggs are from hens free to choose their diet, insects and plants from the bush, as well as grain thrown down for them. There is fish pâté made from fish smoked over a certain acacia wood. Jams and cheese and cereals are all made locally. The yoghurt comes from the farm.

The men are talking about the day's work, as if no one else around the table exists. Just like *then*. But the women are discussing a trip into Harare for the day. This emphatically is not like *then*, when women were imprisoned on the farms, and a visit to a neighbour was a great event. This is such an assault on my memory I postpone the problem till later. Besides, the farmer is talking again. About the AIDS virus. He admires this virus. 'That is the most cunning little virus. I read the other day that the Devil could have designed it, but no, it is God, giving us a warning. We have all gone mad over sex – the whole world. So God is saying, Now, be careful, I'm warning you again! Next time it will be worse than AIDS, if we don't listen.'

This takes me straight back to my Old-Testament-dominated father. In his view it was the forthcoming Second World War that was God's punishment for sin. He and Churchill alone knew what was rushing towards us: it was the Wrath to Come. There I was, sitting in the same landscape, if from this awry perspective, listening to a reincarnation of my father thundering warnings of God's new punishments, after fifty years, the Second World War, the Bush War, and all the other wars and disasters. A kind of continuity, I suppose.

OVER THE RAINBOW

In Harare they talk endlessly about the new agreement over Namibia in the same way we do about the ending of the Iran–Iraq War, and the end of the invasion of Afghanistan. With every war there is this feeling that it is impossible, it can't be true, we are dealing in lunacies, there is no reason why it should be happening, it could have been avoided. Yet it is happening, and it seems nothing can stop it. Then – it stops. If it can be stopped, then why did it start? This line of thought goes back to primitive fears, beliefs: is there a God, a Power, that needs the smell of blood? After all, we believed this for thousands of years, and perhaps the old belief helps to create the helplessness that can be sensed when war is seething up and seems unstoppable.

But now the mood is optimistic. If They can stop the Namibian War, then They can stop the slaughter in Mozambique. Obviously it is only a question of time.

And even cocky: 'Now the Third World Groupies will take themselves off to Namibia and we'll get them off our backs. They are packing their bags already.'

'Perhaps they will find their paradise in Namibia.'

'Somewhere, over the rainbow . . .'

IN THE OFFICES

I have spent a day . . . two days . . . three days, in offices in Harare. Not an easy business: security is a problem. At the entrances to government offices there may be guards, in Aid offices doors are anxiously unlocked to let you in, and then locked again. 'Skellums' of all kinds abound, the young unemployed, some of them children, and the ex-soldiers, subsisting somehow in holes and corners of this populous city on petty crime and not so petty crime. 'None of that kind of thing under us, under the whites,' you hear, in the sniffy voice of the black-disliker, '*we* used to just stroll in off the street any time we liked to have a chat about our problems.' '*Who* strolled in? The whites strolled in, the blacks were seen as potential thieves.'

Government offices, Aid offices, in both the words most often heard are Infrastructure, Extension Worker, Aid Money and – of course – Comrade Mugabe.

I sit and listen. Not only for the facts and figures which are after all in the pamphlets and reports that now cover every possible surface in my room, but for the tones of a voice. Passionate Protagonists to a woman and a man, but some sound as desperate as parents with a sick child, and others are, there is only one word, cynical. The new rich class, the corrupt élite, that's the problem.

'You go down to the villages, you see how they are working;

you see how optimistic they are, and the poverty, the terrible poverty, then you come back to Harare and watch these fat cats swanning around I tell you, it makes me want to . . .'

On the wall of a government office I see a poster.

> The Boss drives his men,
> The Leader inspires them.
> The Boss depends on authority.
> The Leader depends on goodwill.
> The Boss evokes fear.
> The Leader radiates love.
> The Boss says 'I'.
> The Leader says 'We'.
> The Boss shows who is wrong.
> The Leader shows what is wrong.
> The Boss knows how it is done.
> The Leader knows how to do it.
> The Boss demands respect.
> The Leader commands respect.
> So be a leader,
> Not a boss.

They say this exhortation is on the walls of every government office in the country.

FAT CAT ADMONISHED

In a certain Aid office I was told this story, to persuade me – persuade himself? – that things were not so bad, really.

A very high-up official, a woman, 'one of the good ones, you know' – kept close contact with her village, which is in a remote area, far from Harare. She insisted a male colleague should come with her to visit it. 'How long since you visited your village? – Very well, you must come with me to mine.' He agreed, grumbling. The first night she broke him in gently, at a decent hotel, but the next night it was a terrible hotel. 'People have to use it, don't they?' she said. 'Why shouldn't you?' He complained and suffered all the way. From the last little town on the road they had to walk through miles of bush to her village. She introduced this man to women working in the fields, and they at once started to shout at him that if he was a Chef then what did the government think it was doing? He complained, 'They shouldn't be talking to me like this, they should show respect.' A child had been sent to fetch the old men. Ten or twelve of them arrived, together, and the oldest said, 'Sit down, my child, and now you must listen to us.' The great official obediently sat. 'My child,' said the spokesman, 'you have done very badly. Your thoughts have not been with us. All we hear about you is bad. How is it that we had that terrible war and now all we see is people like yourself, who have forgotten about us, getting rich in Harare?'

The official had to sit and listen while one old man after another, and then the women, scolded him. But on the way home he said it had been a wonderful experience. He had been reminded of where his duty lay.

'So you see,' says my interlocutor persuasively, but sighing, 'things can't be so bad, can they?'

'And has the official changed his ways?'

'That I am afraid I don't know.'

A POLITICAL OFFICE

A young woman of medium rank (black) lectures me about the disadvantages of a civil service. 'We are going to make sure the civil service has no power,' she says. 'Otherwise they hold things up when we make decisions. Did you see "Yes, Minister"?'

'It has been argued,' I suggest, 'that a responsible civil service can prevent the excesses of a bad government.'

'But our government isn't bad, it is good, and it will only do what is best for everyone.'

This particular department is manned and womaned by a host of attractive young people, all in their thirties and committed to any 'line' put forth by Comrade Mugabe. That means they must sound like marxists, even if they are not, must support a one-party state, and – this is the important point – support the ever-spreading control by the ruling party over every part of administration. The new bureaucracy doubles every year – exponentially, people claim, it is like the Sorcerer's Apprentice, it is like a fungus devouring everything. That these intelligent people are unaware of the bad things that go on is impossible: what they say to each other behind closed doors can be guessed at. But they present a smiling united front to anyone from outside who might be a critic.

I remark that Lao Tzu said, 'You must govern a country as you would fry a small fish – lightly.'

They exchange looks, hesitate, then laugh. 'Is he Chinese?'

I see they think he is modern Chinese, therefore marxist, therefore good.

My companion, a woman who spends much time in the villages, mentions the new Sheraton Hotel, built by the Yugoslavs, claimed to be the ugliest building ever built anywhere. It is called the People's Hotel, but no Povo would dare to go near it, for they would be shown the door at once. The officials exchange quick looks: they are aware of all the criticism.

'I heard a village woman from Central Province say, "What they have spent on the Sheraton would give all this province clean water."'

The officials do not look at us, nor at each other. From this I deduce they probably agree with the woman from Central Province.

A bit later in the conversation one remarks, 'Of course we have made mistakes.'

The great new buildings are more than a sore point: in some conversations with Povos, even with Passionate Protagonists, it becomes clear they are a symbol of everything people hate about the new regime. There is not only this luxurious People's

Hotel, used only by fat cats and prestigious visitors, but there
is the new Party HQ, for which money has been collected from
even the poorest people. There is Heroes Acre, which cost a
lot of money. And now there is talk that the new Houses of
Parliament will be built on top of the kopje. 'What is wrong
with the old one?' people ask. And, in fact, it is an attractive
place.

'And now I suppose the Chefs will travel from their nice
homes up to Parliament by helicopter, they'll never touch
ground at all, they'll see us even less than they do now.'

The Povos do not approve, either, of the Chefs travelling
abroad all the time. There is a new joke about Mugabe. 'Why
is Comrade Mugabe like Christopher Columbus?' 'Because he
is always discovering new countries.'

AIDS

In every conversation these days, sooner or later, AIDS
appears. Not in government offices: officially Zimbabwe is not
supposed to have a problem with AIDS. The Minister of Health
has just announced publicly that talk of AIDS is put about by
ill-wishing whites to destroy the infant tourist industry. This
has filled doctors, or anyone with information, with despair
and rage. Doctors say that half the children brought to the
Outpatients are HIV positive. Fifty per cent of the army and
the police force are HIV positive. People are dying of AIDS
out in The Districts, but the doctors don't say AIDS, they use
euphemisms. Sometimes they don't recognize an AIDS death,
really think it is TB, malaria, 'flu'.

Shortly after this the government changed policy, and Zimbabwe began an efficient campaign.

An official: you have to remember Zimbabwe is one of the
successful African countries. Ten per cent of the population
have clean water, eighty-six per cent of the children are immun-
ized against measles, polio, tetanus, whooping cough. Infant

mortality is sixty-one per thousand. Life expectancy is fifty-seven years for a man, sixty-one for a woman. Literacy rate is seventy-five per cent. There is a country-wide network of clinics, pretty basic, but the infrastructure is there. And now for the bad side: there is periodic malnutrition, associated usually with poor rainfall. The population growth is equal to Kenya's, the highest in the world. This is partly due to the government claim – at the beginning of Zimbabwe – that any suggestion women should not have as many children as possible was a plot on the part of the whites against the blacks. Without AIDS the population will treble in twenty years. AIDS is the joker in the pack, just as it is in every African country south of the Sahara.

It is said that the Cuban soldiers now going home are all full of AIDS.

SERVANTS

Dorothy is asked what kinds of people make the best employers. She says the ex-pats are the best. Then, the old Rhodies: 'At least we understand them and their ways. On the whole they are fair.' She hates, with all her heart, the new rich black class who, she says, treat servants badly, underpay them, do not give them proper time off. She tells all kinds of stories about bad behaviour. For one thing, they exploit relatives. A Chef, asked about this, says she is biased: 'Of course we make mistakes.' But she must know that every successful black person is besieged by out-of-work or out-of-luck relatives, whom he is bound to support. Every Chef's house is full of poor relations. In return for their board and lodging they do housework and odd jobs. The Chef pays school fees for the children and buys their clothes. Sometimes a Chef will be sending as many as thirty children to school. Back we go to Dorothy. 'Sometimes that is true,' she says. 'I didn't say they were all bad. But these days a lot of the rich people behave like whites, they don't help their families.'

AID WORKERS TALK

'I don't know what it is about this country. It just gets you. I've worked in a lot of Third World countries but this one . . . you really care what happens to it – perhaps because they have a chance of making it. But I think it is the people. I don't want to leave them. I know when they send me on somewhere else, I'm going to spend half my time worrying about what's going on here, if they are getting it together.'

'Why do you get so fascinated by this place? That's easy! Are the good guys or the bad guys going to win!'

THE BOOK TEAM OF THE COMMUNITY
PUBLISHING PROGRAMME

And now that stroke of luck travellers dream of, which we cannot plan, expect, order, or foresee: I was invited to go with a team of people making instructional books for use in the villages. These people, their ideas, their work, are revolution-ary, truly so, not in a political sense. The originator, Cathie, a South African who had worked in rural areas there, was shocked by the ignorance of village people in Zimbabwe about modern living, even the household technology everyone in Europe takes for granted. Besides, what of the waste of talent, of potential? 'The most important resource of the country is being wasted – the intellectual and creative energies of the people living in the rural areas which no one recognizes or bothers to develop.' There was a gap here, an insufficiency, something needed to be done, so she decided to do it.

There came into being – though not at once – a team consisting of herself, with two small children, Talent, the young mother of three children and former Freedom Fighter, Sylvia, a handsome and vibrant lady, mother of eight, and Chris Hodzi, a shy and sensitive young man, in the way artists are supposed to be and still sometimes are.

At the time they invited me the Team had already finished two books. Each book is in fact several, for they are translated into six languages. The first was, *Let Us Build Zimbabwe Together* (the title had been suggested by the village people themselves), a handbook on overcoming civic problems, and how to co-operate in a practical way, ignoring the slogans and rhetoric that cause political activists to believe that if you shout sequences of words long and loud enough, that process in itself is enough to change things.

The second book was still being put together. It explains economic problems in detail. How to get a bank loan, open a bank account, use book-keeping, assess the chances of success for a dam . . . a new borehole . . . a vegetable garden . . . a village store, or even a roadside stall. Each book is a mix of text and cartoons, like a book of comic strips.

Now the Team was planning the third book. It is for women, and will be the most controversial because while rural women are acknowledged to be the liveliest agents for change, they have to contend every minute of every day with traditional attitudes about the inferiority of women. Zimbabwe is not the only country in the world where a new government has announced that old attitudes about women are retrograde and inefficient – 'We will give women equality in law and in the work-place' – and then had to contend with the past. One is Libya. Another, Iraq (whether we like it or not). But if you speak to women from Libya, from Iraq, you learn that theory is one thing and practice another. So with Zimbabwe.

'As we all know, we can change laws, but then we have to change hearts.' (Who? Lenin? Stalin? Mao? Rosa Luxemburg? Emmeline Pankhurst? Mrs Thatcher?)

Making these books is not at all a question of sitting in an office in Harare and writing down inspirational precepts.

With the first it was Cathie and Chris who travelled around and across and back and forth all over Zimbabwe, seeking out and talking to people they had been told were outstanding in local affairs, or who had the potential to be. Sometimes they had to contend with antagonism from local officials. They had very little money. They often lived on bread and oranges. They were fed by idealism and the response they got from the villages. What they were offering, expertise, information, was what these people, still recovering from the civil war, half-educated or uneducated, yet expected to be modern people in a modern world, were hungering for. 'I knew there was a need,' said Cathie. 'Not until we actually got into villages did we realize just how enormous a need it is. Every time we got to a village we were welcomed as if we were actually bringing the goods then and there – that was because of all that hot air from the government. But what we were saying was, This is how you do it. As soon as they understood that, the word went around and then we were inundated with demands to visit them. So then the Team became four instead of two.' And, soon, officialdom noticed them, saw how good these people were, and offered support.

Making the book for the women was being done in stages, just like the other books. First, the Team went around the whole country, finding women who already represented others. Each had to be persuaded to take on even more work: many said they had too much to do already. Yet now their task was to go around the villages, to other women as individuals or in groups, and persuade them to take part in the making of this new book. Having set the women's book in motion, the Team went back to Harare to finish the second book, and arrange for the translation of all three. Then out they went again, for the women's book, all over Zimbabwe, to meet the women. At the point I joined them they had been on the road five weeks and were tired. They had travelled by local bus – no joke, this, since buses are overcrowded, and tend to break down; by train; by car when they could, and, occasionally, comfortably, in official cars. This was happening more often: local officials were beginning to see how valuable these people were. In every district the attitudes of local bureaucrats varied. A hostile local official could ruin everything. Time had to be spent on courtesies, even flattery, in the offices of district Party bosses.

'But,' said Cathie, in her breathless way that combined enthusiasm with apprehension because of what she had taken on, 'they help us more and more, they even send us messages to come to their districts.'

We were off down the Mutare road, five of us together, late for a meeting, while I gave up any idea of watching for landmarks – balancing boulders, rivers, crags – for while I sat by Sylvia, who drove, my head was turned so that a flood of information and statistics emanating from Cathie in the back could enter my right ear and, with luck, assemble themselves usefully in my already swollen-with-facts brain.

The meeting is in a local government office. An office is an office is an office. We have sped from Harare in what seems a few minutes: some of these women have travelled hours, even a day, to get here. Twenty of them are waiting, a serious, sober, attentive little crowd. I understand the phrase 'to hang on' words: they are hanging on every word spoken, in this case by Cathie, who is using English. Every syllable, hesitation, nuance, is being assessed. These are poor women. They feed and clothe families on very little – some on twenty or thirty pounds a month. (Yet the Team has said these are comparatively well-off women: wait till you get to Matabeleland next week, *then* we will be with really poor women.) It is pleasant watching these shrewd, humorous faces, and how they turn to their neighbours with a joke, a comment, and then laugh – and the laugh spreads around the room. One woman and then another says the weeks she has spent covering a ward or district were heavier than the organizers seem to realize. Am I sensing: 'It's all very well for you, rushing around the country in a car, while we use our legs, or bicycles.' I think I am. But 'you' does not only mean Cathie, the white woman, but Chris, the black man, as poor as they are, and Talent who lives on Simukai, a farm which can scarcely be described as rich, and Sylvia, who has as many children as they do.

Cathie has said that everything about making this women's book is revolutionary, cuts across custom: now I begin to see what she means.

She is telling the women the response to the book is very good, women everywhere are working on it. Now she wants every woman in this room to talk to the women on either side of her, and discuss ideas they want to be in the book.

This way of conducting a meeting is revolutionary. In fact, what it reminds me of is stories about early days in the Russian Revolution, when idealism still governed events, and young activists went out into the countryside to ask villagers to take charge of their own lives. One difference: there is not one word about politics. Not one slogan. No rhetoric.

These women are not only being asked to take control of their lives, without submitting to men, but to overcome reluctance to talk to women who might come from an area a hundred miles or so from their own. Here, we are cutting across tribal and clan divisions. This is Mashonaland, certainly, but the Mashona are an infinitely subdivided people. This women's book is subversive in ways immediately evident to the women themselves – and the local officials, who are sitting at the back of the room, watching.

Soon the women are in lively discussion. Then each one in turn puts forward an idea. These having been written down, the initiative is again passed back to them with, 'And now we want you, the women, to write the book. If you don't know how to write, tell a neighbour who can write to take down what you say. You can send in stories, poems, songs, jokes, articles, it doesn't matter what. When all the material is in from all over Zimbabwe we will bring it back to you and we can decide together what will go into the book.'

The women have not expected this. At first they are confused, then they are pleased. Soon they are telling us and each other what they will write. Many of the suggestions are criticisms of the local Party officials. The Team has told me rural people speak their minds about anything and anybody. Behind me sit the Party officials, listening to what, in a really communist country, would be a cause for prison or death.

THE RUINED HOUSE IN THE TRANSVAAL

This meeting was in Marondera, my brother's nearest town for most of his life and near, where, long ago, the family lay out under trees and were part of the night-time bush. To match that past with the women's meeting in the local office – impossible, two different worlds, just as it was not possible to imagine telling my brother about the women's meeting. But I could not have done that anyway, for he was dead. He died in the Transvaal in the car that was taking him to hospital. If it had been an ambulance of the kind we take for granted in Europe, they would have known how to stop him dying of the heart attack.

My brother had visited me twice, in London, and we spent many hours, and days, saying, Do you remember?

He talked about his new life but he did not like the Transvaal. One doesn't grumble, of course.

One story he told me several times. Every evening he went for a walk into the veld, with – at first – the two dogs, and then with one. He came on a ruined house in the middle of the tramped-down, over-grazed, dirty grass.

'It's not the same, not like England, if you found a ruined house here someone would know about it. But there – it made me feel really funny, that old house, someone lived there didn't they? I wonder what happened to them. I was poking around and there was a potato plant. It had finished flowering so I pulled it up. There was a cache of good potatoes under a cracked bit of cement floor. But that place must have been there empty for years and years. I couldn't make sense of it. I went poking about in that ruin and I kept coming on potatoes, more potatoes, that plant had put down roots under everything – old bricks, slabs of cement, I couldn't come to the end of it. There was something about that place the potato liked.'

'But I thought they didn't like too much lime?'

'Not much lime left, I should think. Not after so many years. Anyway, I just went on pulling up bricks until all the potatoes were exposed. There must have been a couple of big sacks of them. Then I didn't know what to do. In the old days there would have been baboons, or birds, but now there's nothing. I took some potatoes home. I went back every evening, and there the potatoes were and then one night – they had gone. Probably a herdsboy. At least someone got the benefit. I didn't like to think of those potatoes working away there, season after season, and no one getting any good out of them.'

IN THE NIGHTCLUB

The next meeting was in Jamaica Inn, once a nightclub for whites, now a Rural Women's Training Centre. In an office wait thirty women, who at once let us know they have been kept waiting. Cathie humorously apologizes. They humorously accept her apologies. The nearer you get to Harare, I have been told, the better dressed and more confident the women will be: this is a smart and self-possessed crowd.

Three men, local officials, are greeted as allies by the Team. They sit at the back. Now the proceedings are in Shona, and Chris Hodzi, who is sitting beside me making sketches, translates for me. Chris sits through every meeting, listening, choosing moments of tension or drama or humour.

The men interrupt with comments and criticism. Cathie sends me a note saying the men are playing devil's advocate, giving the women experience in handling hostility. It seems to me one man means every word he says: I am sitting just in front of him. He is a large middle-aged man, a pillar of society in his three-piece suit. His face is calm and confident.

The three men are polite and formal, while the women bring up all the points we have heard at the other meeting – and will hear again. From one end of Zimbabwe to the other, the Team say, the women raise the same problems. Nor do the men react much when the women demand that government representatives – in other words, themselves – should come to the villages to explain their new rights to them: often male officials take advantage of their ignorance. The men start serious heckling when the women talk about prostitution. The Team have said they have found prostitution in every rural area, no matter how remote. Before their travels they believed, like everybody else, that prostitution was a problem for the towns. The man behind me says village women are greedy these days and are not satisfied with their husband's earnings. Women are not as they used to be. They want careers and they neglect their families. For example, who is looking after your children while you are all enjoying yourselves here? The women laugh, and say neighbours are caring for their children. And what about your husbands? Who is cooking their food? Not one woman asks why the men should not cook their own food; they say their husbands are being looked after.

Women spend money on making themselves up, on clothes, all they care about is we should think they are beautiful and love them – says the conscientious dissenter behind me.

Not at all, says one woman, the others clapping softly to applaud her, it is a question of self-respect, of making yourself look nice.

I hear the male voice behind me, low, intimate, as if spoken into the ear of a woman in his arms, 'You know what I am saying is true.'

I make the point that these arguments can be heard in every country in the world, but feel 'the world' enters this room as an irrelevance.

The women's demands go on: the men heckle: it is all good-natured enough, and they joke and laugh.

Then the women sing, clapping their hands: it is a song they have made up especially for this meeting. 'We have come together to work with our hands. Lying under a tree sleeping we have left to the dogs.'

This is the end of the meeting. Just as the women rise, and gather their belongings, the man behind me remarks softly, 'One of the reasons a man rejects his wife is because she is a witch.'

A silence, a change of atmosphere, a chill. No one laughs.

The silence is a bad one. Everything about this meeting until now, the tone of it, the style, is rational, reasonable, the modern world. But witchcraft is from the past. Yet everyone knows how strong it is. The women do not look at the men. They do not laugh. I would say they are afraid. When I turn to look at the men behind me they seem complacent: they have had the last word.

Again the Team says they will be back here at the stage of the discussion of the submitted material.

And off we go back to town.

THE TRAIN

People telephone to say how much they envy me going off with the Book Team. 'You get cynical in Harare with all the corruption and bureaucracy. But you won't feel cynical when you meet the people in the villages, particularly the women.'

We are to go by train.

In 1982 they said the railways were dead, because of lack of capital investment, because white skilled labour had taken itself out of the country, and no one knew how to make the trains work. I stood by the railway lines with a farmer from Mutare and heard his lament: 'Under our government the trains came through here, dozens of them every day on their way to Beira. They ran on time. They were efficient. Now you get one or two trains a day, and they are filthy, and full of hooligans.'

There is investment again, and the railways are recovering. But when I said in Harare we were going by train, several people said, 'You can't do that, it's dangerous. It's just possible if you go first class.'

Hearing this, Dorothy remarks that she often goes to Bulawayo, by train, third class. She is serving a table full of people dinner at the time. Ayrton R. has taught her to be a *cordon bleu* cook. She stands there in her smart dress, this plump handsome lady, watching us to make sure we taste everything she has cooked, and she smiles when we commend her food. She likes the idea that I am going to Matabeleland. So does Ayrton R. She and he exchange nostalgia about the beauty of their homeland while we eat mango fool, and for the hundredth time everyone congratulates Mugabe on the Unity Accord.

Dorothy remarks that she thinks I will find the train to Bulawayo 'not very bad'. She thinks it is a pity people sometimes condemn things without knowing enough about them. It turns out that no one present has been on a train recently.

The Team is travelling second class. At the station queues wait to collect already booked tickets, but at the time an official should have appeared – no one. The queue doubles up on itself, and soon the room is so full the queue loses definition. 'It is not corruption that's going to do this country in, it's the inefficiency,' I hear, not for the first or the twentieth time.

We solve our problem by approaching an official standing at the edge of the crowd, apparently without function. His job certainly is not to deal with us, but he does, from good nature, not for a bribe. And there we are on the platform which I swear has not changed by so much as a nut or a bolt. It still looks as if made from a giant Meccano set . . . and can that be the same coat of battle-grey paint? The long platform seethes with people. *Then* the train consisted of half a mile or so of coaches, most of them with a few white faces at the windows, then, further along, a couple of coaches with brown faces – Indians and 'Coloureds' – a forced conjunction of people guaranteed to cause resentment to both, which it did for all the time of White Supremacy. Finally came a couple of coaches where all the blacks were squashed. This arrangement meant that most of the platform used to be sparsely occupied by whites.

I amuse the Team by a description of those times. They find the past improbable, and laugh at it. Cathie says that South Africa's segregation patterns, in her time, have never been as rigid as that. Talent who spent all her youth as a guerilla fighter has never known old Salisbury. Chris is still in his early twenties.

Just in front of us is a black woman so burdened it is as if she is there to illustrate some statistic. In her belly is a baby, on her back another, and clinging to her hand a small child. She spreads a blanket on the platform and places on it three more children, twins of about eighteen months, and an older child of about five. The three sit there while tall people mill about them. They are uncomplaining, not fidgeting. I remark that it would be hard to find white children who would sit there stolidly, not making a fuss. Cathie says the children are taught to behave well, but she is convinced it is bad for small children to be forced to sit silent and obedient for so long. I say that if one woman has to cope with several small children it is just as well they have learned to behave. Talent listens to this exchange without comment. We ask her what she thinks, and realize she does not find the sight of this exhausted woman remarkable. Or perhaps she is herself tired. The Team have already said that at the beginning of the present tour of Zimbabwe, five weeks ago, they were all full of high spirits, but now they're waiting for a second wind. 'It will be all right when we actually start work.'

The long platform eddies with people, nearly all black. Among them are perhaps a dozen white faces. Chris, yards away, waves to show he has located our places, and pushes his way towards us as the crowd ebbs into the train. The mother of the children is frantically running about, weeping – one of the babies on the blanket has wandered off. She has babies all over her, in her arms, clinging to her knees. They do not cry. Large solemn eyes in small serious faces stare around them, unfrightened, Chris goes to alert some official to her predicament, we go into the train. They have put us three women into a coupé, and Chris into a compartment with five others. We do not want to be separated: already we feel like a family.

Inside the coach I see it is identical with those of *then*: solid, respectable, shining with brown wood and yellow and green paint. Yes, I am told, it probably is the same: they haven't renewed the coaches yet. Here is the fold-away metal basin, here the exactly placed hooks for keys, or belts, or to pull yourself up to the higher bunks. I run through the sequence of thoughts appropriate for the occasion: can this be the same coupé where in '48, in '38, I – etc., and so forth. Meanwhile the bedding official has appeared. You buy your bedding tickets when you buy your ticket. This official used to be white, now he is black: a fatherly manner goes with the job, and he is full of advice about not leaving belongings near windows where station thieves can reach in. Sometimes they employ long sticks with hooks. And remember that it can get cold, with so much rain, so keep yourselves warm. While he makes up the beds, appears the inevitable clash of cultures. Talent wants the windows tight shut. In her village she would have slept in windowless huts, the door fastened against thieves and prowling dogs, even wild animals. Cathie and I are convinced we cannot sleep without fresh air. A compromise is reached, while the bedding official listens. He would adjudicate if we let him. He departs to the next compartment, leaving us feeling tucked up. We stretch ourselves out, one above the other, I on the bottom shelf, Talent in the middle, Cathie on the top. We plan to sleep the moment the train moves, but the train does not move. On the platform the people who have come to say goodbye stand in groups, talking, laughing. Bottles of soft drinks are passed in and out of windows. The scene could be Italian in its vivacity, its enjoyment of the moment. What I am remembering is a hundred farewell scenes during the War, poignant scenes, full of that reckless elation which is war's secret and dangerous accompaniment. But now such scenes take place at the airport, so the atmosphere of the platform has lost an ingredient. How many times had I watched the train pull out, listening to the long shrieking note of the whistle, a sound that monitored our emotional lives through all the years of the War, heard from one end of Salisbury to the other. But this engine has a new voice, it makes brief hectoring hoots – not to signal departure. Not at nine, nor at ten; not at eleven, or twelve o'clock.

Jealous for the honour of Zimbabwe Cathie and Talent keep assuring me that they often make this overnight trip to Bulawayo, work the day there, returning the next night. Never has this happened before.

At two-thirty the engine emitted its fussing hoot, moved a couple of hundred yards, and stopped. We slept.

At six the same attendant arrived with coffee and biscuits. His glance at the window – humorous, tactful – directed my and Cathie's attention: it had got itself closed in the night. Had we slept well? he wanted to know. Cathie at once went into the exchange in Shona, I have slept well if you have slept well. We were stationary somewhere half way between Harare and Bulawayo, where we ought to be arriving about now. Cathie and Talent were anxious, knowing that groups of women were travelling long distances to meet us: the first would be in the office at nine-thirty. The train went on standing, fretting a little. Hours passed. We had not brought food. 'My mother always said, never travel without food and coffee,' said Cathie. 'Imagine, I used to laugh at her.' Trips along the corridor showed, through doors left open for sociability's sake, people enjoying fruit and chicken. Some grumbled: the steady low-key complaint used to relieve anxiety. Talent lay calmly on her bunk. She told us she learned how to wait in the War. Sometimes they were hiding in the bush waiting for a safe time to move for days, without food or water. They ate fruit from the bush, when there was any. Once, after rain, the whole company of a hundred or so stood around a tree and each sucked the water from a single small bunch of leaves. Five leaves each. Talent said, 'Sometimes I look back and I don't know how I did those things. I couldn't do them now.' She was one of the team that collected bits of body after a bomb went off. 'You'd find a hand or a foot or a bit of liver, or a heart, and you'd think, But this is one of my comrades . . . we used to bury just bits of people. You have to get hard, you make yourself not care about what you are doing.' For a time Talent was defusing bombs. Where was that going on? 'In Zambia – they used to bomb where they thought our camps were. Sometimes they hit us, sometimes not.' I could tell from how Cathie was listening that Talent did not often talk about the War. 'I was lucky,' said Talent, 'I wasn't one of the pretty girls. The pretty ones used to be taken off into the bush by the Commanders.' This remark surprised me: I think she is very attractive.

Her war went on for years. She was never a girl and then a young woman with clothes and make-up and flirtations: she was a soldier when she was a child. She was a soldier when she met her future husband, for she was one of the men and women who agreed, at the Collection Point, to make a communal farm of ex-guerillas, at Simukai. She remarked that she lived with her husband for years before marrying him. 'I can't understand how girls can marry men they don't know.' Now she has three small children and her husband looks after them when she is on one of these trips. So does Cathie's husband. Both say they could never do this work if they didn't have such good husbands.

'Sometimes I can't believe I am doing this work,' says Talent. 'I can't believe I am alive. When I was in the bush, I often could not believe the War would end, and I would live an ordinary life.'

But it seems the War has never really left her: she has terrible headaches and sometimes cannot move for days.

Listening to Talent was like sitting with my brother talking about war.

A war ends, you bury the dead, you look after the cripples – but everywhere among ordinary people is this army whose wounds don't show: the numbed, or the brutalized, or those who can never, not really, believe in the innocence of life, of living; or those who will for ever be slowed by grief.

Meanwhile rumours enliven the train: the trouble is the brakes, the engine has broken down, rain has flooded the track. Puddles lie everywhere, and the sky is full of lively clouds, blue appearing only intermittently.

The train moved forward, stopped. Round about Gweru it summoned enough energy for a short move forward of a mile or so, then another, stopping in between like a wounded centipede.

People left the train and strolled about or sat on the embankment, Chris among them, first in ones and twos, then in groups, then it seemed everyone on the train was out there. It looked like a picnic, but without food. The scene reminded me of what I had been told of the old days – in this case before I was born, up to about the time of the First World War, when the train running north to Sinoia (Chinhoyi) would stop long enough for a man to leap down and shoot a duiker, a bush buck, a koodoo, if game appeared near the railway line. The meat was distributed among the passengers. When the booty was a lion the sportsman was given time to get the skin off. If in a good mood, the engine driver might halt long enough for everyone to have a picnic.

When our train gathered enough energy for a short move forward, it summoned the wanderers with short nagging snorts, and everyone ran back to it. Soon, when we stopped, people lugging suitcases ran to the road, hoping for a lift. But there were dozens of them, and hardly any cars, and these days people don't easily give lifts.

During one long wait two white youths from first class sat by themselves under a tree watching the lively scenes they could not allow themselves to be part of.

Round about midday the train stood idling near a village. People ran in crowds to buy soft drinks, biscuits. While they streamed one way, a small half-naked black boy ran from his hut where his mother stood watching him. He carried a plastic container, and jumped up into the train to fill it from the train's water taps. Having drained one container, he ran through the train, stopping at one tap after another. Meanwhile his mother waved her arms and shouted, afraid he would be whirled away from her. But soon he proudly went back, with his container filled.

The train stood quietly puffing. What was to stop us being here all day . . . another night . . . for ever? Time was behaving as it does when there seems no reason why a long wait should ever end. No, much better not to look at our watches, for by now not one but two groups of women were in the Bulawayo office wondering where we were.

There appeared two white officials with the look of those volunteering for martyrdom. They stopped in every compartment doorway: their task was to defuse aggression. When we asked what could conceivably be holding up this train, they said there was an electrical fault in the signalling system, because of the heavy rain. At every set of points the driver had to wait for written permission to proceed. 'It is in your own best interests,' they insisted, in the self-righteous and threatening manner of officials at bay. Shrieks of laughter accompanied them all down the train, like a bush fire behind an arsonist. What written instructions? From whom? Was a man running from the next station with a written message in a cleft stick from some punctilious station master who had looked in an instruction book under the section, 'What to do in the event of rain fusing the signalling system'? Had the radio not been invented yet? Nor the telephone? No one believed in this nonsense, probably invented by the officials who, said Talent, were obviously pretty stupid.

Soon the train that had left Bulawayo that morning for Harare stopped alongside us. The windows were full of jolly faces, offering us sweets, biscuits, Fanta, even sadza. 'Shame, better go back to Harare and try again tomorrow.' In no time our despondent populations had cheered up and began laughing and joking back. At about two our train suddenly shot forward and soon the thorn trees and acacias of Matabeleland appeared. Trumpeting gently we arrived in Bulawayo station nine hours late. The exuberant noisy crowd poured out of the train and on to the Bulawayo platform, once proud of being the longest in the world. (It used to add a few feet to itself every time it was outdone by a platform in the Andes or Cincinnati or somewhere.) Among them pushed the young mother with all her small children in her arms. The women looked like butterflies. The cotton industry in Zimbabwe flourishes, cotton is the second crop, after tobacco, and somewhere there is a designer who fills the shop shelves and covers the women with brilliant swirling patterns that look wonderful on dark skins. At the exit I stopped, for I had heard a voice from the past. A fat bad-tempered white man was using it on a small crowd of patient blacks – the hectoring, bullying voice that . . . 'But why,' I demanded, 'is that man allowed to talk like that now?' For I realized I had not heard that voice, not once, since I had arrived in Zimbabwe. 'Can't you see he is a South African?' said Talent. Then I did see: the characteristic belly-forward, chin-out stance which goes with the voice. But why? Was this a religious group? What was a group of black South Africans with their minder doing here? But it was a mystery that had to remain one, because we were hurrying to see if the women were still waiting.

Embassies had been sent to the station at half-hour intervals all day. They sent commiserations and good wishes. They would be waiting for us next morning.

Grey's Inn Hotel has a sign showing sprightly coach horses, Dickensian – oh, lost England!, lamented no less in unexpected parts of Africa than in England itself. Inside, this amiable hostelry is far from English. But perhaps, so I am beginning to think, this explosive, irreverent, witty, selfish society does resemble eighteenth-century England? But then surely England is more like eighteenth-century England with every up and down of the national mood? You walk along a London street and look at the youngsters – for more and more London seems a young town. If you are wise you hold tight to your handbag because of pickpockets. Cocky, jolly, full of self-conscious style, with a swagger to the hips and a set to the shoulders that says, You can't put anything past me! These attractive barbarians, full of relishing word-play – based on quips and slogans from television – do not resemble anything that was in these same streets when I came to London after the War. A dreary self-regarding respectability was more like it, to match the dreary unpainted streets and the last days of rationing.

The hotel is old-fashioned, with an atmosphere that tells you it has been enjoying itself for decades. I hope that does not mean it is due for demolition. My bedroom is large and has four beds: a family room for a society that prides itself on having plenty of children. The others have large rooms too.

In the heart of this hotel is a patio, or court, part-covered, furnished with umbrellas for the sun. But the sky is grey: the long cold spell hasn't given up yet. For a couple of hours we sit at a table that expands as people join us, friends and their friends, relations, aides and admirers acquired on previous visits of the Team. The courtyard is crammed. More blacks than whites, and many mixed groups. I know that while I have to note this, because of the past, everyone here has long ago got used to the easy mix of races. In fact a young woman – Persian

by origin – tells me her generation are surprised at the racism
of their elders. It is in this hotel, a local politician, in opposition
to Mugabe's government, holds court most evenings. People
come to listen to him. He is famous for saying everything he
thinks: in the years before the Unity Accord that was certainly
a brave thing. But this is Matabeleland, I am reminded, this is
the home of *The Bulawayo Chronicle*, the newspaper never afraid
to challenge the government on corruption and inefficiency.
People are proud that the only newspaper 'everyone' reads is
in Bulawayo.

What I remember is that Bulawayo and Salisbury were
always in competition. Salisbury said Bulawayo was commercial, crude, lacking in the graces. Bulawayo said Salisbury was
boring, and 'civil service', respectable, snobby. Now Bulawayo
is saying Harare is full of Chefs getting rich and the smell of
bad money. Harare says Bulawayo is a backwater. To the outsider both cities seem to fizz with energy and interest.

Again and again people say how lucky I am to come to Matabeleland now. Everyone here is happy. First, because of the
Unity Accord, and because Joshua Nkomo, their man, is an
important man in government. Then, the drought is over, and
last year was a good season and this year, too, it is raining
well. If I had visited before the Unity Accord everyone would
have been despondent and suspicious, people were afraid, and
then it seemed the long drought would go on for ever.

Cathie tells me: 'The Communal Areas where we will be in
the next few days are poor, the poorest anywhere. Forget the
money-fed areas around Harare. Yet people are full of energy,
full of spirit, that's what's so marvellous. These women . . .
it's the women . . . they won't let anything get them down.
You'd think they have it so bad the guts would be knocked out
of them. Don't you believe it.'

In this court, and later around the table at supper, and, for
that matter, anywhere where people talk, the same subjects
come back and back. It is women everywhere in what is called
the Third World who are changing things. If you want to get
things moving, go to the women, say Aid workers who have
been in a half a dozen countries. Sometimes you have to go

along with what seems to be the infrastructure – men in power;
but really, it is the woman. Why is it that poor women everywhere are taking hold of their lives like this? asks someone. No
one replies: *Why* questions are not as interesting as the facts,
as reports on *how* things are being done.

They talk about Aid, Aid money, exactly in the same way as
the people on the verandahs talk. With regret. With bitterness.
With accusation . . .

The worst thing is that so much of the Aid money was
wasted. This was partly because of all those fine words at Liberation: people believed that the fine words were the same as
getting things done. Now when the government has a Party
rally few people attend: it is a sign of maturity, and let's hope
Mugabe realizes that. There was a big rally here last month,
and when the government spokesman – she was a woman –
talked, the crowd did not respond. But when a local Chief got
up to speak everyone went wild. Yes, the old Chiefs are back.
Mugabe needs their support and he has returned them their
courts: they can try local cases. But of course they want everything back: they want the power to allocate land.

Countries dishing out all that Aid money have got wary:
their fingers have been burned too often. But it was their own
fault. They handed out money to anyone and anything before
making sure there was an infrastructure to build on . . . and a
lot of the Aid money was stolen.

I hear another version of the 'what is the most dangerous
job' joke: distribute Aid money – you'll get away with ten years
if you're lucky.

But have people actually been imprisoned? Well, not many.

Back comes that question: how is it so many get away with
it, *expect* to get away with it? Everywhere people have helped
themselves as openly as if they were taking honey out of an
old tree in the bush. Aid money has founded the fortunes of
many a Chef.

Yet there is always another set of initials, signifying another
fund, agency, organization, in arcane conversations impossible
for a newcomer to crack. 'If we can get X of XY to fund KA and
BC then the IWP will come in and underwrite CBD and WSP.'

A well-known East African, once Minister of Economics, says he thinks Aid money is the worst thing that ever happened to Zimbabwe. (I have to emphasize that he is black, otherwise, 'Well, he would wouldn't he?') 'Mugabe should have insisted on pulling up the country by its boot-straps. The infrastructure was all there. Now the automatic response to any problem is, "Give us some Aid money". All right, it would have taken longer. Aid organizations have turned the African nations into a pack of beggars.' Or, a newspaper editor talks – black: 'Aid hasn't done us any good. Look what happened in the Second World War when imports stopped: secondary industry developed, Rhodesia became self-supporting. Then Sanctions: they were very good for this country, the same thing happened. Though of course it isn't fashionable to say so.'

Another friend, South African (black), says the most disgusting thing he has ever seen was Nyerere on the television, 'smiling like a dear sweet little angel', waving in Aid money with both hands. 'Send it along, send it along,' he cried.

I have tried these ideas on various groups of people during this trip, but the response is, 'That's all very well if you haven't seen the poverty for yourself.' I haven't the heart to say anything of the sort to these people here, so optimistic, so confident. The Book Team uses Aid money. It has also refused Aid money, when an organization has tried to lay down the law, exert political control. 'They fly in from somewhere – Canada, America, Denmark, Germany – they talk to some bureaucrat in a Harare office, then they say, we'll give you money if you do this or that. If we're lucky they'll take a trip to a Communal Area for a couple of hours before they rush back to Harare.' The books the Team are producing are expensive, though not in labour, which is mostly voluntary. Eventually there will be six, each in the main six languages. It will take another six years to complete the project. If Zimbabwe changes as much in the coming six years as it has in the past six, then the books will have to change too.

'Why, do you think Zimbabwe has changed?' I am asked, by people impatient for utopia.

'But surely you must see how much it has changed. Being here is like being in a slow earthquake. I'm surprised any of you can keep a balance.'

'It seems to us everything is going very slowly.'

Early next morning, when the waiter brings the tea, biscuits, it is raining. I sit up in bed surrounded by the Team's books and look through the second one, called *Building Wealth in our Villages: An Introduction to Rural Enterprises.*

All cartoons. An attractive young woman says: Zimbabwe's economy is one of the most heavily dependent on external capital in black Africa. About seventy per cent of the capital is controlled by foreigners, mainly by one hundred and thirty British companies and forty-three South African companies. Foreigners own sixty per cent of Zimbabwe's industries, ninety per cent of the mines, and nineteen per cent of the farms. Between 1980 and 1983 profits sent outside Zimbabwe amounted to at least 3,330 million dollars.

A young woman exhorts: So it will be a slow and difficult process to change the economy in a way that reduces the gap between the villages and the urban modern sector, and reduces Zimbabwe's dependence on foreign capital and technology. Another young woman: As village people we should be very actively involved, well informed and well organized for this process, as it is a task the government cannot carry out alone. And for this we need a basic knowledge of Zimbabwe's economy.

What is economics? One reply is spoken by a middle-aged village woman, another by a middle-aged man.

What is production? Production is the act of transforming the things that come from Nature into usable goods. In order to produce we need the following: Natural Resources, Labour, Capital.

When Chris Hodzi makes these cartoons, he uses people he has seen, watched, listened to, at the meetings he sits through, usually unobserved, sketching. It occurs to me that the books will be a record of the types and kinds of people of this time, everywhere in Zimbabwe, what they wore, how they looked, stood, talked.

No one planned it: but usually the most valuable things just happen.

1. What is the most important product in your village?
2. Describe the natural resources that went into its production: labour, capital.
3. Do you have any difficulties in getting the natural resources, labour, or capital you need for producing your main village products? If so, describe your difficulties and think of the ways in which you might begin dealing with these problems.

The books will be in every village in Zimbabwe. The first one is already in every village. Even where schools are bad these books, if they are read, will be as good as an education in citizenship. That wasn't planned either.

By eight we were in an office for the delayed meeting. It was conducted in Ndebele: both Cathie and Talent speak it. The women come from the poorest areas that have suffered years of drought. They all know about the women's book, and there is the sense of an important occasion, of hope.

Two memorable moments, both from the past. One when an older woman put the conservative view – there is always one who does, and always the younger women listen in a way that says part of them has to agree. 'Not all the old ways were bad. We must keep what is valuable in our traditions.'

And the other, when an old woman rebuked a girl who said the law should protect women against rape. Women, she said, have forgotten how to protect themselves. How about that old technique: a girl in a forest is being chased by a man. She lifts her skirts as she runs, shows everything, the man gets weaker and weaker, cannot run, cannot catch her . . . Everybody laughs, then they remember Chris is there, the only man present. He laughs too, saving the situation.

The meeting ends in laughter and in last minute exhortations from the Team: Matabeleland South is famous for music, remember we need songs and poems for the book. Make up poems and songs if you like.

Then down the stairs we go and into a Toyota Landcruiser

supplied by a local office: the work of the Team is valued here. This vehicle is a development of a landrover, larger, more comfortable, high off the earth. You float in it. It can carry a lot of people, and today this is useful because every minute someone else asks if they can come too.

It is still quite early. If you wake at five or six, with breakfast at six-thirty, it can seem the day is half done when it is only eleven. It is grey, it is chilly, and there are puddles. Bulawayo, however, has a festive and even frivolous look, because sky-blue lamp posts adorn every street, so you expect them to have holiday garlands or coloured ribbons.

One woman with us represents yet another organization, but it is not possible to keep count of them all. Long before Liberation she married a black man – she is white – brought up his children, and has gone through all the harassment that went with this situation. She says that bad old Southern Rhodesia has quite gone.

We are on the road north, which would lead to the Victoria Falls if we stayed on it. It was the road where, in 1982, Terrorists kidnapped tourists and then killed three of them. No one remembers this now. The bush on either side is fresh, young, glossy, full of juices. Last time I saw Matabeleland everything was brown and dusty, which is its usual condition. At every turn of the road there are fat goats and cattle. The goats wander about apparently untended, the cattle are behind the fences: these are Commercial Farms, and so the bush is whole and healthy. No game, though: plenty of animals, but they are cattle, goats or donkeys. Animals are animals, I try to tell myself. But sometimes a pair of guineafowl run beside the road, or partridges. At this time of the year the guineafowl are not in flocks, they are pairing, but someone remarked that last year, up near the Wankie coal mine there were so many guineafowl it seemed the earth was moving: there were hundreds of them.

THE GARDEN

People talk about the garden as they did about that potent little shed near Harare. Something about this garden delights them all, but they say, Wait and see. Half way to the Falls we turn off into a Communal Area. In spite of all the rain the bush is thin and scrubby, semi-desert, with low dry hills. Suddenly, in this apparently infertile waste, there is a large lush garden. Out we all pile, and stand together to listen to the story of this garden . . . we stand shivering, for you simply do not take jerseys to baking Matabeleland and none of us is properly dressed.

All around here are extremely poor villages. On the radio there was a government-inspired talk about 'projects', that is, how villages can improve their situation. A garden was mentioned. But this is dry country, with pale Class Four soil . . . but there was a worked-out gold mine, which had a borehole . . .

This time it was men and women together who started the garden. It is growing tomatoes, onions, cabbage, mealies, carrots, spinach: you would never believe this soil could do it.

Twenty-four women and nine men invited anyone interested to join the new co-operative. Women work harder than the men, but the men help them, because the family eats better, both because of the garden and what it earns.

We stand looking at half a dozen women working, bent double, knees straight: impossible to work like this, you think, but they do, for hours. Their feet are bare, because of the mud.

When this garden was started there was only poor dry soil. An Extension Worker came and told them how to make irrigation trenches, and contour ridges, and a fence around the whole garden because of the goats. This commune is now closed to new members, but if there was money for a new borehole, another garden could be started. Now everyone wants to start a garden. The whole district is improved because of this one garden.

How are they to get a new borehole? The village representatives men, and women, are hoping the Aid representatives among us will help them.

One of the women with us, representing a modest, not one of the rich, international organizations, was asked for money a couple of years ago, and offered one hundred dollars – about thirty pounds. The man talking for the village is reproachful, if humorous. 'One hundred dollars,' he says. 'What could we do with that?'

The Aid woman says, 'But I think you told me you had done very well?'

The man continues to stand in front of her, accusing.

'You bought chickens, and within a year you had made that one hundred dollars into five hundred, so you told me . . . well, is that true?'

The man laughs and says it is.

'There you are. How many people have been given hundreds and hundreds of dollars and there is nothing to show for it?'

'Yes, we know that is true, but we are not that kind of people.'

'What we are talking about is money for a borehole and my organization doesn't deal in that kind of money.'

'Then what are we to do?'

'You should talk to this man here – if you can talk him into it, he's the person.'

This man here, one of those who had come with us from town because he knew there would be a visit to the garden, goes aside with the villagers to talk about the possibilities of the borehole.

Our group is now scattered about, and I am standing by myself, when an Extension Worker – in this case a man of about forty, muddy because he had been helping to clear a flooded irrigation ditch – comes hastening up to me. He is laughing in that way which says you will soon be laughing too.

He comes to a stop in front of me, puts on a grave look, and says, 'You see, Mrs Lessing, you do not understand our problems.'

These words, used by the whites in the old days every time some visitor criticized them, duly make me laugh, and he nods, to register that I had got the point and he could proceed.

'We are now a civilized country,' he pronounces, and waits for my response so he can go on with the punchline.

'I can see that for myself,' I say.

'Like every other civilized country we have a corrupt ruling élite,' says he, and starts shaking all over with laughter.

We laugh. Then he goes back to supervize the irrigation ditch, shaking his head and laughing.

The point was, there had recently been another corruption scandal in Britain.

The people who work this garden are proud, like the people of the shed, that their facilities are free to people who are not members. They can get free seedlings. In return for contributing manure from their beasts, they are given free vegetables.

The gardeners have decided to give up using fertilizer if they can get enough manure. The vegetables grown with fertilizers don't taste good, they say. If you have one line of vegetables grown with fertilizers and one with manure, you can tell the difference from the first mouthful.

We are shown, with pride, how inside the fence where the garden has been left room to grow, there are holes full of wilting weeds left to rot and make food for the pawpaw trees, guavas and oranges that will be planted soon. With pride, we are shown how, outside the garden, the Blair toilets are half-concealed by masses of feathery pink and white cosmos. The fence is well-kept. The village huts are well thatched.

As we go off towards the Landcruiser, the women come up to sell us vegetables. The housewives among us buy eagerly: vegetables like these cannot be easily found. The women have made a few cents, and they are pleased and proud. This garden, this achievement, which is changing all their lives, has put two thousand dollars into the bank. This is a very great sum to them, even though it must be shared by many people. Nothing could bring home the level of the poverty here more than this: the pleasure of these women because of these few coins, a couple of dollars altogether for a great heap of vegetables. In this poor district, sharply improving the level of a family means being able to buy a pair of shoes for a child at school, or a jersey for a cold day like this one, or a kerosene lamp so that the children can do homework.

I am told there are two good primary schools in the area. The two secondary schools are in the same condition as the one I saw a week ago. The headmaster of one is being charged with embezzling school funds.

All the time we stop to pick people up from the side of the road, and set them down again. The Landcruiser is being seen as a bus, and on this bush road no one seems afraid of giving lifts. What we are discussing is every kind of problem and crisis, but we laugh all the time, particularly at the corruption scandals, and everyone tells stories.

A politician from Harare meets an old friend, an ex-Freedom Fighter, now a Chef, in the street in Bulawayo. This Chef had been in the papers that week for a particularly flagrant bit of theft. The first one says, 'I don't think I can afford to be seen with you this week.' The delinquent one says, 'What a pity, I was going to ask you to dinner.' 'Another time,' says the first. 'No, I have the solution,' says the Chef. 'Come and stay the night with me, you won't have to be seen with me in public. And I'll take you to the house I show the government watch-dogs when they come around to see if I am infringing the Leadership Code. I wouldn't compromise you by showing you my farm, my store, my hotel, my other house, my . . .'

The Leadership Code imposed by Comrade Mugabe, is supposed, like the Romans' Sumptuary Law, to check this greedy tide.

They tell a story from Manicaland. 'Aren't you ashamed to be so rich, so quickly? Aren't you afraid the government will punish you?' 'No, this government is on the side of the poor, isn't it? Well, I was a poor man and so the government must be on my side.'

A story about a politician whose wife is infamous for her greed: 'Oh, he's a good man, we all know that, he's incorruptible, who could ever say a word against him? But if you sleep with corruption, then what do you call that?'

In the middle of the jokes and anecdotes there is always the moment when someone says, 'They think we are stupid because we are poor people. The Chefs forget we are watching them. We know who is good and who is bad.'

'A lot of corruption is small corruption, but behind every small corruption is a big man's approval. They should remember it is dangerous to take a government car to ferry rhino horns to the dealers. Rhino poaching has powerful people behind it. The poachers carry powerful guns. Who can afford to pay for such big guns? Only the Chefs.'

'During the Bush War the Comrades used to listen to the people and take our advice. Now they have forgotten to do this.'

'The once-honoured word Comrade should be shed or used for crooks and criminals. They have given up using it in some communist countries. When people start using the word sarcastically, then it's enough.'

They talk about Joshua Nkomo, with affection, with approval. It is forgotten he was so long in the wilderness, accused of every kind of rebellion and sedition, and it is as if he has always been up there among the Chefs, an architect of Zimbabwe, and a good man.

There is a story going about. Nkomo visits a certain shrine in the Matopos, and there the ngangas greet him as Lobengula: he is the old king reincarnated, or at least, he is animated by the old king's spirit.

'You would not listen to us when you were Lobengula,' he is chided by the wise ones. 'You did not listen when you fought the British and were defeated, as we warned you would happen. Are you now that Lobengula who was disobedient to the voices of the ancestors, or are you he who will do what we say?' Joshua says humbly: 'I am he who will do what you say.' 'Then you will have honour, a long life and a great public position.'

Is this story true? It illustrates a feeling about Joshua Nkomo, as much as it does the need for continuity in a society that has been so violently and so often disrupted in the last hundred years.

In the hotel at dinner there are a lot of us, and we sit a long time talking. Sylvia is at the head of the table; her daughter, who is learning the hotel trade, is at the bottom. It is Sylvia's turn to tell us the story of her life. We listen as people seem to do at this time, judging it as a strand in that epic, the Making of Zimbabwe.

Sylvia was the child of a polygamous marriage, was brought up to obey, to say no more than Yes or No in the company of her elders, never dared to criticize her parents. But she is married in the modern way with a husband who helps her, takes equal responsibility for everything, and when she is on these trips is responsible for the children – women's work, according to the old ideas. Her daughter has taken just as large a step forward. I cannot see any difference between her and any seventeen-year-old girl from Europe. She is pretty, lively, independent.

We ask her to tell us what the new generation is thinking.

She replies smiling, with a relish and pleasure in what she is saying, knowing how it must strike us, and particularly her mother. She is not being unkind, her manner says, but she has been asked to say her piece: clearly all this has been discussed with her friends. She is indeed speaking for her generation.

'First of all,' says she, taking sips from her glass – Zimbabwe wine, which she is judging as a student in training – 'we stay at home with our mothers as long as possible, because that means we don't have to get married and have a husband telling us what to do. We aren't going to get married until we are independent in our work and can do as we like. Secondly, we aren't at all grateful for all the sacrifices our parents have made for us – we don't care about the War of Independence and all the people who have died for our sake, and the people who went without an education because they were fighting – all that. We want to have a good time. We are going to have a good life. We know we are selfish. But that's how we are. You asked.'

Her eyes are bright with mischief. We have listened to her with, we hope, good grace. Talent is the one who has sacrificed most for Zimbabwe, but tonight she is tired and only smiles. Cathie, I think, is genuinely shocked. Sylvia, the mother, a handsome queenly downright woman, who you might expect

to react strongly, is looking humorous. Chris, the same generation as the girl, is regarding her from the point of view of one
much less privileged. He has a hard life, for you don't earn
much money drawing cartoons for these books.

The girl goes on to tell us how she has planned her life.
When she has graduated – very well, this goes without saying
– she will make sure she is in a really good hotel in Harare and
then she will go to a good hotel in Europe.

When she has gone to bed I point out that her speech could
have been made – is being made – word by word, by young
people in the Soviet Union: I read about it only a week ago.
'We don't care about your war, your sufferings, your sacrifices
. . . we don't care about you. You've made a mess of it, and
now we are going to look after ourselves.'

Has it occurred to you – someone said – that it was the
generation with all those high ideals and beautiful thoughts
that did make such a mess of so much? What makes us think
these selfish children will do worse?

Before I go to bed – late, it is nine o'clock – a visiting United
Nations official buys me a coffee and supplies me with the
international point of view.

There is a new word for certain African governments: they
are kleptocracies, he says. But yes, Zimbabwe does have something the others don't. Let's hope Mugabe recognizes it. There
has never been a country that began with such a fund of goodwill. But he treats his people as if they were enemies.

I say it is because – from what people say – he never meets
any of the ordinary people, he lives in an ivory tower surrounded by sycophants.

But, says he, that's what all these leaders do. They meet no
one but each other, at international conferences, and since they
are all crooks they think everyone is.

Mugabe, I say, is not a crook. I tell him this story - heard from
guess who, an Extension Worker - that morning: 'Comrade
Mugabe? Yes, he has his faults, he is a human being. But look
at Tanzania, there they have a saint for a leader and look at the
trouble they are in. How about Zambia? – you could say Kenneth Kaunda is a quarter of a saint. Who would want to be in

the trouble Zambia is in? No, we don't want a saint for a leader.'

'That's quite sophisticated,' concedes the United Nations.

'They are sophisticated.'

'Village people, you said?'

'You should try meeting some.'

'If they're still telling jokes then they're lucky. You can't make jokes in Zambia. If you so much as ask them the time they look over their shoulders to see if the secret police is listening. They are not only authoritarian and corrupt but it's a mess and a disaster.'

'This country isn't.'

'Not yet.'

'What an optimist.'

'I've spent too much time in Africa.'

We discuss why African states become corrupt. 'After all, no new Party or leader decides, Now we are going to have a corrupt country.'

'No, corruption just creeps up on them,' he says.

'Perhaps it just crept up on Zambia and Tanzania and the rest, but it can't just creep up on Zimbabwe, because they have the example of the others.'

'It *has* just crept up on them.'

'But Mugabe is trying,' I said.

'I see you've succumbed to the place. People do,' he said. 'What you don't see is that Mugabe can't really do anything because if he put all the crooks in prison he wouldn't have any supporters left.'

'Nonsense. You never leave Harare or Bulawayo, you people.'

And next day at breakfast very early in the dining-room, I hear an Aid worker, American, telling the same United Nations man, 'If Mugabe misses this chance, if he screws it up then it'll be a tragedy. How often does a leader have all this energy behind him? The Revolution might have gone bad up there . . .' (he means Harare) 'but down in the villages it is still the future. What will it be like if all this optimism goes sour? This level of expectation is not something you can call into being with a few speeches or a Party rally – no, what goes on in the Communal Areas and Resettlement Areas has all the War of Liberation behind it. It *is* the Revolution.'

'Well,' says the United Nations, 'I'm going to have to take your word for it.'

But this corruption everyone talks about, day and night, obsessed with it, which, so it is claimed, makes investment in Zimbabwe an impossibility: compared to the financial scandals that perennially rock Britain, Japan, the United States, France, Germany, it is rather like some delinquent adolescent robbing a child's piggy bank. Later, in London, I put this point of view to a money man, a City of London man, and he said, obviously surprised at my inability to grasp essentials, 'Don't you see? Before a country can go in for that kind of thing it has to have a decent infrastructure.'

And now it is the next day and we are driving south through the Matopos, handsome granite bush-covered hills and I find myself agreeing with Dorothy and with Ayrton R. who say this is the best part of the country. It is not only beautiful, but full of shrines and magical places. Then the hills are left behind and we are in a part even poorer than yesterday.

'This lot complain all the time, they're not like the people we met at the garden.'

Someone suggests that there isn't that energetic individual who so often originates change. Cathie, that fireball of a woman, who sparks off effort and enterprise anywhere she is, does not find it easy to agree because she is committed on principle to groups working together. But in the end it is agreed that when you go to an area and find 'projects' successful and people optimistic then the reason often is that some woman, some man – an individual – has been the yeast.

Soon we are in a Growth Point and the office is in fact the old farmhouse of a bought-out white farm, and sixty or so people, mostly women, are on and around the big verandah where for so many years a thousand tea trays, drink trays, were brought by black servants for the farmer, his family, his guests. Presumably that square shed at the back was the kitchen. In front the bush is sparkling and fresh, and a dozen goats are making the most of it.

Just as the meeting begins, one of our company says she has heard there is a meeting about AIDS just down the road, and off she goes to find out about it.

There are five men present, one the village chairman. They sit quietly while Cathie and Talent say this book for women will be written by the women themselves, and ask them to suggest subjects. Which turn out to be the same as we have heard at the other meetings.

The tone changes when a woman demands to know why they are not allowed to do other kinds of work: why can't they drive buses, for instance?

The chairman says that women are not built physically for driving buses: they can't climb up to the top of buses to lift down luggage.

A woman: 'Suddenly we hear about our weakness. No one mentions our weaknesses when we are planting the crops and growing the crops and hoeing the crops and harvesting the crops and cooking the food and bringing up the children and building the houses and putting roofs on the houses . . .' she would go on, but the chairman stops her: he is not the chairman of this meeting, and some women shout at him, saying so.

He says, 'It is your duty to do these things for your husband.'

'And whenever we criticize the men for being lazy, then suddenly the talk is of Duty.'

'But,' the man insists, full of calm conviction, 'it is your duty.'

At this, in comes that older woman who has to speak for tradition: she says there was good in the old days and the baby must not be thrown out with the bath-water, freedom for women is for outside the home, but inside the old ways are best. 'Well spoken, mother,' says the chairman.

Groans and laughter. There seems to be something in this particular mix of people that makes for confrontation. Yet it is not ugly: there is laughter, joking, nothing of the cold vindictive hatred of men some feminists make their rule and try to enforce on others.

'Why is it there are still so few women in leadership?' a man asks. He is not being provocative.

'Because men say that equal rights do not mean *they* should look after children and cook food.'

'My husband sits around waiting to be served even when I have done all the work and I am sick and he hasn't worked all day.'

Another woman says, 'I came home from the field yesterday, my husband says, Why isn't the water ready for me to wash? – I put on the water, and he says, Why is my food not ready? – I take the washing water off and I put the porridge water on and he says, What is this, why have I not washed?'

The traditionalist woman says severely, 'Some women are too lazy to build a fire large enough to take two pots.'

'But I did not have time to go for firewood because the goats were in the field and I had to protect the plants. You forget, now the children are in school, we do not have their help.'

A silence. Everyone wants the children to be in school, but their labour is missed. The women's lives are even harder.

'And,' goes on the complaining woman, 'my husband would not help me with the goats when I asked him.'

'Because it is not men's work,' says the chairman.

'What then is man's work?' enquires a woman sweetly. She is one of the large formidable females who, I am told, are often the will behind a local women's group. She is typically middle-aged, her children are grown-up, she may well be without a man. She is likened to the market mammies of West Africa, financially resourceful, hard-working traders. But here she does not have her niche, as she does in West Africa: she still has to make a place for herself.

The chairman confronts her, 'God has ordained the differences between men and women.'

At this one of the white participants, from America, asks, 'Then why are the roles of men and women different in every part of the world? Now everyone moves about the world so much, we know how different all the cultures are and we can no longer say, God has ordained this and that.'

A woman remarks, with humour, that she has never travelled further than Harare, to visit her sister, and there her sister complains about her husband just as she does.

And now the subject of Maintenance, which has been discussed with passion at every meeting. There is a new law, welcomed by liberals and progressives, that men abandoning women must be made responsible for the children. In the villages this law is seen differently; the respectable married women are angry.

'Already our husbands have two families, a new one in the town, leaving their real wives at home. They spend all their money on the new women. Our children go hungry. These town women are prostitutes. If they are given money for their children by the government then our husbands will find it even easier to abandon us.'

Says the chairman, 'If you want to know why your husbands take new women then you have only to look at your wedding photographs.'

This cruel remark causes indignation, not anger as some of the observers thought it deserved.

The women exclaim, exchange irritated remarks. 'These bad women have only themselves to look after.' 'They can afford a new dress and lipstick.' 'I can't afford even to buy soap to wash my children with, let alone myself.' 'I haven't had a new dress for five years.' 'Yes, and sometimes a prostitute is maintained by four or five men who give her their money. No wife can compete.'

The chairman, 'Women are beautiful when they marry, then they neglect themselves.'

'We are overworked, don't you understand?'

'No, he doesn't understand, because men never work.'

'Why do you say that when you all know I work hard for you as village chairman?'

'I wish I had your job.' 'Yes, and I do too.' 'And I.' A lot of laughter. The women are looking at him as they might at one of their naughty children.

Then, the question of disabled women. Often men rape these women, then there are children and no one to look after them. The government should help disabled women to get work. And men should be considerate: they shouldn't sleep with disabled women.

The chairman remarks, 'She may be crippled but she is all right.'

All through this he maintains a calm, smiling, magisterial look, never loses his dignity for a moment. Is he being deliberately provocative? I can see that Cathie and Talent are whispering together, looking at him, and wondering exactly that. Sylvia is as calm and authoritative as he is, while she disassociates herself from this brutality. Chris the artist – goes on drawing.

'The men who do these things should be arrested,' says a woman, challenging the chairman direct, but he merely smiles.

Cathie and Talent suggest the women should make up a song about a man who impregnates a crippled woman and abandons her.

'And we will make him sing it,' suggests someone – to the chairman.

'Yes, I will sing it,' says he. 'I have a good voice.'

A pause. Then a middle-aged woman remarks that the old laws were not always good. If a girl fell in love with a man her parents did not like, she could not marry him. The women look at her in a way that says she is telling her own story. There are murmurs of sympathy.

This meeting ends, like the others, with promises from the Team to be back in a few months to collect all the material.

Then, as always, there is a song. The message is vigorous but the tune is sad: it is an old tune. Some of the African songs are as naturally sorrowful as Russian songs, designed to break your heart even when on jolly subjects.

> People are slow to change, but they do change.
> So go slowly and they will change.

That is one song. Then another:

> Tell them about development,
> Tell them about health.
> Don't tell the people to do what you say,
> Tell them to do what you do.

And now, a hymn tune:

God's love is so wonderful.
Love, love, wonderful love of God . . .

And there is a great circle of women dancing. Women come in from everywhere around, hearing the music. Some drop out and stand ululating and clapping. A few have babies on their backs.

As we go to the car, escorted by everybody, the woman returns who has been at the AIDS meeting. She is half-laughing, half-furious. There is in existence a proper well-made educational film about AIDS, giving facts, explaining dangers. But the local mission nuns have vetoed it. No one seems surprised the nuns have the power to do this. The same nuns, I was told, burned *The Grass is Singing*, my first novel, having remarked it was a good book, but dangerous.

The film actually shown said that AIDS was a danger to homosexuals and to drug-users. But homosexuality is not part of African culture; in Africa AIDS is a heterosexual disease. No one here has heard about drugs stronger than marijuana which grows everywhere and is part of the culture. Several hundreds of school children, some as young as nine or ten, have sat uncomprehending through this film and are at this very moment dispersing, bewildered.

The local doctor has said that five people died of AIDS in the last few weeks, in this area. That is, the acknowledged deaths from AIDS. Since no one knows anything about AIDS, a person may die of it and all you hear is: my brother got too thin, and he had swellings and then he died.

As we climb into the Landcruiser a village man says to me, 'You have chosen a good time to visit Matabeleland. The Unity Accord has made us happy. The Dissidents have stopped making our lives a misery. We had a good harvest last year. The rains are good this year. And – of course! – there will never be another drought in our Matabeleland.' Everyone laughs, and to the sound of laughter we leave the Growth Point.

The train to Harare left on time. In the early morning, after coffee and biscuits, I went to stand in the corridor. Six women seemed a lot in that one compartment.

Two windows down a young smartly dressed girl stood watching the bush go past. A couple of duiker grazed their way into a gum plantation. A partridge ran madly beside us, as if racing the train.

A young man, handsome, a dandy, watched the girl from the end of the corridor. He came sauntering down, politely apologized as he squeezed past me, and began with, 'Where are you going? It's a nice day, I think. Haven't I seen you before?' She jabbed her toe into the corridor wall, and hung her head: maidenly bashfulness a culture away from her dress, her shoes, the pink beret. He chatted on – whimsical, frankly trying to charm her. But the courtship made slow progress. She would not respond, she simply would not, but went on poking her toe at the wood, and hung her head.

Suddenly she could not prevent herself letting out a giggle. He laughed out loud with his victory, clapped his hands and spun around on his heels. After that it took him five minutes to get her to say yes to meeting him in Harare that night, in a bar, for a drink. 'And who knows? We may like each other and go and eat some sadza together.' As if that hanging head, the sulky indifference, had never been, she chatted animatedly with him for the remaining hour into Harare.

THE TRAVELLING CLASSES

An evening in Harare spent with academics, journalists from various countries, politicians in and out of office, some farmers, musicians, a mixed lot black and white. What do they all have in common? They travel, they make comparisons, they are of the travelling class.

If it is hard for most of the white people to leave Zimbabwe, then for nearly all the black people it is impossible, and the world outside Southern Africa hardly exists.

The academics present have been out on scholarly missions.

The journalists, by definition, get about. The farmers have relatives in Europe. The politicians, like their kind everywhere in the world, are always off on Committees, Commissions, Conferences.

Something extraordinary has happened.

The young Zimbabwe began with the naïvest, most untutored enthusiasm for communism. The newspapers printed nothing critical of communist countries. The Gorbachev revolution was hardly mentioned. The self-criticisms of the Soviet Union went unnoticed. That Stalin is no longer the Father of his people but rather a murdering maniac has passed most people by.

Sometimes one is tempted to believe that the mental attitudes of a country have something to do with its sun and soil. Old Southern Rhodesia was the same, complacently indifferent to the outside world. Leaving it was like leaving a stunned or a drugged country. The only comparable places are in certain Mid-Western States in America, where curiosity about the world ends at, let's say, the borders of Iowa or Nebraska. A university audience will hardly know where Afghanistan is – or Sri Lanka, or Pakistan. In California sun-drugged youngsters will stare at the mention of Gorbachev.

Similarly, Zimbabwe. You may spend an evening with a professor of history, or of literature, whose attitudes towards the Soviet Union or China are identical with those of thirty years ago. Someone may remark – wearily, since they have learned the uselessness of it – 'But the Russians themselves are debating the forced collectivization of the peasants, Stalin's purges.' 'Nothing but capitalist propaganda' comes the prompt reply, with all the self-righteousness of the True Believer. An inaugural address to a new year of students may begin with a set-piece of praise for the achievements of our great brother the Soviet Union, but these do not include the courageous self-examination of the last five years, because the illustrious academic has never heard of them. If some intrepid person remarks, 'But you can hear the Soviet Union's criticisms of itself, on the shortwave radio, at most hours of the day or night' – then the faces of these survivors, the Stalinists, put on the shrewd seasoned look of those who have known and seen it all: they aren't going to be fooled, not they!

One of the bad effects communism has had on the West, perhaps the worst, is that generations of politicoes have learned politics from what is described as 'the communist style of work'. 'The Leninist style of work'. This style of work demands a sneering jeering language, based on a moral contempt for opponents, which suffuses the mind and character and prevents any kind of thinking that isn't on the level of the school playground. I grew up when 'everyone' was a communist. ('Everyone has been a communist; no one remains a communist.') People like me can recognize from one look at some representative of the 'hard left' on television, that scarcely-concealed glitter of mendacity, the pride at cleverness that knows how to outwit opponents with election rigging, or the fixing of statistics, character assassinations, the whole 'bag of tricks'. This immediately recognizable look, the equivalent of laying a finger against a nose with a slow wink is, unfortunately, not recognized by people who were not young when 'everyone' was in 'The Party'. And that means they have no defence against it.

The upheavals in the Soviet Union and Eastern Europe send shockwave after shockwave to undermine the old guard, but in more isolated parts of the world, tucked away in university departments and institutes of higher learning, they survive, proud of 'the bag of tricks', the 'style of work', deliberately refusing to know not only that their great exemplars have self-destructed, but that all the mental attitudes associated with them have gone too. These little crooks can never see themselves as others see them, since they identify with Lenin the pure. They do great damage, because the idealism of young people who learn to see through them goes sour, for they become angry, then cynical and are often turned away from any kind of politics, or even ordinary service to the community.

In Zimbabwe, 1988, the travelled ones know what goes on in the Soviet Union and China, the communist world to which, in theory, they belong, and will discuss it all with sophistication and worldly wisdom. But the ordinary citizens know nothing.

Privilege in our world often resides in this: that people have information. Did anyone plan this? Of course not. It just happened, this mental tyranny; and it is perpetuated by Stalinist woodenheads who are fighting to hold their places in the seats of high learning, for they would not get jobs anywhere else. They are infinitely skilled in political intrigue and infinitely unscrupulous. The decent and informed people in their departments succumb to despair, and take their skills elsewhere, when they can, because their energies have to go not on teaching, but on trying to maintain a position against colleagues they despise, but cannot ignore.

Meanwhile, in schools all over Zimbabwe children dream of the distant shores of learning, in the University of Zimbabwe, which they probably will never reach because they are not clever enough.

Research into the workings of the mind shows that a percentage of people are incapable of changing their minds, no matter what the evidence. If they have been imprinted at some point in their lives with, let's say, the information that all cats are black, then for ever after they will say all cats are black, even if white cats are paraded before them with labels saying White Cats.

This is hard to believe – unless you see it. Most of us by now have seen it . . . for instance, there was a young woman brought up in the top echelons of the Communist Party of East Germany, and knew it all from the inside, who then was for seven years at the Moscow University; she married an Englishman, and lived at an English university. Knowing all about communism, she was not a communist, but would have been happy to discuss what she knew. But left-wing circles in the university refused to have anything to do with her. She was a reactionary, a fascist; she was probably CIA.

'Mugabe ought to do something about it.'

'What, precisely?'

'Well, he could make a speech of some kind.'

'But he is a marxist. And the revelations of the Gorbachev era didn't emerge in a single speech, they unfolded over months and years, people had time to get used to them.'

'Then he should instruct the newspapers . . .'

'But we don't approve of him instructing newspapers, do we?'

'Then he shouldn't discourage lively and critical editors.'

'How do we know *he* does.'

Oh surely it can't be Mugabe himself: Mugabe is *of course* on the side of the good, which in this case means the availability of information. Conversations can go on for a whole evening where it is assumed that Mugabe has been misinformed: he is surrounded by yes-men and they don't tell him the truth.

Someone remarks that every leader that arises anywhere is assumed – in the West, particularly in Britain – to be a giant of liberal democracy. If Ghengis Khan appeared now in no time the London leader-writers would be reassuring us that he liked Western films, subscribed to the *Guardian*, supported Amnesty International, had a wry sense of humour.

We – that is, Europeans, people with an experience of democracy as practised in Europe – assume the countries we colonized were taught democracy. In Southern Rhodesia a lively democracy was enjoyed by the whites, but was never extended to the blacks who experienced only various forms of repression under the whites. Why then should they not have turned to communism?

Robert Mugabe is the product of an authoritarian culture. He was educated by the authoritarian Catholics. People who taught him, and fellow pupils, say he was clever, always reading, did not mix easily with others, but watched and listened: 'A typical intellectual.' He was brought up under White Supremacy, which was like living under a cold lid, like a frozen sky. His culture, his people were always criticized, disparaged, despised. When they say now, 'But it is our culture, it is our custom' as a last word, what you are hearing is self-respect, a people's pride, that has survived decades of contempt. When Mugabe became part of the liberation struggle, it was British rule he opposed, and the language of marxism was common to all liberation movements then. They say it was Samora Machel who finally made him a communist, and that was quite late in his career. Because the Soviet Union made the mistake of backing Joshua Nkomo, Mugabe was orientated towards China, whose history since 1949 has been continuous, success-ive, waves of mass murders – millions upon millions killed for ideological reasons. (I actually heard a Chef say about this, 'But you can't make an omelette without breaking eggs.') He led an army that fought not only against Smith's forces, white and black, but sometimes against the armies of opposing political groups, Bishop Muzorewa, Nkomo – for while these armies had the same aim, they often competed for future power.

Mugabe was put in detention by Smith. To be detained or a prisoner was a harsh experience. The prison was the scene of hundreds of executions, many of them Mugabe's friends and comrades. All kinds of atrocities were committed by Smith's men, which are talked about but have not been officially exposed: this is because of the need to bury the past and its 'mistakes'. Smith refused Mugabe permission to visit his son – his only child – when he was ill, and when the child died he was not allowed to attend the funeral. It is sometimes argued that this was the stupidest thing Smith ever did. When Robert Mugabe came to power it was after more than a decade of war fought, as wars have to be, with brutality on both sides. The attempts on his life have isolated him, made him suspicious. Why then do people expect Robert Mugabe, with such a his-tory, to be this combination of Abraham Lincoln, Jefferson, Gandhi? But people do expect this: Comrade Mugabe, like God, is on everybody's side. And he does sometimes behave with magnanimity.

What has there been in Mugabe's experience to make him admire democracy?

Yet as communism, and marxism as an idea collapses, as communist societies give up and go, it is likely that the 'marxist' leadership of Zimbabwe will be pleased their communism has always been more rhetoric than fact.

What will supplant marxism?

Christianity is strong in Zimbabwe, stronger than marxism ever was.

From a letter: 'The Pope has just visited Zimbabwe. Thou-sands of people turned out. Don't run away with the idea they have all become Catholics, it was all more exciting than a Party rally, that's all, and they *love* parties. Comrade Mugabe was there. He said "This is like being baptized again." Also, that he could see no conflict between Christianity and what his government stood for. At least that's what people say he said. The newspapers didn't report it.'

As marxism fades, the Chiefs become stronger. There are jokes that in the long run the Chiefs will turn out stronger than the Chefs. Slowly, they are getting their powers and privileges back. They are conservative, taking their stand on 'our culture', 'our customs'.

But not always. And Robert Mugabe, that man conservative by temperament and authoritarian by upbringing, is not at all the traditional African male. He is sympathetic to women, and – they say – much influenced by his mother, a remarkable woman whose life was as hard as African women's lives nearly always are.

LEADERS

Always and everywhere citizens sit around wondering. Why does he – she – they – do this or that? and in the same tone of frustrated incredulity of 'But why does Mugabe . . . ?'

There surely must be a secret ingredient, information with-held, a palmed card, the joker in the pack? – for the citizens simply cannot believe what is going on.

Let us take a recent event in Britain. (But it happened in the United States too.) It was decided to close mental hospitals and throw out all the inhabitants, who would thereafter be 'cared for in the community'. Anyone who knew about the services which would be caring for these poor people, could foresee what would happen. The unfortunates would be living on their wits, or be exploited by landlords, or drink or drug themselves to death. But if ordinary sensible people could see this, the experts could not. It was obvious that quite soon, people appalled by the sordid fate of the expelled ones, would cry 'Eureka! I've got it! What we need are a-s-y-l-u-m-s, what we need are r-e-f-u-g-e-s where they can be looked after. Why is it people didn't think of that before?'

Over and over again this kind of thing happens, always to the bafflement of people who are not experts or officials.

There is an ingredient X. It is that as soon as people get into power, even on an ordinary level, they only meet people like themselves and who think the same – they succumb to a kind of gentle group hypnosis. Nothing is more rewarding than to spend an hour or so in the company of, let's say, Labour officials, and then an hour with the same level of Conservatives. They live inside different mental landscapes, which they continually reshape to make them fit with their beliefs. So powerful is this mechanism that politicians seem able to persuade themselves of anything. At the time of the miners' strike – Arthur Scargill's – members of the hard left all over the country were sure Britain was on the verge of red revolution, and were already choosing the government posts each would fill. A couple of years later they would be secretly thinking, 'I wonder what got into me?'

THE FARMERS IN THE MOUNTAINS

And now, again, the road from Harare to Mutare. Again we sped through rolling open country past all that magnificence, and those other slow journeys when we watched how a clump of boulders appeared far ahead, grew large, dispersed itself at a turn in the road and came together, rose up, seemed to topple, then fell behind as another clump approached – the slow unfolding of the landscape, like a well-known tale or reminiscence told with pauses for effect, was part of the past, and even the journeys of six years before were in another time. The place of the accident? Conversation in the car was so entertaining I forgot to look for it. In 1982 every stretch of bush, each hill or mountain was a memory in the topography of war. That war had gone, together with all the other wars, into the memories of people growing old; a new lot of young people are already looking at each other with humorous grimaces as their elders intone, Do you remember how the government troops came that night and . . . ? *Can't they leave it alone? We don't want to hear about that.* The car carried a load of optimism: the rains, the good rains, were here, the end of the drought; a green countryside, fat beasts, well-fed people. All of us in the world are dependent on the rains coming as they ought, but in Zimbabwe you remember it in every other conversation. 'If we have another three years of decent rains then Mugabe will be safe. Another drought like the last one and we will be in trouble.' *We?* I am listening to whites who so recently meant we, the whites, when they said *we*, but now they mean Zimbabwe.

The road is almost empty. Is the standard of driving better? Yes, much. Have the unlicenced rattle-traps been cleared off the roads? Yes, but there are still plenty of licenced ones. Do you remember there was no petrol in the pumps, because the South Africans – well, all right, Renamo – kept cutting the pipeline?

'Yes, you're right, they did – but now our troops guard the pipelines.'

'If you live in a country you hardly notice changes.'

'What changes? Are things really so different?'

In London I wait for visitors, and then ask, 'What changes have you seen since you were here last?' They tell me, and I say, 'Really, are you sure?'

In Mutare we stop to shop, and then off we go into the mountains. I am watching for baboons.

'Do you still have a man out with a gun shooting wild pig and baboons?'

The Coffee Farmer replies, with that small smile that goes with the pleasure of deflating sentimentalists, 'No, I don't need one. Luckily the leopards are back in the hills and they keep the baboons down for us.'

And now the hillside in the mountains, and from the

verandahs we look down on mountains and hills, the lakes, the rivers – water, water, because of the rains. And so close you'd think you could throw a stone at it, the mountain that is in Mozambique.

'Do the Mozambique rebels come through here?'

'They were around a few months ago, we think. But all during the War the 'terrs' were coming back and forth across our farms and we never knew it. Now they tell us and we have a good laugh.'

'Do the Mozambique peasants still come across the border to get food?'

'Poor bastards, yes they do, they're starving down there, don't forget they are coming to get food from their own brothers.'

The ghosts of the two young white native commissioners dicing over a map, one Rhodesian, one Portuguese, almost appear, but decide not to.

'And the battalion that was here, driving you all mad?'

'They've gone, thank God.'

'What other changes?'

'Let's see.'

The servant, a new one, brings out tea, brings out drinks, sets it all on the table, we are introduced, and off he goes to cook dinner.

We sit and watch while the evening light models the landscape.

'Let's see.'

There are a couple of newcomers – whites.

'Any blacks?'

A quick look. A laugh. 'Didn't you know? Tekere got rid of all the Squatters. It was Edgar Tekere who threw them out. The hillsides where they were trying to grow mealies and making all that erosion – they are healing themselves. I'll take you to see them. The forest is coming back.'

'So you don't hate Tekere any more?'

'Hate Edgar Tekere? Certainly not. He's a good chap.'

'How many Squatters were there, do you suppose?'

'Probably several hundred. Well, it was ridiculous wasn't it?

No idea of conservation, no idea of . . . if you're going to farm
in mountain country then you've got to know what you are
doing.'

'Yes, yes, all right . . . Did you know the blacks think of you
as very rich? Those rich Vumba farmers, they say.'

'Do they! Well, most of us nearly went bankrupt last season.
It was a terrible season. Did you know that the X's just saved
their farm? They had the best crop of kiwi fruit ever, but the
prices went to nothing because all the Third World countries
are growing kiwi fruit, it is grown so easily – as for us coffee
farmers we are surviving only because we grow quality coffee
– Arabica. Did you know our coffee is a favourite with the
buyers?'

The pride of old Southern Rhodesia, the pride of new Zimbabwe, rings in his voice. We always did know how to do
things – is the unvoiced message.

What else?

'We are putting in another dam. Another drought like the
last and we'll be done for.'

He tells this story. A certain new length of pipeline was
losing its rubber seals and gushing water. Someone was stealing the rubber. 'We put our chaps on to find out who was
stealing . . .'

'Wait a minute, what exactly does that mean?'

'Never mind. Well, if you must know, we found out which
of the kids had new catapults in the school playground. We
went to the headmaster. We told him he had to punish the
boys. The trouble was, the kids had already been beaten by
their fathers. So they were beaten twice. They won't go stealing
our rubber again. But I keep remembering what fun I used to
have with my catapult when I was a kid.'

So I tell the Chekhov story about the peasant who steals nuts
from the railway sleepers. The local landowner is the magistrate
and he asks the peasant why he does this dangerous thing?
There have been train accidents, has he never thought it is his
fault people have been killed? 'Well, your honour,' he says,
'it's like this. I like to fish. Those nuts from the sleepers make
perfect sinkers for catching some kinds of fish.' 'Do they?'

exclaims the landowner. 'What kinds? I didn't know that.' He likes to go fishing too. The peasant and the landowner discuss the different depths certain fish are to be found in the rivers, what bait they like, the best sinkers to use on the lines. They are expert, know everything about fish and their ways. But the time comes when the magistrate has to take over from the landowner, and he sentences the peasant to so many years exile. The man goes off, incredulous: he cannot believe that this fellow fisherman who has been talking to him man to man about the ways of fish, is now turning on him. 'But I have no alternative,' says the magistrate. 'You stole the nuts, didn't you?'

The Coffee Farmer listens to this tale with his characteristic small smile: Yes, well, that's how things are, whether you people like it or not!

Easy to say, 'A story that could have come from old Rhodesia' if it were not that savage beatings regulate the new schools. It is against the law, but in some countries – Britain for one – adults seem to feel beating children is their right.

Jack later wrote, 'He has gone, and the new headmaster is in. He works hard, and so far spends all his time in the school. But he drinks and beats the kids. He beats them so hard we . . .' (meaning the white ex-pat teachers) 'go to him to ask if it is necessary. He beats the small kids too, even if they are late because the rivers are up because of rain.'

Whenever you meet teachers they talk, horrified, of the beatings.

'Did they beat their children in the old days?'

'Yes, they did. And the women too. Incredible beatings. Horrible. Terrible. When we expostulate they think, oh, that's just a Honkey talking.'

All right, so what else has happened?

It takes hours of gossip to catch up with it all.

We eat supper early. We go to bed early. We get up before the sun. I look to see if the vervet monkey is in his tree down the hill, so we can watch the sunrise together, but the tree has gone the way of all trees, and perhaps the monkey too. Vervet monkeys do appear briefly on the edges of the clearing, play, chasing each other, in the branches – disappear. Youngsters. Not a philosopher among them.

The animals I met last time? Clever little Vicky was run over by a drunk driver at the Club. Old Annie the bull terrier was killed by a wild pig. The lanky ridgeback with legs that splayed and slipped about over the polished cement turned out to be too stupid to live, and found an early grave. The little black cat was allowed to keep a kitten from her last litter but the father was a bush cat, and this kitten, a strong brave young male, took to the bush. He comes to visit his mother, and they sit nose to nose where the trees start behind the house.

A new bull terrier lies on his back and moans with pleasure when the fires are lit in the evening. There is a young black dog, Seamus, part Newfoundland.

What about that great black dog, Tarka, who used to wake me every night by putting his nose into my hand, or my face, lonely because his people were away? He is too old to be running around at nights now, he stays at home. When there is a party at the Club, he stands on the edge of the room, a stiff old dog with a greying muzzle, looking in at young Seamus prancing and jumping among the dancers who say, 'Look, Seamus is dancing with us – come Seamus, dance with me . . .' And the young dog, almost weeping with pride, is steered for a few steps, his front paws carefully held up, while people applaud him. This is the dog who, a few months ago when the Coffee Farmer fell off the dam wall on a black night and could not walk, having cracked his hip, stayed by him, and when the Coffee Farmer was recovered enough to crawl home, adjusted his pace and positioned himself so the farmer could put his weight on his back. It took hours to cover the mile of rough road.

A PARTY

A big dinner party: everyone comes. You would not easily get this food in Britain. The vegetables have never heard of insecticides, fertilizers: they live on compost. No one has heard about hams being injected with water. The smoked beef has not had hormones fed into it.

It is a noisy enjoyable party, with a lot of young people. The little girls of the previous visit have grown up, and are in different parts of the world: there are new little girls, and they are all in love with a handsome young man visiting from Sandhurst. What has happened to the parachutist? Oh, he's off farming somewhere, doing well, they say.

Not a suggestion in any of this talk of the peevish complaint of six years ago. They might be different people: they are different people, all involved with development projects.

Even more than last time they plan to diversify: the crash of kiwi fruit prices was salutary. And they might be growing one of the most sought-after coffees in the world, but there is a coffee mountain . . .

These few families are also growing soft fruit, macadamia nuts, pecans, vegetables for the Mutare market, the new small pawpaws. In one kitchen a farmer's wife began making cheese from the surplus milk: now she cannot produce enough of her cheese to satisfy the hotels and the embassies in the cities. Last time I watched her work on her kitchen table: now she has special rooms kept at the right temperatures, and employs others.

The talk goes like this:

I heard Bob is doing well with his eland, how do you think eland would do up here? (Eland grown like cattle, for meat.)

Zebra . . . would it be too high for zebra here?

If camembert is a success here, why not try . . . ?

I'm putting in five acres of granadillas this year.

Ostrich feathers are back . . .

In Peru they . . .

In Mexico . . .

In Arizona . . .

I'm getting fifty more hives of bees. Killer bees they call them in America. They get hysterical about the slightest thing in America.

I said: 'My brother had two hundred hives. When I told him they were called killer bees he only laughed.'

'Anyway, you can breed aggression out of bees. I don't see the problem.'

Mangoes . . . pineapples . . . strawberries . . . papayas . . . Some of these are grown to dry and crystallize: there is a good market for them abroad.

The new sheep . . . the new pigs . . . the new fish . . .

The whole world comes on to these verandahs when they are discussing how to find new crops, new ideas.

And then, which certainly could not have happened last time: 'I don't understand why the Africans don't try this . . . try that.' 'I don't see why in the Communal Areas they shouldn't . . .' 'I'm going to have a word with the Minister next time he's down and suggest . . .'

A GOVERNMENT OFFICE

In fact, on this trip, not much time was spent in the mountains.

Down the mountain road we go to Mutare where in a certain office we tackle Bureaucracy. Today we are three: the Coffee Farmer, a woman visitor from South Africa, and me. These days white people don't just wander around villages whenever they feel like it: too much of a reminder of the old days. Besides, one is South African: the fact she does not admire her government is not written on her face. But the Coffee Farmer knows one of the officials well. During the War, the peaceable character sitting behind the desk was a well-known Commander, and he and the Coffee Farmer were enemies. Many a time had the Commander crossed the farm, at night . . . The two men enjoy the Ho-ho-ho type of male friendship. 'You never knew how often I was back and forth across your farm.' 'Then it was probably you I was taking a pot shot at that night.' Sometimes they go off to a bar and drink on it. My father used to visit a German smallworker not far from our farm. The two men were in the trenches opposite each other early in the First World War. In Harare I was told of a certain famous guerilla leader who regularly allowed a government security officer through his territory because he was taking medicines to villages; this mission of mercy completed, they resumed hostilities. The two men are now good friends. Clearly there are few closer bonds than having tried to kill each other.

This young man is thoroughly enjoying his position of being able to say yes or no. You can positively see him thinking that it will do the South African good to be petitioner to a black. The Coffee Farmer does not enjoy having to beg. Not for himself: as a conservation officer he can go where he likes. I am the worst problem: a really suspicious character, it seems. It is no good saying I have a journalist's pass. The young man says, 'That does not recommend you. We have given permission to journalists before, with bad results.' 'But she is a friend of Zimbabwe,' says the Coffee Farmer. 'There are friends and friends,' says the official. With relish. With the robust enjoyment that goes with certain kinds of political debate. I say that I was a Prohibited Immigrant in this country for thirty years and it is a bit hard to be under suspicion again under this government. 'Ah,' ripostes the official, 'then you are in that area, the political area, and we have to be cautious.' 'Surely not as cautious as all that?' 'And after all there were many Prohibited Immigrants.' 'True, but I have the honour to have been personally Prohibited by Lord Malvern himself.' 'And how do you happen to know a thing like that?' 'He told me so.'

We eye each other; seasoned politicos. His face is full of dramatic disbelief, eyebrows raised, chin forward, lips compressed. His hand is lifted, palm forward, as if to say, This far and no further. He slowly lowers his hand, places the palm judiciously on the desk, sits with eyes lowered, thinking. He says 'Excuse me' and goes out to make a telephone call from another office.

He comes back, smiles all round. Now he confides that he is a writer himself, and would like to be a novelist. We discuss the problems of literary creation. In his case, he has to spend too much time on administration. Shaking his head at his fate, office life, he sends us off with underlings into the bush.

There are two cars, the one from the office, one the Coffee Farmer's lorry.

THE RESETTLEMENT AREA

Off we drove on the road east, then turned off on to a bad road, unsurfaced, then, many miles further on, were on a rutty track, all the time in wild and beautiful country. The soil is pale: this is Class Four soil, and was not bought from white farmers Taking the Gap, for it was unallocated government land. This government, always cautious about resettling people, making sure that there was at least some kind of administrative focal point, water, transport, is now even more so, because something is coming to the fore that was not thought of earlier. Conservation. The precious, precarious, so-easily destroyed soil.

The Coffee Farmer is now a conservation representative for Manicaland. He works under a Chief, whom he describes as a very sound type, a good chap, you know. It is his task to keep an eye on the sufferings or health of the earth. As we drive rocking along the track he keeps exclaiming, 'Look at that! See that field! It's gone to hell since I was here last. See those ruts – that's erosion.' Or, 'Look, that chap there, he knows how to do it, that's a perfect field. But look at that one on the other side of the road, it's a mess, there won't be any soil at all next year if . . .' He clutches the wheel, he suffers, he could easily, we soothe, have a heart attack. But it is no good: if he sees a patch of sick soil it is as if he himself were ill. A happy and well-looked-after piece of earth makes him content. 'Look at that gully. It wasn't there last year. *What does that chap think he is doing?*' And he stops the car, so the car behind has to stop. Everyone gets out of the car, to look at him standing over the raw scar in the earth. He points at it like the judgement of God: '*Just look at that.*'

'I simply do not understand it,' says he, pointing first at the eroded field. 'It's just as easy to do things well as badly, so why doesn't this chap do it as well as that chap?'

He appears to think that this is a simple question, one that can be answered with a sentence beginning, Well, you see, it's like this . . .

On, on, on we drive, many miles from Mutare. We pass Growth Points, all new ones. We pass notices that say 'Welcome to——School'. We drive past lines of women and children selling mangoes. This is mango country. You may have tasted mangoes but never mangoes like these. Why are they not known world-wide? Transport, that's why: great distances, bad roads.

We are giving lifts all the time: the once-bitten-twice-shy cautions of the sophisticated areas are not appropriate here.

One elderly man, who sat for a few miles holding tight to the side of the jolting lorry, a quiet, unremarkable, smiling man, who walked off into the bush with a smile and a wave when we set him down, has three sons. One is being trained in Czechoslovakia to be an aircraft engineer, for he did well in his examination. One has just taken his O-levels and everyone is waiting for the results. The third failed his exams. The contrast between the futures of the first son and the third was in all our minds; one will live in the modern world, the other as if it scarcely exists.

I remark how strange to pick up a poor man in the middle of the bush whose son is at university in Europe, but am rebuked with, 'There are many like him.' I wish I believed there were many like his oldest son being educated in Britain.

We are now miles, worlds, away from anywhere. Leaving the cars, we walk into the bush and sit around on rocks under the light airy dry trees that shed a shifting fragrant shade. It is midday. An emerald spotted dove calls: is answered.

There is a village near here, though we cannot see it. People come from the village and sit with us. Children. Men. No women. But there are women, with us, officials; two people we gave lifts to are here to take a census and they sit apart under a tree with the headman, conferring earnestly over charts and notebooks. An Extension Worker, a woman, is here to check on the state of the rains, the crops. During the hour we sat and lazed there, a good deal of business was done. As much, certainly, as if it were a meeting in an office.

The talk turns to Mozambique, which is so close, and to the people who keep coming here through the bush to get food. 'How can we feel safe in Zimbabwe when the Mozambique War goes on and on?' 'It will never end. It is in South Africa's interests to keep it going.'

A Mozambique joke: What is a sardine? A sardine is a whale that has gone through seven stages of socialist transformation.

An old man tells the children that once Mozambique was a rich country, and there was plenty of food. The children sit shaking their heads, disbelieving: for all their lives Mozambicans have crept through the bush to beg food from them.

'Why are they so poor?' asks a boy of about ten.

'There's a war,' says the old man.

'Wasn't there a war here?' asks a teenage girl, who dimly remembers something of the kind.

'No, we haven't had a war,' says the ten-year-old.

The adults look at each other, black and white, shake their heads, laugh.

I ask: 'If there was one single thing you could have here, in this area, what would you ask for?'

'Money,' said the headman. They all laugh.

'Well all right. You have fifty thousand pounds. What would you spend it on?'

The vastness of this sum makes them laugh again. They argue for a while, and finally agree, 'A dam. That's what we need most. We should dam that river that runs under those hills.'

I tell them about the garden I saw in Matabeleland: poor soil, but successful, because of the water. They are at once interested, come closer, ask questions: how much water? Is fertilizer being used? Where did the money come from?

I ask what people in this village do for entertainment.

'The government sent its film unit around last year,' was the grave reply: then they all laughed about something in the film that was shown them. They did not say what was so funny about the film.

And when there is no film unit?

They sit in their homes and talk and tell stories in the evenings, and sometimes there is a dance.

There is a bus that comes, takes us to the Growth Point. We can shop there.

Sometimes we go into Mutare and visit relatives, but it is a long way off, over a hundred miles.

Later that day in another place, another meeting, conducted under a tree.

The local village representatives came to meet visiting Extension Workers and a local Extension Worker, who is a woman, one of the twenty per cent now coming out of agricultural colleges. She is young, smartly dressed, married, with three children. Around a table set under the tree there are about ten people conducting village business.

They do not seem pleased to see officials from Mutare. When one of the men goes from the lorry to the table, they all at once begin joking about some advice he gave them last time he was here. There are two kinds of people here, it is easy to see: the villagers, and the experts and officials.

I was told in Harare, 'These new experts coming out of agricultural colleges, think they know everything. They go into the villages and tell people who have farmed in those conditions for centuries what to do. You have to do so and so – say the experts. But it won't work – say the villagers, and it is hard to know when this is peasant conservatism talking, and when it is the voice of experience.

I have been given research papers, much of it from the university, defending traditional agricultural practice. The villages know everything about how to look after soil in a drought year, how to grow crops on this and poor soil, how to keep beasts well when fodder is short. But if the experts on a university level are full of praise for traditional practices, this does not mean these are being taught in agricultural colleges. It always takes a long time for the results of research to reach school and college syllabuses.

When I said to the Coffee Farmer, 'Even the old missionaries
and explorers talked about what good farmers these people
were,' he replied, 'You don't understand. That was then – very
few people and plenty of land. They haven't changed their
practices to suit the new conditions. I keep telling them . . .'

It is the evening of the same day, the sun gold and low,
making shadows. We are standing by a strong new fence, paid
for by some foreign Aid source.

Handsome black and white cows are crowding up to the
fence to look at us.

The Coffee Farmer is holding forth. 'Look at this fence. I
know what it costs. You don't get fence of this quality under
X pounds a kilometre. To fence this bit of bush must have cost
ZY pounds. It will last Z years. Yes, first-class fence, bloody
marvellous. But if you had slung that wire from tree to tree,
doing it properly so the trees are not hurt, then it would have
cost XZ pounds and you could have fenced in three times the
area.'

He stands on his two solidly-planted feet, hands on his hips
in front of a group of Africans, who are listening gravely. I and
the South African woman, both appreciating this traditional
scene, white man lecturing blacks, catch each other's eyes, carefully do not smile, turn our attention to the cows who both
wish and do not wish to become acquainted. That is, they
come, drawn by curiosity, to a point about five feet away, then
stand ready to jump back and off at the slightest movement
from us.

We hear, 'That is the trouble with all this Aid money. They
just waste it and waste it. But why didn't you tell them . . .
why didn't you simply put your foot down and . . .'

All this is nonsense, because everyone knows that when
international experts descend on an area they will decide
exactly what they want done, and the locals will like it or lump
it. We can just imagine saying to some well-conducted Swede
or German, 'Never mind about steel fence stanchions, just sling
the wire from tree to tree and . . .'

'It's all heartbreaking,' we hear. 'The one thing that is essential, the key to everything, the *priority* is fencing land properly

so the mombies can't get on it and so it can rest and come back and there won't be erosion . . . just look at this.'

He is leading his class to look at a fenced area that has no mombies on it. 'Look. That soil has rested for two years and you can see how the bush is coming back. See that plant? When you see that plant it means there hasn't been a beast on it for at least two seasons. You see my point? If you use trees instead of metal stanchions then you could enclose three times the area.'

Across the fence where the beasts are is a commotion. Another group of cattle approaches the first, pale dust rising about their hooves and dulling the shine of their hides. It is led by a bull. The first group is led by a bull. The invading bull comes forward, presumably to negotiate with the first about sharing this bit of grazing. The two bulls stand nose to nose snorting while the cows meet and mingle and begin to graze. A newly-born calf, as loose and sinuous and shining as an empty black silk glove stands with his nose to the fence, his back to the herd, staring at us with a look of wild affront.

'And there's another thing,' says the Coffee Farmer. 'Money wasted, wasted, wasted on status symbols. Now the fashionable thing is to have a house made of burned brick. But making bricks means you have to burn wood. You waste wood. Why not kimberly brick? It is perfectly good. Did you know there are countries in the world that never use burned bricks, they use bricks made of mud and water and they last for centuries. Why do you people insist on . . .'

The two bulls have come to some agreement and are now peaceably co-existing.

'It makes me absolutely wild,' says the Coffee Farmer. 'I go around the villages and everywhere I see these kilns, what for, money wasted, all the wood wasted . . .'

When the Coffee Farmer is out of earshot we ask the officials and the villagers if they mind being lectured.

They do not look at each other. Then they smile and after a pause one of the villagers says, 'No, we don't mind. We know he wants to help us. He is a good man.'

It is impossible to know if they are being polite. We discuss the incident and decide they mean it, that is, the villagers do, but the officials may be a different matter.

We go back into the cars. We drive back on the long long roads through the sunset bush, back to Mutare and up the mountains.

To supper comes the man who used to do the job of the official in the office in Mutare. For years he was resettling people all over the Eastern districts. He knows it all. What I have to remember, says he, is that in the early idealistic days Mugabe envisaged collective farming, like the Russian kolkhozes, where land was owned in common. The idea has worked no better here than in Russia, or in Tanzania where they tried it. It is a failure and everyone knows it. But to know it is one thing, to admit it publicly another. What works is when farmers are given land and then pool machinery and facilities. Is it really their land? Well, here is another of the famous Grey Areas. It is government land but it is also theirs. What they want is to own land, with proper title deeds, which they can hand on to their children. Things seem to be developing along these lines, while the legalities remain ambiguous. And there is another thing, immediately much more tricky. A condition for being given land in a Resettlement Area is that a commitment must be made to that way of life: you agree to be a farmer, nothing but a farmer. But they want the same conditions as in the Communal Areas where at least one member of a family will have a job in the nearest town. The poverty in the Resettlement Areas is worse than in the Communal Areas – and that is why, say the resettled farmers.

But the government says: If you commit yourself totally to this way of life, give all your energies to it, then the Resettlement Areas will be transformed, they will be rich . . .

Well, yes, in time. A generation? Two?

In the Resettlement Area we were shown the house of a good farmer, who satisfied the Extension Workers, and who is a credit and an inspiration to everyone. His house is a little brick house, with a couple of rooms and a kitchen. It has a nice garden. The field at the back is green and properly contoured. But the youngsters growing up in this house, a hundred miles from that metropolis Mutare, will do everything to go into town. At any cost. Even if it means living crowded with twenty other people in a poor room.

LEGENDS

Now we are driving south from Mutare along the edge of the Resettlement Area we were in yesterday. We are on our way from one centre of order, comfort – civilization – to another. For an hour the pale dryness of Class Four soil accompanies us, and we know the many villages hidden from us in the bush are the same as the few we looked at. We know because the Resettlement Officer of *then* is with us, and he knows every inch of this bush, every hut, every new Growth Point. He identifies with the efforts of the resettled ones with the same passion as the Coffee Farmer suffers in his own flesh the struggles of the soil. When we say we have been talking about what we saw yesterday, and found it discouraging, he says if we had known the area before we would be impressed.

This former Resettlement Officer is also an historian and knows all the history of this area. This means that the frontier with Mozambique, so close to us, is in his mind no more than a temporary political whimsicality, just as it must seem to the villagers who see their tribe arbitrarily divided.

One view of a future Mozambique reflects the past. The eastern districts of Zimbabwe and Mozambique are a historical and geographical unity. When? These ideas need something of the quality of those stretches of time that will see the Indian Ocean spilling into Mashonaland. No, the new Monomotapa will hardly need a million or a thousand years to take shape, but a hazy landscape of Time is best suited to a region already populated with legendary kings and old ruined cities waiting unexcavated in forests and jungles along the shores of the same ocean. One of the worst things about taking power, if you are a leader, a party, a junta, must be that henceforth your dreams have to narrow themselves to the necessities of power-keeping. The Freedom Fighters in the bush may sit around the fire at night talking: 'I wonder if one day this frontier will disappear and this tribe can live as they did. All these frontiers are arbitrary anyway, invented by the whites, so why should we take any notice of them?' But, the War over, and you are no longer sitting among trees watching firelight make moving patterns on leaves and grass, conversations of this kind must be held in closed rooms, when you have made sure no one, not even a servant, is listening. How many armies have come out of the bush, forests, mountains, to find they have lost the freedom to dream they had when they owned the rags they wore and the weapons they carried?

PLEASURE

Today rain threatens from every quarter of the sky. Rain fell in grey sheets behind us, then around us, then – as we ran through the hills – we emerged into sharp stinging downpours that kept pace until we left them in sullen purple-black masses that blotted out the mountains: saw an intense orange sunlight ahead and thought we would reach that but no, at another turn of the road the bruise-coloured clouds were ahead, and we were into a new storm that lashed the car with hail. At midday, in a space of sun, we stopped by a river at a place that combined wildness and remoteness with the convenience of a picnic table and a bench. While we sat there three men emerged from a landrover and came to look at the river. Two tourists and their tour-guide. We guessed Swedish, German, Danish, American, but heard Italian. These were rich Italians in elegant clothes, and they could afford an individual guide who had brought them to stand above a tempestuously-running river, full of rain, before speeding on up to Mutare. Then on we drove in the opposite direction, through wilder and more mountainous country, with never a car in sight, while the storms still deployed around us until finally everything was grey rain. We arrived at the Chimanimani Hotel in rain and found a vast fire burning in a vast living-room. The hotel is spacious, every room large with high ceilings, the bedrooms large with verandahs from which you look at mountains and more mountains, and, close to, the decorous blue swirls of a swimming bath. Old Colonial, which has made some of the pleasantest hotels in the world, but it was nearly empty. How can such a hotel not be permanently full? It seems one of the problems is that it is near Mozambique and a couple of years ago a party of Renamo Terrorists came through these mountains. Well, and what of it? No one stops using the roads when they read the statistics for car accidents. There is no accounting for what people choose to be afraid of.

We ate dinner in the capacious and almost empty dining-room, listening to the laughter and hullabaloo of general enjoyment coming from the outside bar – for that is packed every night, even when bars inside the hotel remain underused. That night the hotel was enclosed in a hush of rain, but by morning the rain had become mist. We drove around and around mountains, each known intimately to the two men who had walked over them. Then, from the mountains, to the Bridal Veil Falls. (In every part of the world savagely beautiful falls of water are diminished and domesticated by being called bridal veils.) The water smashes, crashes, plunges, in cascades of white hundreds of feet over rocks into a pool. On either side of the falls are steep escarpments full of the homes of birds, and the place is enclosed in that silence that is made by a continuous rushing noise. Banana trees grow there showing all the cycles of their lives. For when they have flowered at last they die: new saplings spring up among giants whose sagging limbs show they are due to rejoin the soil. They have red ribs and a glossy jewelled look. We were sitting on a grassy lawn between rocks when the Coffee Farmer remarked, 'During the War a bunch of 'terrs' murdered some tourists here. The locals won't come near the place. Just near where you are sitting actually.' We did not rise to this. Whatever vibrations of fear or horror there were have long ago left this place: a more exquisite one cannot exist. Besides, we remarked there must be few places in the world where there have not been murders, battles, deaths. Also, of course, love, kisses, picnics and good times. Then off we went on yet another road through mountains, seeing no one at all, only some fine cattle who stared nervously at us as beasts do who seldom see vehicles clambering past their lonely altitudes. All morning we drove, with the mountains of Mozambique on our right hand, sometimes along ridges looking down into valleys where there are farms, dams, plantations, sometimes through forests that are still whole and healthy. We drove slowly and kept stopping because we did not want the journey to end. When we joined the main road we knew we left behind one of the few places in the world still owned and managed by Nature. Well, more or less.

THE MASHOPI HOTEL

On the way back from Mutare to Harare I stopped in Macheke, outside the old hotel, which was no longer boarded up and derelict but again recognizable as the hotel of those long-ago weekends. I asked to see the manager, who turned out to be a young black man orchestrating a team of enthusiastic helpers. I told him that in the old days this hotel was popular, always full. But this could only mean popular with whites, and he didn't care about that. I said that in the War the RAF used to come out from Salisbury for weekends: sometimes there were parties that went on for days. But he thought I was talking about the Bush War, and had never heard of the RAF: the Second World War was over before he was born. I asked if I could go over the place for old times' sake. He was polite, amused. At the back the bedroom block was again visible and identifiable, and being added to, and the flight of steps I could not find in 1982 appeared among the new rubble of building work. A garden café with sunshades and tables had replaced shrubs. The bar was where it had been, but extended, and curved into the place where we had danced, now a drinking room. In the dining-room, exactly as it was, I had lunch, and could have believed the door would swing open and admit ghosts brought back by this resurrection of old haunts. 'You see?' I silently addressed them. 'It has all happened, just as we said it would . . . well, not just as we said . . .' Rather I could have addressed them, imagining the precise degree of irony each face would show, if I was not in such a hurry. I thanked the manager. I looked across the road to the scruffy gum trees, making sure those miserable baboons had not reappeared. Then I left, on the road to Harare.

GOOD OLD SMITHIE

It occurs to me that no one mentions Smith: six years ago they could not stop talking about him. He has been in America, saying that Zimbabwe is more of a tyranny than South Africa. People think that he wants to be arrested, wants to be a martyr. 'But Mugabe is too clever for him.'

They tell a story of an incident at the local post office. Mr Smith, Mrs Smith, queue up to be served 'just like everybody else' – they say, with approval. One day Mrs Smith said to a black woman that she hoped her little girl was well. 'Do you remember, I used to give her sweets.'

'Yes, I remember, Amai . . .' a term of respect for older women. 'But you see, sweets were not enough.'

A THINK-TANK

'They' say that there exists an unofficial Think-Tank, composed of high-level people from both parties. They are all of the travelling class, and do not use the rhetoric of a marxism dead and discredited. Two languages or modes of speaking are used in Zimbabwe, just as was the case in the Soviet Union before Gorbachev: the public, the official one, used as self-protection, and a living language which acknowledges the falseness of the first. It is said that 'Mugabe himself' sometimes comes to the Think-Tank evenings. This means that people wish he did, if he does not. The ideas of the Think-Tank filter down, have influence, like a stream of fresh quick-moving water in stale water. But the language used in the Think-Tank would not be used in public, and never in the newspapers. 'If you get a Cabinet Minister by himself you find they all know what the real situation is. When they are all together in the Cabinet or one of those committees of theirs, then they are afraid to say what they think.' 'They' say that this Think-Tank enjoys so much prestige that very high-level people indeed from South Africa come up to sit in and listen. 'Who are these people? Liberals?' 'Oh no, better than that, you'd be surprised, oh no, the real thing, people from the government.'

THE OLD FARM

And now it was time to stop being childish. I had to go back to the old farm. To make sure that the driving wheel would finally be turned on to the right road, I was not going to be behind it. This business of writers' myth-countries is far from simple. I know writers who very early build tall fences around theirs and afterwards make sure they never go near them. And not only writers: all the people I know from former dominions, colonies, or any part of the earth they grew up on before making that essential flight in and away from the periphery to the centre: when the time comes for them to make the first trip home it means stripping off new skin and offering exposed and smarting flesh to – the past. For that matter every child who has left home to become an adult knows the diminishing of the first trip home.

A child's world is full of enormities, every neighbour or uncle or auntie or the shopkeeper on the corner is easily transferable to the world of fairy tales or of comics, but once grown up, she or he goes home to find they are just people after all. And that is the point, finding oneself so diminished because those powerful arbiters are. But in The District – so we referred to it, as if there could be only one district (just as there is no people in the world who has not called itself, in its beginnings, simply, The People) – in The District, Lomagundi, they were all outsize and fit for tales and epics, because the white farmers lived at distances from each other, and everything they did was visible, and everything they said too, because those were the days of the district telephone lines when there might be up to twenty farms on one line. They still exist. Lonely people listened in to conversations, or even joined in. There could easily be a three-way or four-way conversation going on, as if they were sitting together in a room. It was as if they all lived on stage, every characteristic or event enormified by storytelling: the word *gossip* is surely suitable only for small streets and crammed populations? And the Africans assisted this by their custom of giving the whites names, like those in epics: Angry Face, The Woman With Two Husbands, The Fire-haired Son, The Man Who Barks Like a Dog.

Take the Matthews, our nearest neighbours. He was Big Bob because he was six foot six, weighty, looked as if he had been carved out of beef well-marbled with fat. She was Little Mrs Matthews, being five feet tall, plump, dainty. His brutalities to the natives were discussed with disapproval. 'He doesn't know his own strength, that's the trouble,' was the nearest anyone came to acceptance of Big Bob's excesses, fifty, sixty years ago. He had been a policeman in Glasgow. Easy to imagine him strolling along wet dark pavements, hands behind his back, truncheon under his arm. Easy to imagine her in a pretty-curtained parlour. When my brother and I dropped in on our bicycles she would be in the kitchen cooking: tea cakes, girdle cakes, pancakes, oatcakes, fruit cakes, sponge cakes, tarts, pies, gingerbread, fruit bread, parkin. All these would appear on the table for that supremely Scottish meal, tea. Their house was full of 'store furniture', in other words, glossy heavy suites and wardrobes. Sometimes nieces visited, and then Little Mrs Matthews and the girls danced Scottish sword dances, kilts flying, slippered feet as neat as cats' tripping around the sword hilts. If they had stayed in Scotland would they have been remarkable? But what about the weight of Bob, the height – he would have been material for notoriety wherever he lived, and those fists . . . 'Good Lord, it would be like colliding with a steam-hammer, being hit by Big Bob.' The blacks called him Thunder and Lightning and put marks on trees near the paths people used looking for work, meaning, This is a bad farm.

But the question is, what was it in Big Bob, and in Little Mrs Matthews that took them out of Glasgow before the First World War to farm in old Southern Rhodesia among all those wild animals and the savages? What restlessness, or ambition, or crime, or romanticism, well concealed behind conventional looks, took them so far from home? And, similarly, with all the rest of our neighbours. If you saw them at Church on Sunday – Presbyterian and Church of England services alternated at the village hall – those sober Sunday-dressed-and-hatted people, eyes down over hymnbooks, their voices measured to 'Rock of Ages' and 'All Things Bright and Beautiful', it was easy to imagine them back 'Home' from where, surely, they need never have taken flight? But that wasn't true. Every one of them had something concealed, not evident but powerful, which had brought them out here to The District to spread themselves over so many acres of land stolen from the blacks, farming with all the energy of poor people who remember poverty.

The District was full of misfits, for better or worse, who had found England, Scotland, too small.

Now when I think of these people, among whom I grew up, this is what interests me: what were they before they sold up their furniture, put themselves on the slow boats to Cape Town or Beira, and then on the trains to Salisbury, there to scatter and look for land, risking everything in a country they knew nothing about? Every one of them arrived in The District in the same state as the families stepping off ships on the shores of

New England or Virginia, their minds full of tales of danger
and riches. And, too, of thoughts of freedom.

Going back to the farm, so commonsense told me, not to
mention friends, was bound to be an anti-climax. This turned
out not to be true, though I did not expect to have my ideas
shifted about as they were.

First, there was this business of the weather, or, if you like,
the climate. On that day I was driven by Ayrton R. to The
District, everyone was worried about the rain. After those satis-
factory but brief rains weeks ago no rain, none. Yet it was late
in November. Tucked away at the back of our minds is the
notion that our new weather sciences should be bringing the
weather to heel: that when we say the Inter-Tropical Convergence Zone the words should be enough to force the masses
of warm wet air that rise off oceans and forests into the right
place so they may clash with the high pressure areas south-east
near Mozambique. But the skies were a bright calm blue, not
a sign of rain-tension, black silver-edged clouds unfolding up
into the zenith, lightning flickering low on a horizon, thunder
like a promise. Everyone was thinking 'a drought', but no one
was saying it, yet: superstition. If you say 'drought' then that
makes it real.

I did not want to see the old farm thinned by dryness and
dimmed by smoke from bush fires: a harsh and denuded thing
is the bush before the rains have come, like a literal depiction
of a state of mind I was afraid of – though I had dreamed it
often enough. Isolation. Being excluded. Exile from the possibilities of the world outside the farm. I wanted the bush in its
lush and luxuriant aspect, the rainy season landscape, and I
was almost sure I would find it. After all, reports did say it had
rained in the north-east, if not enough. Above all, the migrant
birds had arrived. Even when the dry season dust was still
velvet on your skin, those travelling birds announced the rainy
season. And, better even than that, in that long-ago *then* storks
and swallows brought news of places it was hard to believe I
would ever see, for England was situated in a region of the
mind as different from Africa as the atmosphere of one recur-
ring dream is from another. *There* were snows, mists, shallow

305

sunlight, long twilights in a pastel country where birds cried
along chalky shores they never left. *Here* the sun got up and
went down pronto at six and six, the colours were strong,
the heat burned and snapped, you lived high on the Altitude,
among dramatic skies. It never snowed. When I was young I
was infinitely separated from Europe. Except through literature. When I came to England and became Prohibited, the
Africa I knew was out of reach. Separation of my landscapes
has always been my fate. But, a few days after I returned to
London after this trip in 1988 I saw a weatherman point to the
weather map on television and remark that the Inter-Tropical
Convergence Zone over Southern Africa was influencing the
air masses, hot and cold, to the north of it, and they in turn
were shaking and shocking the weather in our skies, the skies
of England. I sat on my London sofa, the curtains drawn tight
to keep out December, and the certain and immutable walls
that had kept my inner landscapes apart vanished in a chart of
rivers of wind and oceans of air, the two worlds joined more
swiftly than Concorde can do it, or those machines still being
evolved which one day will travel from London to Harare,
London to Tokyo, in a couple of hours.

But this resolution of impossibilities was still a month ahead.

No, it was distance, what had happened to distance, which
was the real theme of my return to the farm.

It was a brilliant day, when Ayrton R. and I set off. We
went through the northern suburbs of Harare while I ticked off
events and people: this happened here, this happened here;
no, it is not possible that people survive what they do survive,
what we all survive, that is the point – and thank God we do
forget it all, except on voyages like this one.

But wait . . . is that true . . . perhaps it isn't true? Suppose
one was able to keep in one's mind those childhood miseries,
the homesickness like a bruise on one's heart, the betrayals –
if they were allowed in lie in the mind always exposed, a cursed
country one has climbed out of and left behind for ever, but
visible, not hidden . . . would then that landscape of pain have
less power than I am sure it has? There is a fish called the
Angler Fish, that looks as evil as if it has chosen to illustrate a

morality tale. It cruises just under the surface of the sea, watching for migrating birds who decide to risk a few hours sleep rocking on the waves. Then this brute of a fish sneaks up, snatches at sleep-loosened feet and drags the bird down, down . . .

On we drove over the good smooth urban roads, but when memory expected a sudden bumpy encounter with the country roads nothing happened, on we went rolling high and safe, infinitely far from the bush and the past. Yes, I had been in The District only a few weeks ago, and on a farm not far from ours, but the approach had been on a different road, one that did not share my childhood, or those journeys of *then*, the interminable journeys in child-time . . . 'When will we get there?' 'Soon.' 'But *when*' – as the valleys and hills jogged slowly by, the road twisting among clumps of tall grass and piles of rock. It was over this road I drove my father into Salisbury, in the old car, he a diabetic in danger of coma, my mother beside him in the back seat, watching his face, her calm fingers on his pulse. The road *then* was a track, corrugated in long slow waves of soil from Salisbury all the way north to the Zambesi. If I drove fast, the corrugations jarred the sick man so that he gasped out pleas for me to stop. So I stopped, then drove slowly at about five miles an hour, up and down, from the ridge of one corrugation to the next, dodging between potholes . . . essential to get him to hospital fast, at once, but if I went fast those corrugations would kill him. How many times did we make that journey? But I have forgotten. And then they built the strip roads. Roaring north now on this wonderful road I searched for the old strip roads, broken threads that appeared by the railway lines and disappeared into grass. Those fragile foot-wide ribbons of tarmac marked a stride forward into a new technology – Southern Rhodesia invented the strip roads – and thereafter journeys into Salisbury were no longer nightmares, took only three or four hours of careful driving. As for the old dusty and muddy tracks that were the first roads, they are no longer visible, though I daresay if one stopped the rush northwards, got out of the car, climbed down the embankment and searched in the thick after-rains grass, there would be traces of those roads we dawdled, slid and skidded over, or waited on patiently for hours so a river might go down. But now you don't notice the rivers running full with rain or sluggish under the bridges. Soon, long before memory and dream landscapes say is possible, there is the Dyke. That chain of mountains full of crystalline lights and blue distances, what a pity my mother did not know they are linked with the Rift Valley and the Indian Ocean, or are for romantics who refuse to listen to pedantic objections. Her memories, her talk, were full of the sea. She was London-bred, made by streets, but the sea was her mind's hinterland, and a tumble of granite rocks, or ruffling sweeps of white cloud high above a red sunset brought out of her talk of waves crashing on reefs or storms at sea. Later I discovered that her mother, Emily Flower, she who died in childbirth with her third, was the daughter of a lighterman on the Thames, so seas and rivers were in her blood. As we say. She was proud she was such a good sailor, that on that terrible journey on the oil tanker on the Caspian, when her husband and children were ill with seasickness, and later on the voyage out to Africa when the gales were so bad all the other passengers lay in their bunks longing for death, she was up on the bridge with the captain. On the farm, six thousand feet up, she yearned for the sea but we could not afford it. She was shockingly imprisoned on that farm. No one we knew went to England for holidays. If someone in The District went Home then it was for medical treatment or to say final farewells to aged parents. Even the 'cheque-book farmers' on the other side of The District went Home seldom, and we all talked about their trips as travellers' tales out of our own experience. The richer farmers did go to Durban; we did not.

But if it had been known then the continent would split and the Indian Ocean . . . then sea-spume and sea-winds and Arab trading ships would have been added, in the talk we listened to as children, to the gold-bearing reefs, quartz outcrops, Arab trading safaris and Arab miners who in those days were supposed to be the reason for the ancient mine workings that we stumbled on as we picked our way through long grass.

If only we had known the real history of that area . . . We

believed it had been inhabited when the whites came by people not much more advanced than hunter-gatherers; yes, they did have unimportant little fields of grain and gourds. The fact was that for centuries it was a tale of large and small kingdoms, wars, conquests and coups, traitors, treaties and spies, with the Portuguese there not only as traders, far from it, they were sometimes king-makers and more than once rulers, too. It was all like Shakespeare's plays about the Plantagenets, much more satisfying than sentimental notions about the Arabs.

From Harare to the Dyke was a moment, while I kept trying to slow the journey to match this turn of the road, that descent of a hill, with the past, but it was no use, the Dyke was behind us and in no time at all we would be in Banket.

It was on this trip that I understood, in my own self, in my bones and my blood, how this had happened once, long ago, in Europe. Big towns were so far off that people might go there once in their lives, or they knew people who had. The village where they bought what they did not grow needed a day to reach, walking, or on horseback. A fearful or excited night in an inn, and then home, with tales to surprise the neighbours. And then suddenly, happening within a generation, good roads, coach travel, and the world shrank. What had been out of reach was within touching distance. The rough tracks that had followed paths discovered by the necessities of walking, of getting somewhere on foot, paths that wound and hesitated and curved and detoured around hillocks and searched for shallow places in rivers – they disappeared, were swallowed in grass, and then in scrub and then in trees. This revolution has still to take place in some countries of Africa. It has still to happen in some parts of Zimbabwe, for you can speed to the end of the tarmac and see before you the sandy bumps of a bush road whose course was determined by feet walking a path. The car that was speeding straight through the infinite variations of the bush has to slow and match itself to a walker's landscape.

And now we were in Banket itself, grown to a little town, with the old Banket, 'the Station' visible only to the eye of History – mine. *Then* the centre of 'the Station' was a long low

narrow strip of building like a shed with verandahs, called
Dardagan's, the Greek who owned the hotel, the butcher's, the
grocery, the kaffir truck store. A little room at the north end of
the brick line was the butcher's, with its zinc counter and the
great metal hooks behind it where the bloody joints dangled.
Outside, under the tree at the back, they cut up an ox or a
cow, with its four stomachs spilling out sweet-smelling cud. A
fly-covered carcass might be hanging from a tree. After the
butchery, came the store, the next along the verandah, with its
tinned fruits, its bully beef and its biscuits, and too, the bolts
of cotton stuff. Sacks of sugar, flour, mealie meal, stood about
on the cement floor, and trickles of tiny black ants had to be
swept up by the store 'boy', always vigilant for these foragers.
Next to the store on the same verandah, was the hotel, which
consisted of the bar and the half dozen tables to provide meals
for the commercial travellers or people going north to Northern
Rhodesia. The bar, like all country hotels, was the money-
maker, with people in it, mostly men, every night. There were
a couple of bedrooms. The kaffir truck store was separated from
this building by a few yards.

Here, on the verandah a half-grown girl dusty from having
walked in the seven miles from the farm stood and looked
through the fly-wire-screened door at a commercial traveller all
long burned legs and burned arms and throat and in the khaki
shorts and shirt worn by the farmers he visited selling cattle
dip and wire and creosote and paint. He was sitting extended,
legs out, so the chair under him was like a tilting temporary
prop while he ate his way seriously and fast through a whole
packet of Marie biscuits, and gulped the orange-red tea, strong
enough to rip the lining off any stomach, and often wiped the
sweat off his face: it was hot under that corrugated iron. The
girl from the farm stood staring at a world of unattainable
sophistication: a man who appeared on this verandah and then
jumped back into his car and sped to stations further along the
line, or to Lusaka, or back to Salisbury, a man who *moved*, just
as he liked, and – it was necessary for the adolescent to believe
this – chose a woman to share his bed when he did stop for
the night. The fact was, since it was the 1930s, and the Slump,

the traveller had grabbed hold of a job he was lucky to get, and he had a wife working somewhere as matron or housekeeper – anywhere she could have the children during school holidays. The traveller felt the pressure of that hungry stare, looked up and was just able to discern through the glare against the screen, the shape of a girl. Looking more closely, adjusting his gaze to the dazzle on the wire gauze, he saw she had long burned legs ending in 'veldschoen' – those ancestors of the shoes known as hush puppies, and bare burned arms; a .22 rifle dangled from her hand, and her dress, incongruously, was a neat little number smart enough for town. For she had brought into the butcher six guineafowl, shot from the vast flocks that covered the farm with their clinking and their movement, running like dark shadows through the bush until they lifted themselves into the air to settle in the trees away from that pursuer, the .22. For the six guineafowl she had been paid just enough to buy a cotton dress-length from the store, which she would run up that night on the sewing machine in her bedroom – a dress that proved she was grown-up. But if this man actually came to open the gauze door, the girl would be gone, for she needed to watch, to observe, to dream, and the last thing she hoped for was a conversation which, she knew, would diminish the traveller into some captive of necessity, like her own parents.

These little strips of building now stood locked and empty, ready to be demolished. Just as with the hotel in Macheke, I could not believe that such thin, shallow bits of building could have held so much life and so many people. Why, on mail days, or when there were dances or gymkhanas, hundreds of people might pass along those verandahs and in and out of the bar. The post office I knew is still there, among all the other buildings, a pretty little place. And, for the rest . . . energetic Banket is spreading fast, the new townships have black people in them properly housed – or at least, there are good houses, but who knows how many each has to hold?

Two roads run off to the right of the main road north, fine new roads, and one follows the line of the old railway to the Ayreshire mine. We called it the Ayreshire track, though the

railway sleepers were long ago displaced, or stolen, or might
be stumbled over in the bush where they lay filling with water
for mosquitoes to breed in.

In the 1890s the Ayreshire mine was a big mine with its own
hotel. Then and later it was notorious for the casual or cruel
treatment of its workers. In our time it was no longer being
mined properly, but was an open-cast working, owned by a
man called McCauley. The men who worked for him hated him
so much they sometimes strung wire from tree to tree across
the track when he had been in Salisbury or in Banket and they
knew he was coming back. The idea was that the car would
run into the wire at windscreen level and turn over. But we all
knew these wires were sometimes there and we watched for
them. No car was overturned, and he died in his bed. He used
to say that he had survived the trenches in France, and he
wasn't going to be killed by kaffirs. I remember wondering why
such a wicked man was always so pleased with himself.

To go from Banket to the farm, by car, might take an hour,
not only because of my father's idiosyncratic attitudes towards
speed, but because, if it rained, the road would be red mud,
in which we got stuck, over which we skidded. Or if it was
dry, the wheels could sink in drifts of red dust. 'Going into the
Station' was a state of mind, an odyssey. But if I walked then
I might dawdle along the track for a couple of hours. Now the
journey takes a few minutes.

This new road, obliterating the old turns and twists and ups
and downs, runs through field after field of the rich Banket
soil, surely as beautiful as any in the world, red, soft, rich and
mellow. The bush has been cleared to make these fields, leaving only strips here and there. Once this soil was proud to go
sixteen bags of maize to the acre, and people all over the
country used to quote it as an example of merit, but now,
because of genetic miracles, it would scorn to go less than thirty
or thirty-five, though forty is more like it. 'This district could
feed half of Zimbabwe on its own,' says Ayrton R., who might
be from Matabeleland, but clearly feels about Banket and its
accomplishments like a parent.

We passed the Matthews' house, still in appearance just the

same, and I waited for that moment when the long low grass-thatched house would appear, confirming so many dreams and nightmares, but there was the hill, yes absolutely and veritably a hill, it had not been vanished away, and on the top of it not the long house, but another, further back, a graceless greyish bungalow. But it was the field, the big field, rather, the Big Land, that was holding me. There it was, the Hundred Acres Field, stumped out by my father in 1925. We all stood there, my father, my mother, my little brother, then three years old, and a little girl. Four oxen, yoked together, dragged felled trees in chains, like criminals, to the edge of the cleared space, where they would burn.

'It's a shame,' my mother said, with the social inflection she gave to such summonings of that *real* world of hers, England. 'This part of the bush is just like English parkland.' There we stood, the English family, while the black men swung their axes and the trees toppled, and the great bonfire roared, exploding sparks and black smoke where birds flapped and swung. They say birds are attracted to smoke because it gets rid of their parasites for them; wherever there is smoke, there are birds. My mother saw parkland, but I had been in that England of hers for six months, aged five, and I remembered my horror at the dinginess, the blackness, the wet, scene after scene that stuck in my mind meaning England, for years. Black wet ganglia of railway lines, under rain. A fishmonger's slab where a black wet lobster futilely moved its legs. A room in a boarding-house, and dark rain streaming down the windows. A row of little gardens, each as neat and pretty as an illustration in a child's book and in one of them a sad man grinding his teeth and snuffling, and digging a fork into the soil as if he wanted to kill it. He stood in cold drizzle wearing a trench-coat soaked with patches of damp, and through the straps on the shoulders (made to hold the gloves officers wore) he had pushed limp hide gloves. They dangled from his shoulder like dead grey fingers.

The Hundred Acres Field, or the Big Land, stood on that November day bared for planting, a dark rich red. Across it curved the contour ridges made by my father. For sixty years that field has been growing crops, so something must have been done right.

And now the turn up to the house, a place where the cattle kraal had been, from where manure was taken across the track to be laid on the field. The kraal was gone, and gone the little patch of bush that for some reason was full of bauhinia trees, with their flowers like scraps of white silk crêpe and a dry enticing smell. The hill was ahead: the road was now solid and good, and there was no need to balance and crawl over ruts and ridges. And then we sped up the hill among thinned trees, and were at the top. Gone was the big muwanga tree that once dominated all this landscape, full of honey which we cropped once a year, leaving enough for the bees. My parents used to say, 'Well, you can bury us under the old muwanga tree', meaning it was certainly not as good as an elm or an ash or an oak, but the next best thing. The old tree had been felled by lightning: even in our time the white trunk had a black lightning scar down one side.

There we stood at the top, and we turned our backs on the new ugly bungalow.

'What did they mean, the hill has gone?' Ayrton R. and I asked each other.

Yes, the top has been sliced off, making a flat and amenable place: stony ground sloped down sharply from the walls of our house. Quite a lot has been pared off: ten feet? Twenty? It is a sizeable plateau. Because the month was November, the bush was heavy and green – what there was left of it. The relief that came from finding myself standing on the top of a hill, one not imagined or invented, softened something else: on the hill the bush was sparse and damaged, and whereas once we looked out on thick trees and vleis, where a few fields lay scattered, now the bush has gone, and the scene is of wide fields climbing and stretching everywhere, with some modest strips of bush left in it. Here it is, the Banket soil, the red rich wonder-worker, and I suppose the question has to be, How is it this wealth of soil was allowed to stay so long unproductive under unstumped bush?

The country brings itself to a height here, at this hill: the landscape heaps itself up. The hill where once the farm compound stood is only slightly lower. A mile or so further, going towards the northern mountains, is Koodoo Hill, where my brother and I used to walk all day. It was full of game. The wild pig particularly loved it. Just as I remembered, this is a group of hills or high places, making a centre for the wide ring of mountains. The Hunyanis to the north-west, the Umvukwes (or the Great Dyke) to the south-east, and, in front, the Ayreshire Hills, that stood up on that afternoon sharp and clear . . . unchanged. Well, of course . . . but why of course, when so much has changed? No, they could not have blasted the tops off those hills, but at their feet, where you can't see it from this hill, is the new dam which will be the third biggest in the country. Looking out from where the front of the house was to the Ayreshire Hills it seems the bush is unchanged, but hills and valleys hide the new farms.

I stood and looked out at 'the view' which was why my parents had built the house where they did, and which fed their eyes and their hopes for all the years of being on that farm where nothing went as they wanted.

It is beautiful. It was more beautiful than I expected, because of those inexplicable warnings from my brother. 'Don't go back, it will break your heart.' What had broken his heart? Soon I understood. Not that our old house had gone, for it had to, being built of mud and thatch. Not that they cut the top off 'our' hill. No, it was the bush. It had gone. Where he had spent his childhood were interminable red fields, *his* bush – gone. When the forests that covered Europe after the end of the last Ice Age made way for fields and herds do you suppose that people who had spent their youth under great trees, wary equals with wolves and bears, returned after absence to find their own real place gone, and went about warning others still exiled with, 'Don't go back. Whatever you do, don't go home or you'll break your heart.' And spent the rest of their lives in mourning for trees that had expired in smoke?

I stood there, needless to say limp with threatening tears, unable to believe in all that magnificence, the space, the marvel of it. I had been brought up in this place. I lived here from the age of five until I left it forever thirteen years later. I lived *here*. No wonder this myth country tugged and pulled . . . what a privilege, what a blessing. And yet my poor mother spent all those years grieving that her children were being badly done by, should be in some conventional school in England.

But now it was time to turn myself around and look at that new house. If somebody tried to build a house that embodied everything my parents hated, it would be this one. A graceless lump of a dark bungalow, painted to look dull, it crouches twenty feet or so back from where our house was, and perhaps fifteen or twenty feet lower.

Past it down the hill were some women and children. Ayrton R. went to talk to them, and returned to say they did not or would not speak English. It could be seen through the windows that the place was full of children, staring out, as we smiled, gesticulated our need to talk to them. A lot of children.

We gave up and wandered over the back of the hill. Once it had tall thick grass, where no one ever went except my brother and I, to reach the big vlei at the back of the hill, full of birds and game. There were also, though we did not know the plant then, thickets of marijuana and sometimes a mile or so of bush was saturated with the reek of it, a rough hairy smell, like sweat.

Here was the scene of the pawpaw drama. My mother planted pawpaw trees tastefully where they would look nice, but found they languished. Pawpaw seeds thrown on to the rubbish heap produced a grove of trees that dropped the pinky-yellow globes all around them, so many they were not gathered. The earth there was fed with pawpaw flesh.

Not far from where the women stood watching us was where our lavatory had been. It was a deep pit, and over it an inverted packing case that had a hole in it, and over that a little hut, screened by grass fencing – like the lavatories of nearly everyone in The District.

Everywhere over the flat place that tops the hill are disused brick buildings, and, half hidden in grass, a brick and concrete line with rusty iron rings which had been for pigs, or perhaps cows. A barn was up here, too: surely unintelligent, for everything would have had to be dragged up the hill by cart or lorry. Where our barns had been down near the track – nothing at all. The bricks had been brought up here to make these now ruinous buildings. But there were not enough bricks lying about to make the statement: here was a cow shed, here a garage, here a pigsty. Here were only the spare bones of buildings, for the bricks had been taken off somewhere else to make new buildings, and this was a lying melancholy.

What I was looking at was not only the scene of our old life, that had left no traces, nothing, for the ants and borers and termites had demolished it all, but at the remains of another later effort, which had failed. Everything here spoke of failure.

They have planted fruit trees, my brother had complained – fruit trees!

And there they were, lacking water and in bad shape, orchards too big for a family, a homestead, but not large enough to be commercial. From these trees they could have picked enough peaches to take into the Station for resale to farmers coming in for their mail – and who almost certainly had their own peaches – but no one could have made a living from them. No, what we were looking at, I was sure, was just such another effort as my parents' – who were always trying a little bit of this and a little bit of that. One might believe that their spirit had infected the people who came after them.

Did they too dream about finding gold? We searched in the scrub for my father's old prospecting trenches, and there they were, though the shafts he had dug everywhere so he could inspect a promising reef were all filled in. If our successors carried a prospector's hammer so they could chip a bit of a rock off an outcrop then it was no more than most farmers did, in The District, which was named Banket after a gold-bearing reef on the Rand.

We walked back to the new house. There was a little strip of newly watered marigolds. My mother's passionate, knowledgeable gardening, that always had to fight with the rocky crown of the hill, was being continued here, in this brave little display.

Again we tried to communicate with the children. Were these

Squatters? Was the farm being run as an annexe to one of the enormous high-tec farms of The District? Was this the black manager's house, and in it his many children, relatives, friends' children?

Strongly present were the ghosts of my parents. My father, I knew, was laughing, for this scene, so admirably contrived by the Grand Storyteller confirmed everything he had always known about the vanity of human wishes. My mother's face was brave. 'It's just as well,' I could imagine her saying, in her sprightly social voice, looking at the awful suburban bungalow, at the crowding black faces in the windows where the panes were cracked, where torn curtains hung – 'It's just as well we don't know what is going to happen, isn't it?' And then, taking firm hold of the situation, 'I wonder if they've tried growing pelargoniums? They do well up here. Perhaps I'll just have a word . . .'

As for me, I stood trying to see into that dark room, past the many faces, and thought that these children were no more remote from civilization than I was, as a girl, with the wonders of the world in books and even the cities of South Africa far off because of our poverty.

But there was a difference. In the living-room of our house were bookcases, and newspapers and magazines came from London.

No books here. Nothing in that room for those children, not a book, a toy, a magazine, an exercise book, a pencil, a picture.

Then we stood looking out, over the fields and the bush, just as we used to do *then*, first at this range of mountains, then that, for if your eyes stayed too long on one group of hills, where the light was changing, then you might miss the drama of the Umvukwes (or the Dyke) where a peak was being touched by sunlight while its fellows were still defined by shadow.

And here, but above our heads – well above – was where we sat every night it didn't storm or rain to watch the stars and the comets raining down, for the sky was so clear *then* that . . .

Enough.

My heart hurt, not for my parents, who after all hadn't done too badly, though that was not how they saw it, but for my brother, who had so suffered from coming back here. Well, every day there are more people everywhere in the world in mourning for trees, forest, bush, rivers, animals, lost landscapes . . . you could say this is an established part of the human mind, a layer of grief always deepening and darkening.

After that we drove fast, taking only a few minutes, to the Ayreshire Hills, where the new dam is. Mazwikadei, the name is. In 1956 I stood on a hill above a landscape soon to be flooded by the Kariba dam, then just completed, the tall curving white walls standing high about the Zambesi. All that magnificence soon to be drowned. 'Why not? There's plenty of Africa, isn't there?' And now the Kariba lake is enormous, it dominates the map and the minds of the people of those parts, just as the Dyke does further south.

After one good wet season this new dam is nearly full.

My brother and I used to take the rifle and walk through the bush to the Ayreshire Hills, moving silently like the black people, having learned from them, listening to the cicadas and for the movements of animals, watching the birds. The big vlei on our farm, full of thorn trees, is as it used to be, but it is silent. It used to sound with the cooing of doves, the ones with the delicate black rings around their necks. Everywhere in that bush were doves and go-away birds and other louries and above all that sorrowful enchanter the emerald spotted dove whose cry, the Africans say, sounds like, 'My mother is dead, my father is dead, all my relatives are dead, oh, oh, oh, oh . . .'

We crossed the Menene river on stepping stones, watching for crocodiles. After that came the Mukwadzi, just below the hills, the river that is newly dammed. We used to squat on a certain long slope of rough warm granite and look across a small gorge and wait, keeping our voices a murmur, trying not to move. Soon the baboons would come, dozens of them, guarded by a big male who kept his eye on us, warning his people with grunts and barks if we moved carelessly. We watched them all go down to the river to drink, perhaps fifty or so of them, the little ones on their mothers' backs. Then they merged back into the hills, the big male going last, sending us across the river a final admonishing bark.

All that land is going under the water. Going, going . . .

Well, what of it, says the voice of commonsense – mine, at least sometimes. This happened in Europe centuries ago. A continent does not have to be inhabited by its own real animals, its original indigenous trees. Europe is doing fine. It is beautiful. People come from everywhere in the world to admire it. Well, then? We are doing all right – aren't we?

and,
Again . . .

1989

One world generates another.

Santayana

I am sitting next to a Chef, a mini-Chef, with a new job in some department, and he has been out of Zimbabwe for the first time in his life. To New York. To a conference. His story is, must be – how could it be otherwise? – rags-to-riches. Yes, he went from his village near Rusapi when he was eighteen to join the Comrades in the bush, but he was lucky, he only once saw something bad, when a friend was killed by a mine exploding, but for months and months he did not get enough to eat. 'I was so thin my mother cried when she saw me. But the girls didn't cry. I was too good-looking.' After the War he was a clerk in an Harare office working for a Chef who had been his commander in the bush. Then when this man was promoted even higher, he was offered the empty place. 'Three of us hoped for that job and when they said it was my job, I went home and told my wife and we cried so much!' He was a fat and self-important man, but his delight at the fine world now his kept dissolving his pomposity into a sighing laughter. An excess of pleasure pressed his plump hands together, and he could not prevent them softly clapping, applauding his good fortune. Or he shook his head, smiling, in disbelief. Have you ever visited New York? Do you know the White Plaza Hotel? Do you like the food from Thailand? Have you seen *Les Misérables*? That was so sad it made me cry. Had I been to Paris? He was going to Paris soon for a conference. I asked him, if he could have his heart's desire, what he would choose for Zimbabwe. 'How can you ask me such a question! Of course, it would be prosperity.' 'Suppose a fairy godmother offered him on behalf of all Zimbabwe . . .' 'Who is this fairy godmother? Is it the World Bank?' Fairy stories, I said, often are about good or evil spirits who grant wishes or put curses on people. I began with Snow White. He was enchanted, that is the word, never has there been such a listener. He pressed his hands together, he clapped them, he laughed, he sighed, he listened with his whole self. And that is how I spent that night, until he slept, telling fairy stories to a Chef.

At Immigration a sarcastic and unpleasant official gave me a hard time – thus proving how thoroughly Zimbabwe has entered the modern world. Zimbabwe does not like journalists. It is not unknown for journalists and writers to get themselves special passports that do not have these dangerous words on them. Later I argued with a Chef who said if he had his way no journalists would be allowed in. I asked if by chance he admired *The Chronicle* in Bulawayo? He had to admit that yes, he did. Did he ever read newspapers from Britain and America? Yes, but we are a new country and we can't afford criticism. I said, Why can't you? It's a sign of weakness to be so touchy. Did he really admire those articles in *The Herald* which usually go something like this: 'Our great leader Comrade Mugabe inspires Zimbabwe with his example as he leads us forward into . . .' At the first few syllables he brightened, but then he was angry at my levity.

THE HOUSE IN THE RICH SUBURB

Ayrton R. and I are again standing in his garden, looking up at his house, and then at the airy screen that hides the servants' quarters, the two rooms and the courtyard where food is cooked, and from where come the sounds of voices, laughter, and, often, music.

Until a couple of weeks ago there were also the sounds made by the gardener's eleven children.

This is what Ayrton R. began to talk about as soon as I arrived: he is infinitely distressed.

Every afternoon at five o'clock there were screams and tears, as the mother lined them up and washed them in a tub in the courtyard. The neighbours complained.

'But, George, why does your wife have to wash the children

just when everyone has come home from the offices and want some peace and quiet?'

'Because they should be washed before they go to bed.'

'But why does she have to wash them so hard they cry?'

'Children hate being washed, everyone knows that.'

Eleven children make a lot of noise. They need a lot of space. They often spilled out of the little courtyard into Ayrton R.'s garden and he pretended not to notice. The neighbours complained again. They were invited to come over and meet the criminals, the gardener and his wife, two abashed but stubborn people, whose defence was, children make a lot of noise. Tense conversation over the teacups: these negotiations were going on in Ayrton R.'s living-room. 'I insisted on them all sitting down in my living-room so it wouldn't be a white boss–black servant confrontation.'

'And it wasn't?'

'Of course it was. The point is, the children ought to be with both parents. George ought to have his whole family with him. On the other hand, you can't really have eleven children in one room. And two parents.'

'A bit of an impasse, then.'

'But George has a house in his village and there's a school nearby. The children don't go to school when they are here.'

The eleven children and their parents, thirteen people. Dorothy and her man and her three children, who are intermittently here. Eighteen people in two rooms. Impossible.

'I am terribly sorry, George, but you simply cannot have all your children here. Perhaps two . . . well, three or four then. But not all eleven.'

'This is not your voice I hear, it is the voice of the neighbours,' said George, with dignity, with reproach.

'No, I am sorry, it is my voice.'

Later his wife took the eleven children back to the home in the Communal Area. Soon there would be twelve, proving that she is still a woman, so she had stopped being depressed. But she returned almost at once with the new baby and some of the smaller children.

Ayrton R. looked the other way.

'You would think that in eight months nothing much could change.'

'Things have certainly changed in this household – no, not George having too many children, and anyway that's only our way of looking at it.'

George's oldest daughter, she who has the Spirit, is now in competition with her cousin, George's brother's daughter, about which of them has inherited their grandfather's Spirit: he was an nganga. The real ngangas have finally refused to accept the gardener's daughter as a medium. The fact is, she is now evidently crazy and getting worse. Her parents want her to go home and live in the village, but she says, at first calmly, then shouting and screaming, that the house in Harare is her home and she has no intention of ever leaving it. She sleeps on the floor in the kitchen separating the gardener's room from Dorothy's room and there she entertains men. It is a shame and a disgrace for parents to overhear the love-making of a child, but that is what they are forced to do. Dorothy is also forced to overhear. Her man, whom everyone deplores, begging her to throw him out, has sex with the gardener's daughter just through the wall from where Dorothy has her bed. Why does she not throw him out? But this woman with three children who has never been married hopes he will make an honest woman of her. If you remember, the gardener's daughter had sex with all eight security guards at an institution where she was cleaning. The security guards are policemen. Fifty per cent of the police and the army rumoured to be HIV positive. (This figure has not yet been released by the government: meanwhile there are those who say it is much higher.) It was Dorothy who said that all people with AIDS should be put to death. This is the tragedy that is silently unfolding in the crowded servants' quarters.

'The government may be coming clean about AIDS at last, because AIDS isn't a plot by the Honkies any longer, but they still pull their punches. The new AIDS poster you see every-where has a prostitute standing in the shadows while a man debates whether to have sex with her. But it is the army and the police who are worse infected – well, as far as we know.

The poster ought to be of a man in uniform and a woman deciding not to have sex with him. But everything is slanted against women in this culture and that is too much to expect, I suppose.'

And now, to 'cheer me up', Ayrton R. takes me to the supermarket.

'I am afraid we have to accept the fact that citizens everywhere are going to judge their government by how well they eat, never mind about democracy.'

THE SUPERMARKET

Zimbabwe goes short of very little. People who cannot live without olive oil, tinned fish, some spices, arrange for friends to bring them. Everyone who goes out of the country comes back again with whisky. But there are always new goods on the piled-high shelves as food enterprises start up. The freezer units are full. Stacked high from one end of the shop to the other are some of the best beef in the world, bacon and ham that is not injected with water, and first-rate sausages and salamis. There are ranks of chickens and ducks. The cheeses are good if limited in variety. The bread is excellent, and so are the fruit and vegetables. The maize meal for sadza is here in its different varieties, but this shop has more black people than white in it and they are not confining themselves to sadza. Row after row of shelves are loaded with spirits and liqueurs, all brand names made on licence. (On a van outside a store in a small town near the Zambesi Valley: Cinzano, the Drink of Africa!) The beers are good. Zimbabwe wines, not long ago undrinkable, are winning international prizes – that is, the white wines do, the reds are still learning. All this is produced inside the country. You may think it is not such an achievement for a country to feed itself, but this is more than surrounding countries do. Zimbabwe's food shops would seem unreachable luxury to Mozambique, Malawi, Zambia, Namibia, Angola, let alone countries further north, some in a state of disaster. 'Zimbabwe is not to be judged against other African countries: it is more like a South American country' (United Nations report).

Trading practices in this part of the world would not satisfy political moralists. Botswana has favouring trade agreements with Zimbabwe and South Africa, imports goods from South Africa, relabels them, sells them to Zimbabwe. South Africa puts Zimbabwe labels on fruit and sells it overseas. Zimbabwe's citizens travel to Botswana to buy goods in short supply in Zimbabwe: these are often South African.

'And why doesn't Comrade Mugabe . . . ?'

Comrade Mugabe doesn't approve of all this, and says so, but King Canute couldn't stop the tide rolling in.

MOZAMBIQUE

And what else are people talking about?

Last year Mozambique sooner or later appeared in every conversation. Now few people mention it. This is because the problem is on the way to being solved. Maputo is coming to life again: people are beginning to travel. Some of the braver Mozambicans are going home to ruined villages. Yet the refugee camps in Zimbabwe and Malawi are still full and more refugees arrive all the time. People starve in Mozambique. Bands of bandits threaten the villages. Policing the oil pipeline to Beira and bolstering the Mozambique army still costs Zimbabwe over a million pounds a day. No one seems to grudge this aid, but there are jokes that Zimbabwe, ex-colony, has a colony of its own: Zimbabwe is proud of itself and its support for its ruined neighbour. For instance, the pipeline. It is reckoned that if 'they' – that is, Renamo, blow up the line the Zimbabwe army can get it back into working order in seventy-two hours. It is impossible to guard the line for its whole distance, hundreds of miles. The most recent blow-up was last month, and it was back in operation almost at once. The Zimbabwe troops are now trained by the British: the infamous days of the Fifth Brigade are over. 'They are good chaps now, our Zimbabwe soldiers . . .' (It is the Coffee Farmer who speaks.) 'Well, look at who trained them! They're ready for anything, anti-personnel mines, bomb attacks, air attacks, the lot. Do you remember when you were here the pipeline was cut and there was no petrol for weeks? That couldn't happen now.'

According to the politically-correct, 'bandits' in Mozambique are always Renamo. But the tale of the crocodile hunter suggests otherwise. The hunter was issued a permit to trap crocodiles in the lakes in Mozambique for live export. He took a boat out into the lake, but first Renamo, then Frelimo, bands shot at him, forced him to the shore, demanded a percentage of the earnings. Several times he was nearly killed. So he gave up. 'So neither Renamo nor Frelimo got anything out of him. Serves them right.'

CORRUPTION

From one end of Zimbabwe to the other, people talk about corruption.

It seems people have come to terms with it. On a white farm verandah: 'What are we blaming Mugabe's lot for? Smith's lot all feathered their nests. The only honest man was Whitehead and he died a pauper.'

'And Smith?'

'Oh, he was honest, but he's all bone behind the ears,' cheerfully says a former enthusiast for Smith's cause. 'Look at the trouble Smithie got us into! We need never have had a war at all! Only a minority of whites wanted that war but then we had to go along with it.'

Or: 'The whole country is on the fiddle. No, I don't blame Mugabe. We all learned it under UDI. You had to lie and cheat then to survive and now it's our national style. You can't survive under Mugabe's financial laws without fiddling. Everyone does it.'

A variation on the old joke: Two Zimbabwe Cabinet Ministers are standing outside the Pearly Gates. 'Zimbabwe?' says Saint Peter, 'never heard of it. I must go and consult the Boss.' He goes to find the Boss and says, 'We've got two Ministers from Zimbabwe.' The Boss says, 'Oh yes, an interesting little country. I'll come with you to interview them.' They reach the entrance to Heaven. 'They've gone,' cries Saint Peter, and the Boss says, 'I can't see anybody either.' 'No, no, the Pearly Gates, they've stolen them.' (A United Nations official.)

A United Nations report: 'All of Africa is bedevilled with rhetoric. There is no connection between what is going on and how it is described. And Zimbabwe is the worst of them all.'

THE TOYOTA SCANDAL

The enterprising editor of *The Chronicle* who exposed this scandal was sacked, or, as the government put it, promoted, to a job where his journalistic talents cannot be used. *The Chronicle* is now almost as bland as *The Herald*.

But – say the Passionate Apologists – *The Financial Gazette* is well-informed and critical, and there is a magazine, *Parade*, which is not afraid. Cynics reply, Why not? The *Gazette* and *Parade* are only read by intellectuals, the Povos never read them.

As a result of *The Chronicle*'s exposures, the Sandura Commission was appointed: the resulting hearings in court were attended by jeering, shouting, laughing crowds, while the defendants reached heights of imaginative perjury described by one member of the audience as 'a combination of Baron Munchausen and Cecil Rhodes boasting about the annexation of Mashonaland. I tell you, comrade, only Zimbabwe could have come up with that one – it was better than any theatre.' All of Zimbabwe applauded Mugabe for appointing the Sandura

Commission: at last he was behaving as he was expected to behave, a bulwark against corruption and a defender of the good and the right. The students were particularly full of praise. But then the guilty ones were pardoned by the President, and the people who committed perjury in court and who expected jail sentences were pardoned too. 'One law for the Chefs and one law for the Povos,' said the cynical. Said, by the by, the now very cynical. As we all know, there is no one more furiously cynical than an idealist betrayed. Needless to say, the rumours about why the President did this ill-judged thing flourish. 'They' say that people very close indeed to the President were implicated. 'They' say that the President cannot afford to offend the corrupt Chefs who keep him in power. The charitable say it hurts Mugabe to see old comrades who fought with him in the bush disgraced and in prison.

Maurice Nyagumbo
Zimbabwean hero who fell from grace

Maurice Nyagumbo, who was Zimbabwe's senior political affairs minister until his resignation last week over an illegal car deals racket, has died in hospital after taking poison. He was 64. He resigned after a judicial inquiry set up by President Mugabe implicated him in a scandal which involved helping people to buy new vehicles, to resell them on the black market at inflated prices.

Before his fall from grace, Nyagumbo had been a prominent figure in the struggle for Zimbabwean independence, and spent many years in jail for opposing white minority rule. After independence was granted in 1980 he became a leading figure in the government of Robert Mugabe, rising to be, effectively, number four in the cabinet, and number three in the ruling ZANU-PF party.

Maurice Nyagumbo was born to peasant parents in Rusape, Southern Rhodesia, in 1924. He received some primary education at mission schools before leaving for South Africa in 1940 to seek work. He slept rough, worked at various jobs including waiting on tables, and found a home among black ballroom dancers. He then joined the South African communist party until it was banned in 1948.

He was deported from South Africa in 1955 on the grounds that he was in contact with the Mau Mau in Kenya. Back in Rhodesia he helped form the African National Youth League before becoming secretary of his local branch of the Southern Rhodesia African National Congress. In 1959 he was detained for his political activities, and was then restricted to Gokwe district until 1962.

On his release he joined the Zimbabwe African People's Union (ZAPU), led by Joshua Nkomo, but broke away the following year with others including Robert Mugabe to form the Zimbabwe African National Union (ZANU). When ZANU was proscribed in 1964, he was arrested and spent the next 11 years in various prisons and restriction camps. Released in 1975, he was soon convicted of recruiting young people for guerrilla training and was sentenced to 15 years imprisonment.

He was released in 1979 in time to observe the closing stages of the Lancaster House Conference in London which led to Zimbabwean independence. Afterwards he held several government posts including minister for mines and minister of state for political affairs and cooperative development.

In 1980 he published an autobiography whose credo was: 'Some of us must remain to be with the people, even if it means to be in jail with them.' Undoubtedly he was a courageous man, prepared to suffer for his beliefs. After Independence, in his cloth cap at President Mugabe's side, as senior minister for political affairs, he was one of the symbols of the struggle.

He is survived by a wife and six children.

The Times, Obituary

TWO-BOY TEKERE

Edgar Tekere, the maverick, the outsider, is discussed with the
relishing, sardonic disbelief we use to salute disreputable but
entertaining possibilities.

If you play that private game, of sitting rather outside a
conversation and listening to the sound rather than to the
sense of it, Tekere Tekere Tekere clicks through the talk like a
cricket.

He is mounting a one-man opposition to Mugabe, and has
been thrown out of Mugabe's party Zanu PF because of his
criticisms of corruption and Mugabe's toleration of it. His new
political party is called the Zimbabwe Unity Movement. (It is
interesting how often the word Unity, or United, is used for
political movements that are in fact divisive.) But Zum is
making an impact because everyone knows his criticisms are
just. What sort of impact? No one knows. He appeals too, to
some people – not a few – who would like to see more whites
in Parliament, because of their expertise and know-how. (When
whites are valued in black countries it is seldom for their charm,
their wit, their delightfulness, their kind hearts, but rather
because they are equipped to deal with the modern world.)
Everywhere campaigning goes on in preparation for the next
election, on lines familiar to Zimbabwe – to Kenya – to India –
to communist countries – and, of course, to England in the
eighteenth century. Every kind of dirty trick is employed to
outwit or discredit opponents. Gangs of bully boys break up
Tekere's meetings and threaten possible supporters with violence or actually beat them up, and are never rebuked or punished. This is because they are members of Zanu PF's youth
section. (Why doesn't Mugabe . . . ?) By-elections are rigged.
Tekere himself is publicly vilified and there is a cleverly managed whispering campaign.

It was Tekere who, when drunk, murdered a white farmer
just after Liberation. This certainly darkened the shining image
of a Soldier of Liberation. The incident is again being discussed,

and, too, his willingness to work with Smith. In addition, the authorities leaked Tekere's medical records, which made him sound like a schizophrenic. That he is an alcoholic does not seem to discredit him: it is this fact that makes some people think that 'they' (this time, the Povos) don't take Tekere seriously.

Tekere has turned criticism to his own advantage, describing himself as a 'Two-boy', which is how schizophrenics are known in these parts. On campaign posters he is describing himself as 'Edgar Tekere Two-boy, the Christian Alcoholic', and making everyone laugh.

Tekere is in fact playing a familiar political role, or allowing himself to be in a position where other people ascribe the role to him. He is seen as the opposite of everything Mugabe is. Mugabe has never made anybody laugh. Mugabe needs a whole motorcade and darkened bullet-proof windows if he so much as sets a foot out of his home but Tekere is available to everyone, he isn't a fearful man, 'he lives dangerously, just like us'. Tekere doesn't go rushing off to conferences everywhere all the time. Tekere drives a little car and he never wears a three-piece suit.

During this kind of conversation politicians' tribal origins always come up. Tekere is from Manicaland, which makes him a representative of Eastern Zimbabwe, just as Joshua Nkomo represents Matabeleland.

But someone gives me a lesson on ethnology. All this talk of the Matabele and the Mashona and the Manicas! There is no such thing as the Mashona. There are four main Mashona groups, the Karanga, the Manyika, the Zezuru, the Kore Kore. The main group is Zezuru from around Harare. Mugabe was Karanga by origin, and brought up as a Zezuru. The battles that go on inside the Party can often only be understood by the balances of power between these groups. At the moment the Karanga are losing out: it is the Karanga versus the rest. But Terence Ranger (Zimbabwe's prestigious historian) says that before the whites came these divisions were not important: the missionaries exacerbated them. Then each group insisted it was the most important: 'We are the real people.'

'Tekere', says someone, 'is just as much a Mashona as Mugabe is. They'll say anything to discredit Tekere.'

During an evening of informal talk with a high official, he insisted Tekere was 'a Nazi'. Protests at this silliness from everybody. 'Oh yes, it's just the same. At first Hitler was just right wing: it was only later that people discovered he was a Nazi.' (The word 'objectively' is implicit.) 'And so that makes the students who support Tekere Nazis.' (The university students have again demonstrated – 'rioted', according to the government press – against corruption. Some carried Tekere party cards and shouted 'Tiananmen Square!') The official went on insisting that the students were Nazis. Not once did he admit that the students' complaints were just. There was an unreasoning hysterical insistence in his talk about the students. Given the law that the same kinds of people say the same things at the same time, then it is likely this students-are-Nazis talk goes on at high levels.

AIDS, AIDS, AIDS

Only eight months before, the atmosphere had reminded me of Brazil in 1986. There were people saying, but privately, 'AIDS is a time-bomb, ticking away, but our government doesn't want to know. Brazil might have been invented to please the AIDS virus. It is a permissive hedonistic society, male and female homosexuality – anything – goes. A blood transfusion is a death sentence. Drugs are everywhere.' A few months later the Brazilian government understood AIDS would not just take itself off, and limited information campaigns began on radio, on television, in the newspapers. Poor countries cannot afford the money for serious propaganda. Compared with Brazil Zimbabwe is well-off with its infrastructure of hospitals and clinics. The point is, no one knows how much AIDS there is. Doctors say there is far more than the government admits to. Politicians let slip damaging figures, but they are not likely to be accurate.

Everyone knows that up north, in Zambia, Kenya, Zaire, Uganda, other countries, a whole generation may die of AIDS before the end of the century. Already in Uganda and in Kenya there are empty villages where so many people died of AIDS the survivors fled, from what they see as witchcraft, the evil eye. Zimbabwe believes itself to be fortunate, compared with these countries. But is it? When a subject is *almost* in everybody's consciousness, is still a question of 'I met a doctor who says . . .' or 'They say that in the Communal Areas . . .', but is not a matter of accurate facts and figures as is the case in Europe or the United States, then it hovers on the edge of conversations, makes an appearance and takes itself off – people look embarrassed or uncomfortable, as if afraid of an accusation of scare-mongering. And AIDS is still monstrously distorted in political left-wing mythology. Thus, in a group of ideologues, the mention of AIDS will at once inspire denouncements of the CIA who deliberately created the AIDS virus to weaken the Third World. The suggestion that the disease may have evolved from monkeys in Central Africa is a malignant invention of Western scientists who allowed the virus to escape from their test tubes by mistake, and who are now covering up their carelessness by lies, putting the blame on Africa . . . 'as usual!' These people are at the same stage as the Soviet Union was until very recently, saying that AIDS was impossible in a communist country, only possible in capitalist societies: evil is the attribute of The Other; demons and dangers and threats can only come as the result of ill-will. Or of the Evil Eye.

Meanwhile blood transfusions inspire terror – and many stories. Zimbabwe soldiers guarding installations in Mozambique were given blood transfusions. All became infected and brought the disease home to their wives and children. Mozambique is full of AIDS. (This is true.) 'Not only do we, Zimbabweans, have to spend our wealth guarding Mozambique and defending it, and feeding hundreds of thousands of refugees, but then they poison our boys with their AIDS. *We* have an efficient medical infrastructure, *our* blood transfusions are safe. But the Mozambicans are hopeless. We have to look after them all the time.'

Meanwhile some of the ngangas have not been helpful, saying that if men sleep with a virgin this will cure or prevent AIDS. Most have understood that AIDS is something outside their competence and are allying themselves with science.

HEALERS, SPIRITS AND CONDOMS
from the *Observer*

It comes as a surprise to see the elongated white cardboard boxes amid the rest of the paraphernalia – the spears, the dried animal skins and the tin trunk packed with potions inside the musty hut. Each box contains 100 condoms, and in the past three weeks, Stephen Njekeya has distributed about 25 to his clients. 'I am a doctor,' he says, dreadlocks flapping as he nods his head.

To hundreds of people around the small southern Zimbabwean town of Gutu, he has been just that since the late Fifties when, while working as a waiter, he was seized by a fit that was interpreted as 'spiritual possession'. This deemed him suitable for apprenticeship as a traditional healer.

His herbs were used by 'my fore, fore, forefathers and they are still useful', he says. Njekeya, and the 35,000 other members of the Zimbabwe National Traditional Healers Association (Zinatha), a group of spirit mediums, herbalists, traditional midwives and faith healers, have assumed a new importance as Zimbabwe struggles with an AIDS epidemic.

As attention yesterday was focused on World Aids Day, much of the concern centres on Africa. And Zimbabwe's 5,086 cases reported to the World Health Organisation in September represents the fastest growing rate on the continent. A survey of random blood donations indicate that 4.2 per cent of adult Zimbabweans are infected with the HIV virus, but several experts believe the figure to be much higher.

Some 75 per cent of Zimbabweans live in rural areas, many of them illiterate and too poor to afford a radio. This constitutes a major hurdle for health workers trying to spread an awareness programme. Since February, however, Zinatha has been running a pilot project in the Gutu district, bringing the healers known as nganga together in workshops to teach them about the disease and enlist their help.

About 80 per cent of Zimbabwe's 10 million people would prefer to consult a traditional healer before a Western doctor. Nganga have their roots deep in popular culture and are widely respected in the community. 'Given the sheer numbers of traditional healers, they have an enormous value for involvement in Aids awareness,' said Celine Gilbert, projects officer for the Zimbabwe Trust, an independent aid organisation backing Zinatha's project.

Njekeya claims that he first detected Aids symptoms in people during 1985 and was troubled because unlike other forms of sexually transmitted diseases, it wouldn't go away. He says he diagnosed it as runyoka – an illness that is supposed to manifest itself in ants crawling inside a victim's body and one that is contracted by adulterers.

One of the nganga's concerns after learning that Aids was contracted through contact with infected blood was the fear they could catch and spread the virus through unhygienic practices. Njekeya says how now he makes his customers pay for a new razor each time he uses one, mostly for small incisions into which the healer rubs mushonga (medicine).

Anna Dondo, another healer, says they have stopped the practice of biting into the flesh of a patient, and sucking out what they have diagnosed as the cause of illness. Instead, she cuts a tennis ball in half and uses the concave side as a 'mouth'.

They have accepted they cannot cure Aids, but Western medical experts here believe that the healers, with their experience of treating sexually transmitted diseases, have a knack for identifying the symptoms. In Gutu, they have begun to refer patients to the local clinics, telling them that they have gone as far as traditional lore can help them, and that Western medicine is needed.

THE SCHOOL IN THE BUSH

'The man without character', dismissed as headmaster and now
a primary school teacher, was ordered to return the money he
stole from the school and from the pupils. Everyone knows he
cannot do this because of his small salary. Everyone argues
about whether it was a good thing he was not put in prison.
'It would teach him a lesson!' 'Yes, but how would his family
live if he was in prison?' 'But it is already a terrible punishment
to be a primary school teacher after being headmaster.'

The new headmaster began well, working furiously, 'from
dawn to dusk, making all us teachers jump'. Then he turned
out to be an alcoholic. It is this man who so terribly beats the
pupils. Jack tackled him: 'How can you beat a child for being
late when he couldn't cross the river because of rain? How can
you beat the big girls? It isn't right! Besides, it's against the
law.'

The beatings continued, by the headmaster, and by other
teachers. Jack went into the local office and reported the headmaster, who was formally rebuked.

Later Jack had to ask this same headmaster for a report on
his work as a teacher. 'Mr Jack Pettifer' (this is a made-up name)
'is a hardworking and conscientious teacher. God forbid he
should ever be employed at the same school as myself again.
He has no loyalty to his colleagues.'

Jack said to him, full of reproach, 'Now, this isn't right. It
isn't just. You were breaking the law and I had to do my duty
by reporting you. How can I get another job with this unfair
report?'

So the headmaster gave Jack a fair report, but went on beating the children.

Jack wonders if he should stay another year. 'What's going
to happen to the school library when I go? No one is going to
keep the school newspaper going. No one is going to stand up
for the kids.'

Three months later Jack left. Within a month most of the

books were stolen from the library. The school newspaper ended. Jack asked his successor if he would like Jack to set up a couple of issues for him, but he said No, it was not necessary. All the machinery for keeping the grounds in order was stolen. But: there were six qualified teachers instead of only one.

On a hot November afternoon Jack, Ayrton R., and myself are again in the classroom that still has a cracked rafter and a broken windowpane, though the dust has been swept away. We are with fifteen strong young men and buxom young women, who are in their penultimate year in school. They look like adults and they are adults. Often on this trip and the last one I have misjudged ages, thinking youngsters years older than they are. This goes for infants too. You see a large and energetic baby strenuously reaching all around itself for new experience, and with alert, observant eyes – you think it is ten months old but no, it is five weeks, or two months.

An irrepressible physical vigour – that's what you see everywhere.

The young people are noisy, laughing, uninhibitedly full of enjoyment. They have just returned from Harare where most of them had never been. Jack took them, at his expense, on the bus, and to visit a printing firm and a newspaper and to a meal in a restaurant. The bus trip both ways, many hours of it, was part of the experience.

We are here in the classroom because Jack has said it would be a good idea for them to interview us all, as part of learning how to be journalists. Jack himself, Ayrton R., one of the teachers, and I, we each are surrounded by a group who ask us, what is our favourite colour, do we like this school, how do we like Zimbabwe, do we think it is fair girls should always have to do so much work (the girls). But it is noticeable that the pupils writing down our replies in notebooks are every moment less assiduous, for they are looking past us at where the handsome young teacher is talking about his problems. In a moment, they are all crowding around him and we, the interviewees, are with them for we are as rapt as they are.

This teacher is the star among the staff, with two A-levels, more than any teacher has, not only at this school but at any of the others round about. He has been accepted at teachers' training college and so he is at the foot of the ladder which may take him at last to Harare. He talks dreamily, and often, about living there 'one of these days'. But now what he is talking about is his wife. He leans against the wall, arms loose by his sides, as if they ache with emptiness, and as he talks, he does not look at any of us: his eyes are full of tears and he addresses the wall.

'This is my sad day,' he says. 'It is a too too sad day, for this morning I heard I am now a divorced man. My marriage is finished.' He cannot go on, and pretends he is waiting for the apprentice interviewers to write it all down.

His wife has an office job in the little town about fifty miles away. It is the town with a hotel that has electric light, a bar, a dining-room, and a courtyard with coloured lights strung among the tree branches. And, often, music. She lunches at the hotel. This is permissible. But she has been seen at the same hotel in the evenings, very late. (Ten o'clock perhaps? Eleven? – everything is relative.) Friends have told him she is there having a good time with men. This means she is no better than she ought to be – as my parents used to say. He has had to divorce her.

It is occurring to more than one of his listeners that there is something here . . . A handsome young woman says to him (while her eyes swoon with love), 'But when you go to teachers' training will not your wife be . . .'

'My ex-wife . . .' He openly sobs.

'But she will be left alone in Kusai and is she not alone all the time when you are here? She must be lonely.'

'But I am lonely too.'

And now the hot silence confined in the dusty air of the classroom while outside thunder and rain lurk about hot skies announces without words – in fact positively shouts – that if he is lonely then he has only himself . . .

He is leaning against the wall in a limp curve, his arms dangle palms out down his sides, his head is slightly back, his eyes are shut. Thus a man might stand waiting for the final bullet . . .

And it is not my fault. I asked her to take another O-level and she could be a teacher too, but she likes the hotel in Kusai better. I said to her, It is your duty to get more qualifications and help Zimbabwe.'

A couple of the young men supported him with, 'Shame', 'That was not well done.'

'Besides,' says he, with the fine appearance of justice that accompanies such remarks, 'women must obey their husbands, it says so in the Bible.'

Moderately dizzying, this conversation is, switching from level to level, as is so common when – as the phrase goes – cultures are in the melting pot. Between the young man who lectures his wife on becoming qualified, and the one who says, Women must obey their husbands, lie cultural gulfs, not least because he cites scripture when it suits him.

Ayrton R. says, 'You know, women all over the world are finding men's claim to God's support in these matters increasingly unconvincing.'

This contribution is being judged as a far from equal one: it is as if Harare itself has spoken.

The teacher stands facing Ayrton R., being judged and sentenced.

A pretty girl saves the situation by asking, with a giggle, her pencil poised over her notebook, 'What do you think about love?'

He replies with severity that children at school should be thinking only of their books and of learning: love is for older people. On the girls' faces now appear properly sceptical smiles: recently two senior girls have married teachers.

'Yes, it is today that my divorce is final.' He made this sound as if unpleasant things like divorce are a natural result of thinking of love when you should be studying.

'And now,' says Jack, 'you must ask him how much of what he has said can be written down and how much is off the record. Because a good journalist has to respect the interviewee.'

'No, write it all,' cries the handsome teacher, 'I do not mind. It will warn other people not to marry for love.'

Tears well into his beautiful eyes and the pretty girls long to kiss them away, one by one.

Meanwhile, somewhere in the office fifty miles away in Kuṣai, a that-day divorced young woman is planning an evening with a local admirer, or even with a passing-through Harare Chef. Over a table in the restaurant that has such tactfully dimmed lights, she will say how unhappy she is, and how disappointed with a husband who neglects her and thinks only of himself.

'Poor little thing,' it is only too easy to imagine. 'Never mind. What a shame. I'd never treat you like that, not a clever pretty special girl like you.'

THE LOST ANIMALS OF THE BUSH

Next morning Jack's minute room was filled with pupils and teachers coming to say goodbye to us, and to be with people sustained by the blessed ichors and zephyrs of Harare.

The handsome teacher was there too. He remarked that what he liked best was to go for walks in the bush by himself. 'I am a serious man,' he said to me severely. 'People do not understand me.' We were standing at the door. He waved his hand at the ravaged trees and the eroded earth and it occurred to me that when he said 'bush' and I said 'bush' we did not mean the same thing. I told him that the country around here had stayed in my mind for thirty years as an ideal of what forest could be, with musasa trees perhaps hundreds of years old, and full of every kind of animal. He was silent, surprised. I was experiencing that suspension of probability that accompanies moments unforeseen when you begin a journey, a pilgrimage – moments when things slide into place: it had never, ever, entered my mind that there was a generation in Zimbabwe which did not know how their own country had been, and so recently.

'Animals?' he asked. 'What animals? You mean mombies? You mean goats?'

'When I was a girl in Banket the bush was full of koodoo, sable, eland, and all the smaller buck, particularly duiker. There were stem buck and bush buck, anteaters and porcupines and wild cats and monkeys, and baboons and wild pig. There was every kind of bird. There were still leopards in the hills. Elephants had gone. Lions had gone. But you couldn't take one step in the bush without startling some creature.'

'Did you live in a game park?' he asked.

'No. That was how the bush was then. Everywhere. In every part of the country. And the birds . . . the dawn chorus – it split your ears. There were flocks of birds sitting all along the telephone lines . . . every kind of bird. And if you looked up in the sky any time of the day you saw the hawks circling. Five, ten – or more. Then you saw that everywhere in the sky were groups of hawks spiralling in the thermals. There might be twenty or thirty groups of them. The sky used to be full of hawks and kites. The groups further away were like little black flies against the blue. Now when you look up . . .' We walked away from Jack's little house and stood on the track outside it, with the Blair toilet a few yards in front, the still derelict water tank on its rise, and sparse trees dotting the land off into the distance. We stood looking up. There was not one bird in the sky. 'Hundreds of them,' I said. 'Now you're lucky if you see one. And in the morning when you went to see what had happened in the night, you examined the dusty road, and the tracks and the spoor of birds and animals were so thick in the dust it could take half an hour to sort it all out.'

He lowered his eyes from the empty blue, he stood gazing around, he was sombre, of course, because of his unhappiness, but now he was bewildered too.

'You say that wasn't a safari park?'

'No. Don't you see – that's how things were everywhere then. That was how all the bush used to be. And now on that road all you'd see would be the marks of bicycle tyres.'

'Probably my bicycle,' he said, and laughed.

A few days later on the verandah of a certain club in the mountains, referred to – what else? – as a watering hole, I am introduced to a man who would not have disagreed if I had described him as the – once – hardest of hard-line whites. For that is what he had been.

'I nearly packed up and Took the Gap when we lost the War. The worst mistake of my life, if I had.'

'So you like the black kids, do you?' prompt his boon companions, encouraging him as one does a child you hope will show off nicely.

'I like them all right. They are a fine bright lot of kids.'

He had chanced to discover that black children in the townships knew nothing about the bush, or the animals that live in it, and little about the lives of their grandparents. He set up a camp in still unspoiled bush far from any town, and now takes batches of town children there for a week or so, and he teaches them about the trees, the plants, the animals.

When not with the children his job is culling elephants.

'Keeping them down to the right number, you know.'

'Right number in relation to what?'

An ironical grimace. 'Yes, that's it. But remember, we're the only country who has handled the elephants well. Anyway, there are too many of the buggers. We aren't going to go short of elephants.'

But what he likes best is the time he spends with the black children.

'I had the wrong idea about the Affs, you know.'

'I seem to remember quite a few people were saying something along those lines.'

'Better late than never.'

I tell this story to a couple of black friends, poets. We are on a verandah in Harare, one that is netted and barred like an old-fashioned meat safe: we are sitting inside a cage. The house was burgled last week. The world is more and more a paradise for thieves, we reflect. Will there soon be more thieves than honest people? Should we all join the prospering profession?

These poets are poor: most writers are, here, unless part of the university.

When I am with them it is only a few moments before I begin to feel what they do: it is a sombre mood we share, for these are not people deprived of information – far from it. Africa, the continent, does not inspire anyone with happy and optimistic thoughts, these days. No one likes marxism and the censorship that keeps the newspapers so infantile. They know that in Europe and the Soviet Union communism is very ill, but most poets in this country are young, which means they were part of the euphoria of Revolution, and they are sitting by the death-bed of communism as if by a dying mother or father.

What I have told them about the watering hole in the mountains and the elephant hunter has, it seems, silenced them. Often on this trip, on the point of asking a question or adding a comment, inhibition has sat on my tongue, as if this organ were the Culture Gap embodied. Besides, everyone I meet seems to have a raw place where the skin has only just grown over.

'Excuse me,' says Poet A. 'Are you saying a white farmer is taking *our* kids on trips to show them the bush?'

'Yes, that is what I am saying. An ex-farmer, actually.'

The two young men face me with angry eyes – but that is not the point. They are despondent, hurt.

'Why should he want to do that?'

With difficulty I make myself say, 'Because he cannot stand the idea that black children shouldn't know anything about their bush.'

This remark in itself is taking a lid off impermissibles: it is believed by every black person that all white farmers are as bad as Simon Legree, with never a human impulse between them.

'I'd like to meet that paragon,' says one, trying to be humorous, but he laughs, most unhappily.

'No, I think you probably wouldn't,' I say, attempting to match his humour. 'You have to be brought up with this lot, you know, to understand . . .' I definitely falter.

'Hidden hearts of gold?' says Poet B. Rather, sneers.

'No, not exactly. But you know, some of them are trying hard.'

'I haven't noticed it.'

'If they are all paternalists these days then just think what they were like before.'

'It's a bit late for paternalism.'

'Well, you're all stuck with each other –' I say, allying myself, as it happens, with Comrade Mugabe, and his 'We are all citizens of Zimbabwe now.'

The two young men show the signs of being trapped, restless checked movements, restless eyes, and their faces darken even more.

Poet A says, 'And what does a Honkey know about the bush anyway?'

Here is another moment when my tongue has a weight on it.

'He knows. My brother was the same. He had an instinct for the animals. If you went out into the bush with him, he would know where a duiker was, or a koodoo – he knew the paths they would take.' Silence, because I was talking about my brother. Another strand was being woven into the webs of inhibition: family.

'His cookb – his servant.'

'OK, his cookboy,' says Poet B bitterly. 'Oh don't worry, my sister's husband's got a good job, and she told me a man came asking for work, he said, "Do you want a cookboy, madam?"'

Laughter, this time shared absolutely, with all the history of the country behind it.

'Your brother's cookboy?' invites Poet B, his hands spread open in a gesture of acceptance of fate.

'He used to come to my brother, and ask him to go with him, and his brother – go hunting. Because my brother always knew where the animals were.'

Silence.

'When was this?'

'When there were still animals,' I say, and my voice is as bitter as theirs.

'Yes,' says Poet A.

Poet B says, 'I was brought up in Harare, so I would have to ask your brother too.'

'I haven't been to my village for . . . well, quite a time, two years . . . no three . . . well, it's probably about five,' says Poet A.

Here I could have gone on to say that my brother might have

understood the ways of animals, but knew about Africans only
through the veils of his prejudice – but what was the point,
they knew that. My brother, and other white bush-lovers I
tried, did not know that a certain tree, the muhacha tree, is
sacred to the Mashona, though they must have walked under
the tree, with blacks, a thousand times.

'Really?' says my brother, as if I were talking about another
planet, 'that's interesting, I didn't know that.'

He, like other white bush-lovers interpret the bush – no, not
as white people, for that is not the point, but as modern people.

An anthropologist said, 'When I'm with the old people, I
have to remind myself they live in a different landscape. Each
rock, tree, path, hill, bird, animal, has a meaning. If an owl
calls or you see a certain bird, that is a message from another
dimension. A pebble set near a path is part of a pattern.
You see a bit of rag tied to a bush – watch out! It's a bit of
magic, most likely. *Don't disturb!* We don't live in that world,
but the point is, their young people don't either. They know
as little about it as we do. But when I'm with the old ones
I sometimes get a glimpse of a landscape that existed
everywhere in the world before modern man arrived on the
scene.'

In 1964 at the Independence Celebrations for Zambia, there
was an exhibition of Southern Rhodesian art. Near the door as
you went out was a large picture of an ancient tree. The artist
stood by the picture with that look often seen in Southern
Africa, 'If you choose to notice me, choose to ask questions,
you may get interesting replies.' My companion and I stop,
say, what a fine tree, and wait. The artist, an oldish man, looks
closely at us, sums us up, as you may see Africans doing, and
says, 'That tree was the telephone for our village.'

At this point, other people had laughed and walked off.

'What kind of a telephone?'

'You people have telephone lines. We had trees. Through
this tree the women sent messages to the men out hunting,
when are you coming home, what have you killed for us to
cook? And the men sent messages, We'll be back tonight, or,
We can't get back until tomorrow, we are stalking a fine eland.'

'Why don't you tell the government how it is done?' we joke. 'They'd like to know how to save some money.'

'Ah. But that's it, that's the trouble,' says the artist. 'All our old people knew how to do it. And sometimes children can still do it. But young people can't do it at all. It's gone.'

'Can you do it?'

'When I was a child, the old people used to send me to the tree.'

Similarly, the Bushmen of the Kalahari had, and a few still have, capacities that the young have lost: they knew days beforehand when people were going to arrive, for instance. And in a book about travel in Haiti it was recorded that the people there used trees in the same way: and again, young people had lost the art.

The anthropologist mourning lost landscapes (for the impartiality of the scientist wore transparent when he talked about them) told me this story – not of the past, but of last year, 1988. 'A young girl refused to marry an old man chosen by her family. They put a spell on her. She weakened and grew ill and tried to drown herself. They pulled her out of the water. She agreed to marry the old man and her family removed the spell.'

'A horrible story!'

'Yes, but that is not the point. Have you wondered how often in our culture people put spells on other people – no, no, not witches and that sort of thing . . . what are spells? Strong wishes. Well, how often do you think families or just spiteful individuals bad-wish someone? Well, think about it then . . .'

It is certainly true that witchcraft has unsuspected dimensions of usefulness. Ayrton R.'s little cat, now very old indeed, was his mother's cat, much loved by her. Now Dorothy and George both believe that Ayrton R.'s mother's spirit is in the cat, who is her mudzimo. 'A good thing,' says Ayrton R. 'It means they treat the cat well when I am away.'

Indifference or cruelty to animals is sometimes a reaction to what is seen as white sentimentality. Or rage at how whites will love animals but are unkind to blacks.

ANIMALS

A joke that is also a popular song. A white man sets off on a car journey. His dog is beside him in the front seat, and his black servant is in the back seat. There is an accident and the man is killed. The police ask the servant what happened. 'Don't ask me, ask the dog.'

Some time in the last few hundred years the Zambesi changed its course. Its old exit to the Indian Ocean was where Beira is now. The present delta is a hundred miles or so to the north. 'What I wonder is, how did the animals take it?'

A small battle in the War between humans and animals. A certain farmer, growing citrus, got a poor crop because of the vervet and simanga monkeys. He put up an electric fence. The monkeys easily jumped over it. He heightened the fence. The monkeys discovered that electric shocks did not kill them. They learned to jump in such a way that the electric shocks knocked them into the orchard where they ate their fill, and then positioned themselves so they were knocked back out of the orchard. The farmer could not bring himself to increase the electric shocks to the point where the monkeys would be seriously harmed. He went back to employing a man with a gun: expensive as well as being less effective.

Simanga monkeys are being resettled in areas where they have gone.

A Story of Two Unimportant Creatures

In a house in Harare a large black dog, half Newfoundland, half Rottweiler, welcomes the visitor with a determination that you notice him: bold, not to say commanding, eyes watch your every movement. He accompanies you as you walk about the house, then the garden, always one step to heel, his nose at your hand. When you stop to turn, his head is there to be stroked and patted, and his eyes never leave your face. Another dog, a small Alsatian, is lying in a dusty hollow near the back door. He watches, his whole body saying, I am not worthy to be noticed, while his eyes crave affection. When you go to pet this dog, the big dog's nose, head, then shoulders are interposed between your hand and the smaller dog's head. Again and again this happens: it is not possible to caress the Alsatian, for the big dog will not allow it. The Alsatian knows your goodwill, but knows too it has no alternative but to ask for nothing as it lies in its dusty place. It came as a refugee to this friendly house, full of people of all colours, and of cats, monitored by this jealous dog. Its owners went south to The Republic – they Took the Gap, and left it behind. This Alsatian, say its new owners, making a joke of it to black guests, is a racist. It has been taught to attack black people. Now its skills, for which it was valued, applauded, and given titbits, are reproached: when it performs as it was trained to do, it is chastised and rebuked. This confused and unhappy dog is determined on one thing: that it will not lose this home where at least it is fed and has a place to sleep. As it watches the confident and successful dog, the Alsatian seems to be silently weeping. If it were human, it would be saying, 'I am sorry, I can't help it, I don't know why I am wicked.'

THE BOOK TEAM

We take a coach to a town in Central Province. The coach is efficient, well-driven, punctual. Gone are the days when the Team went on long journeys by bus, for the authorities saw a humorous cartoon by Chris of the Team standing bedraggled in the rain near a broken-down bus, and insisted they should travel less dangerously: in the five weeks of my trip the newspapers reported four major accidents with buses. 'We don't want to lose the whole Team all at once!' cried the officials. Nor is their diet restricted to oranges, bread, milk. 'It was a healthy diet, at least,' says Cathie. But even on this trip, at the end when funds ran low, I heard the Team telling Cathie that she really must not expect them to put up with it, if she fed them all on five dollars after a hard day's work. 'I lose pounds on every trip,' says Chris, who is too thin.

At the half-way stop, we sit around under trees in a café garden, and I listen while Talent, Sylvia, Cathie, and Chris give each other information – through chat, gossip. An apparently casual process. The Team are at that stage when they must be conscious of what their strengths and weaknesses are. These four small vulnerable people are besieged with demands. Every village in Zimbabwe would like the Team to visit. In Harare the telephone never stops ringing. Aid organizations, government departments, 'Third World Groupies' sense that here is something extraordinary. The Team now begin to see that they are strong, because of how other people see them. And how can they cope with what is asked of them if they are weak? They discuss their 'styles of work', and gently criticize each other. I realize I am watching a process that was the aim of the old communist activists. But not one of these people is a communist: they share an ironical patience with the political circus. When I ask if they have read how in old Russia idealists 'went to the people' with their skills and their enthusiasm, they say no: but they are interested to hear about it. 'I don't think it's strange that we are the same,' says Talent. 'They had people who needed a lot of help and so do we.'

Contemplating the extent of help needed, the depth of need, the four involuntarily laugh, and look at each other, sharing humorous incredulity.

It is the level of expectation that surprised them . . . that supported them . . . that inspires them. And, often, dismays them. What they are doing is, in fact, impossible.

Two springs, or rivers – or floods – fed that expectation. One was, that the whites had gone, with their persistent denigration of everything black, their cold, sniffy, self-righteous disapproval. The Africans, with that pressure off them, felt that now everything was possible. The other was, the rhetoric of Revolution, promising everything. 'In that dawn . . .' There wasn't a woman, man, or child in Zimbabwe who did not expect the good life to begin almost at once. But nothing much happened, except that the new bureaucracy creaked and groaned and tangled them in old and new regulations. Then, up there in Harare the fat cats . . . Into this vacuum came the Team who said, 'You can do anything you want to do, all you need is the expertise, and this is what you have to know. And now, learn how to do it for yourselves.' In the case of the women's book, they were told, *You* decide the topics, *you* bring in the material, you write the book.

Now, while we drink Coca-Cola and eat meat pies, I listen while they share scorn for the big Aid organizations. 'They sweep into Harare, can't even begin without offices, word processors, computers, a staff, and enormous funds.'

Cathie says, 'I still only have a desk and we use the house telephone, and I only have a typewriter, no machines at all.'

'And yet we have a network of people working for the Team all over Zimbabwe.'

'It works because we have the goodwill of the people themselves.'

They make many jokes about the experts known as Consultants. 'Many of them have never set foot outside Harare. If they get down to village level they stay in a three-star hotel and visit the local district offices. They know nothing about local conditions but they lay down the law about what we should do with their Aid money.'

'Just imagine! We get back from a month's trip all around the villages and then some Dane, or German, or American tells us, No, the main *thrust* of the problem according to our information is . . .'

I have a cutting with me.

They lean over the table, reading, their faces slowly spreading into smiles.

'If we had only a fraction of that money . . .'

'Even a thousandth of it.' 'Even a millionth of it.'

Advising Africa has become a major industry, with European and North American consulting firms charging as much as

$180,000 for a year of an expert's time. At any given moment sub-Saharan Africa has at least 8,000 expatriates working for public agencies under official aid programmes. More than half of the $7 to $8 billion spent yearly by donors goes to finance these people. Yet in the two and a half decades since African Independence Africa has plunged from food self-sufficiency to widespread hunger. Is Africa getting the right advice?

Lloyd Timberlake, *Africa in Crisis*

Cathie produces from a string-bag material for the forth-coming seminars and shares it out. There will be this problem and that problem, says Cathie. The four are leaning forward, looking into each other's faces, intent. Sylvia speaks, then Talent. If they did not know how to concentrate these moments when they are together, not actually working, nothing would get done. This break under the trees is the equivalent of an organizing meeting, but it is not called that, nor do they think of it as a meeting. If this fragile little organism, so full of life, developing on its own inner impetus, allowed itself to fossilize and demand a structure, then they would need hours-long meetings to get through what they do now in a few minutes.

They are all people under pressure in their ordinary lives. Talent has three small children and takes a good deal of the responsibility for the running of the collective farm. She can only come on these trips because of the support of her husband – it was he who said, 'There are no men and women, there are only people on this farm.' Sylvia with her eight children finds the going hard. She is a large, queenly woman, confident, competent. Cathie whose energy incandesces not only her, but everyone else, is the queen-pin of the Team, one of the world's natural organizers. She has children, and says she could do none of this work without her husband's help. When the four sit together like this, the 'family' – for they say they are one – their differences of temperament and style show in every gesture, in how they sit, how they talk. Cathie leans forward, smiling, always smiling, and her hands present her ideas in sympathy with her breathless, tumbling words. Sylvia sits four-square, nodding, or sceptical, magisterial. Talent claims she is

shy, and finds it hard to speak, but with her friends she is
funny, satirical – a comic. Chris is mostly silent: he watches
and he listens, and five minutes later he will pass around a
sketch he has made of the three in energetic verbal combat.

A young man comes towards us. He is shy, he hesitates,
he waits until Cathie and the others recognise him, welcome
him. Last year he worked with the Team in this district, and,
knowing they were bound to stop here today has been
watching for the coach. He needs advice.

This is his problem. His family are insisting that he marry.
He is thirty, and that is old not to be married, in Shona
culture. But how can he support a wife? On a tiny salary he
earns as a junior welfare worker he already supports an old
mother, an assortment of unemployed friends and, too, his
brother's family. This brother, himself fifteen, made a four-
teen-year-old girl pregnant. Both youngsters were expelled
from school, thus guaranteeing for both a future of unemployment. The girl's father demanded marriage. These two are
still under twenty and have two small children. This young
man here supports them all. He is afraid of marriage. His
mother was left by his father, and for a long time she fed her
children on what she could find in the dustbins of white
houses. (I have now heard this tale several times and it is still
happening. 'But now the really good dustbins are multi-racial,
so I suppose that is progress.') This young man wants a real
marriage, he says: like Cathie's, like Talent's. He has heard them
talk about their husbands. He does not want to marry the girl
chosen for him by his family, because he does not know her.
What should he do? He seems confident they will know the
answer. Talent and Cathie consult together. Then Cathie says
marriage should never limit you, but add to the possibilities of
life. Yes, says Talent, you should have a partner like my husband who makes you think about everything.

The young man says, 'But how do you know beforehand? I
do have a girl and I like her, but how do I know she would
turn out to be a real wife, like Cathie and like Talent?'

At this point we are summoned back to the coach.

There are five of us, finding our places in the crowded coach, but we joke there are really six. Everywhere the Team goes, they take a big drum. This is because no meeting can be expected to go well without music. 'This is the best travelled drum in Zimbabwe,' says Cathie.

When we reached the coach terminal in the town there was an official car waiting. Cathie says, 'You don't know what this means, look, this is the District Office car. They said they wanted us so badly they won't let us pay in the training centre. And look – those men are the big bosses for the area. They've come to meet us. You don't know what a change this is.'

We were taken to the training centre, which is built not in the town but well outside it, a large, light, five-year-old building surrounded by expanses of grass, then trees, making an uncompromising statement: Here is Progress, here is the modern world, here is Zimbabwe. It is full every day of the year, with people from every part of Central Province, taking courses on management, book-keeping, accountancy, dressmaking.

The Centre takes a couple of hundred at a time. For the Book Team's week of seminars thirty women have come, and nine men. That the men should be here, supporting women, for the women's book, is another revolution and not a minor one. These men must all be extraordinary in some way, for not only are they going against traditional ideas, but must expect criticism, perhaps derision, from other men. The Team congratulate each other about the men's presence. 'There you are, Chris, you aren't going to be the only man now.'

As soon as we got there, the forty or so of us sat in a big circle and introduced ourselves, first the Team, Cathie, Sylvia, Talent, Chris. As each offered little autobiographies to the company, everyone leaned forward, in the absolute silence of concentration. Not all had been here months before, when the Team came to say that the women's book was to be decided by them. Impossible for them not to think, What an unexpected combination of people: how did they come to work together? just as the observers – myself, and two area officials – wondered how the people who were prepared to give so much time, so much effort, to the book had chosen themselves, or were chosen, for they were very different, well-dressed, poorly dressed, confident, or fighting shyness. Two women can illustrate the range of difference. Mrs Berita Msindo, with eight children, said she had always worked, first as a teacher, then as a senior development officer. She was proud of being the first woman in the Province to ride a motorbike. She has just returned from a study tour in Rome. 'All my children are successful,' she remarked, just as if this were not an extraordinary thing. The two oldest are university graduates, one in England studying agriculture and economics. Another two are school teachers. The four younger ones are doing well at school. Mrs Msindo says her husband is proud of her: without him she could not have done so well. She is a large, handsome woman, humorous, pleased when everyone claps as she finishes.

The other woman is thin, tentative, anxious: she comes from an area debilitated by drought. She and the other village women get up at three or four every morning to walk to the borehole some miles away to fetch enough water to drink and to cook with: washing has become a luxury. In her area they are all short of food. Her eyes shine with passionate admiration when she listens to Mrs Msindo talk about her life. She says that when the rains come and things get easier she wants to take an O-level. She knows she could pass examinations well if she had time and opportunity. And now everyone applauds her and it seems as if she gently fills, as she sits there smiling gratefully, with their sympathy, their encouragement.

This business of our becoming a company, a communion, takes about three hours. When a woman claims an achievement, people softly clap, when the men speak they are especially applauded. The local officials who sit slightly apart, watching and listening, never opening their mouths after the first formal welcome, are impressed and say so. 'You people are doing wonderful things,' says the district representative. He sounds bemused, probably wondering how this atmosphere of mutual help, trust, community, is achieved, when at other times, with other people, it doesn't happen at all.

These introductory proceedings over, the women dance, singing their welcome to the Team.

The evening meal was in progress when we got to the food hall. It is a large hall, with four tables down its length. At the end is the serving place, and queues of women and men, mostly young, were being handed plates heaped with sadza, meat, green vegetables. As usual I was astonished at the amount of sadza on every plate, at least two pounds of it. It is a thick porridge, not unlike polenta. The meat was beef, braised, very good, with a rich gravy. The cabbage was well-cooked. The meal would please a hungry Italian. But the surprising thing is, this amount is eaten three times a day, and often with plenty of thick-cut white bread. Unless a stomach is full and heavy there has not been a real meal. Often Africans invited to a 'white' meal will go home and fill themselves up with sadza. When Jack took his aspiring young journalists to a restaurant in Harare they complained, only half-joking, there had been no sadza. This surely must be an emotional thing. In Japan, because of the starvation after the Second World War, when even a few grains of rice were precious, rice has become an emotional necessity even though food is plentiful. The rice bucket is there, and people will eat a little spoon or two after a long meal. It is a reassurance, a manna. Sadza is served at every meal cooked in the homes of the new rich, though the menu is usually 'white' food.

But sadza is no longer a 'black' food. The son of a privileged white family, asked what he wanted for his birthday meal, said nothing would do but sadza and stew. Sadza is served in every restaurant, every hotel, at every barbecue. In the courtyards of the country hotels, along with the barbecues, are the great pots for sadza. Nothing is more satisfying to the ironies-of-history nerve than to watch those whites who stay in Zimbabwe but preserve their feelings of superiority, filling their plates with sadza. *Then* – in the old days – sadza was kaffir food and no white would dream of eating it.

The meal in the hall that night – and all the other meals – was noisy and exuberant, with an atmosphere of holiday. To most of the people here taking courses, this training college in the bush represented a time of affluence. Few people can afford to eat meat at every meal, or even every week, and certainly not great slabs of it. And when we went off to the bedrooms, the shower block was full of women showering. Like a party it was, a water festival. There they stood under the streams of hot water and called out to each other their pleasure and their surprise at the lavishness of it all. No one in the villages has unlimited streams of hot clean water. Some women had showers several times a day, just as they ate as much as they could.

Chris was sleeping on the men's side of the building. Talent and Cathie were in one room, Sylvia and I in another. The four of us crowded on to Talent's bed, for discussion on next day's strategies. It was an atmosphere pleasantly reminiscent of after lights-out at school.

'We must take things slowly,' said Cathie. 'We forget, we've done this so often, but for nearly everyone on this course it's new. It's worth taking the trouble to explain and explain. This is the first time ever people have been asked to choose their own themes, and then write their own articles and poems and stories and then comment on it all. We mustn't let them be shy. We must watch out for the ones who don't speak and encourage them.'

Talent has had her experience in the army and then at the collective farm. 'We must split them into smaller groups to discuss the material, between every session. Then they will support each other, and it'll be easier for them to criticize us.' She is always the first to translate theory into practice.

Talent and Cathie began a close, expert, detailed discussion on the right sizes of groups for different purposes. Sylvia was tired, she wasn't sleeping: she wanted to go to bed. The room was divided by a partition for privacy but it was easy to talk. We talked until late, just as Cathie and Talent were doing in their room. From every room in this women's wing, until late, came voices, laughter and, once or twice, singing. Sylvia was not laughing. She was telling me about a close friend whose marriage had broken up, and in a way she often uses: she does not want me to make quick judgements about manners and mores she is sure are hard for me to understand. They often are.

There are several children, the oldest nearly twenty, the youngest still a baby. The husband is a civil servant. The marriage was always difficult: he was for some time an alcoholic, she saw him through it, protected him, interceded with superiors. Then there was another woman and a baby: she took him back. Only a few weeks ago she discovered that he now not only has another woman but a new baby: she knew nothing about this until someone told her the baby was being christened. She accused her husband: he said he wanted her to accept a polygamous marriage. She said, 'When we married you had the choice of a Christian monogamous marriage, and a marriage according to our customs. You chose a Christian marriage.' 'I have changed my mind,' said he. She refused to accept a polygamous marriage. He is spending all his time with the new wife and baby, and if he does come home it is only to shout at her. Meanwhile she is supporting the children, almost entirely, because his money is going on the new wife, the baby, a new house. The new wife's relatives say he must not have anything to do with his old wife and come to threaten her. Under the new law she could force her husband to support the children, but she is afraid. Sylvia says she is ashamed to tell me this story. I say I don't see the difference between many men in so-called Western culture and this husband. Monogamy, polygamy, what's in a word? Many Western marriages are polygamous, and more and more couples break up, remarry, and the children may have a place, even a room, in two homes. Sylvia does laugh at the idea of a child having a whole room to itself, let alone two, in two houses.

She says the pattern is only superficially the same: she does not mean, either, the difference in standards of living. It is no use, she says, judging things by what is happening now, you have to look at the history, too. When she was growing up, there were four wives, each one married properly, according to form. A woman who is not married is seen as a prostitute or a loose woman. Her father had to marry the wives of a brother who died. Not until his fourth wife did he love a wife.

'Our custom is that a brother's widow must be married to a
surviving brother; this is a good thing, because it means women
are supported, but it is a bad thing too, because they are not
loved by their husbands.' I ask if the four wives got on. At first
Sylvia says yes; then she admits that she has never heard of
the wives of one man being real friends. Though they might
pretend to please the husband. 'Polygamous marriages are bad
for women,' she says at last, making an admission she would
rather not make. When people these days say 'our customs',
'our culture', you are intended to take it seriously, even when
they are seeing these phrases like unsafe life-rafts in a stormy
sea.

I was lying there in the dark, listening to the women all over
the building talking, laughing, splashing and singing in the
showers, and I was thinking of the man who had to marry
three women not chosen by him, before he could marry one
he loved. But it was not possible to mention this. What atmos-
pheres forbid you to say, an invisible clamp on your tongue,
can often tell you how stupid you are being. This was not a
nice dispassionate chat about cultural differences, nor could it
be. Sylvia was too unhappy, a heap of misery just the other
side of the partition, because of this failed marriage, when she
was so afraid for her own.

A *New Yorker* joke came into my mind: a boy of about fifteen
in his first grown-up suit approaches a worried-looking rather
drunk man at a party, saying, 'I don't know if you remember
me? We met here last year: I am your son by your third wife.'

But I couldn't tell her this joke; the atmosphere forbade it.
She would not find it funny . . . well perhaps it wasn't funny
. . . was there something wrong with me, to find it funny? If
so, then what did this say about 'Western' culture? What jokes
could Sylvia tell me that I would find shocking? But Sylvia was
not telling me jokes, not that night, not that trip.

Next morning began the week's work. Every session was
introduced by a little play that encapsulated a problem,
rehearsed for a few minutes after breakfast. Then there was
dancing, a song. Everyone joined in.

Most of the problems were familiar from last year. There

were two, provoked by the existence of the women's book, that were – so Cathie and Talent said – really revolutionary, and challenged the fabric of 'our culture', 'our customs' – and were bound to cause opposition. One was that babies are automatically registered in the name of the father, 'who then goes to one woman after another, and we have no legal control over the children we bring up. Sometimes we don't see the father for years, but by law he can just turn up and take the children.' And another, 'Why should land automatically be registered in the name of the man when it is the women who do all the work?'

And there is another new theme. Last year no one mentioned AIDS, not once, in the meetings, but the government propaganda is being effective, for a sketch by one of the groups about prostitutes and their clients began with a man limping from weakness across the classroom, and at once everyone said, 'He's got AIDS.' This sketch was funny too. All the impromptu playlets and sketches are funny.

In a week as lively as any I can remember, some incidents stand out.

Cathie is standing by the blackboard, making diagrams of statistics. She says that she is going to skip the next page of the draft book because it is too difficult. She means the statistics are too detailed to be illustrated in this way, but one of the women, misunderstanding, says sweetly: 'Just try us. It is possible we may have the intelligence to understand.'

A local official, a man, says, 'I don't know why it is that people who do the most work, nearly always women, working all day, walking long distance, get paid practically nothing, while men sitting in offices get paid ten or twenty times as much.' Because he is one of the men sitting in an office, he is applauded and at once they make up a song about it, which they sing to him, clapping and ululating.

Judges can be very harsh, particularly with women. A woman had a third child and killed it: she was supporting her mother and father and her grandmother. 'I cannot support all these people on my wages.' She got a prison sentence and her children were taken into care.

Another woman killed her ninth baby, was imprisoned, and her eight children were put in care. The welfare official said, 'We decided to find out how they were doing. Eight child allowances were being paid to a relative, who doesn't know where the children are. We have lost eight children. Where are they?'

A discussion on why the judges are so inflexible: the conclusion is because they are new to this job. 'People can only be flexible when they are sure of themselves. But while they are learning to be sure of themselves, we have a bad time.'

(There are several legal systems in Zimbabwe. Shona customary law. Ndebele customary law. Mbacha customary law – which is a mixture of Shona and Shangaan. Roman-Dutch law. English common law.)

Several times in the workshops women complained that poor black women farmers are employed by richer black farmers, particularly women, who pay them badly or do not pay them at all, only giving them some food. 'We have no alternative, we have to work for them, we have to feed our children somehow.'

One evening after supper a woman sat herself by me and asked, 'Have you ever seen people as poor as we are?'

'Much poorer, in some other countries.'

'I have never been outside this province. It seems to me we are very poor. If you do not have enough to eat sometimes, isn't that being very poor?'

I said to her, 'There are parts of the world where people just suffer poverty. But if you people are in a bad situation you try to think of ways out of it. If you have a problem, you decide to solve it. That in itself makes you rich compared to them. And you are all so full of energy and determination.'

She thought hard, for quite a long time: a minute – more. When I believed the conversation was over, she remarked, 'And yet we owe so much money.'

I said, 'The total debt of all the African countries is less than the debt of any one South American country.'

'You mean that Africa is richer than South America? Have you been to South America?'

'In Brazil.'

'It is worse than here?'

'Yes, it is. For one thing, there are greater differences between rich and poor.'

'We've got rich people here too, now. Haven't you seen them?'

'Nothing like as bad or cruel as in places like Brazil.'

She sat quietly beside me, thinking. Then: 'Why is it poor people in some countries don't complain?'

'Sometimes it is because they haven't energy, they are so badly fed or full of diseases. Sometimes it is because of a religion that makes them suffer in silence.'

'But I am religious and I am complaining. I complain all the time. My husband says to me, Woman, why are you complaining? I say, Your life is all right, but my life is very hard and that is why I am complaining.' She laughed, loudly, so that people turned to look and laughed in sympathy.

During one workshop a terrible story was told of cruelty, of official stupidity. The whole room was laughing, forty or so people. I said to the man next to me, 'Why are you laughing? That's a terrible story.' 'That is why we are laughing,' he said.

A certain man who had been hostile to the women during the last visit of the Team, was here again, claiming he had had a change of heart: now he knew he had been wrong. But, said he, it hurt him to hear women criticize men, who all loved women. 'For my part I think women are a gift from God.' For all of that day, when it was felt that the proceedings were becoming too heavy, someone remarked, 'Women are a gift from God,' and everyone laughed, the men too.

These men know they are revolutionaries to be here at all. They like to be asked what makes them special, more enterprising, than other men.

Here is an autobiographical piece submitted to a workshop.

In 1965, on the 9th day of May, a baby boy was born at Masvingise, a small village in the Chivu Communal Lands. 'He shall be called Amos' they finally agreed.

Shining with youthful freshness and innocence the baby could not foresee the misery that was heralded by his birth. He only managed to have a glimpse of his father seventeen years later, and that was that.

Unlike other children in the village I managed to go to a mission school at Bergena in 1980 for my secondary education.

I became a shining example and many male parents sent their children to school. I am now working, and I owe everything to my mother who worked so tirelessly to make me what I am. However, I miss my father, but I am not sure he would have made me what I am now. Amos Sithole. Co-operative Assistant. Gutu.

I take the opportunity of being with so many people of so many different kinds, to ask what they think about Edgar Tekere, whose name is in every newspaper as a threat to the government, to order, to security and to Robert Mugabe.

But no one is talking about Tekere and his new party. For that matter no one mentions the Unity Accord. This is Central Province and not Matabeleland, but the whole country was celebrating the Unity Accord only a few months ago. People soon take good fortune for granted.

Tekere? We aren't going to vote for him. We are just stupid village people, don't forget, and we don't want another war.

Tekere? He's useful in opposition, he keeps them awake for us, but he's not steady enough to be a leader.

Tekere? I like him because he's an alternative. But they say at the next election we can vote for people we put forward ourselves, not from a list Mugabe has chosen. If that happens, then everyone will forget about Tekere.

As the week goes by, the Team visibly tire. They put so much energy into the workshops and seminars, and into the discussions that go on every evening in the bedrooms. And, again, they have already been on the road for weeks. The women are worrying about children and husbands. Chris talks about his girlfriend.

When they get back to Harare there will be rooms-full of material from these workshops and from past ones. Chris will have to make many drawings and submit them to the Team.

No area or district must be favoured at the expense of another.

When Cathie gets home she will not rest, for she has so much correspondence. From all over Zimbabwe requests for the Book Team to visit them come pouring in. Cathie has no secretarial help. How does she get everything done? She herself doesn't know: the more you have to do the more you do, she says. But she is worried. 'Sometimes I think it is not possible to do what we are doing.'

'Of course it is impossible,' says Talent. 'That is why we are doing it.'

The Team is worried, too, because they do not always have this welcome. They have enemies. And it will not be easy to get 'them' to accept this women's book, so full of explosive ideas. 'We don't know who our enemies are. No one is going to say anything openly against us now, because the village people like us, but suddenly you come up against a block and then you know . . .'

'But often the block isn't hostility, it's inefficiency,' says Talent.

On the last night there is a party after supper. Soft drinks, beer, snacks, and dancing, in between sketches contrived by the different groups.

One is about highly qualified girls trying to get jobs, but they fail, because the Chefs prefer unqualified girls who are pretty or with family connections. 'You say you are my mother's auntie's second cousin? Take a seat and fill in this form in quadruplicate.' The qualified girls go off, reciting their hard won qualifications to each other and the audience.

Another is about a charlatan village healer getting rich on the gullibility of his patients.

A sketch shows a woman possessed by the Spirit giving out all kinds of positive and optimistic prophecies for the future of the Women's Book. Then the ngangas are mocked when she begins shaking and writhing and demanding money from derisive bystanders.

One sketch is solemn. 'The way these books have helped us as communities is very important. They have changed our attitudes and our working style and have made us feel part of

Zimbabwe. These books were an eye-opener to the community leaders and to us as development workers.'

When this party ends it is only ten o'clock, but the women say they won't go to bed until they have properly sent off the Book Team. The training centre has a large and formal entrance hall. The women and some men take this over, demanding the Team's drum. They start a wild stamping and leaping dance, far removed from the sedate dancing of the official party. The whole building vibrates with their singing and with the drum. People who have gone to bed descend to reprove them but find themselves pulled into the circle of the dancers. One of the songs they make up says, 'This is our book. We, the women of Zimbabwe are making our book. It will change the lives of our children and our husbands. It will reach other countries. Hear us, hear us, Harare.'

Someone watching these women during the week of workshops would have one image of them, the same observer catching a glimpse of this uninhibited dancing, would see something very different.

It will be noticed that I am making the claim that Africans, or at least these Africans, have rhythm. Why not? – when they claim it themselves. These women are aware of the dramatic value of the thing, when, having introduced a workshop session with a dance, they sit down and say, with severity, 'We feel that sub-clause (d) of clause 2 on page 4 is incorrectly drafted. We are putting forward this alternative sub-clause.' They are conscious of the value of both worlds and intend to keep both.

But, take heart, the politicoes who cannot endure that Africans have rhythm, who cannot believe that it is possible to have rhythm and other things too . . . at a meeting of intellectuals in Harare, a poet who had just come from the rural areas, where everything is sung, danced, mocked, acted, demanded that the writers and poets present sing a song, but they could not, they writhed with embarrassment, reluctance and selfconsciousness, just as civilized people are supposed to do.

And, when I sat for a couple of hours in a car watching a

pavement in Bulawayo, of the dozens of people who passed only two women walked as they once all did – goddesses is the only word. The rest thumped and clumped and flumped and were clumsy and graceless, just like us. As a girl I used to watch village women walking to the well, one hand held up to steady the cans on their heads, and tried to be like them, but I could not do it.

That night the women did not go to bed at all. When they had done dancing, they all had showers and were sitting in the buses that were to take them to villages, by five in the morning. Some were tearful.

The Team sit drinking tea, summing up the week. A success. A woman on another course who has got hold of the draft women's book, sits by us and says, 'It is the Chefs and the bosses who should be reading these books and learning from us. They are always talking about educating the people. But it is they who need educating. They know nothing about us because they never come near us.'

Other women come to sit with us. 'Now everyone knows the women do all the work, the Chef's wives and all kinds of career girls descend on the villages dressed up like fashion models, their hair straightened and their cheeks glowing orange from skin lighteners. They congratulate the village women, and return to politicking in Harare.'

In Harare I heard an Extension Worker say she refused to go into a Communal Area unless she could stay in a village, having heard a song made up about patronizing visitors. 'Now work hard, ladies, keep it up, Zimbabwe is proud of you, here, have a sweetie, have a bit of cake.'

The village women are scornful of the smart city girls who 'want to be white blacks'. The chemists are full of skin-whitening creams, some with chemicals that have been banned in other countries.

The villagers do not admire Harare. The word can mean an attitude of mind. Perhaps they talked of Babylon thus.

Stately Look
Harare
  a
    prostitute
trying
  on
    new york's
oversized
  suit
import
  quality

Simbarashe R. Johnson
(From Tso Tso, a new magazine.
Tso Tso means twigs.)

None of us wants to leave this optimistic, energetic place.

'I don't know why it is,' says Cathie, 'but in the offices in Harare they talk as if these people are stupid. It can take me hours to get a point across to officials there that these people get at once. They are much more quick-witted. The political women are all intellectual and abstract.'

In only one way does this training centre, run by socially concerned and optimistic staff, resemble the school in the bush.

If you look closely, some of the parquet tiles are missing or loose. Curtains are falling down. Shower curtains are torn. Strips of wood are coming off the edges of tables, and some chairs are shaky or useless because screws have come out. There is a look of mild dilapidation. Yet a young man who has attended courses in various training colleges remarks, 'I like coming here best: it is so well maintained.' A mystery. Nothing is wrong here that could not be put right by an efficient housewife with some glue, a screwdriver, a needle and cotton, a step-ladder. One evening a hosepipe ran water for hours beside a path where staff constantly passed, and this in a water-short district.

'They should train a team of young women to cope with minor wear and tear and send them from institution to institution.'

'Why doesn't one of these Aid organizations . . . ?'
'Why doesn't Mugabe . . . ?'
On the way back in the coach, we pass one of the largest black townships.

THE NEW TOWNSHIPS

In the old days black townships around cities were assemblies of any kind of cheap housing, sometimes brick 'lines' – single rooms built in strips, without even lavatories, or sheds of corrugated iron, like factories. Sometimes local authorities built suburbs of hundreds, or even thousands of identical little brick houses, perhaps single rooms with kitchens, and communal lavatories at the back, or, if luxurious, two rooms. Now the new suburbs qualify as towns in their own right. Again they are of thousands of tiny houses, two rooms with a verandah, a kitchen and bathroom. To make such a township, first all the indigenous trees are cut down, the roads are laid out, usually on a grid pattern, and then the houses go up in a dusty or muddy plain. They are crammed as closely as the old houses built under the whites: the new suburbs, like the old, look what they are, desperate attempts at cheap housing. Zimbabwe is hardly short of space, not like Europe where every yard is contested. Why then are these houses massed like so many toy towns? Because this reduces the cost of the services: the pipes, wires, lines, ducts, sewers that make it possible for many people to live together. Is this not perhaps short-sighted? Would it not have been better if Comrade Mugabe had insisted from the start on paying more and laying out towns with enough space between the houses for some kind of privacy? It is hard to see where they find room even for a washing line, particularly since, as soon as people move in, they plant fruit trees. To reach the bush, the trees of their heritage, they have to leave the townships and make excursions into 'the country'. Why didn't Comrade Mugabe . . . ? Surely *he* could not have agreed to this short-sighted policy?

As in the old days, the hour of travel into the big town for work, the hour back, are on roads crowded, jammed, with bicycles, buses, and (but still only a few) cars. The people who live in these townships mostly cannot afford cars. There is talk that railways will be built to link the black townships with the big town – which is not white now, but multi-racial. The cheap suburbs are black, and poor.

If you drive past such a township, or fly over it, and see the ordered, not to say regimented, arrangement of identical houses, an image is created of many units, each for a family. But each house, meant for a family, contains perhaps twenty or so people. Anybody doomed to rural living with a relative in town will claim the old rights of kinship and try to fit them-selves into a house which is already exploding with people, a house appropriate for the nuclear family, for mother, father, and two or three children. But this house could not be more unsuitable for clan or communal living, which was better accommodated in the old days with clusters of huts: it is easy to build a new hut if relatives come to visit, or find themselves homeless. Rather, once it was easy, but now there are not enough trees, or enough grass for thatch.

No, clan living, the extended family, is being done in by the modern towns, and the necessity for them.

The new townships are not cheap. In fact it was cheaper to rent a house in the old days, when they were subsidized.

Two little rooms, a kitchen, a bathroom, limit numbers, even if people do sleep ten or more to a room. 'You know my heart is large,' a certain woman wrote in reply to a request from a country cousin for a corner somewhere, 'but my house is small. There is nowhere left for you to sleep, except under the kitchen table.'

The Book Team worry that they spend their time in rural areas, not these overcrowded, poor, complex conglomerations where people must be needing just as much help.

'But not the same problems. They don't need to be told about starting co-operatives and bank accounts. How to handle bureaucracy is more like it.'

'But we all need to know that!'

THE GARDEN IN HARARE

There is no end to the variety. I ask Ayrton R. to walk around it with me and give me names. Clerodendrum: glory bower. It is dark red. Clerodendron: bleeding heart. The yellow marmalade bush. Mackaya: a mass of pale pink, veined with carmine. Aspidistra as ground cover. Various hydrangeas. The fiddlewood tree. Magnolias. Ajuga as ground cover. Tree ferns. Cape chestnut. Miniature bamboos. The potato tree, twenty feet or more tall, covered with purple flowers. Elephant's ear. Busy lizzies. Indigenous arums. The spur flower: purple spikes. Plectranthus bushes. Flowering prunus. Blue agapanthus. Hen-and-chickens, otherwise the spider plant. Bougainvillaeas in maroon, orange, white and pink. The ginger bush: yellow with red. Different kinds of canna lilies. Mallow: pink. Ornamental cassava. The tape worm plant: segmented narrow leaves. Albizia: an indigenous tree. Geraniums. Succulents. Small heliotropes. The Kenyan croton tree. A tree with oak-like leaves, and panicles of rust colour. Hymenosporum. The red handkerchief bush. From Australia: the brush cherry tree, with bright pink fruits. Thunbergia: a blue creeper. The Pride of India: crepe myrtle. A cactus from Arizona, with a flower like waterlilies, grown with an indigenous canary creeper up it. Cacti with flowers like red fountains. The Beaumontia vine, with enormous white flowers. Strelitzia from Natal, the national flower of California. Red robin: a large bush. The Chinese hat plant: rust colour, purple, yellow. Berberis. Ficus benjamina. The pineapple-guava plant: like Christmas decorations. The pigeon berry tree – yellow. Mulberries. Peach trees. White agapanthus. A daisy from the Eastern districts, indigenous. The pompom tree. Escallonia. Hamelia: rather like a honeysuckle flower, always in bloom. Pampas grass. The kitchen herbs. Indigenous waterlilies. Day lilies. The indigenous red-veined banana tree, from the Bridal Veil Falls at Chimanimani: it is really a plantain. The yellow daisy bush. Penstemon. The Cape honeysuckle: orange. The Mediterranean rock rose, magenta: a cistus. Hebes. Cannas seven foot tall, in orange pink. 'You could garden with cannas alone.' Barberton daisies. New Zealand flax: maid-of-all-work with red currant-like flowers. Yellow lantana. Cape may: a mass of white blossom covering a bush. Miniature white poinsettias. A guava. Acanthus: purple. The wild fig tree: indigenous. The giant ageratum, covered with fuzzy mauve. Lemon and orange trees. Bauhinias, purple and white. A large yellow bush, nameless. The yesterday, today and tomorrow bush. Pomegranates. Sage shrubs, very large. Daisy as ground cover, pink. Fuchsias. Chinese lanterns: orange. An anonymous pink creeper. The handkerchief bush: white. Moonflowers, white and yellow. Cotoneaster. From South Africa, a succulent with minute magenta flowers. Cascades of nasturtiums. Cycad: Japan. The powder puff bush, faint pink, like a delicate thistle flower. Hypericums. The flag bush, grown with the white and the red handkerchief bushes. Aloes with dangling red spikes, from Nyanga. The bottle brush tree, which birds like so much. The Chinese sacred bamboo. Honeysuckles. Azaleas. The mirror plant from New Zealand. The lady's slipper plant, a thumbergia from Mysore, like an orchid, dark rust and yellow dangling panicles. Monstera: a tree-sized creeper. 'I always feel sorry for monsteras when I see them as prisoners in English offices.' Rothmania, a tree with pink bell-shaped flowers. Oleander. Plumbago. Petunias, pinks, cornflowers. The Norfolk Island pine, from New South Wales. Marigolds.

We stand at the bottom of the garden, the list in my hand, listening to the noisy louries. As the bush thins and goes, will the birds come in to the town gardens for refuge, as happens in Britain?

A team of black men are working in Ayrton R.'s swimming bath, which has developed a crack. I am listening to the talk and laughter as I have done half my life, from outside, not part of it. But in the Training Centre I was part of it, and never thought about the colour of anyone's skin.

'A fairly dizzying business, this,' I say, 'swooping from the verandahs to the grass-roots and back again.'

'White master and white madam, watching black people work,' says Ayrton R. 'Whether you like it or not.'

'Would you say that patch of rape down there is bigger than it was last year?'

'Hmmmm, yes, I think it is. Well, that's all right.'

In my mind's eye that paradise of garden slowly submerges under a sea of green mealies and rape. Well, it is certainly the way of the world. Only a week before I was reading how two female explorers travelled across the Gobi desert – that was before it was criss-crossed by military roads – and came on a wonderful walled garden, all flowering trees, plants, and the splashings of water, a paradise in the midst of leagues of stony dusty emptiness. They returned that way some months later. A minor war had destroyed the garden, and all that remained were hillsides full of charred trees and fouled water channels. But: one of the prettiest gardens in London grew vegetables right through the War (Second World) and on the day the War ended began the work of restoring lawns and pools and roses.

'Who do you think will be living in this house in thirty years' time?' I ask, not meaning to be abrasive.

Ayrton R. is terribly upset. 'I hope I will.'

Our eyes travel up past his house and on up the hill to the houses of the new rich black class. We are both thinking that it would not be Dorothy or George or their children who would buy this house, nor the men working in the swimming bath.

This poem criticises the new black rich class.

The Vengeance of the Poor Man
You treat me like dirt,
Pull, push and kick me,
With boots soiled with mud,
And call me a filthy wretch.
When I am dead and buried,
Your deeds will tear your heart.

Your farms, wild and bushy,
I've tamed, fenced and ploughed;
The yield I gather you sell
To spend the cash alone.
When I am dead and buried,
Your deeds will tear your heart.

Your cows I dip and milk,
Your horses shoe and brush,
Your sheep I feed and tend,
Yet I live on crumbs.
When I am dead and buried,
Your deeds will tear your heart.

In your sumptuous house
I toil and sweat for you,
Yet in the heart of Harare
You see a stranger in me.
When I am dead and buried,
Your deeds will tear your heart.

In hotels that glitter,
On fatty steaks you dine,
Honey your tongue with oozy puddings,
And sink your frame on cosy beds.
When I am dead and buried,
Your deeds will tear your heart.

My Kufa is bony ridged,
Your Gutsa is round and plump,
Dull and feeble is Kufa,
Bouncing with energy is Gutsa.
When I am dead and buried,
Your deeds will tear your heart.

S. J. Nondo (From *Tso Tso*)

Gutsa: as it sounds. Kufa: associations of death, deprivation. Ayrton R. says, 'I suppose one ought to be pleased that it's not just the whites who are the villains. But I don't think I am.'

ON THE VERANDAHS

Someone says that Smith, asked in the States what he thought about the black government, replied that the whites had underestimated the intelligence of the Africans. Everyone is delighted with this little morality tale.

Street children in Harare – gangs of petty criminals, as well as ordinary kids, are playing games based on their traditional stories of hare, tortoise and the other animals. They keep the structure of the tales, the plot, but the characters are called J. R., Bobby, Sue Ellen, and so on.

A man who has been at a celebration for the successful building of more Blair toilets, reports that they are taking off, even in the more remote places, because they are status symbols. 'It is salutary to meditate on the theme of how much of human progress has been dependent on "I have a Blair toilet, but you don't have a Blair toilet."'

The Minister of Justice was in prison for ten years under Smith, tortured, beaten. He is planning to abolish the death penalty, and 'they' say he is a good man and concerned about the prisoners. 'I know what it's like,' he is supposed to have said. The dissidents who were in prison at the amnesty at the time of the Unity Accord, and not let out because they had committed crimes of violence are, it is said, shortly to be released. There are no political prisoners in the Zimbabwe jails. Everyone I ask says, 'No, conditions are good. We are doing all right. We don't have to be ashamed like South Africa, or Zambia.' 'How is the food?' 'I've never seen an overfed prisoner,' was one reply.

THE WINDS OF HISTORY

'What is the most dangerous job in Zimbabwe? "Minister for Internal Affairs: your conscience will kill you."'

We were talking about the man who ran the prison outside Salisbury during the War of Liberation, when so many people were hanged, beaten, tortured. 'No, you can't blame the prison governor, he was only doing his job, it's the Minister who is responsible.'

But it is probably a mistake to imagine responsible officials with consciences made swollen and tender by remorse.

In London during the 1950s were numbers of men who headed the Liberation movements of British Africa's colonies. All were poor and many were unable to return home, where they could expect to be put at once into prison, if they had not already escaped from prison. Some kept themselves fed on post office jobs, ever a life-line for people educated above their job possibilities. Others subsisted on hand-outs from well-wishers. There were households where these men could get a meal and meet revolutionaries from other parts of Africa.

My visitors included a school teacher Orton Chirwa who would shortly return to liberated Malawi but there he would spend many years imprisoned by that cruel man President Banda. He is still in prison; a future President; some future Ministers; a trade union leader who would soon die of malaria; a man who, on returning home to the struggle, would spend time in a British jail and then, on Liberation, be made Minister for Economic Affairs but was imprisoned again, as a threat to his country. He was in prison seven years, mostly in solitary. And, too, a youthful hero, round, sweet, radiant with idealism, the pet of all the older men for he was a poet and often moved to spontaneous Odes to Freedom, Liberty, and Justice.

Roll on the years, not to say decades, and this former idealist poet and I are in the kitchen of a farmhouse in Devon. Improbably, but that is another story.

He is now a fat man glistening with success. He is Minister

for Internal Affairs in one of the more conspicuously unsuccessful of the former colonies.

I am particularly pleased to run into him, for only last week I was talking to the man who – now again at liberty and lecturing to the universities of America on African affairs – spent the seven years in prison. As it happened, one of these years was in a prison in the territory of this Minister: another fairly improbable story, but Africa is full of surprises.

'Do you remember M.?' I enquire.

'How could I not remember that very fine comrade?'

'Did you know he was in prison for seven years?'

'I believe I did hear something of the kind.'

'Did you know that for a year he was in one of your prisons?'

'Really? Oh – I am surprised to hear that.'

'As it happened he shared a cell for some months with——' I mentioned the name of the current President of yet another African country.

'President L.? Yes, I heard that he too had been in prison. In the same cell? That must have been nice for them, to be together.'

'M. told me that the British prison he was in before Liberation was a holiday resort compared with your prison, which nearly killed him and President L.'

We stood facing each other, while the Devon spring rain darkened the windows. We were far indeed from the hot skies of Africa.

His eyes had become evasive. He sighed. He glanced at his watch but decided ancient friendship was due another minute.

'Ah, if we knew when we were young how cruel life can be . . .' And he gazed mournfully back through the mists of time at our youthful enthusiasms.

'But,' I persisted. 'Your prisons. Surely you must know how terrible they are?'

His eyes hardened, almost certainly on the thought, Once a trouble-maker always a trouble-maker. Then he allowed himself to be overtaken by tears. 'I often say to my wife, my dear, I say to her, if we had known in the dawn of our struggle what we know now – ah, life is cruel, life is a cruel cruel thing.'

'Not as cruel as your prisons where our old friend M. and President L. nearly died.'

'Sometimes I think there is some kind of curse that turns all our wishes into their opposites.'

'Just a minute. You are Minister for Internal Affairs, aren't you? Well then! *You* are responsible for your prisons.'

'And suddenly you are told you are responsible for the suffering of old friends.'

'Well, why don't you improve the conditions in your prisons? There were days they didn't get anything to eat at all. They didn't even have a blanket. They . . .'

'Cruel . . . cruel . . .' and his eyes shifted over the whitewashed wall he was facing, looking for some place of consolation or comfort.

'*You* are Minister for Internal Affairs.'

'I am glad we have spoken of these things. Sometimes I think my subordinates do not tell me what they should. I am grateful to you.' And with this he smiled, but wanly, because of the sadness we both knew ruled Life. He shook his head, gave a brief sobbing laugh, which was cut short by a glance at his watch. He hurried out of the kitchen to his car which nearly filled the country lane.

One may imagine asking Genghis Khan, 'How do you feel about killing twenty million people?'

'But it wasn't my fault,' he would say indignantly. 'I was nothing but a straw blown in the winds of history.'

POLITICS

In 1956 when I visited Southern Rhodesia and Northern Rhodesia, the 40,000 or so Tonga then living on the shores of the Zambesi river were being moved from their villages on the river bank. Because they most passionately did not want to leave their homes they were forced into lorries, sometimes at gun-point, and driven away to high dry grounds miles away, and there dumped to get on as best they could. Many died. This operation was not one the governments in question could be proud of. The enforced migration of the river Tonga was because of the shortly-to-be completed Kariba dam, and was a big issue with the then young national movements of Southern Rhodesia, Northern Rhodesia, Nyasaland. Countless political speeches were made to audiences who cried Shame, Shame, and groaned and even wept. There were riots. There were petitions. The white liberals of the time (or 'Kaffir-lovers') were eloquent. The bad treatment of the river Tonga was a symbol of everything wrong with white government.

When in 1989 I told people at the Training Centre I was about to visit the Tonga, they said, 'You don't want to go *there*.' 'They are primitive people.' 'They wear skins and sleep in the ashes of their fires.' I said I had friends who actually knew the Tonga, and they live in huts and wear clothes, but the response was, 'Then the clothes must be the ones collected from us for charity.'

It is true the river Tonga are as poor as any people I saw in Zimbabwe. They are thin and some are stunted. Their villages are shabby. (Not however the villages of the Chiefs, which are of fine big huts, well built.) The lives of the Tonga since they were taken from their land, their shrines, and the graves of their ancestors, have been hard, have been painful, a struggle year in, year out, and from season to season. Unable to fish, removed from the rich alluvial soil that produced two or three crops a year, they tried plants that withstand dryness, like millet, rapoka and other small grains, but flocks of quelea birds waited for these to be ripe and even when women and children stood for days and weeks banging bits of iron and saucepans, the birds descended in clouds so thick they darkened the sky, and ate up everything, as thorough as a swarm of locusts. The quelea are those multitudinous flocks that we watch swirling so attractively about on our television screens. Then the Tonga tried maize, but had to reckon with elephants, who love maize. The elephants had visited just before we did, and had devastated the fields.

These were near the villages behind Binga, which is on the

other end of the Kariba lake away from the Kariba township on its hills, with its tourist hotels and tours and tour guides – quite one of the most attractive places in Zimbabwe, where you think these are shores in Greece or Sicily, wild pale rocky hills and islands and the blue water and the blue sky, and with all the attractions of elephants who appear even in the town itself, or herds of buffalo, and birds and buck . . . these shores and their delights are for the visitors who bring in essential foreign currency, and take photographs of the game, and on the lake itself, of crocodiles and hippos.

But crocodiles tear the frail nets of Binga's fishermen, and hippos threaten their boats.

Binga is expanding fast. It consists of several acres of small two- and three-room houses of the kind described as medium-density housing, and here set at angles in the thick pinky-white dust where soon gardens will spring up. The air smells of donkeys and goats and cows, and roosters wake you at their appointed times through the night. It was full moon in Binga. Outside many of the little houses flickered the cooking fires found more attractive than the kitchens and stoves favoured by the whites. Binga is crowded with every kind of Aid worker. They are a dedicated lot. They would have to be. For one thing the temperature can stand at over a hundred for days at a time. To get there you drive miles on a dirt road that demands serious vehicles, like landrovers.

Electricity was soon to arrive in Binga: the great power lines were in place, ready to come to life. People will no longer have to sleep at eight-thirty, their eyes strained by candlelight. A new hospital, a fine place, a gift from the United States, was just finished. It is a high-tec hospital, and needs electricity to work as planned. But this electricity will not benefit the villages. The great dam which deprived the Tonga of their homes has not benefited them. The lake does not irrigate the land around its long shoreline: Kariba is a vast lake, like a sea. I can recommend travellers to visit Kariba, for there is nothing like it anywhere else in the world. But do not visit the river Tonga, for they will break your heart.

We sat in the shade with the Tonga fishermen under great

trees like green towers, on the Tonga stools that fetch high prices in the tourist shops. The fishermen tell us their story: two of us speak their language. Settled far from the lake and ordered to become farmers, they did badly, and a few crept back to the shore to catch fish, for their families were starving. At last the authorities stopped arresting them, and they were permitted to make a fishing collective. There are forty of them, and they have four boats. No more fishermen nor boats will be permitted to join the collective. Some children were energetically playing around the huts. Because these children ate fish they were healthy, unlike the apathetic children we had already seen in villages a long way from the shore. But these were not really supposed to be here: the fathers bring them into this man's village, to feed them up, in the school holidays. The fishermen themselves eat little fish: they sell it to pay for their children's schooling, for like every parent in the country they are determined their children will get the education that will admit them to the modern world, far from this poverty.

Because families are not allowed into the fishermen's village, it is men who mend the fishing nets draped everywhere over lines, and which are often torn by the crocodiles. The nets are expensive and a torn net is a tragedy. The fishermen's lives are a guerilla war with crocodiles and hippos, just as their wives miles away fear elephants. The spectral trees that still stand up everywhere in the water, the remains of the forest that was drowned by the rising waters, are a bonus: the fish like the old trunks, and the fishermen row quietly from one dead tree to another, after the fish. But the crocodiles know fish like the dead trees and they are there too.

The fishermen are humorous. They are philosophical. They laugh as they talk of their poverty and the indifference of officials. Told that one of their visitors is a writer, they suggest that their lives should be described because – they seem to feel – if the authorities *really* knew, their hearts would be less hard. They laugh when they tell us how they may not now row their boats across the lake to visit their relatives on the Zambian shore. 'The police there will only talk to us with guns.' 'Passports are not for poor people.' 'Why should I have to get a passport to row half a mile to villages where my own family lives?' One fisherman remarks that he enjoys seeing photographs in the newspapers of Presidents Mugabe and Kaunda embracing with fraternal emotion: it makes him feel so much better about not being able to visit his Zambian family.

These men are the second and third generation away from the people who were forced to move. Asked if the Tonga talk about their past, the reply is that old people do, but the children don't believe their tales.

'Once we lived on the edge of the water: it was a big river then, it was the Zambesi river. We fished and we hunted and we grew three crops a year in the rich soil. Now we grow one crop a year and we are not allowed to hunt – we are sent to prison if we do. And only a few of us may fish.'

Once we lived in Eden where Nature was so kind we hardly needed clothes and fruit fell from the trees. But then an angel with a flaming sword . . .

At the beautiful hospital, that has a Spanish feel to it, with tall curving walls and open-work patterns in the red brick, a perfect building for the climate – designed, for once, by a Zimbabwean architect – we sit in a room with a young woman, Shona, who is responsible for the health of the district. She is highly educated, full of energy. She could get a job anywhere, with her qualifications, but she is here, with the Tonga. This makes her unusual, for it is hard to persuade nurses and teachers out into these remote places. This hospital, designed for thirty-six nurses, still only has eighteen. The doctor, much liked, came to grief through drinking too much, and will not easily be replaced. 'Almost certainly it will be an ex-pat. They don't mind how hard a job is, they take on the dirty jobs. God knows what these remote hospitals and schools would do without them.' 'But,' says this man's interlocutor, 'remember that the ex-pats choose hardship for three or four years and then go back to the flesh-pots. It is understandable these people, experiencing the good life for the first time, find it hard to give it up and sweat it out in the bush somewhere.' 'Why shouldn't they choose hardship for a year or two and then have a good time?' 'Ah but you're forgetting, if you step off the ladder, it's hard to get back on again.'

The young black nurse is clearly thinking that she has better things to do with her time than sit and talk with us. But she is polite, and smiles. 'I treat women who have been malnourished since their conception. You never see women like this in any other part of Zimbabwe. You see an adolescent girl, and then you realize she is a woman with five or six children: she has been dwarfed by bad food. We have terrible problems with childbirth. Ninety per cent of these people have bilharzia. There is still some leprosy. Nearly fifty babies and small children died of malaria this last wet season. Malaria is getting worse. Oh yes, AIDS – I knew you were going to ask.' She makes herself smile. 'We know about AIDS. But it's not the worst thing. Are you surprised I say that? Look, you can tell illiterate people that a mosquito will give them malaria. They can see the mosquito. But you try explaining a sophisticated disease like AIDS. "There is a very small thing, but you can't see it, called a virus, and it can adapt its shape to become like another small thing, which is just a bit bigger and it lives off it and kills it . . . and remember it can take eight years to become fatal." These people don't believe us when we talk about AIDS. We have shelves full of condoms – unused. Yes I see people dying of AIDS all the time but we don't call it AIDS. No we don't routinely test for AIDS – that is regarded as an infringement of the liberty of the individual.' She laughs, but she is angry. I think it is probably a generalized anger: the one we all feel: how can *they* be so stupid? 'They tell me the campaign against AIDS is beginning to work in other parts of the country, but here . . .'

Soon she says she has to go, she must, she'll never get through her work.

We are told that this young woman and a male colleague continuously travel over a large area, exhorting, teaching, holding clinics: that is, when they aren't holding classes and clinics here. 'They never stop working. When I see them I believe everything will be all right, Zimbabwe will make it.'

The Outpatients of this hospital is a large space under trees.

There is a shed-like building where people can sleep if they want, but most prefer the open air. Women come in from the villages to wait for labour to start, or for treatment. They are all, every one, undersized, apathetic. The comparison between them and the exuberant noisy people at the Training Centre hurts. I wonder if they have ever, in their whole lives, eaten plates loaded with sadza and meat and gravy and vegetables.

A young woman sits directly in the dust under a tree. A small child sits quietly beside her. The woman is making a basket. The Tonga baskets must surely be the most beautiful anywhere. Between her thin dusty hands this miraculous thing is coming to life. Inside that head of hers, which seems more like a child's head, and is dusty, are the subtle patterns that her fingers are making. The baskets are famous and sell for two, three, four Zimbabwean dollars, to enthusiasts who travel through the villages. The baskets get sold for another dollar or two to the local shops. But by the time they reach the smart shops in the towns they cost many times more. The Tonga stools are also famous. We sat with a Tonga stoolmaker who squatted in the dust near his fire where tools were pushed to become red hot. Blocks of wood stood about under the trees waiting for him to transform them. A new stool is sometimes buried, to give it a look of age: tourists prefer them like that. This stoolmaker is asking five, six, seven dollars for a stool. It takes him two days to make one, so he earns less than the minimum wage. In the National Gallery in Harare I saw the same stools selling for one hundred, and a hundred and twenty dollars.

Everyone agrees the Tonga are wonderfully artistic. The baskets and stools will find themselves in rooms all over the world, where visitors will say, What a beautiful stool, what a beautiful basket.

The young teachers, in whose house I am staying, have bought a few things to take back to the Mid-West of America, as presents.

They are religious, and work very hard. Other teachers in other houses are not religious and also work hard.

One ex-pat teacher, from near Chicago, is appalled because

most of a mathematics class don't understand what she has
been teaching. 'They sit there, it seems they understand – then
you discover they haven't understood a thing.' Eight of the
class of forty she believes have a chance of passing O-level if
properly coached. It is holiday time, but every day she drives
herself on terrible roads to the school, and there is met by the
eight pupils who have come in from their villages, some walking miles. She sits with them for hours, going over and over
the problems. This same girl tells me a story. In Harare she
was standing for the three or four hours that it is customary to
have to wait for anything of a bureaucratic nature. She was the
only white person in a line of hundreds. The young black clerk
who was pushing people's fingers into ink to make prints did
not look up at the faces of the people who moved past her.
When she saw the white hand, she did look up, then said
sharply, 'Have you washed your hands?' 'No.' The clerk had
said this to no one else. 'Then go and wash them.'

This incident is a mirror of the arbitrary white treatment of
blacks in the old days.

It must not be thought that all the ex-pat teachers or Aid
workers are useful. I was in a village when a young Englishman
who was working in the fields with the villagers came over.
He was leaving that day and he was miserable. 'It was the best
thing I ever did, coming here. It's taught me everything. They
are a wonderful people.'

I asked the Extension Worker who had brought me about
this youth. Some villagers were there. He said, 'They send us
these young people. They are supposed to be teaching us. They
want to help us. But we have to teach them what they are
supposed to be teaching us. When they arrive they have no
manners, they don't know how to behave. What do they learn
in their schools? This one had a breakdown. Sometimes they
drink because they are so lonely. They find it hard to be friends
with us.'

The woman in whose hut the young man had been living,
with her son, said, 'But he is not a bad person. He wants to be
kind.'

The Extension Worker: 'These young people get paid to come

here and teach us. But we don't get paid for teaching them everything.'

The hostess woman, who is large, literally shining with health, has suddenly become someone else: she has become the young man. Every bit of her body pleads as she stands in a curve, head poked forward, chin thrust out, eyes moving from one face to the next in a mix of aggression and apology. She is the poor young man who can be seen at this very moment, a forlorn figure, holding out his hand that has a store biscuit in it, to a small child who is shyly taking it. Becoming herself, the woman stands laughing. Everyone laughs with her.

LOVE OR SOMETHING. I

In a remote part of Zimbabwe, two American ex-pat teachers live together in a minute house on the edge of a dusty village, near a school that is built in the middle of a vast dusty space. They both come from well-off families, in a large city in the Mid-West. They are used to an easy life. One evening, having finished supper, they are sitting side by side at the little table they eat their meals off, correcting homework by candlelight. There is a knock on the door. They open it and in step an old man and two young men: a local minor Chief with his attendants. 'Drat,' think the girls. 'It is already eight-thirty, and it is bedtime, if we want to get up at five tomorrow.' The candle is subsiding in a puddle of grease, and they quickly light another. 'Come in, come in,' they cry, 'sit down, take a seat, would you like a beer – tea – coffee – mineral water?' The old man sits, and his two young men stand behind him.

The girls know the old man. He is the father of two of their pupils.

'I have come on a serious matter,' says the old man.

The girls exchange looks: this must mean that it is Gwenda he wants to speak to, for his daughter is a girl who often gets into trouble with her teacher, Gwenda.

The girl who is not Gwenda discreetly withdraws to the kitchen where she stands correcting exercises by the light of another candle.

Gwenda smiles encouragingly.

'I have come to ask you to be my second wife,' says the old man.

'Excuse me?'

'I love you. You must be my wife,' he insists.

At last: 'Do you think we could work out a relationship?'

'Yes. I love you.'

'But your first wife would be unhappy. She would be jealous.'

'Jealousy is unknown among us.'

Oh yes? – the girl in the next room, eavesdropping, can positively be heard thinking: the house is so small everything done and said can be heard by everyone. This makes Gwenda even more nervous.

'But you are older than my father.'

'That does not matter. In our culture it is not important.'

Gwenda stands with an unopened beer bottle in her hand, staring at him. Then, an inspiration: as she speaks she knows she is saved. 'But my parents would never hear of it, they would never agree to my living so far from them. They would not give their permission.'

'In that case,' says the old man, 'I have no more to say.'

The beer bottles are opened. The two young men are urged to sit down. The two young teachers and their guests converse for an hour or so, and then all agree yes, they will be good friends.

LOVE OR SOMETHING. II

It is in the same little house, the same two girls, and about the same time at night. A commotion outside. They draw back a curtain. A young man they know professionally, a community worker, is staggering about in the dust, drunk. 'Gwenda,' he howls, 'Gwenda.'

'But I haven't done anything to encourage him,' protests Gwenda, to her colleague's satiric look.

'Don't you dare go out,' she says.

Gwenda is not, as might be thought, an extraordinary beauty. She is pretty. So is her friend, who has also had her opportunities.

But Gwenda is kind-hearted: if not succoured, the young man will probably fall down.

'Well now,' she says smartly, 'it is time you were in bed.'

'Gwenda,' he shouts, embracing her, 'I've had a terrible day. I've just been helping to rebury six Freedom Fighters who were killed in this village. I love you. I want to have a white girl-friend.'

She pushes him off, with, 'But I don't want a black boyfriend. Inter-cultural marriages are very difficult. Besides, I have a boy-friend at home.'

'Yes, yes. You must think about it. I love you.'

She says severely, 'You are very selfish. You have to learn to see other people's points of view.' And goes indoors.

Next day they meet in the supermarket. It is a small super-market, which you would easily mistake for a village shop. It is not a place where you can avoid unfortunate encounters.

He says, 'They tell me I behaved unkindly to you last night.'

'Yes, you did.'

'Then I'm very sorry. I feel really sad this morning.'

'Your apology is accepted.'

A Jesuit priest said, 'The Feast of All Souls has a new mean-ing. The souls are the souls of the dead fighters, killed in the War, and left unburied.'

All over Zimbabwe teams of former Freedom Fighters are being sent to areas where they fought, to try and remember where fighters were killed and carelessly buried, or not buried at all. The corpses or bones are buried with appropriate rites. It is believed by many that the country is full of dissatisfied and vengeful ghosts, and it is they who are responsible for Zimbabwe's many problems.

TWO WHITE FARMERS AND
THE BOOK TEAM

We are back with the farmer who last year sang us his hymns
to the soil, and we are watching gangs of seasonal workers
plant tobacco. This is far from the chancy operation of the old
days, which depended on the coming of the rains. Pierced
pipes and long hoses now make planting possible weeks
earlier. 'Water, we have so much water now,' cries the farmer,
meaning the new dam, full because of the good rain, and
already irrigating the farms around here. This soil is producing
three crops a year. 'Soilmining,' says the farmer, irritable
because of his conflict, loving real earth, but working with this,
which is like brick dust and soaked with chemicals. This earth
is no pleasure to look at or to touch. Not in this field are we
likely to see the farmer bend to lift a handful of earth and
marvel at it – an act of worship. But he is pointing at another
farm just across a river. 'Now there's a farmer! *He* never wastes
time lying awake at night wondering what Nature's going to
wham us with. His farm is really high-tec, they've got everything, you should see it. I tell you, Israel's got nothing on us
in this district . . . yes of course he's white. The Affs don't have
any feel for this kind of farming, and good for them. I'd like to
believe they never will.'

He goes on, irritable and discouraged in a way I remember
from *then* because of 'trouble' with his workers.

It was all his own fault, said he: he brought it on himself. Last
season he suddenly couldn't stand seeing the female casual
workers sitting on the floor of the work-shed hour after hour
tying up tobacco, with their babies on their backs. Eight hours
a day. It was insane. He offered them a crèche and two trained
nurses to run the crèche so the women would not be burdened.
The women refused, saying they wouldn't trust their babies to
strange women, because of the danger of witchcraft. 'Witchcraft! It's unreasonable! It doesn't make sense! It's irrational! I
tried again this year but they wouldn't hear of it, and there's

bad feeling but they won't tell me why. All I know is, I'm some kind of a villain.'

I asked the Book Team about this. There we sat, five of us, under a tree, talking about the affairs of the world. Both Sylvia and Talent took it for granted that the farmer, being white, wanted a crèche because the women would be more efficient. I said it was not so: he was upset because of the over-burdened women. They wouldn't have that. 'Do you realize you at once assume the worst just because he is a white farmer? You won't credit the whites with any human feelings at all?' It was no good. When I persisted, they said, as if this was proof of the man's illwill and not his incomprehension, 'And anyway, he is starting at too high a level. He should have made enquiries in the farm village and found women who are already trusted by all the other women. It wouldn't be easy, because of course they don't trust each other. They are from different tribes.' 'But,' I ask, 'handled differently, do you think he could get them to accept a crèche?' A long discussion: on the whole, probably not. Cathie was unhappy because of the witchcraft and wanted the others to agree it is being exaggerated. But Talent and Sylvia and Chris insisted that witchcraft is a serious problem, and won't go away just by being ignored.

I took the original incident and the comments of the Book Team to the Coffee Farmer.

'I wonder how often good intentions on the part of us whites go wrong out of sheer bloody ignorance. I'd never have thought of going to find a woman in the village and talk to her about setting up a crèche. Witchcraft wouldn't have crossed my mind. Why should it? Why don't they ever come and tell us when we go wrong about this kind of thing.'

White farmers are villains – and that's the end of it. It is true that some are not the most endearing people in the world. But what of the others, who are trying hard? Too bad about them. I think of Alan Paton's 'I am afraid that when they turn to loving, we will have turned to hating.' The word 'loving' is not one I would choose. But I remember arguing with a black friend of mine who wanted to preserve a picture of white farmers as cruel savages: he retreated back and back until he cried out,

'But they don't love their homes as we do.' But if there is one thing that has distinguished the whites, right from the beginning, it is love for the country. I said this . . . he could not bear it. I think of Proust's duchess (I think it was) who, when faced with some unpalatable truth, cried out, 'Then at least don't tell me about it!' There is a point in political feelings when some invisible balance turns and thereafter people don't want to be told about it. *Basta*. Enough.

The blacks talk about the whites as if there is, and always has been, a layer of people who remain the same, clinging on to privileges no matter what. Yes, some left to Take the Gap, but those who remain are those who have always been here . . . but in fact there has never been a homogenous, stable, white minority. Since the Occupation in 1890, 600,000 whites have passed through the country. At the height of White Supremacy, under Smith, the figure was 250,000. In my time, *then*, there were 100,000 or 150,000 whites. Only a few, some farmers, civil servants, politicians, businessmen, were permanent. The rest came, and then went. They left because they hated being part of the white oppression, or because they were bankrupt. Few blacks even now would be prepared to see any white as poor: in the past the gap was too great; all whites were rich. In the 1930s, when young men came out from Britain because of unemployment and the Slump, to take any kind of job they could get in Rhodesia, and often failed, and went Home again – that is, if they could get relatives to send them their fares – returning to unemployment, drink, every kind of demoralization, they were seen by the blacks as rich.

A Catholic lay-worker told me she had been given a trip to Ireland, and had been astonished to see poor people, 'people as poor as we are', giving money for missions and church work. 'Where did you think the money came from, then?' 'Oh,' she said gaily, 'I thought everyone white was rich. I felt really ashamed when I saw those poor people counting out their coins to give to us.'

A SAD, TRUE STORY

A black girl, clever, ambitious, with parents proud of her, passes exam after exam, and gets a scholarship that takes her to the United States, to university. No sooner does she reach there, than in every mail there are letters, not only from her family, and her clan, but from her village and even nearby villages, demanding money, clothes, goods of every kind. Also, books. She has set up a library in her village, and donated a great many books, sending some from the States. This has been an expensive business: the United States postage is not cheap, and the Zimbabwe Customs charges on every parcel according to whim. She appeals to various foundations for books, because her stipend does not allow much for extras. Still the requests come. She does her best to meet them. She lives more frugally than most students, eats little, dresses poorly, because of what she has to send home. Driven to desperation, she puts an appeal in a local newspaper, for donations of clothes, and money for her village. A representative of Zimbabwe in Washington warns her that she is blackening the name of Zimbabwe, and if she does it again, she will lose her scholarship.

Her straitened lifestyle makes it hard for her to have the usual student social life. She is lonely. At home she has been close to a sister. With difficulty she saves up money to pay this girl's air fare to come for a visit. The girl arrives, takes one look at the small flat, the meagre food, the simple clothes of her sister and starts abusing her for deceiving her. 'You have deceived us all.' What had she expected? Well, obviously, the same as she has seen in 'Dallas', 'The Colbys','Dynasty', which is how people live in the States. She stays three days, then insists on going back to her village in Zimbabwe. The poor student is depressed: it takes her a year to get over the shock of this rejection. She decides she can never return to Zimbabwe, there is no way she can satisfy these demands. Or perhaps she should become a nun?

The same girl, invited to a Thanksgiving dinner by a teacher, and asked to say Grace, prayed, 'Please, God, forgive us for having as much food on this table as would feed my village for a whole week.' Some of her fellow guests were offended, quote the story as an example of bad manners and ingratitude.

I told this story to a Jesuit Father who was silent for a while and then said, 'Quite soon those villagers will be saying, as they sometimes do to me, "Forgive us, Father, it was our ignorance."'

But surely the question is, how after all this long time can this ignorance exist?

The answer has to be that the blacks have put their thoughts of the whites, their beliefs about the whites, into some region of legend or myth, where nothing has to be earned.

When sitting alone on the verandah on the mountainside that overlooks mountains and rivers and lakes, a young black man came cautiously up from the trees, and, smiling, sat down with me. I ordered tea. His name is Never Harare. Why Never? He believes it is because it took him a long time to get born. What is his real name? Ungana: he is surprised I ask. Although he has done several years in school, he has one O-level, and he is now a seasonal worker. He speaks good English. He is very intelligent. He is going to apply to become a policeman, but he hasn't got the qualifications. Why, then, apply? I recognize the look on his face: *It might happen, mightn't it*? I ask what he would like to be, if he could have his heart's desire. This is not a question you may ask in Britain without expecting an embarrassed smirk. In Africa, not burdened with such inhibitions, the question at once opens the door into . . . in this case, and at once, fantasy. He brightens: he thinks I have a magic wand and can give him his heart's desire. He would like to be a farmer. I ask why he doesn't apply to be given land under the settlement schemes. He becomes limp with disappointment: what he meant was, a farmer like the white farmers, and live the life of the verandahs. Recovering, at least a little, he enquires what it would cost to buy a farm like this one? Thousands, many thousands. We sit looking cautiously at each other, both making adjustments and assessments. I am trying to find out if he thinks he could farm without any experience, let alone without capital, and be ready to deal with bank loans and overdrafts. I have in my mind's eye the farmers of this area, with their expertise, many with a background of farming – a father, brother, or relative in one of the counties of Britain, with, many of them, money of their own . . . as we say. How then does this young man with the hopeful bright face see them? He doesn't. He wants to live this life, just like all the others who were promised it – they thought, when they were still fighting in the bush. How does he see himself? As one who has been made promises. If he were actually here, sitting on this verandah as its owner, how does he imagine himself? Well, of course, living as the white farmers . . . but he knows in another part of his mind, that the whole farm would at once fill with his relatives to the tenth generation and he would not in any case live the life of the verandahs. It doesn't matter. He is dreaming . . . when he walked up out of the bush to sit down by me, the farmer himself having driven off somewhere, he was walking into a dream, and now he is living it, drinking tea on this verandah with an old woman who says, What is your heart's desire? even if she is not going to fulfil what he hears as a promise.

If I said, Never Harare, I happen to have with me the title deeds of a farm even better than this one, and here they are, he would find nothing impossible. The whites are all rich, and sometimes they are kind-hearted. They may impulsively bestow a farm on some young friend, if in a good mood.

On my visit in 1956 I read novels by black writers – in those days all men – and every novel had in it a scene where the hero was invited by a white employer to come into the house. 'Lie down on this nice bed, eat this nice food, and here are some nice clothes.' Thereafter the hero lived like Oliver Twist, a favoured protégé, to become, at last – though this process was not described – rich and powerful. One minute a poor boy living rough, the next the favoured son or godson of a white benefactor who is rich.

Before Never Harare walked away into the trees I asked him if he ever thought about the fighters who were killed in the Bush War. I did not say, they died that you might be free – but

that was in my mind. He smiled – polite, nervous. He did not
know why I asked this, but, to please me, said he liked to think
of them. Then: 'I did not know any Comrades. I was at school.'

THE FIGHTERS

Two veterans of the Bush War are talking in the sardonic but
wistful way of their kind.

'General So-and-so said the other day . . .'

'General? General? There are Generals and Generals.'

'I mean a real General, from *our* War.'

'I see, you mean a General.'

'The General said, why don't the young respect us? I said,
It is because they don't know you. There's a generation who
cannot remember our War. He said to me, But we won Zimbabwe for them. I said, But we Boys in the Bush are history
now. He said, But what were we fighting for? I said, Yes, I
often wonder myself.'

'Virtue has to be its own reward,' said the second veteran.

'Ah, I see. I hadn't thought of that. When I see the General
next I'll tell him, General, I shall say, virtue is its own reward.
He'll say, Shit to that, I want to be in the history books with
full honours. I'll say, We might be in the history books, but are
these kids going to read them?'

A priest who ran a mission far from Salisbury all through the
Bush War says, 'The boys used to drop in when the Security
Forces were looking the other way. They wanted an evening
of being ordinary. We had a meal, they drank, they danced –
had a bit of a party. They taught me how to jive – want to see
me? They were very young men, boys some of them, sixteen,
seventeen.'

Another man who saw the Freedom Fighters often, playing box
and cox with them and the government troops said: 'The War

didn't end because of the bravery of the Boys in the Bush. They were demoralized, drinking themselves silly every night because their lives were so hard. The War ended for economic reasons – sanctions, and because everyone was fed up with it.'

A former Freedom Fighter says, 'They made use of us. We fought for them. We listened to what they said and we believed them. Suddenly no one believes it any longer.'

A book called *White Man, Black War* by a white combatant is just out. It is like the books by American soldiers in Vietnam, full of horror at what they were part of. The author was whole-heartedly for the whites, but he has had a conversion. What he admired he now hates, all evil was on the white side, all the blacks blameless. This is not an uncommon psychological switch, but what is interesting is his castigation of the whites now, presented as – every one of them – arrogant, racist, ill-wishing the blacks. I know that many such must exist, but on this trip I haven't met any. Whites who were like this, have become good citizens. Considering that only six years have done it, what changes can another six or ten achieve?

The Freedom Fighters in the War of Liberation were advised by the ngangas, who told them how to conduct their campaigns. Is this fact in the history books? It is in the books written by serious historians. What is taught as history to that boy or girl in the secondary modern school? Unless they are lucky in their teachers, political slogans, political myths. But if you are talking to a fighter about the Bush War he or she will give credit to the ngangas.

I say this to an ex-combatant from Smith's armies, and he says, 'The ngangas were advising us too. Probably that's why we lost.'

An evening party. The guest of honour is a female Chef. Although many women fought with the Boys in the Bush, few became Chefs. Some have turned out well, some badly – just like the men. The people in this room all know each other well, and this Chef was a friend long before she became a Chef or even before she was a fighter.

'They' say she didn't want to be a Chef, but Comrade Mugabe said, 'It's an order.' He likes her because she speaks her mind and he is surrounded by sycophants.

She talks through dinner and then afterwards, while we sit about drinking coffee and Zimbabwe wine. I had been told, 'She has to choose her words these days . . .' but she talks as people do who normally watch their words, but now need not, because they are with friends.

She was talking about the camps in the bush, where she had been first as a girl, then as the War went on and on, as a young woman. Her formative years had been with the guerillas. Her job was to teach girls and boys deprived by the War of schooling, and, too, young men and women who had escaped from the miseries of village war-time living, and who would have to face competitive life after the War – without training. How very far ordinary life must have seemed, then, in those classes held under the trees, always alert for an enemy.

Her talk sounded for minutes at a time like an official history of the War, full of licensed phrases like, War against Imperialism, Forces of the People, but then other phrases and words came in, and soon the Authorized Version had given way to her own thoughts and words. She was remembering . . .

Certain official figures, now presented as perfect, with the finality of statues . . . Such and such a famous soldier, now a Father of the Revolution, the best soldier of them all, knew nothing about politics – he despised politics. One was always drunk . . . Another's behaviour to women soldiers was so bad they had to be hidden until he went away. Once a woman Commander said to this man, who had sent to her demanding a girl for the night, 'I am responsible for these girls. They are here to fight for freedom, not to be whores for you.' Then she talked about 'the trials' in the camps, modelled on the 'treason trials' of the great communist exemplars. These trials went on in the bush, in the wilderness, people hanged and shot because they were convicted of – well, what? Treason, of course, but it was a power struggle, that was the point. 'It was really about power,' she said and said again – had to say, and say again, distressed, unable to stop talking. All those Comrades, good Comrades, had been killed and it was for their suspected ambition.

The room in that quiet Harare suburb seemed full of the ghosts of young men – very young men, boys really, murdered by their comrades to the accompaniment of judicial phrases, the judgements of the People. How many? No one knows how many now. These killings went on in the camps, dozens of soldiers, perhaps hundreds. That was a time when 'now I think we all went mad'.

These murdered people were one of the bricks or stones that had built this 'communist' state, just as long ago the corpse of a sacrificed person, later an animal, was put into the foundations of a temple or sacred building, a cornerstone.

Listening to her, who, presumably, had been at least 'on the side of' the killers, we all had to reflect how we have become accustomed to barbarity. She had been sucked into some madness, as millions of people all over the world have been, like being dragged over a waterfall, and now there was left only, 'now I think we all went mad'.

Next day the evening was discussed – a strange occasion, it had been. Why, now, so many years after the events, did she have to talk and talk, the way an animal slowly licks and licks a sore place.

Then slowly details hardly noticed came forward . . . for instance she had remarked that she was wearing a pair of trousers allotted to her from a common store of clothes, after the clothes she had on were blown off her by blast from a bomb. She could not make herself throw them away, those old green pants that had had their day.

What we had been listening to all evening was the monologue of the old soldier about a time so vivid, every minute so strong in memory nothing can ever be as real again. How could I not have recognized it at once? After all, I had been brought up with it, with my father talking, talking, about *his* war. It suddenly occurred to me – and why had it not before? – that all the men and women in the machinery of government, Big

Chefs and Little Chefs, have come out of camps, out of the War in the bush, and they spend at least all their working lives together. War bound them, and memories of war bind them now. They sit talking, Do you remember? – but there is no need to ask, for they know they all remember and cannot forget. A great deal of their talk is about that war even when it is apparently about something else: this is always true of people who have been scarred by violent emotions. Nothing will ever happen to these people as powerful as what they lived through, before many of them were even twenty years old.

That evening a curtain had been briefly lifted for us on the loneliness of the old soldier, whose war is in the past, and now the world is full of new people and they don't want to listen.

But what is most interesting, is the future. The official histories, the Authorized Versions, are given out as fact, are part of official ceremonies, taught in schools. A whole generation of young people have been brought up on them, as the sacred Foundation of Zimbabwe. But the people who fought in that war and know what it was like are in their twenties and thirties. Soon at least some will be writing their memories, autobiographies, reminiscences. Then the truth about the War will be exposed, and there will be two versions, the official histories and the truth. It must be obvious to everyone that this is going to happen. Yet the Authorized Version continues to be insisted on, to the point where a novelist writing about the War mildly enough, suggesting that the Comrades were not always perfect, was attacked by all the critics. In fact there is already a verbal history and an official one and, inevitably, the Chefs will be made to look silly.

If there was ever a case of, *How do these politicians' minds work?* – then it is this one.

EDUCATION

I am interviewed by a clever young woman, product of the University of Zimbabwe. She was one of the best students of her year. I am so impressed I mention her to various people, and what they say adds up to this: She wouldn't do so well now. First, she is white. Second, she is not political. Third, she is a woman. Any one of these, by themselves, all right: put them together and she wouldn't make it. I mustn't think this is what Zimbabwe is like everywhere. On the whole it is good-natured, friendly, easy-going. No, the bigotry is where the Stalinists are entrenched. And by the way, have I thought how extraordinary it is, the white politico who identifies with black racism? They hate and persecute their own kind, while, of course, complaining about racism.

Nor are some ideas from the past going to be shifted easily. Already a generation of young people studying literature or history have been imbued with Stalinist, or socialist-realist, ideas. An historian, the father of Rhodesian–Zimbabwean history, told a class in the university that he had made a mistake in certain interpretations. The students would have none of it. 'But that's not what we were taught.' 'But I'm telling you, what you were taught is wrong. I wrote that history and now I know parts of it are wrong.' But it was no use: what they knew was history. As marxism, communism, is rejected everywhere, the people who were marxists and communists will remain, but calling themselves something different, and even thinking of themselves as different, but with large blocks of ideas that belong to marxism, to communism, intact and unexamined in their minds.

A friend visiting an American university where history is taught as it was twenty or thirty years ago, said he kept thinking of *Fathers and Sons*, the chapter where Bazarov takes his friend to visit the past in the shape of two little old people who are embodiments of the Enlightenment, unchanged by everything that has happened, living in a dream of past righteousness, triumphant rectitude.

Straws in a Variable Ill Wind

On this trip – not the previous one in 1988 – I have heard the word 'intellectuals' used pejoratively from many different kinds of people.

'What is meant by intellectuals?'

'The students, they are rocking the boat.'

'The dissidents.'

'What dissidents?'

'Oh you know, negative people who criticize.'

Similarly, people talk about 'sell-outs', used as mindlessly as the phrase is here. 'Sold out *what*?' 'If you have to ask then I'm afraid I can't help you.' The 1960s still cast a long shadow.

In Zimbabwe the term comes from the War, when dozens of people were murdered, 'got rid of' because of its power to destabilize the thinking processes. Now it can mean people you disapprove of, not unlike our recent use of the word 'fascist' as an all-purpose term of abuse.

'Sell-out' is often indistinguishable from 'South African spy'. In Zambia, where things fall apart and scapegoats are needed, South African spies are glimpsed everywhere. Eight months ago in Zimbabwe I heard nothing about South African spies but this time some obviously harmless citizens are 'spies'. Of course there are South African spies, but South Africa need never employ spies at all: if the aim is to 'destabilize' its neighbours, their paranoia would be enough to cripple them.

On a road between Bulawayo and Harare, at a road block, a policeman was suspicious because a map was spread on my lap. What did we need a map for? We replied this was not the main road, and therefore we needed a map. Thoughts common to such occasions, such as, that real spies would hardly be likely to spread maps open on their laps, seemed to lack force, faced with the man's furious hostility. That region of romping farce, so useful for the theatre, is because of the contrast between the seriousness (we have to suppose) of the spy processes, and its manifestations lower down; for instance, a petty official told to keep an eye open for spies from The Republic. South Africans abound in Zimbabwe but mostly as tourists. In every place of beauty or interest, which means nearly everywhere, are groups of South Africans taking the air and admiring the view. All of them, when driving on little-frequented roads, would have maps spread open on . . . but already we are in farcical area that characterizes spies and spying.

Tekere is of course in the pay of the South Africans: government propagandists and the C.I.O. spread rumours that he is, and he makes an advantage by joking about it. When Joshua Nkomo was out of favour he was supposed to be a spy. No one believed it. Any effective critic, the student leaders, people who show signs of talent and originality – any or all of them may find themselves suddenly described as South African spies. This is not, as we know, an uncommon thing in totalitarian societies. And envy was ever a great breeder of spies.

There are sane people in high places who try to combat this lunacy. Canaan Banana, at the university, is one. He has just said publicly that Zimbabwe is a democracy and everyone is entitled to say what they think at all times.

The university has been in trouble ever since Liberation. First, it has students. Second, people work in it who think. Third, a great many academics come from other countries with ideas and information. Every kind of effort is made to keep the university subject to the control of the Party, but it is like an ebullient ox that has no intention of being inspanned. The latest restriction causing shame and fury is that people coming to do research must have permits from the Ministry of Internal Affairs. But often this kind of thing is ignored: all the time, in every way, on every level, you see people desperate for the honour of Zimbabwe trying to save it from its own follies. 'One of these days Mugabe will get the point.'

Everyone is uneasy about the new Ministry of Political Affairs. At its top levels the Ministry is staffed by impressive men and women, all young, at least scarcely middle-aged. They are dedicated, efficient. But in a country like Zimbabwe, with not enough trained people, what goes on at lower levels does not necessarily reflect the competence of its Chefs.

Sometimes I think that Chefs in every country formulating policies that sound so brilliant as they enunciate them among clever colleagues, might stop and wonder how these same policies will sound – well, for instance, in the mouths of some local official. 'Why have you got that map on your lap?'

A newspaper editor: 'Mugabe should take the Central Intelligence Office dogs off our heels. You wouldn't notice it because you are a visitor, but they are always around sniffing things out. For instance, a novelist was planning a thriller about a country where a coup was being planned from outside. He talked about his idea to a friend: a few days later the CIO came around and warned him not to write the book; people would think he meant Zimbabwe. So he didn't write it. It is easy to say he should have ignored them. If I lived in Britain I wouldn't take any notice either. But it's no joke when those CIO men drop around for a chat. They know how to scare you. And don't forget the best editor this country ever had – *The Chronicle* in Bulawayo – got the sack. If there's a tricky issue, just when you're thinking, I've got a wife and children to look after, it's funny how the CIO boys just happen to be around, "Let's have a drink and talk things over."'

In London an international expert talks about the disaster of Zambia, the demoralization. 'They are always looking over their shoulders to make sure the secret police aren't listening.' I said I saw nothing like this in Zimbabwe. On the contrary, everyone I met said what they thought at the top of their voices: hard to imagine these exuberant, irreverent, witty people putting up with the Thought Police. 'That's not what I've been told by my people,' she says. 'I reckon Zimbabwe has only a short time to decide whether it's going to be like Zambia. Their culture is authoritarian, it's hierarchical, not easy for them to challenge authority. Big political movements are one thing, but it's another to challenge a petty boss out in the sticks somewhere. There is something in their traditions, or their culture, or their history which makes them helpless when they encounter ours. Our organization gives out money for projects, but part of that money will always be stolen, unless you can arrange for checks all the way – and what example do they get from their leaders? All they see when they look at Harare is the Chefs getting rich on fiddles. And what would happen to them if they complained? And now Mugabe is insisting on a one-party state and then there won't be any opposition at all.'

I asked if she ever went out of Harare when she visited Zimbabwe. She was uncomfortable: 'No, I've never been out of Harare, I'm afraid.'

A poem from *Tso Tso*.

> Strong strings tie my . . . my
> Strong strings tie my tongue tight
> Strong strings tie my taunting
>   tongue straight and silent,
> With no might nor right or curling
>   and lick the doors of its cave-empire.
>
> Tongues! Who thought even tongues
>   could be spiderwebbed silent?
> During those days of blighting bullets
>   amid slogan chants
> Those years of the bloody bayonet
>   to the lull and soothe of 'honest' promises
> Who could ever have the thought –
>   – of those tight cutting strings to masses?
> Tongues-UES-UES-UES-.

S. Kumbirai Rukuni

PATTERNS

I am shown a piece of stone that has the outline of a leaf impressed in it. The leaf is like the little fish on my mantelpiece, its form obstinately preserved, through so many thousands of years. The fish, the leaf, make me think of something that happened in the 1960s, in London. For some reason, I forget why, a group of people got into the habit of meeting most evenings, to sit around my big kitchen table, to talk and drink wine. We were old, and young, and from various parts of the

world. We played this game: every person who sat down was
given a drawing block, and different coloured pencils. We
doodled. I don't know how this game began. I found a heap
of these drawings recently, and at once knew who had drawn
what. We each had a characteristic style, and themes that
repeated night after night, week after week. Some of us got
desperate, trying to escape this cage of necessity, that made us
produce the same patterns, no matter how hard we tried to
change. One man, brought up a Roman Catholic, who then
became an atheist, drew tight, small patterns, and in every
one, somewhere, was a cross. There was no way he could avoid
that cross. When he refused to let his pencil make a cross, we
pointed out that the pattern of the drawing was a cross. A
young girl, in one of those psychological labyrinths it seems
impossible one will ever get out of, drew convoluted knot-like
patterns like intricately braided tresses. She could not draw in
any other way. When she put her pencil to the paper, it
seemed, of its own accord, to make these black, swirling knots.
A woman then at the height of her life, full of content and
optimism, drew patterns of leaves and flowers. She tried to
draw different things, but an animal, or a person, or a cup
became half vegetable, growing leaves and fruit. A woman in
a state of indecision – should she leave her husband or not –
put her pencil to the paper, made a line or a shape, scratched
it out, started again, scratched it out: at the end of an evening
her sketch pad would be full of jagged erasures. And so it was
with all of us: we were set in modes, by organizers and gov-
ernors unknown to our conscious selves.

BOOKS

President Mugabe has said there will be a good library in every
village. I have been visiting more schools, some as bad as the
one run by 'the man without character', some good. But in
very good schools there are empty shelves in rooms that call

themselves libraries where books ought to be. Books written by African writers are all read to shreds. There are rejects from better libraries, and among them might be books the children would enjoy, but no attempt is made to differentiate between them. Perhaps the idea is, better any books than none at all. But there is such a hunger for books, for advice about books, in this country where the electronic revolution is yet to happen. Radios may or may not pick up the BBC or South Africa. There is little video, and a few programmes from The Open University, but only a minority benefits from these, since most schools do not have television. Books remain as influential as they ever were, in countries like Zimbabwe. It is not possible to exaggerate the influence of books, even one book. Dambudzo Marechera, the author of *House of Hunger*, described how, when he was a hungry child scrabbling for bits of food and clothing on the rubbish heaps attached to white houses, he found a thrown-out Arthur Mee's Children's Encyclopedia. It changed his life. Yet even the big libraries in Harare and Bulawayo are short of funds. If you send them books, you may get a letter: I am sorry, please don't send any more, we cannot afford the Customs duties. Even the University of Zimbabwe library is not funded to keep itself up to date with books.

MUSIC

A Sunday morning mbira party. The mbira is a base of wood with metal strips of varying lengths and widths set on it, in tiers. It can be held between two hands and played while walking. When I was growing up the gentle sprightly tinkling of the mbira could be heard as you walked through the bush, and then the player came into sight, usually a young man with a hoe slung over a shoulder, his fingers conversing with the hand piano (which is what we called it) while his eyes searched the bush for game.

When played seated, the instrument is held inside a

calabash, for resonance, and metal beer tops are used to add depth and tone.

There were a lot of people, perhaps forty, on the verandah enclosed on three sides by rooms. A swimming bath was watched in case toddlers went too close.

Pupils of a school some way out of Harare sat in tidy rows, wearing their dancing costumes, consuming soft drinks and peanuts. They are well known and entertain visiting Chefs, at parties and banquets. Now they are playing for fun. The meal was sadza, with relishes of peanut sauce and green leaves; rice and curry; stewed chicken, bread, and Mutare's famous mangoes. Ice-cream. Oceans of Coca-Cola.

The mbira orchestra consisted of three black players, one described as Zimbabwe's best player, and some white amateurs who joined in the accompaniment. The children danced to the mbira. This kind of dancing is deceptive. It begins with simple padding movements, the feet flat, the body quiet, then grows, but slowly, into a frenzy of movement where you cannot follow the variety and speed of the rhythms, for at the dance's height it seems the dancer's feet are always in the air flying after energetic arms and shoulders, every part of the body answering a different beat. There was one little girl, perhaps eight or so, watching the older girls' movements and carefully following them. She was all concentration as she adapted her arms, her feet, her body, to the dance. Once I watched flamenco dancers in Granada (this was before every flamenco group was tuned to the tourist industry). Four or five women danced together, of different ages, the oldest being perhaps sixty. They were initiating a new dancer, a girl of twelve or thirteen. The older women watched her, making almost imperceptible gestures of correction and encouragement. The audience all knew this was an occasion for the new dancer, joined in the clapping, and called out to her. One day she too would be a famous flamenco dancer, like her grandmother, her mother, her aunt, her elder sister . . . And she danced for hours, absorbed in her rituals. So, too, the little girl that Sunday morning on the verandah.

People called out for this mbira piece, or another: soft, delicate music, subtle music, the rhythms outside one's capacity, just as the energetic patterns of the dancers were too fast to catch.

'This music is to us what your New Testament is to you,' said the famous mbira player. 'It is sacred to us.'

Later, in London, I switched on the radio and heard the most seductive of the pieces I had heard that morning being played with a Western orchestral backing, as part of a concert. They say the Zimbabwe mbira players are honoured outside Zimbabwe, but hardly known there: there is a centre for mbira music in New York. Similarly, young people will often have no time for their own songs and music until they hear them played by visiting bands, who have fallen in love with them and adapted them.

When I was a girl there was a man called Hugh Tracey ('That man Hugh Tracey!') who went around the villages recording and collecting music. The whites regarded him as some kind of a freak, even a traitor. Some of that music would not have survived without him.

AN OUTLINE FOR A PLAY. A FILM?

A Woman of Our Time
The young man who will one day command a national movement/a guerilla army/his country, represent his people while in exile or in prison, shows none of the qualities of a popular leader. He is shy, scholarly, an observer. The man best known to the Party and the People has all these qualities. When he speaks crowds go wild. He stands in front of them arms held open as if in an embrace, while they shout Viva, or Shame. It is expected he will lead the country, but the capacities that make him so popular also undo him: he likes to be liked, secretly values his reputation with the whites as 'reasonable'; hates unpopularity. He agrees to a deal with the whites that make

him a 'sell-out' and even a traitor. At any rate it is the shy
and scholarly man who takes his place and proves himself as
a skilled and tenacious negotiator/leader of an Army/President
of the Party/a powerful presence, all the years he is in prison.
(Men who have led African countries have all been in one or
several of these roles. As for the uncharismatic second-in-
command coming forward to take power, this has happened
more than once.)

When his Party wins an election/the War in the Bush/gains
Independence from a European power because the Winds of
Change have blown his way, he at once becomes the only man
who could possibly ever have led the country: hindsight is a
persuasive writer of history. But while he finds himself able to
handle the former Colonial power, the leaders of other African
countries, and trips to meet world leaders, being a popular
leader does not come easily. He never had the gift of eloquence,
and does not have it now. He has never swayed crowds. He
watches colleagues, some of them brave figures from the fight
for Independence, easily gather to themselves hearts and
minds which they seem to wear like badges or medals, for when
they stand on platforms it is as if they are surrounded by an
aura of confidence: I love you, you love me. Secretly he yearns
over his people like a shy lover. It is not unknown for him to
weep while speaking/stutter/appear pedantic because over-
controlled.

The man so isolated inside his shyness soon seems proud
and austere and even cold. Some call him a saint. He is known
for his integrity. He lives simply and makes sure everyone
knows it. He tries to moderate the excesses of associates who
are energetically getting rich.

His first love/wife dies, or he finds her simple village ways
(which match his own) a handicap. He meets a woman who at
once attracts him. She has everything he lacks. Large, ebullient,
beautiful; loud, laughing, extrovert,' she commands everyone
with her charm. (It might be interesting to make her from
another part of Africa or from another tribe, adding to her
attractions for him, but to the suspicions of the populace about
an outsider.) This man feels as if he has been in prison all

his life and this woman has released him from it: suddenly
everything that had been difficult for him becomes easy. When
they are with friends in the evening (it seems now there are
parties every night) she communicates with them all, using her
whole body: no one can take their eyes off her. When she
stands on a platform (which she increasingly does, claiming
her right to be Mother of the Nation) she holds crowds with
her majestic breasts and thighs just as much as with her beautiful
face, her full voice. He watches her, admiring, full of love, but
uneasy. How does she do it? What is this gift which he has
been so absolutely denied? He jokes with her – but in his way,
which is as if jokes might turn out dangerous when unmoni-
tored – that she has not been elected, and while it is all right
to be Mother of the Nation in her role as his wife, she must not
go beyond that.

'Nonsense!' she cries, and, seeing she has hurt him, for he
withdraws like one of those acacia leaves that fold themselves
up even at the approach of a finger, she embraces him and he
again feels life flow through him.

She is crying 'Nonsense!' often. When he says that their rule
of life must be modest. When she returns from some Conference which she has spent talking with other wives, and now
says she has opened a Swiss bank account, and he says No, it is
dishonest to spend the People's money. When an opportunity
comes (pretty often as the country develops) for her to take
part in deals that are increasingly shady, and he remonstrates.
It takes him a long time to understand she has not one molecule
in her body of what he has always taken his stand on: his
honesty, for which he is known all over Africa and the world.
She really does not know what he means when he says, We
must set an example, or We must not let our country become
corrupt like the others. 'Why not? Corrupt? But everyone does
it,' she might carelessly say, laughing. And she teases him
as she sometimes does for his inhibitions in more intimate
ways. She even uses the same words: 'Where do you get these
ideas from? Who says no? Is there a law which says we
mustn't . . . .'

Yes there is a law, for he passes it, making it illegal for

Ministers and Public Servants to own more than a certain
amount – one house, for instance.

They take no notice of this law. The citizens wait for him to
enforce the law, and stand by them, his people, who put him
into power, who trust him to be on their side and with the
Purity of the Revolution/the Party/the War of Independence.
He does nothing. They do not understand why not. They do
not yet know the Mother of the Nation has her fingers in many
tills, though they keep a cold eye on the Ministers and Party
Bosses and know exactly what they are up to.

The Leader watches his wife whom he loves, whom he
depends on for vital contact with the world, gaily and even
proudly and certainly shamelessly making herself a rich
woman. There is a scandal and it is impossible to avoid putting
certain public figures on trial. They are proved guilty. The
nation waits for them to be punished And now the whispers
begin: he cannot let Justice take its course, because the guilty
ones have said that if they are punished they will expose his
wife.

What hurts him more than anything is that she never understands how she is damaging him, always talks as if it is his
'shyness' that makes him so finicky. It is not until the corrupt
regimes of Eastern Europe and the countries of the old Soviet
Union begin to fall, one after another, because of the loathing
of the citizens, that she – for the first time – wonders if her
husband's 'stick-in-the-mud' ways might be an advantage. She
is in fact secretly angry about the criticisms of the old communist leaders, whom she has admired for precisely those qualities
her husband has sometimes expressed doubt about. She likes
ruthlessness. She is not shocked by tortures, 'the strong
methods', of dictators. She thinks their own country would be
better, 'make a good impression' – as she puts it, if they, too,
made citizens fear their government. And she encourages the
bully-boys of the Party to intimidate opponents, rig elections,
beat critics up.

Now, suddenly, her husband is putting his foot down, saying Enough – and shouting at her, with the barking desperation
of a man who feels everything is slipping away from him. The

regimes that he has chosen as allies are all collapsing, to the accompaniment of choruses of hatred and contempt, and now this woman, this force of Nature, who is everything to him, has had to be checked . . . as she shuts herself down, banks her fires, sulks, shows her hurt in a thousand ways, he closes up more and more, just like that acacia frond, subtly trembling even at the approach of a finger. When he shouts at her, forcing her because of his position of authority into obedience, he feels he is cutting himself off from all the secret powers of Nature, while she, obedient, feels that the rush forward of her life, which is based on a confident instinct that lays hold of everything it touches has been checked . . . unkindly checked, above all *unfairly*, so now she is a prisoner of his cold cautions.

The final scene could be in an airport. He, she, and their entourage are on their way to some International Conference. A terrorist bomb has wrecked the Distinguished Persons' Lounge, and they are all in a hastily-contrived fenced-off part of the ordinary Departure Lounge. Today they have heard of yet another country's collapse, and she sees about her faces that were until recently those of Prime Minister, Cabinet Ministers, still among the small gathering of Distinguished Persons, though probably they will not be entitled to be here for much longer. Into this area comes that day's fallen Leader, with his family, and he goes straight to her husband, begging him for shelter. He is bluffing and boasting, pretending it is only a temporary rejection by his People, and he will soon be back in power. She whispers to her husband that on no account must this fugitive be given asylum, because they will be associated with him in the public mind. She is speaking out of the ancient instinct that to be near defeat is bad luck, though she uses the language of reason. Her husband, principled as always, offers the hospitality of their country to this disgraced leader: 'Of course one must help friends in trouble.'

She knows that his 'friend' is one that in fact he does not much like; it is she who has liked him, admired him, and still does, though he is regarded (the newspapers say) as a tyrant, a thug, a murderer, a hangman.

She is standing rather to one side, looking at this man she

has married, in conversation with the refugee President and his family. He is awkward, unbending, stiff . . . 'arrogant' they call him, though she is pretty sure he isn't that . . . . what exactly is the word that goes with all these qualities of his that have turned out to be right all the time? As she stands there, a pathetic figure, though she is not aware of that, holding herself upright and defiant, a group of women from their own country comes into the Lounge – that is, into the area for common people, just on the other side of the quickly contrived rope that keeps them out. They are off on a delegation to Indonesia, for a Woman's Conference on Alternative Technology. They see her, the Mother of their Country, and stop, stand whispering to each other. She was at school with the two women leading the delegation, who come forward to the rope barrier, softly clapping their hands in greeting.

She claps hers, in the manner of one waiting to see what is expected of her.

'Do you remember us, Mother?' asks her ex-school fellow.

'Yes, I remember you. Of course.'

They stand looking at each other, the Great Lady and the humble ex-schoolfellows.

Then one says, 'Remember us, Mother.' Softly and turns away.

The other says, 'Remember us, Mother.' And turns away.

One after another the women come forward, stand in front of The Mother, but on the other side of the rope, and say, 'Remember us, Mother' – and turn to walk back to the group, where they stand with their backs to her.

(There are several women of this type in high positions in various parts of Africa.)

VIEWS ON THE FUTURE OF
SOUTHERN AFRICA

A prominent South African lawyer, a liberal: 'Everyone is hypnotized by the political stereotypes. All they can see is the injustice of apartheid. But the country is roaring ahead, the blacks are roaring ahead in spite of everything, and they are so full of talent and energy. Yes I suppose there will be some bloodshed . . .' here he impatiently waves his hand, 'but not nearly as much as everyone expects. You'll see, we'll come to an agreement. And then – the sky's the limit. In fifteen or twenty years it will be one of the most exciting parts of the world. The brakes will be off, full steam ahead.'

Visiting European politician: Not a hope! Not because of Zimbabwe but because of South Africa. South Africa's going up in flames and Zimbabwe will have to be involved. Look at the past if you want to see the future: Zambia weakened itself helping Zimbabwe and now it's a disaster. Zimbabwe weakens itself helping Mozambique. It's no good being a strong swimmer surrounded by drowners.

South African liberal: Why should South Africa solve its problems? It never has. It has been a brutal and repugnant and successful tyranny ever since I can remember and that's fifty years. Look north: Botswana has a tiny population and an atmosphere of get-rich-quick. Zambia can't feed itself. Zimbabwe can feed itself but it is not taking care of its soil. Namibia and Angola and Mozambique are ruined by war. The whole of Southern Africa will be another disaster area, full of repressive corrupt governments.

A Zimbabwe academic has been on a visit to Zaire and reports: 'Towns that ten years ago were operating as towns are derelict. No electricity, no transport, no mails, the hotels don't work, no petrol. I visited the central library. Once it was a good library. The librarians haven't been paid for years and they have fed their families by selling the books. Empty shelves – nothing. The schools aren't working . . . no textbooks. You can't say, It's gone back to Africa, because the infrastructure wasn't African. It's weird, it's creepy, it's like a fantasy film . . . you go into a suburb you remember as a rich suburb and all you see is the smoke from hundreds of cooking fires outside every house burning up the trees and the shrubs and when those are gone, what then? How did it all begin? Electricity cuts. One by one, the services collapsed. Now no infrastructure left at all.

'Can't you see what is happening in Zimbabwe? We have been having electricity cuts for weeks. The railway system is not working. The telephones work or not.* They can't even get coal from the coalfields to the hospitals – this week no operations in Harare's main hospital. No coal for the tobacco barns and tobacco is the main foreign exchange earner. They borrow six locomotives from South Africa, and in the first week two are a write-off – two more are disabled and need repair. At a time when Zimbabwe is grinding to a halt Mugabe hands over fifty-five per cent of the railway capacity to ferry Zambia's freight to the ports. The roads – there is no way this country can maintain its road system, not without handouts. I go to X province, the roads are being done up, I hear. The Swedes are paying for it. Next day on a new road: the French are paying for it. Are we going to go on like this, living on handouts? Gimme, gimme, gimme, give us libraries, give us new locomotives, give us the bloody lot.'

SO WHAT SHOULD BE DONE?

Marxist student: The Bourgeois Revolution has failed. Now we must have a Revolution of the Proletariat.

Black farmer: Transport, it's all transport. If only Comrade Mugabe would organize our transport . . .

White man, (born in the country, plans to stay in it, on innumerable boards, committees, charitable governing bodies):

---

* The Japanese are building Zimbabwe a telephone system.

First you take the brakes off investment. But that won't change anything until something else happens. Money has been poured into this country – millions. Most of it wasted. The Aid agencies, they don't understand the priorities, they don't understand the level they should have started at. The railways will work when these chaps have been trained to understand the mechanics. Industry will work when there's a trained personnel. Look at Zimbabwe airlines – they fly, don't they? They don't just fall out of the sky? No, they decided to have an airline – all these countries have to have one, they're prestige. But they put money into training the chaps to teach. Because they had to. If I had my hands on this Aid money I'd set up colleges to train the teachers. There's a gap – that's the gap. And make it prestige. Mugabe should be right in there making speeches and dishing out prizes. Do you know what has happened? These young black chaps, they want to study literature, God help us, they've inherited all that snobbery from England where engineers are dirt. When I was in the States last year I kept meeting engineers in the aeronautics industry, English, Scottish, they are working in the States and in Europe where engineers are valued. But here it is a matter of life and death for engineers to be trained and then valued. Until we've got this layer of properly trained black chaps it's pouring money down the drain.

'Did you know that every year the Japanese train 400 times more engineers and technicians than we do?' ('We': The British.)

'Training, training, training, TRAINING, **TRAINING** – it's **training that we need. TRAINING.**'

POLITICS

A Commercial Farmer (white) in the high-tech district, where not so long ago Selous bartered with Lo Magondi, applied to become a member of Zanu PF. He was interviewed by two important members of the Party.

'First of all,' says he belligerently, 'I have to tell you three things. One, I have a big mouth and I'm not going to change.' (He had been famous for attacks on government policy.)

'And what else, comrade?'

'I've been farming thirty years in this country, and I'm going to go on farming the way I know best.'

'And what else?'

'I'm never going to leave this country. If you burned my house down around my ears and told me to live in a mud hut I'd stay.'

'Welcome to Zanu PF, comrade.'

GIVING UP

People leave Zimbabwe for apparently minor reasons: straws that break . . .

'You are leaving because of *what*? You're mad.'

'If you like. I moved house. I put up a dura wall around the garden.' (A type of cement fencing.) 'All day in the department I hear, "So you've put up a dura wall, just like a white, you all put up fences." But everyone knows the first thing a Chef does when he buys a house, before he even moves in, is to put up his dura wall. All I hear is the whites this, the whites that. I've had enough of this racism. It's getting worse. I'm off.'

A scientist left because, having many times applied unsuccessfully for some laboratory equipment, refused on the grounds of shortage of foreign exchange, he stood at the airport watching 'Dozens of these damned Chefs off to one of their conferences somewhere. There's always enough money for that.'

The last straw for another was a new history book for use in schools, designed to correct the errors of the white version of African history. First. There is one short chapter on the hundred years of white domination, which transformed black culture. 'It's called Positive Discrimination.' Then, hunter-gatherers are described as inhabiting the Middle East until one thousand years before Christ. 'You can't have black kids knowing there were scintillating civilizations around the Mediterranean long before they were ever heard of.' And then, that polyglot band of desperate, penniless, hard-drinking adventurers who arrived to take their chances in the Kimberly diamond mines are described as 'capitalists'. And then, in a book meant for both girls and boys, the pupils were invited to imagine themselves king in medieval Africa, loaded with finery, and waited on by his wives. 'Not a word about all the important roles the women had, they were not just wives to the king, that's just rubbish. No, I'm a historian. That means *facts*. If these people want to go in for all this political rubbish then – I'm off.'

But: the man who left because of the fence is back. 'I'd like to take the bloody place by the shoulders and shake some ordinary bloody commonsense into it. But I don't want to live anywhere else.'

Nor is it unknown for black Zimbabweans, and even a Chef or two, to be found far from home. After an evening spent playing that game known as *choosing one's words*, you may hear, 'Yes, that's how it goes . . . funny how things turn out, sometimes.'

THE VERANDAH IN THE MOUNTAINS

Again I look down on hills, lakes, rivers and forests and above them is a baby aeroplane, owned by a local farmer, and in it with him is the Coffee Farmer. They are circling the mountains, and the valleys, and the Communal Areas looking for signs of soil erosion, which will then be reported to the Soil Conservation Committee.

Through the days and the evenings I sit listening to the ideas bubble.

Everywhere in the Communal Areas you see these fat goats. How is it the blacks don't make goat cheese? They like strong tastes. Surely they'd like it. Why don't . . . ?

A woman has just come back from Argentina, with, 'They grow the same crops as here. Maize, pumpkins, tomatoes, legumes, potatoes. But the poor people make dozens of different dishes with them. Why can't Argentinian know-how be introduced here?'

It has occurred to an old-timer that the shifts and contrivances, the improvisation, of the white homesteads of the early days, where there was no electricity, refrigerators, running water, could be used now in the poorer Communal Areas. For instance, the coolers that were supplanted by refrigerators. Shelves are enclosed by walls of chicken wire, but doubled, an inch or so apart, the space filled with charcoal. Around the top of this safe is a metal groove that has very small holes in it. It is filled with water that slowly trickles down through the charcoal, so the walls of the safe are always wet, and the evaporation cools the inside of the safe, where butter and milk and meat wrapped in pawpaw leaves to tenderize it are kept at temperatures degrees lower than outside.

Canvas water coolers were hung from rafters or tree branches, and had in them lemonade and cold tea as well.

I said, 'Outside our house was an enormous metal tank where on hot days the water got so hot you couldn't put your hand into it. Now I find it hard to believe it never occurred to us to use the water for baths or washing clothes.'

'Why don't they . . . ?'

'Why don't we . . . ?'

'What if . . . ?'

In the coffee valley the government AIDS campaign is working. 'Not just the government, we are at them all the time too. But it's sad, because at the beer drinks and dances they are afraid to get drunk and have a good time. Now they're all getting religion instead, you know, the song and dance religion. A good thing, because they have hard enough lives without not having any fun at weekends.'

The Coffee Farmer has been mugged in Mutare in the middle of the day. He had just been to the bank to deposit cheques. The muggers thought he had been in to collect the month's wages for his workers. 'They certainly knew what they were doing,' says the Coffee Farmer, with more than a hint of admiration. 'One tripped me, and the other frisked me. They were off before I got up off the pavement. I ran to the corner but the car was too far off to see the number plate. They must have been watching for the moment when only one person was on the street. Well, bad luck, I only had a couple of dollars on me.'

A PASSIONATE PROTAGONIST

In Harare's beautiful park I was the victim of clever pickpockets. Two engaging youths approached me and a companion and asked if we would sponsor a walk in aid of something or other. One suggested I should spread the form where I would note my contribution on his back, which he helpfully turned so I could sign. While I signed, my hands were occupied, and he slid his own back and into my bag, where he lifted over a hundred pounds. Meanwhile his associate engaged the attention of my friend.

When I told this story to a woman who cannot endure the slightest criticism of Zimbabwe, she at first looked anguished, but rallied. 'You say it was a clever operation?' 'Oh yes, brilliant, I can't imagine pickpockets in London with such charm, such persuasiveness.' She sat back, with a satisfied sigh, like a proud mother.

HOT SPRINGS

Under the whites this was a popular resort, but it is ruinous now, the pool and bathing cabins unused. Of the old amenities only a kiosk remains for the sale of cold drinks. Young men are crowded on benches around trestle tables drinking beer and playing draughts with paper boards and beer tops for

counters. At a separate table an old man holds court, surrounded by young men and boys listening to his reminiscences.
They sit as if hypnotized by their attention to him, sit motion-
less, but often laugh and then sit silently again for fear of missing anything. This scene, in its wildly beautiful surroundings,
reminds me, again, of Italy, the zest of it, the enjoyment. Only
sit near the draughts players and you are charged with the
spirit of enjoyment.

I think of Guy Clutton-Brocks', 'They are the happiest lot in
the world. They get enjoyment out of anything, anywhere, at
any time. And we are the most joyless.'

Ever since I can remember, I've listened to groups of whites
speculating about why this should be so, every level from
'What the hell's wrong with us, anyway?' to, 'What is there in
our culture, where did it start, what happened to make it so
hard for us to enjoy ourselves? The northern climate? Prot-
estantism? The Industrial Revolution?' ('When in doubt blame
the Industrial Revolution.')

So bullied are we all by ideologues, it is hard to say the
Africans have anything whites do not, or that we have anything
they do not, but the fact is, up and down Africa, as travellers
have always averred, they enjoy themselves.

Missionary Moffat (the elder) wrote in his diary how he lay
awake in his camp bed on a moonlit night and listened to
how across the river the poor black savages were dancing and
singing to their drums and generally enjoying themselves. He
saw it as his God-given task to put an end to all this sinful
pleasure. Well, they certainly tried.

For hours on that afternoon young men came drifting in to
drink beer and play draughts; some went over to join the old
man's audience.

Where in Europe now would you see young men and boys
crowding to listen to an old man telling tales?

If it is being asked, And where were the women? – they
were building the fires and cooking the supper for these men,
washing the children and putting them to bed, having hoed
the fields and weeded the fields and harvested the crops and
mended the hut walls and thatched the roofs.

THE STORYTELLERS, THE WRITERS

Tales, stories, jokes, anecdotes come spinning off people's lips like soap bubbles. You could say gossip, too, but there is always an epic quality to it, because Zimbabwe is felt to be important, and that is because memories of the old kingdoms, like Monomotapa (rather, Munhumotapa) are still near. When, later, the white colonialists said, God's own country, they did not know their pride was from long before they came, and would continue when they were gone.

Zimbabwe has good writers, surprisingly many, and they have written good novels, but the form of the short story suits them well, perhaps just because when a group of people sit together and the entertainment is 'gossip', then accounts of what neighbours or the Chefs are up to fall naturally into shape as tales. As well as the writers who write in English, there are many who use the other languages, Shona, Ndebele and the rest, and these are seldom translated. What are they like? Violent, is the report: they are full of murder, crime, passion, incest, and are bought and read in large numbers.

When the women who came to the Book Team meetings were invited to make up stories, poems – women who first exclaimed, Oh no, and were shy, but almost at once began to suggest ideas, the beginnings of tales – then I was seeing the birth of writers whom we may well hear of sooner or later. Or at least an atmosphere where writers may be engendered.

There is already a good novel by a woman, Tsitsi Dangarembga, but it did not have an easy birth. *Nervous Conditions* was rejected by four Zimbabwe publishers. The Women's Press in London published it, and only after that the Zimbabwe Publishing House had the courage to do it. It was criticized for being 'negative', presenting an unfair picture of the lives of black women, who for their part say things like, 'This is the first time I have seen my life as a Shona woman clearly.' In short, it is a revolutionary book. The critics were all male, all hostile. They continue to be.

Zimbabwe critics are mostly bad, but they have the strength of their ignorance, and the backing of ideology. Not only did the academics not have access to news about the Soviet Union and communist countries, but they knew nothing of the many novels where the jargon and pretensions of marxism were mocked. These novels were not allowed in.

There are groups of new writers who deny any talent to 'the fathers of Zimbabwe writing', such as Charles Mungoshi. One might be tempted to cry Impossible! – if the phenomenon had not so often been observed in other countries.

For instance, in the 1970s in Sweden and Norway, newly-arrived writers dismissed all their elders as talentless, using marxism to justify their envy of them: marxism was ever envy's most useful accomplice. The information about the state of literature in communist countries, where 'socialist-realism' and marxist criticism had been reigning for decades, was available to them all, yet their drive to do down their predecessors was so strong they were able to persuade themselves that 'socialist-realism' was alive and well. The '70s in Sweden and Norway are now referred to as the Dark Ages, not least by the writers who helped to create them.

In Britain in the '80s something similar happened, in this case fuelled by the competitive slash-and-burn known as Thatcherism. *She* spoke of 'one of us', of 'us and them' 'not one of us' – and so did the new young group, who claimed talent only for themselves and their cronies, and imposed a style of criticism so vindictive that European colleagues often enquired, Just what has got into you people? Thatcher! the reply often was, but it was only an old phenomenon in a different guise. A whole generation of new readers and writers now believe that malice and rancour is inseparable from literary criticism and reviewing, just as in Zimbabwe a generation believes that criticism has to use the jargon of marxism.

In Britain, if a review or critical piece gives off that unmistakable odour of hate, of envy, it is easy to throw it aside and reach for something more intelligent. Not, however, in Zimbabwe, for there is no alternative.

I was invited to a meeting of Zimbabwean writers. There

were more Party officials and Party watchdogs than writers. The 'heavies' – never was there a more appropriate word – large and ponderous men in their three-piece suits, looked a different species from the writers. They were. They are. It was painful to watch serious writers patiently and with dignity suffering such thrusts as 'I see you believe in the ivory tower conception of literature, comrade' – from a young woman activist quivering with pleasure at her political sophistication and know-how – darting looks at us all to invite admiration. All this is so stupid, you think, No, it simply cannot still be going on, but it is going on and good and serious writers are being hurt by it . . . by this revenge of the second-rate, always finding new ways – particularly political ways – for the operations of Envy. In 1989 the pronouncement went like this: 'Any writer or novel or poem that gets attention or a review from outside Zimbabwe is by definition petit-bourgeois and betrays the needs of the black people – the writer is a sell-out.' Seldom are we able to observe Envy so perfectly displayed, a glittering and poisonous circle of hate, excluding everything but itself, ascribing merit only to itself. This particular formula makes sure that any writer in Zimbabwe, past or future, attracting serious attention, is automatically discredited. (This formula is used in Nigeria, for any writer whose novels are taken seriously outside Nigeria: he, she, is a sell-out.)

In Zimbabwe writers tend to take to drink, or die young, or give up writing altogether. I would too.

Here are some of the Zimbabwe writers, some of the books I have admired.

Charles Mungoshi	*Waiting for the Rain*
	The Setting Sun and the Rolling World
	Coming of the Dry Season
Tsitsi Dangarembga	*Nervous Conditions*
Shimmer Chinodya	*Dew in the Morning*
	Harvest of Thorns (this is the novel, about the Bush War, which was disapproved of.)

S. Nyamfukudza	*The Non-Believer's Journey*
Musaemura Zimunya	*Country Dawns and City Lights*
William Saidi	*The Old Bricks*
Tim McLoughlan	*Karima*
Chenjerai Hove	*Up in Arms*
	Bones
Dambudzo Marechera	*The House of Hunger*

TIME TO GO HOME, FROM HOME

I decided to make a quick trip to my myth country, perhaps to make sure it was still there, and even visit the dark stuffy bungalow on that hill always steeped in moonlight, starlight, sunlight, and aired by the hundred winds of earth and sky. 'Hello!' I might say to those little kids peering out through dirty glass. 'Hi! How are you doing? Tell me, what is your heart's desire?'

But at the turn-off up to the hill where once there was the acacia grove on one side and the mombie kraal on the other, is now a large notice, 'Trespassers will be Prosecuted'.

Quite right too.

The Scriptwriters certainly know their job.

Before I left Zimbabwe, not far from Harare, just after sundown, I glimpsed the past – all our pasts – in a light-stepping youth returning from a range of low hills, his eyes alert for the ghosts of vanished game. On his back was a spear, in his hand was a catapult, and he was accompanied by three lean hunting dogs.

THE YEAR OF MIRACLES, 1990

A young woman is on a plane coming from the eastern Mediterranean, and is joined by a man who says, 'Tell me what's been happening in the world. I've been in the Himalayas for months, and I've not seen a newspaper nor heard the news. Thank God.'

'Well now, let me see,' says she. 'The Soviet Union has given up communism, the Soviet colonies have given up the Soviet Union. The Berlin Wall is down and Germany is united. In South Africa they have given up apartheid.'

'Very funny,' says he, 'and now tell me what has really happened.'

In Zimbabwe the election was won by Comrade Mugabe and Zanu PF and no one talks of Tekere. '*Who*?' they will soon be asking.

Mugabe still wants a one-party state but his colleagues won't hear of it.

1991

Comrade Mugabe formally abandons communism.

Who says no one learns from other people's mistakes?

But the University of Zimbabwe is still subject to Party control.

Why? – everyone wonders.

I try to put myself in Mugabe's place and find I am suffering all the emotions of the elderly who experience what they valued quietly slipping through their fingers. This is a proud man, an austere man, a man of principle. That shield and buckler, the Fifth Brigade, became the most hated people in Zimbabwe. The People's Hotel and Party HQ and the Sports Stadium, all copied from the communists, are white elephants. His colleagues and comrades have taken to thievery as if born to it. Communism has gone, the one-party state has been rejected, the economy of Zimbabwe is in disarray, just like every other communist-influenced economy. But, there is the University of Zimbabwe, and at least that can be controlled.

and Again,
in
Passing . . .

1992

Kenneth Kaunda is no longer President of Zambia. He resigned. Voluntarily. His successor's task in that mismanaged country is unenviable.

In Zimbabwe they are not saying, 'Why doesn't Mugabe . . . ?' 'Mugabe should . . .' The people have given up hopeful expectation.

The currency has been devalued. The Zim dollar is worth a quarter of what it was. The already desperately poor are even worse off. A new acronym, ESAP, sums up a new economic policy. It means, wait for it, Economic Structural Adjustment Policy. Or, how to get the advantages of capitalism without giving up socialism. The Povos, instructed to tighten their belts, say it means Extra Suffering for the Poor, or, The Sugar is Over. (A Shona phrase.) The sugar crop failed because of the drought. The leaders are begging for international investment while still heaping abuse on the multinationals. They, perhaps, are waiting for the telephones to work and red tape to be made less. In the farming districts some farmers have given up expecting anything from telephones and have reverted to the radio networks set up during the Bush War. Jokers say, 'Why not use talking drums? The Africans did well enough with them.'

At a meeting a man called out to Mugabe, 'We did better under Smith.' He was hauled off to prison. But up and down the land they are saying the same. And, 'At least Smith was honest.' And, even, 'We need a new leader', for, like other apparently more sophisticated countries they believe a change of leader must mean a change for the better. It is likely, so rumour goes, that they will soon have a new leader: Mugabe, they say, will resign. They are saying, 'Poor Robert's heart has been broken by the bad Chefs.'

The word Chef is heard less often. Was it after all a term of affection?

Sally Mugabe, Robert Mugabe's wife, has died. They say that pity for him united the country – at least for a time.

Famine threatens. In the past there was a policy to keep a year's supply of grain in the silos. This year's reserves have been given away, notably to the famine areas in Ethiopia, or sold to Mozambique. Meanwhile the government discouraged the growing of maize, the staple crop, telling the farmers to grow crops that bring in Foreign Exchange. It seems advice from the experts of the IMF and the World Bank was partly responsible for this stupidity. Then the rains failed. So now Zimbabwe is buying grain from South Africa, herself short of maize because of drought, and paying Foreign Currency for it. This inspired bit of planning will insure that Zimbabwe will be holding out a begging bowl this year. And if the rains are bad again next year?

The Book Team has had a difficult twelve months. Two Ministries found the women's book unpalatable. High level intervention saved the book. Its title, Building Whole Communities, reflects the women's belief that they are not valued in the community. Eight local Book Teams have been established. In some areas local Book Teams are spontaneously forming themselves.

The young teacher in the bush school is reunited with his wife.

The farm assistant, the champion parachutist, is now a preacher in a charismatic Christian sect.

Dorothy's two younger children are being sent to school by Ayrton R. Under ESAP school fees have been introduced for many children. He buys them clothes and books. They are angry: they do not like school, mostly because their school friends bully them, saying, 'Why should we be at the same school as the children of domestic workers?' But: they will be educated and their parents are not. They are angry too because Ayrton R. has a nice house and they do not.

The Herald, the country's main newspaper is lively and critical, no longer sounds like *Pravda*. There are good magazines, and new independent newspapers and magazines are planned.

In a crowded government office an official was rude to an old white woman who complained she had been waiting for five hours. A black man said to the official: 'Don't speak to the old woman like that, we don't like it.' The others agreed with him, 'Yes, we don't like your behaviour.' The official became polite.

An Irishman, Declan Gould, who has spent seven years helping the homeless and the poor, has been deported, made a Prohibited Immigrant, under the same laws Southern Rhodesia used, which have been kept, unchanged.

When something goes wrong it is still being blamed on South African sabotage. Many Zimbabweans have apparently not noticed that there is a new situation in South Africa.

Things are not well at the University of Zimbabwe. When it was set up, under Federation, it was given a liberal constitution of the kind usual in democratic countries. Under a new law, The University Amendment Act, the university will be controlled by the government, that is, by Zanu PF. The Vice Chancellor will be able to get rid of any academic who doesn't please him – without appeal. Students will have a worse time. Academics who can leave are leaving, or plan to leave. People are hoping this retrogressive law will be done away with.

The writers of Zimbabwe held a meeting this month, January, to protest the harassment of its members by the Central Intelligence Organization, whose stupidity and heavyhandedness is probably due to their having been trained by the secret police of the infamous Ceasescu. People want to know why a democracy needs a secret police.

On a Commercial Farm – white, I was told disgusting racial jokes, inspired by the government's incompetence. But: there should be 200 people on this farm, the workers and their families. There are seven hundred. The farmer says: 'I would have 4,000 by now, but I have to send them away. I don't like doing it. They want to be here because they do better with me than in the Communal Areas. All the white farms carry more people than the same amount of land in the Communal Areas.' He is irrigating large fields, using precious water he could use to grow the profitable crops the government asks for, so as to feed the seven hundred through the drought. 'I'll see my own people fed, at least, since those fools can't do it. And what about all the others that keep coming up begging for food? I have to send them away or I won't have enough for my people. How do you imagine I feel doing that?'

A new law provides for the taking of land without appeal from white farmers in certain designated areas. The perennial threats to do this means that a productive part of the agricultural economy is kept in a state of uncertainty, farmers beginning to refuse to invest in their farms, and trying to put money into movables. Meanwhile the government has large areas of land still not allocated. It is being said that this law is designed to distract the attention of the Povos from the government's mistakes.

Zimbabwe plans to shoot 30,000 elephants this year instead of the usual 3,000 or 3,500. Otherwise the herds would start to die from hunger. But: an enterprising young man says it is not true that African elephants are untrainable. He is training elephants. So perhaps some elephants may become working elephants.

The herd of free-range pigs, as happy as house dogs, showing how a pig's life must have been in Eden, have had to be penned, for they do too much damage.

The noble and sagacious dog Seamus, his master's friend, has died.

A group of seven zebras at their toilet in the bush. First one rubs her cheeks, and her forehead, then both sides of her neck, against a tree. Then first one side, and the other, most methodically. She stands under a low branch and rubs her back. Then chooses a sapling, positions herself, and walks forward over it so that the branches scratch her stomach. Another goes through the same performance. Then another, and all of them. They are watched by a male zebra who is turned on by this and has an erection like a yard of rubber hose. But he only watches them and when they have finished uses the same trees to rub and scratch himself. The zebras took no notice of us watching them from ten paces away.

The drought is so bad in some areas that not only cattle, but hardy goats and the wild animals are dying. They are shooting calves as they are born.

At the Victoria Falls Hotel, old colonial, one of the world's great hotels, spacious, dreamy, slow, cool in the great heat, like a setting for an Merchant Ivory film, a young black man peacocked in new jeans stylishly slit at the knees, the slits adorned with coloured safety pins. He swaggered, mocking himself, accepting applause with an air.

No one knows how to assess the long-term results of the calamity AIDS, which the government says will kill at least a million people by the year 2000, in a population of nine million. Women in Africa south of the Sahara have the highest rate of infection in the world – one in forty women. In Zimbabwe's rural areas many women sleep with men for money to feed children and dependants, pay school fees. They are described as prostitutes. In an urban clinic recently one out of four babies tested was HIV positive. Most men refuse to wear condoms. Promiscuity is admired. That is, in men. 'A Shona good bull impregnates many women.'

An editor: 'Only one thing would save this country. The government must stop repeating mantras, like ESAP. It should look coldly at the situation, without distorting it by ideology. It should examine criticism, instead of regarding all criticism as hostile. It should then describe our situation as it is. Then act. But is our government capable of it?'

A letter: 'When I think of our dreams at Independence I want to cry for Zimbabwe. Oh it is so sad, so sad, don't you think so? I do cry, sometimes.'

But: A visitor returned from Zaire, Kenya, Tanzania, Mozambique, said: 'Let me tell you! In comparison with any of those Zimbabwe is up to its armpits in jam. In Nairobi the shanty towns stretch for miles and no one cares. In Zimbabwe they are ashamed and try to rehouse homeless people.'

During a game of Epitaphs, it was decided there was only one possible epitaph for Robert Mugabe: 'A good man fallen among thieves.' Rejected epitaphs: 'God will reward him for trying.' 'Here lies a tragic hero: he destroyed himself by paranoia, not understanding how much goodwill there was for him among the people.'

A meteorological expert: 'Corruption? Don't make me laugh. Compared to someone like Robert Maxwell they are babies. Bad planning? So what! They'll learn. No, Southern Africa is drying up, that's the news. That is the only news.' But: 'We survived the War. We'll survive the drought.' A village woman, from Masvingo, where it has rained very little for ten years.

LETTERS, TELEPHONE CALLS, APRIL 1992

'The rainy season is over for this year: seven months to go before the rains. Even if we get good rains this year it will take three or four years to make up the damage. The chicken farmers are killing their flocks – no feed. The pigs are being killed: no food. The mombies are dying in hundreds of thousands already. I've been out in the Eastern Districts: you hear them bellowing and groaning as they die. What are we going to do? No one knows what to do.'

'The Povos are angry. Oh, you can believe me, they are angry! If the Government held an election now there would not be one vote for Mugabe. All over the country they are saying, Why did we fight that war? What for? We might just as well have kept Smith . . . Yes, there's going to be a storm all right, but it won't be a rain storm.'

''Mugabe is trying to distract the attention of the Povos by saying the white farmers are hoarding grain, but they aren't. The Povos are better fed on the white farms than they are in the Communal Areas. They try to get on to the white farms.'

'If Mugabe resigns, who are we going to get instead?'

'Who cares whether this is just a little temporary blip on the weather graph? Or a permanent major shift in the climate? The farmers don't care, hungry people don't care. All people care about is, Are the rains going to come in November?'

A LITTLE MORE HISTORY

Southern Rhodesia became a self-governing colony in 1924, though both Defence and Native Policy remained subject to British supervision. The British never, not once, protested against Southern Rhodesian Native Policy, which was always modelled on the repressive policies of South Africa. When the proposed Federation of Southern Rhodesia, Northern Rhodesia and Nyasaland failed, because of the opposition of the blacks, Northern Rhodesia got its independence and became Zambia in 1963. Southern Rhodesia demanded independence at the same time but was refused, unless the whites promised to grant black majority rule within a reasonable period. The whites rejected this and Britain applied sanctions. Ian Smith, on behalf of the whites of Southern Rhodesia proclaimed themselves independent of Britain, in a Unilateral Declaration of Independence, known as UDI. Minor acts of sabotage, riots, protests, had been going on in Southern Rhodesia for years, but the UDI in 1965 can be regarded as the beginning of the War of Independence, as the various parties and then armies formed and took to the bush. The main parties were ZANU, Zimbabwe African National Union, under Robert Mugabe, and ZAPU, Zimbabwe African People's Union, under Joshua Nkomo, who had spent over ten years in a detention camp, in a remote and desolate place, without amenities. 'Like the dark side of the moon,' he described it. These armies and other lesser armies sometimes collaborated with each other, and sometimes did not during the guerilla war against the government forces, a confused scene not made any clearer by the numbers of black soldiers fighting for the government – a majority of the government forces were black. When it was at last acknowledged by the whites that they could not win this war, Britain negotiated peace terms which included an election in which all the blacks voted, and for the first time. They voted for Robert Mugabe and ZANU, and Mugabe became Prime Minister. Joshua Nkomo was offered the job of President but refused. Then began a time when he was regarded as an enemy of Mugabe and the government. It was easier to see the disagreement like this because Robert Mugabe represented the Shona and Joshua Nkomo the Matabele. The Shona, or Moshona, are the indigenous people of the area. The Matabele were an offshoot from the Zulu nation in South Africa, for they left, trekking north to escape from the tyrannical and militaristic Zulu kings. They set up in what is now the south-west of Zimbabwe a militaristic and tyrannical regime with Bulawayo as their city. Bulawayo means The Place of Killing, and at the time when Lobengula the king was tricked out of his land by the whites it deserved its name. Historians disagree over the extent of the Mata-bele harassment of the Mashona, who were never a warlike people.

PORTUGUESE EAST AFRICA, AND THEN MOZAMBIQUE

While in Southern Rhodesia the black guerilla armies fought in the bush, in Portuguese East Africa the blacks fought against the Portuguese. They won, years before the birth of Zimbabwe. This war was headed by Frelimo, or the Liberation Front, whose leader was Samora Machel, a man with every quality of the popular hero. He was clever and brave, handsome and witty, and it seems would have successfully headed a government able to make Mozambique a comfortable place to live in. He was killed in a plane crash in 1986 that was almost certainly engineered by the South African secret police. When white Southern Rhodesia ended, Renamo, which was a creation of the white Southern Rhodesians to undo Frelimo, was taken over by the South Africans. Renamo – National Resistance Movement – that is, resistance against Frelimo – was armed and financed by South Africa and it destroyed Mozambique, and forced millions of refugees out into Malawi and Zimbabwe. Renamo bands continue to burn, steal, rape and murder: South Africa may have called its dogs to heel, but not effectively.

When Samora Machel was killed, he was succeeded as President by Jaochim Chissano, a man with probably the least enviable job in the world.

Southern Rhodesia, landlocked, had its railway to the port in Beira, and landlocked Zimbabwe has been largely dependent on this railway, this port, and the pipeline bringing in oil. It is Zimbabwe's armies who have protected railway and pipeline, repeatedly repairing both as they were blown up during the fighting. And, too, just as poor and precarious Zambia helped the guerillas fighting the white governments of Southern Rhodesia and Malawi, which meant its territory was bombed and sometimes even its towns from Southern Rhodesia, so, now, Zimbabwe has helped Frelimo against the common enemy, South Africa.

The bond between these countries was nominally marxist, but the real bond remains – how to keep control of their countries and their policies against outside pressures.

And what will happen now that South Africa has had its change of heart? I think it should be asked what those hundreds, perhaps thousands, of men and women are doing whose occupation has gone – trained to sabotage, destroy, undermine, destabilize their neighbouring black countries. Are these clever and cunning and brutal people now sitting back smiling benevolently while Mozambique, which they have destroyed, tries to restore itself? While Botswana, where they sent agents to murder and sabotage, becomes prosperous? While Zimbabwe, where they fomented every kind of disaffection, becomes peaceful and united? Well, how are these people spending their time these days?

THE AGRICULTURE

Under the whites most Africans lived in the Native Reserves, where they were put when the whites took the good land for their own farms. There were also Native Purchase Areas where blacks could buy land. The existence of these prosperous black farmers is one reason for the success of Zimbabwe's agriculture. After Liberation the Reserves became Communal Areas. The Resettlement Areas are where blacks are settled on previously unsettled land (of which there is still a great deal left) or on previously white-owned land. The Resettlement Areas were originally meant to be something like the Kolkhozes in the Soviet Union, never mind that they were so conspicuously unsuccessful. Now the exact terms on which these newly settled farmers will hold their land is being debated.

Doris Lessing

Under My Skin

Volume One of My Autobiography, to 1949

'Passionate and compelling, a book so packed with extra-ordinary images that it has obliterated almost everything else I read in 1994.'　　　　　　　　　　　　ROSE TREMAIN

This, the first volume of Doris Lessing's autobiography, begins with her childhood in Africa and ends on her arrival in London in 1949 with the typescript of her first novel, *The Grass is Singing*, in her suitcase. It charts the evolution first of her consciousness, then of her sexuality and finally of her political awareness with an almost overwhelming immediacy, and is as distinctive and challenging as anything she has ever written. It is already recognized as one of the great autobiographies of the twentieth century.

'By putting her life on the page, Doris Lessing has created her greatest work of art. An immediate, vivid, beautifully paced memoir.'　　　　　HILARY MANTEL, *London Review of Books*

'The book pulsates with life. The intensity of the sensory world is brilliantly evoked. Not just the story of the first thirty years of one life, this is the biography also of an age.'

JANE DUNN, *Observer*

'No mere review can do justice to an autobiography which is not just about a particular childhood, but about all childhoods, not just about white marginality, but about all forms of interior exile, rebellion, subversion and secret self-making. A voice of wise and fearless honesty cuts through this book, the best Doris Lessing has ever written.'　　　　　　　LYNDALL GORDON, *THES*

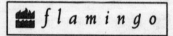

Doris Lessing

Love, Again

'This is a grand novel, boldly hewn, more literary than it declares, and yielding the occasional swooning glimpse of beauty. An encounter with a magnificent mind and temperament in artistic maturity, capable of turning her equal gaze on George Eliot.' CANDIA MCWILLIAM, *Independent on Sunday*

Love, Again is the story of Sarah Durham, a sixty-year-old producer and founder of a leading fringe theatre, who commissions a play based on the journals of Julie Vairon, a beautiful and wayward nineteenth-century mulatto woman. The play captivates all who come into contact with it, and dramatically changes the lives of all who take part in it. For Sarah, the change is profound – she falls in love with two younger men, one after the other, causing her to relive her own stages of growing up, from immature and infantile love (the beautiful and androgynous Bill) to the mature love, Henry.

Love, Again is a fierce and compelling examination of the nature and origins of love, of its remorseless ability to overwhelm and surprise us.

'Lessing's mixture of passionate involvement and the capacity to stand back and take a long look at what was going on, or will go on, is unlike that of any novelist writing now, except perhaps Saul Bellow, and the late Anthony Burgess. It grips, maddens, depresses and excites the reader from the first page to the last.'
                                                    A.S. BYATT, *The Times*

'A wholly compelling book, as vigorous and thought-provoking as anything she has ever written.'
                                    RUTH BRANDON, *New Statesman & Society*

Doris Lessing

This Was the Old Chief's Country

Collected African Stories
Volume One

Includes a new, previously uncollected story.

In this superb volume of African stories, Doris Lessing paints a magnificent portrait of the country in which she grew up. The cruelties of the white man towards the native, 'the amorphous black mass, like tadpoles, faceless, who existed merely to serve', the English settlers, ill at ease, the gamblers and moneymakers searching for diamonds and gold, and the presence, 'latent always in the blood', of Africa itself, its majestic beauty and timeless landscape: Doris Lessing draws them all together into a powerful, memorable vision.

'In story after story, Doris Lessing portrays the helpless collisions and alienations of the races. In "The Second Hut", a Rhodesian farmer is torn with anxiety and guilt about employing a poor Boer assistant with nine children because of the hostility between Boer and native workers. One brings away a sense of the sheer human impossibility of South Africa, as a place fit only for habitation by the imagination of exiles and of children. All else seems lost, betrayed and spoiled, except the glare of the sun, the dust, the boulders. An impressive collection.'

Gabriel Pearson, *Daily Telegraph*

'Doris Lessing's sense of setting is so immediate, the touch and taste of her continent is so strong, that Africa seems to become the universe.'

Newsweek

ISBN 0 586 09113 0

Doris Lessing

A Proper Marriage

'Authentic genius irradiates her pages' *Sunday Times*

The 'Children of Violence' series, a quintet of novels tracing the life of Martha Quest from her childhood in Africa to a post-nuclear Britain of AD 2000, first established Doris Lessing as a major radical writer. In this second volume, Martha, now in her early twenties, realises that her marriage to Douglas is a terrible mistake. Already, the first passionate flush of matrimony has begun to fade; sensuality has become dulled by habit, blissful motherhood now seems no more than a tiresome chore. Caught up in the maelstrom of a world war she can no longer ignore, Martha's political consciousness begins to dawn, and, seizing independence for the first time, she chooses to make her life her own . . .

'Few writers spring such surprises as Doris Lessing. She trusts her own feelings absolutely, and has the rare power of putting feelings straight on to the page, more directly perhaps than any other contemporary writer, so directly that the effect is sometimes like a physical blow.' *Independent*

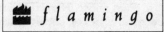

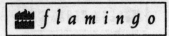

Doris Lessing

Many Doris Lessing titles are available in Flamingo.
Below is a selection.

Fiction

☐	LONDON OBSERVED	£6.99
☐	THE FIFTH CHILD	£5.99
☐	THE GOOD TERRORIST	£7.99
☐	THE GOLDEN NOTEBOOK	£8.99
☐	THE GRASS IS SINGING	£6.99
☐	MARTHA QUEST	£6.99
☐	THIS WAS THE OLD CHIEF'S COUNTRY	£6.99
☐	TO ROOM NINETEEN	£6.99

Non-Fiction

☐	UNDER MY SKIN, VOLUME ONE OF MY AUTOBIOGRAPHY TO 1949	£8.99
☐	WALKING IN THE SHADE, VOLUME TWO OF MY AUTOBIOGRAPHY, 1949–1962	£8.99
☐	A SMALL PERSONAL VOICE	£5.99
☐	AFRICAN LAUGHTER	£8.99

You can buy Flamingo paperbacks at your local bookshop or newsagent. Or you can order them from HarperCollins Mail Order, Dept. 8, HarperCollins*Publishers*, Westerhill Road, Bishopbriggs, Glasgow G64 2QT (0870 900 2050). Please enclose a cheque or postal order, to the order of the cover price plus add £1.00 for the first and 26p for additional books ordered within the UK.

Name (BLOCK LETTERS)_____

Address_____

_____

_____